New Chronicles of Yanagibashi
and
Diary of a Journey to the West

New Chronicles of Yanagibashi
and
Diary of a Journey to the West

Narushima Ryūhoku
Reports from Home
and Abroad

*Translated with a
Critical Introduction and Afterword
by*

Matthew Fraleigh

 East Asia Program
Cornell University
Ithaca, New York 14853

The Cornell East Asia Series is published by the Cornell University East Asia Program (distinct from Cornell University Press). We publish affordably priced books on a variety of scholarly topics relating to East Asia as a service to the academic community and the general public. Standing orders, which provide for automatic notification and invoicing of each title in the series upon publication, are accepted.

If after review by internal and external readers a manuscript is accepted for publication, it is published on the basis of camera-ready copy provided by the volume author. Each author is thus responsible for any necessary copy-editing and for manuscript formatting. Address submission inquiries to CEAS Editorial Board, East Asia Program, Cornell University, Ithaca, New York 14853-7601.

Number 151 in the Cornell East Asia Series
Copyright © 2010 by Matthew Fraleigh. All rights reserved
ISSN 1050-2955
ISBN: 978-1-933947-21-1 hc
ISBN: 978-1-933947-51-8 pb
Library of Congress Control Number: 2010931918

Calligraphy on title page and section divisions by Yanagimoto Katsumi

CAUTION: Except for brief quotations in a review, no part of this book may be reproduced or utilized in any form without permission in writing from the author. Please address inquiries to Matthew Fraleigh in care of the East Asia Program, Cornell University, 140 Uris Hall, Ithaca, NY 14853-7601.

Contents

List of Figures vi
Acknowledgments vii
Introduction ix
A note on the translations lviii
New Chronicles of Yanagibashi (Volume I) 1
New Chronicles of Yanagibashi Volume II 73
New Chronicles of Yanagibashi Volume III Preface and Foreword ... 137
Diary of a Journey to the West 145
Afterword 311
Glossary 337
Works Cited 346
Index 375

List of Figures

1. Woodcut from the second volume of *New Chronicles of Yanagibashi.*
2. Map of Sumida River and environs.
3. Photograph of a *yanebune* roofed pleasure-boat, circa 1871.
4. Narushima Ryūhoku's diary entry for the twenty-first day of the fifth month of Ansei 4 [June 12, 1857].
5. Title page from the first volume of *New Chronicles of Yanagibashi.*
6. Textual excerpt from the first volume of *New Chronicles of Yanagibashi.*
7. Handwritten copy of Matsumoto Hakka's partial transcription of Narushima Ryūhoku's original overseas travel diary.
8. Photograph of Okiku, proprietress of the Yūmeirō Teahouse, circa 1872.
9. Photograph of the Yūmeirō Teahouse, circa 1872.
10. Calligraphic inscription of prefatory poems from the second volume of *New Chronicles of Yanagibashi.*
11. Photograph of Narushima Ryūhoku taken in Japan, circa 1867.
12. Photograph of Narushima Ryūhoku taken at Langerock of Paris, circa 1873.
13. Photograph of Narushima Ryūhoku and David Carr Binnie taken by Shimooka Renjō, Yokohama, July 1873.
14. Excerpt from David Carr Binnie's travel diary for 1873.

Acknowledgments

I would like to thank the many scholars who have helped in various ways with the realization of this manuscript. Jay Rubin, Edwin Cranston, and Harold Bolitho fostered my earliest interest in *kanshibun* and encouraged my work on Narushima Ryūhoku in particular. In Kyoto I was fortunate to work with Hino Tatsuo during his final years at Kyoto University, and was equally lucky to have the chance to read a great many *kanshi* with Fukui Tatsuhiko. I have also benefited from conversations on my work with Kawai Kōzō, Ōtani Masao, Niina Noriko, Nakajima Takana, Ju Chiou-er, and Chia-ning Chang. I have learned a great deal from several scholars of Chinese, including Paul Rouzer, Yu Feng, and Chen Yizhen.

Sumie Jones and University of Hawai'i Press kindly allowed me to pursue the publication of my full translation of *New Chronicles of Yanagibashi* even though a short selection from it appears in a different format in the forthcoming *An Anthology of Meiji Literature*. Her co-editors Robert Campbell and Charles Inouye were also extremely generous in offering advice in various ways.

Robin Feuer-Miller, Steve Dowden, David Powelstock, Harleen Singh, Hiroko Sekino, and all of my other colleagues in the German, Russian, and Asian Languages and Literature Department have made Brandeis a wonderful place to work and I am grateful for their advice and encouragement. Aida Wong, the chair of the East Asian Studies Program, shares my intellectual interests in Sino-Japanese cultural exchange and has been very supportive.

Along the way, my research has been assisted by grants from the Fulbright Association, the Blakemore Foundation, the U.S. Department of Education, Harvard University, the Reischauer Institute for Japanese Studies, the Japan Society for the Promotion of Science, and Brandeis University. I am thankful for the support of these institutions and am pleased to acknowledge a publishing subvention from the Theodore and Jane Norman Fund.

Mai Shaikhanuar-Cota at Cornell has been an enthusiastic proponent of the project and I appreciate her help in guiding the manuscript toward publication. Micah Auerback, Sakano Kayoko, Linda Cheung, Vernica Downey, Barry Hinman, Anita Israel, Dzintra Lacis, Matsumoto Kajimaru, Lauren Malcolm, Eric McGhee, Kuniko McVey, and Emi Shimokawa facilitated my access to various rare library or archive materials. Jonathan Abel, Haengja Chung, Jim Mandrell, Kazuya Ōya, Rebecca Suter, and Larry Schehr gave their expertise and assistance in various domains. I am especially indebted to Paul Warham and Glynne Walley for their generous advice and commentary. Anne Allison, Ishiguro Keishō, Noboru Koyama, Kokumai Shigeyuki, Kuniyoshi Sakae, Nagai Kikue, Christian Polak, Timon Screech, and Tsuruta Tōru kindly shared their own work. Alexander Akin, Steve Hanna, Mark Quigley, and Jason Webb have all provided illuminating suggestions and welcome diversions while I put together this manuscript. Finally, I would like to thank my family for their encouragement, as well as Yanagimoto Katsumi, who has been a wonderful companion over the years that I have been working on this project.

Introduction

Narushima Ryūhoku (1837–1884) was an important literary figure whose career straddled the Meiji Restoration. Born into a family of Confucian scholars who had served the Tokugawa shogunate for two centuries, Ryūhoku held the prestigious post of *okujusha*, which included such academic and intellectual responsibilities as tutoring the shoguns in the Chinese classics and overseeing the editing of official histories. In the tumultuous mid-1860s, he served in even more central military and administrative positions within the Tokugawa government, first as an officer in its new Western-style cavalry unit, and then briefly as second-in-command of the treasury and foreign ministries. After the collapse of the Tokugawa shogunate and the founding of a new government in 1868, Ryūhoku elected not to serve the fledgling Meiji regime in spite of invitations from several of its key officials. Yet far from retreating into obscurity, Ryūhoku built upon his past experiences and endeavors as a poet and writer to carve out a new position for himself as a pioneering journalist, editing the *Chōya shinbun* newspaper, founding one of Japan's first literary magazines, *Kagetsu shinshi*, and continuing to take an active role in Meiji society as a widely read critic, satirist, and commentator.

The continuity of Ryūhoku's literary activities on either side of the Meiji Restoration means that he frustrates the neat categories of Japanese literary history that conventionally take the year 1868 as a decisive pivot. Perhaps the best index of this dual status is the way in which the works of his translated here have been incorporated into the schemas of postwar literary anthologies. His *Ryūkyō shinshi* (New Chronicles of Yanagibashi), for example, is the final selection in Iwanami Shoten's *Shin Nihon koten bungaku taikei* (New compendium of classical Japanese literature), a definitive edition of annotated primary texts from the classical canon that was published in one hundred volumes between 1989 and 2005. Likewise, a generous sampling of Ryūhoku's *kanshi* (poems in literary Chinese) is included in the tenth and final volume of the *Edo shijin senshū* (Selection of Edo-period *kanshi* poets), also published by Iwanami between 1990 and 1993. Despite such classical categorization, however, Ryūhoku's works have also been among the first to be included in multi-volume sets of the modern literary canon. For example, both *Nihon gendai bungaku zenshū* (Complete works of Japanese contemporary literature), a massive collection of 108 volumes that Kōdansha published in the 1960s, as well as the sixty-volume *Nihon kindai bungaku taikei* (Compendium of modern Japanese literature) published by Kadokawa Shoten beginning later that decade, place *New Chronicles of Yanagibashi* in their first volumes. Similarly, Chikuma Shobō's more narrowly circumscribed *Meiji bungaku zenshū* (Complete works of Meiji literature), which was launched in 1965, includes both *New Chronicles of Yanagibashi* and Ryūhoku's overseas travelogue *Diary of a Journey to the West* in its fourth volume, and its volume on Meiji Chinese poetry, edited by Kanda Kiichirō, includes several selections from Ryūhoku's *kanshi*.

Most recently, in what can be read as a recognition of the limitations of the 1868 divide, an affirmation of the interpenetration of "classical" and "modern" texts, and an acknowledgment of the continued significance and relevance of "classical" texts to Meiji literature, Iwanami Shoten launched a new series in 2001. Called *Shin Nihon koten bungaku taikei: Meiji hen* (New compendium of classical Japanese literature: Meiji section), this thirty-volume series includes selections from Ryūhoku's *kanshi* in its 2004 volume of Chinese poetry and prose, and his Western travelogue has just been included in the compendium's volume of overseas travel literature, published in 2009. As the treatment of Ryūhoku's works by these large-scale postwar publishing ventures suggests, Ryūhoku's place in Japanese literary history partakes in important ways of both the "classical" and "modern," a hybridity that is only underscored by the languages in which he wrote much of his work: literary Chinese, in both pure and highly domesticated forms, and Sino-Japanese.[1]

By the time Ryūhoku was writing in the mid-nineteenth century, *kanshibun* (which collectively refers to *kanshi* poetry and *kanbun* literary Chinese prose) had thrived for well over a thousand years in Japan. In fact, the nineteenth century as a whole witnessed an

---

[1] I use the term "literary Chinese" to indicate the language of *kanshibun*. I do so knowing that the word "Chinese" has the potential to be misleading, for it may impute to *kanbun* a sense of foreignness or exclusive geographical specificity that many educated Japanese clearly did not experience or perceive in composing it. John Timothy Wixted, a pioneering scholar of Japan's *kanbun* tradition, has proposed using the term "'Sino-Japanese' for *kanbun* written by Japanese," while reserving "the term 'Chinese' for *kanbun* texts written by Chinese" (23). I share Wixted's concern that the "Chinese" designation for *kanbun* risks perpetuating the exclusion of these texts from the canons of Japanese literary study. Nevertheless, I have reservations about relying on the nationality of the author to determine a text's linguistic status. It may be argued that "Sino-Japanese" is the proper term because the primary mode through which Japanese scholars engaged *kanbun* texts was the *kundoku* reading practice: a means of rearranging literary Chinese according to Japanese syntax. Yet I think it is important to maintain a distinction between *kanbun* texts, in which the constituent characters retain their order and intelligibility as Chinese, and what I call "Sino-Japanese" texts: those that are rearranged and written out in *kundoku*.

unprecedented rise in *kanshibun* composition, its final spectacular flourish before the medium rapidly declined during the first decades of the twentieth century. While facility in literary Chinese had been presumed for Japanese cultural elites for centuries, the late-eighteenth-century Kansei reforms spread this competence to a much wider range of social strata. A basic ability to read the Chinese classics came to be identified with learning itself, and groups devoted to *kanshibun* composition appeared not just in major cities but throughout the countryside. By the middle of the nineteenth century, modern media featuring *kanshibun* circulated in greater numbers and an increasingly diverse and accessible array of reference materials offered guidance for aspiring composers through the first decades of the Meiji period. On the one hand, *kanshibun* was undeniably an antique form, for it was the earliest mode of writing in Japan and served as the gateway to much older Chinese texts. By the very act of writing, Japanese producers of *kanshibun* claimed membership in a cosmopolitan coterie that transcended their present time and space, providing them with an opportunity to engage in literary dialog with illustrious predecessors from the annals of Chinese letters. At the same time, however, *kanshibun* was also significant as the literary and textual medium that dominated many dimensions of nineteenth-century Japan's encounters with the new, in the form of journeys to modern European cities, encounters with new technologies, descriptions of new social and political institutions, and some of the earliest negotiations with Western literary forms.

  The works translated here embody these dual aspects and also illustrate some of the main genres of *kanshibun* popular in the mid-nineteenth century. They are two of Ryūhoku's most representative, widely read, and influential pieces. The first is *Ryūkyō shinshi*, or *New Chronicles of Yanagibashi*, a satirical account of the geisha district of

Yanagibashi that Ryūhoku wrote in installments as the Tokugawa period ended and the Meiji period began. Begun in 1859, *New Chronicles of Yanagibashi* provides not only an informative overall view of the quarter and an explanation of its practices, terms, and customs, but also many humorous sketches of its inhabitants and a series of practical tips for its patrons. At the same time, the work features a relentlessly cynical revelation of the base drives that really govern affairs in Yanagibashi, a comic exposé of the grim and mercenary underside of its success, and a variety of criticisms aimed at targets beyond its confines. If Ryūhoku structured the first installment of *New Chronicles* mainly as a comprehensive, synthetic, explanatory overview of the Yanagibashi quarter, the second installment, which was completed in 1871, is more clearly episodic, organized as a collection of discrete emplotted narratives. The critical tone of the second volume is also more pronounced, and its sights are more explicitly set on recent social changes. In the short span of time between the appearance of volumes one and two, the Tokugawa shogunate, which had ruled Japan for two and a half centuries, came to an end, Edo was renamed Tokyo, and the new capital city saw a host of changes in its customs, material culture, and social structure. Coinciding with shifts at the centers of state power, these transformations were emblematic of the onset of a new era of modernization known as *bunmei kaika*, or "civilization and enlightenment." Using the lens of the geisha district, the second volume of *New Chronicles of Yanagibashi* reveals some of the pitfalls of this program and its occasionally superficial nature. Moreover, in turning to the romantic affairs, contemporary customs, and elegant diversions associated with Yanagibashi's leisure culture for its principal subject matter, the text issued a challenge to an era in which practicality and utility carried the day. Taken as a whole, *New Chronicles of Yanagibashi* serves as both a documentary record and an amusingly nuanced social critique. The work was widely read by Ryūhoku's contemporaries and was a familiar point of textual reference for the generation of writers who came of age in the mid-Meiji period. As novelist Nagai Kafū (1879–1959) noted in the 1920s, *New Chronicles of Yanagibashi* ensured that Ryūhoku retained a place in the memories of Kafū's contemporaries, and even today it remains the work most associated with Ryūhoku's name.

The second work translated here is *Kōsei nichijō*, or *Diary of a Journey to the West*, the poetic journal Ryūhoku kept during the tour he made around the world between 1872 and 1873. The early 1870s marked a time when hundreds of Japanese officials, students, and businessmen traveled abroad to observe and study Western civilization. While many of the Japanese who ventured to Europe and the United States at the time kept diaries or published accounts of their travels, Ryūhoku's travelogue stands apart as being one of the earliest Japanese overseas travelogues to foreground the individual traveler's personal experience of the journey, his lyrical response to the scenes encountered abroad, and his sophisticated appreciation of the cultures visited. *Diary of a Journey to the West* was for this reason read foremost as a literary work and became a model for several subsequent Japanese literary figures who composed overseas travelogues. As many critics have pointed out, Ryūhoku was in important respects "the first Japanese tourist," and the diary's portrayal of his journey as one undertaken by a private individual unencumbered by the responsibilities of an official diplomatic or investigative mission was surely a major factor in ensuring its popularity among early Meiji readers. Yet we should not let Ryūhoku's unaffiliated status blind us to the equally significant ways in which his overseas experience helped to solidify the groundwork for his career as an engaged journalist, a future course we can see prefigured in both texts appearing in this volume.

New Chronicles of Yanagibashi

Yanagibashi refers specifically to the "Willow Bridge" first built in late-seventeenth-century Edo near the confluence of the Kanda and the Sumida Rivers (Figure 1). More broadly, it is the name of the district lying to the south of the Bridge from which pleasure boats would ferry passengers to the entertainment districts that lay on the city's periphery. One such destination was Yoshiwara, the pre-eminent licensed prostitution quarter that had been established by the shogunate in 1617 on what was then the outskirts of Edo. As rapid urban growth soon brought the Yoshiwara district within the boundaries of the burgeoning city, the authorities ordered it to be relocated outside the city limits again; the new Yoshiwara district opened in the late 1650s at a location near Asakusa, where it stayed for the remainder of the Edo

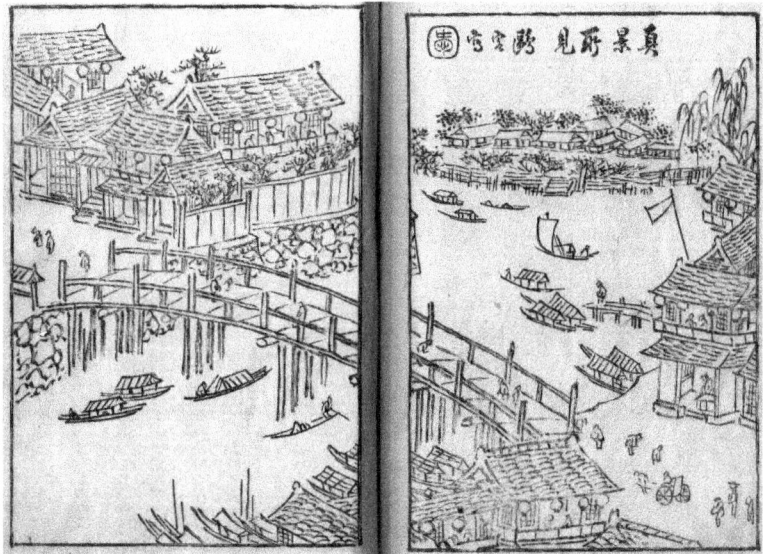

Figure 1. Frontispiece of *Ryūkyō shinshi nihen* (Tokyo: Yamashiroya Masakichi, 1874) showing Yanagibashi in the foreground. The woodcut is inscribed at top right "A true depiction of what is seen. Sketched by Ōkaku." The artist may be Sakata Ōkaku 坂田鷗客, a painter active in the circle of Kawanabe Kyōsai (1831–1899); see Yoshida, 19.

period. A world unto itself with its own culture and even unique linguistic forms, Yoshiwara has been described variously as a "necessary evil" or safety valve for Edo society, a microcosm of that society, and an alternative reality where rigid social strictures could be temporarily transcended and where highly codified rules of connoisseurship and play took their place.[2] Yet in spite of local authorities' periodic attempts to corral prostitution within the confines of Yoshiwara, it was practiced rather openly in other districts such as Fukagawa, which developed their own flourishing nightlife in competition with Yoshiwara. Collectively known as the "flower and willow world" (*karyūkai*), such locales where prostitution was either legal or tacitly permitted were soon to see the emergence of a figure around whom grew a new culture of entertainment: the geisha.[3]

Male and female professional entertainers calling themselves *geisha* first began to appear in Fukagawa and Yoshiwara during the 1750s and 1760s.[4] These individuals could be hired to accompany a customer on a pleasure excursion along the Sumida River, for example, or engaged to enliven a banquet with witty repartee, traditional dances and songs, or shamisen music. Within a few decades, female geisha overwhelmingly outnumbered male geisha, and the term "geisha" itself

---

[2] The articles gathered in Swinton's *The Women of the Pleasure Quarter* discuss these various representations of the cultural space of Yoshiwara from a range of disciplinary perspectives. See also Cecilia Segawa Seigle's essay in *A Courtesan's Day: Hour by Hour* for a consideration of the disjunction between the often grim realities of life for courtesans in Yoshiwara and the glamorous images of "ethereal Yoshiwara" presented in woodblock prints of the time.

[3] Some hold that the "flower" refers to the prostitutes of the licensed quarter and the "willow" to the geisha, but such a clear distinction was not universally observed.

[4] Lesley Downer identifies a Fukagawa prostitute named Kikuya as the first to call herself a geisha; around 1750, Kikuya "had made a reputation for herself with her shamisen-playing and singing and decided to make entertaining her full-time profession" (*Women*, 103). Kelly Foreman notes that in 1762 a woman named Kasen became the first woman to be listed as a geisha in Yoshiwara (*Gei*, 45–46). Tanaka Yūko conjectures that geisha were active in Fukagawa even earlier: by the 1740s (29–33).

soon came to indicate female entertainers specifically.⁵ One important factor that contributed to the initial proliferation of female entertainers in such districts, and that led to the eventual emergence of the geisha, was the banning of female performers from public stages in 1629. The licensed quarters and areas such as Fukagawa thus provided one of the few venues for them to pursue artistic endeavors and earn a livelihood.

In contrast to the Yoshiwara courtesans, geisha were not expected to provide sexual services, and indeed regulations were imposed that sought to prevent geisha from infringing upon the courtesans' custom.⁶ In the same way that a highly elaborated culture of minutely codified social etiquette for patrons and complex hierarchies for courtesans had taken shape in Yoshiwara during the seventeenth century, the latter half of the eighteenth century saw the development of an equally sophisticated culture surrounding the geisha, who began to ply their trade in a wider range of sites around the city. Along with the emergence of the female geisha, in particular, one sees a growing sense of specialization by district, which in turn generated a strong sense of regional identity. In her comprehensive study of the history and aesthetics of the Yoshiwara, Cecilia Segawa Seigle notes the special pride of place that geisha of the licensed quarter enjoyed in comparison to those based in other areas:

---

⁵ By the early 1770s, *geisha* was appearing in Japanese texts as a phonetic gloss for words such as *kagi* 歌妓 "singing female entertainer" and *gisha* 妓者 "female entertainer" (Chinpunkan Shujin, 24). The term 妓 (J. *gi*; Ch. *ji*) refers to singing and dancing female entertainers as well as to those who performed sexual services. It is often rendered into English as "courtesan," and I have followed that practice in general here, unless the term is clearly being used to indicate "geisha." I reserve the word "prostitute" for translating words such as 娼 (J. *shō*; Ch. *chang*), which are unambiguous in indicating labor that is primarily sexual.

⁶ Female geisha were first regulated in Yoshiwara with the establishment of an office called the *kenban* in 1779. Even today, *kenban* is the name for the district offices where geisha register and that often handle the collection and disbursement of their fees.

> Yoshiwara geisha were generally superior artists and more graceful and more dignified in their behavior than their rivals in other parts of Edo. Edo geisha (in Ryōgoku-Yanagibashi, Tachibanachō, Yoshichō, Yotsuya) were known for their easy morals, for example, and Fukagawa district geisha, known as Tatsumi (southeastern) geisha whose high spirits and dash were famous, did not hesitate to participate in prostitution. Fukagawa was full of illegal brothels, and prostitution was apparently a matter of course for the geisha there. These women were regularly arrested and sent to the Yoshiwara. (*Yoshiwara*, 174–75)

The "Edo geisha" mentioned here were also known as *machi-geisha*, or "town-geisha," indicating female professional entertainers in districts within the city such as Yanagibashi who tended to be looked down upon by the geisha of Yoshiwara. The privileged status of the licensed quarters on Edo's periphery meant that *machi-geisha* based inside the city limits had to be careful not to use particular reserved occupational terms, dress too extravagantly, or even call themselves "geisha" too openly, lest they infringe on their Yoshiwara counterparts' special privileges. Kitagawa Morisada's late-Edo compendium of contemporary Japanese customs explains this disconnect between what was supposedly permitted and what actually took place for the geisha of Yanagibashi:

> *Machi-geisha* are also known as "Edo-geisha;" the term refers to those of the city in contrast to the women of Yoshiwara and Fukagawa. There are many in the areas around Ryōgoku and Yanagibashi, Yoshichō, Jinzaemonchō, Horiechō, and Kyōbashi … The *machi-geisha* do not differ at all in appearance and dress from those of the licensed quarters … The *machi-geisha* of Edo are mainly invited to entertain in restaurants or they accompany pleasure boat excursions … They openly call themselves "geisha" but this is ultimately just a private term of reference; officially they are "drink-pourers." (III: 381–382)

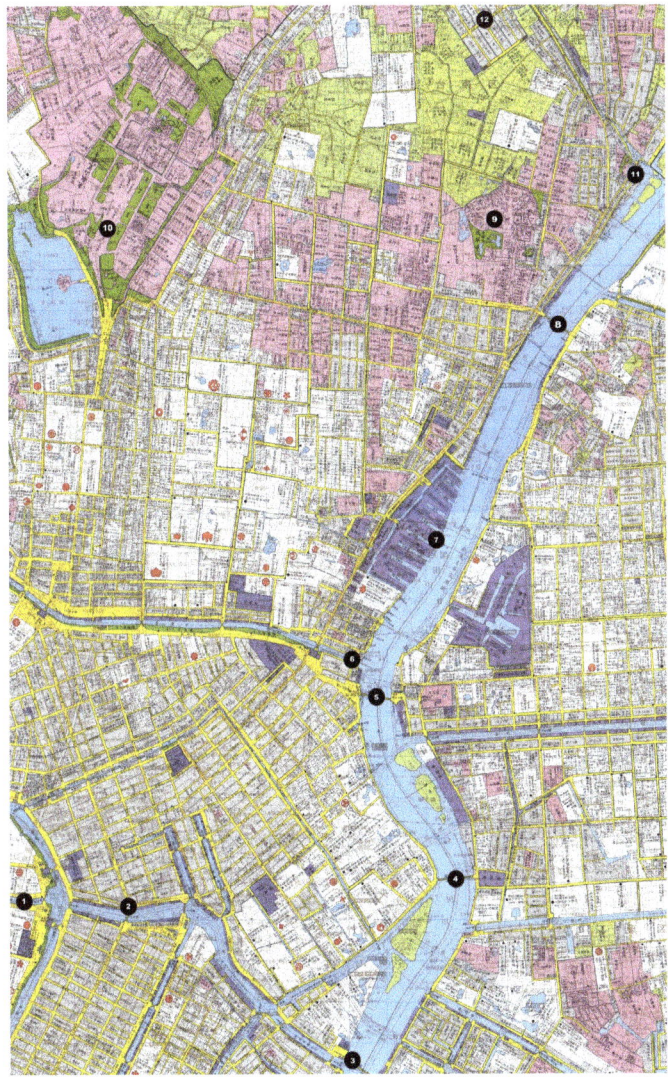

Figure 2: Sumida River and Environs. 1. Edo Castle; 2. Nihon ("Japan") Bridge; 3. Eitai ("Eternal") Bridge; 4. Shin'ō ("New Great") Bridge; 5. Ryōgoku ("Two States") Bridge; 6. Yanagi ("Willow") Bridge; 7. Shubinomatsu "Topsy-turvy Pine"; 8. Azuma ("Eastern") Bridge; 9. Sensōji Temple; 10. Kan'eiji Temple; 11. Mount Matsuchi; 12. Yoshiwara. Modified from a map provided by Timon Screech.

In spite of the somewhat unfavorable judgment initially passed upon Yanagibashi geisha and the ambiguity of their very status as geisha, Yanagibashi emerged as one of the premier geisha districts in the closing decades of the Edo period.

Yanagibashi attained this status in part as an outgrowth of its traditional role as the point of departure for the most popular of the major routes to Yoshiwara: boat passage along the Sumida (Figure 2).[7] Yet by the late Edo period, the Yanagibashi area had become a stylish destination in its own right. Yanagibashi's transformation was decisively accelerated by the government's crackdown on illegal prostitution in Fukagawa, for the prostitutes operating there were forcibly relocated to Yoshiwara while its geisha gathered in Yanagibashi (Nakao, 123). A vibrant recreational culture soon began to thrive in Yanagibashi, centered on its boathouses, restaurants, and drinking establishments. Such forms of diversion were still very much intact in the summer of 1871, when Charles A. Longfellow, the son of the famous American poet, arrived in Tokyo and quickly became a devotee of Yanagibashi, writing the following to his sister about the leisure opportunities it afforded:

> Besides the scenes in the streets which are always curious and interesting, there are a great many magnificent temples to visit and tea gardens where the 'young Japan' delight to spend the day lazing off on cool straw mats in loose dressing gowns, smoking, singing, reading aloud to each other, and listening to the singing girls they often bring with them. Our evenings have been spent drifting about on the river, which is most refreshing after the

---

[7] Through a symbolic reading of various notable sites along the route and the specific qualities of the river-borne passage itself, Timon Screech has argued that the journey from Yanagibashi to Yoshiwara "transformed and so prepared" travelers "for the transient joys of the pleasure world" (255). See also Nakamura Shikaku, *Yūkaku no sekai*, esp. chapter 14.

heat of the day and is most amusing—as the water is covered with hundreds of boats, each one lit by a large round paper lantern and filled with pleasure seekers. I must say the Japanese know how to enjoy themselves most rationally. (Laidlaw, 28)

From the late Edo period onward, Yanagibashi's success was sustained in large part by the local geisha (the "singing girls" Longfellow mentions above) who could be hired to provide companionship and entertainment; see Figure 3 for an early-Meiji photograph of one group of revelers enjoying a daytime river outing on a *yanebune*, or roofed "pleasure boat."

Even when Ryūhoku first took up his brush in 1859, Yanagibashi was beginning to edge out Yoshiwara as the destination of true geisha connoisseurs, in part because it lacked the latter's strict regulations. Just a few years before Ryūhoku's second installment appeared, the prestige of Yanagibashi geisha received one important official endorsement when the Tokugawa shogunate sent three of the district's geisha abroad in 1867 to staff a Japanese teahouse at the International Exhibition in Paris. In some respects, Yanagibashi retained this association with the Tokugawa shogunate even after it was deposed in the Meiji Restoration that took place the following year. As can be glimpsed from the second volume of Ryūhoku's *New Chronicles of Yanagibashi*, some former shogunal officials who patronized the district regarded the triumphant arrivistes who streamed into the capital from the victorious southwest domains as uncouth interlopers. These newly empowered government figures thus began to patronize a separate geisha district at Shinbashi, which quickly became the preferred site of recreation for important officials, a status Shinbashi maintained until well into the postwar period. Whatever preferences individual customers may have had for the rival geisha districts of Yanagibashi and Shinbashi, it was clear by the second decade of Meiji

Figure 3. Photograph of a *yanebune* roofed pleasure-boat, circa 1871. From the collection of Charles Longfellow, whose album gives the caption at top: A "Yanni buni" (Pleasure boat) Yedo. Ishiguro Keishō notes that this photograph, conventionally thought to have been taken by Uchida Kyūichi, may instead be by Felice Beato (Yamada, 370–374). Courtesy of National Park Service, Longfellow National Historic Site.

that the geisha of these districts now had ascendancy over their Yoshiwara counterparts.[8]

---

[8] In 1881, Tsukioka Yoshitoshi 月岡芳年 (1839–1892) began a series of woodblock prints entitled *The Twenty-four Hours at Shinbashi and Yanagibashi* that further testifies to the ascendance of these two geisha districts in preference to the Yoshiwara. See the images and the accompanying essays by Alfred H. Marks and Harue M. Summersgill in Seigle's *A Courtesan's Day: Hour by Hour*. On the outmoding of Yoshiwara, Liza Dalby notes: "Whereas the official Yoshiwara geisha had once looked down their noses at the geisha in the outside areas, now Yoshiwara geisha were deemed second-rate" (Swinton, *The Women of the Pleasure Quarter*, 64).

As Longfellow's letter home hints, the figure of the geisha has been an object of Western attention and fantasy about Japan since the mid-nineteenth century.[9] Yet some of the dominant images and understandings of her occupation and role in Japanese society, particularly with respect to the question of sexual labor, have occasionally lacked historical nuance or have unreasonably generalized the characteristics of a single subgroup of geisha to the profession as a whole. A number of books are now available in English that in various ways shed light on the lives geisha have led from the mid-eighteenth century to the present day. Liza Dalby's *Geisha*, based upon her fieldwork during the mid-1970s in Kyoto's Pontochō district, provides a detailed history of the geisha and remains the fullest treatment of the relations, traditions, and practices that structure the world of the geisha in modern-day Japan. In Dalby's account, the modern-day geisha's avocation combines two ideally complementary roles as artistic professional and banquet entertainer:

> Some geisha feel that their professional lives have two aspects: gei, art, the source of their pride and self-definition as geisha, and zashiki, the night-to-night partying that they are actually paid to do. The geisha who are happiest in their work are of course those for whom these two aspects coincide. (139)

Kelly Foreman's recent *The Gei in Geisha*, based upon extensive fieldwork beginning in the late 1990s, also examines these two roles of

---

[9] Christine Guth's *Longfellow's Tattoos* insightfully explores the various forms of fantasy evident in Charles Longfellow's encounter with Japan. See Lesley Downer's *Madame Sadayakko* for discussion of how the term "geisha" was understood abroad at the turn of the century. Most recently, Anne Allison has devoted particular attention to analyzing the popularity of Arthur Golden's *Memoirs of a Geisha* in the United States at the end of the twentieth century, exposing the rhetorical strategies by which the text not only purveyed certain exoticist fantasies but also convinced readers of its "authenticity."

the geisha as artist and entertainer. As her title indicates, however, Foreman sees the relationship between the roles in a slightly different way. She argues that it is the domain of musical and other artistic training that alone forms the constitutive center of contemporary geisha existence and identity. Whereas Dalby sees the principal aim of Pontochō as lying in the production of the perception that the geisha district "is an entire world created for the delectation of men" (7), Foreman instead sees the entertainment of male customers as a decidedly peripheral concern. In Foreman's view, geisha undertake arts training not to prepare for zashiki banquets but in order to take part in annual arts performances (59); for these geisha, entertaining at zashiki is but a "day job" (63) or a "means to the end" (95) of artistic training and performance.

In addition to these scholarly studies, two first-hand accounts by former geisha are easily accessible to English readers. *Geisha, a Life* is the autobiography of Iwasaki Mineko, a Kyoto geisha who served as a source for Arthur Golden's novel *Memoirs of a Geisha*. Part of Iwasaki's motivation in writing her reminiscences was to correct a misperception about geisha that she believed Golden's novel had only served to re-inscribe: the association of the geisha with commodified sex.[10] While Iwasaki offers with this book an important refutation of a misleading stereotype concerning contemporary geisha, we must be careful not to assume that the circumstances of present-day geisha can be readily imposed upon the past. Women who become geisha today do

---

[10] In the memoir itself, Iwasaki observes that literary and dramatic works set in Gion have sometimes "served to propagate the notion that courtesans ply their trade in the area and that geiko spend the night with their customers ... I understand that there are some scholars of Japan in foreign countries who also believe these misconceptions to be true" (156); elsewhere she claims that the once distinct roles of geisha and courtesan became blurred after the 1872 *Maria Luz* Incident (162). Foreman's "Bad Girls Confined" discusses Iwasaki's characterization of Golden's novel as libelous for its focus on the sexual (36).

so of their own free will, and as Dalby and Foreman have convincingly shown, a contemporary Japanese woman's earnest devotion to the arts is one of the major motivations for such a career choice:

> A woman entering the geisha life today makes her choice of career freely, unaffected by the social conditions that in prewar days sometimes forced families to sell daughters to geisha houses. Unless she has some interest in the arts, therefore, a girl has no reason at all to become a geisha. She could easily save more money and be less restricted in some other line of work. (Dalby, *Geisha*, 218)[11]

Yet to imply, as some have in their zeal to counter patronizing or prurient preconceptions, that the single-minded pursuit of the arts has always been the reason that Japanese women became geisha, that stories of women sold into indentured servitude are "urban legends," and that any association of the historical geisha with sexual labor springs solely from Western biases or misunderstandings, is simply untenable. Another first-person account, Masuda Sayo's *Autobiography of a Geisha*, is a particularly sobering corrective on this point. Masuda worked as a geisha in the years leading up to the Second World War, and as G. G. Rowley, the translator of her autobiography, observes, "the romanticization of geisha life as dedicated principally to the pursuit of traditional arts ignores the poverty that drove many parents to indenture their daughters to geisha houses"; it may be just as misguided and harmful a distortion as that which simplistically equates the geisha

---

[11] In *The Gei of Geisha*, Foreman frames becoming a geisha as the sole option available for many women who aspire to become artistic professionals: "Any woman may choose to study shamisen, voice, or dance, but if she desires to do it as a career rather than simply as an amateur, to avoid teaching, and to feel free not to marry or bear children, then becoming a geisha is the only way for most women to accomplish this goal" (35–36).

with the prostitute (6).¹² If the prevalent images circulating about present-day geisha in various discourses can often color assumptions about geisha of the past, Ryūhoku's *New Chronicles of Yanagibashi* stands as a valuable contemporary source of insight into the status, customs, and lives of geisha in nineteenth-century Japan. While the narrative often idealizes the refined artistic atmosphere that the quarter sought to cultivate, it is also unflinching in depicting its less glamorous aspects.¹³

Ryūhoku began writing his accounts of the emerging Yanagibashi district culture while serving in what might seem to be an unlikely position, that of a rising Confucian scholar in the employ of the Tokugawa shogunate. His official responsibilities in his early life ranged from instructing the shoguns Iesada (1824–1858) and Iemochi (1846–1866) in the Chinese classics, to editing official historical annals such as the *Tokugawa jikki* (Chronicle of the Tokugawa). To acquire the knowledge and skills necessary to eventually carry out these tasks, Ryūhoku had spent his childhood receiving intensive training in the Confucian classics and Chinese poetry and prose composition from his father and grandfather. The earliest extant volumes of the diary that he kept throughout his life in literary Chinese show a staid schedule wherein the teenage Ryūhoku attended various textual study groups, participated in poetry composition circles, and assisted with the compilation of historical records. Around the time he turned twenty, however, Ryūhoku's routine began to include forays into Edo's leisure culture, as the following entry from the summer of 1857 shows (the original text appears in Figure 4):

---

[12] In addition to the other sources I mention here, Lesley Downer has written two books focused on geisha: *Women of the Pleasure Quarters* is a general history interspersed with descriptions of the lives of geisha in contemporary Kyoto; and *Madame Sadayakko* is a biography of Kawakami Sadayakko (1871–1946), a geisha who achieved international fame as a dancer and actress.
[13] For one feminist reading of the text, see Chieko Ariga's "Dephallicizing Women."

[Fifth month] Twenty-first. *Kanoto-hitsuji*. Fine, then cloudy. I set out on a pleasure boat on the Sumida River with Sugimoto Kōseki, Tamura Sōtatsu, Izawa Heikyū, and others. We relaxed in the Kawaguchiya and Hiraiwa. Kokatsu came and joined us.[14]

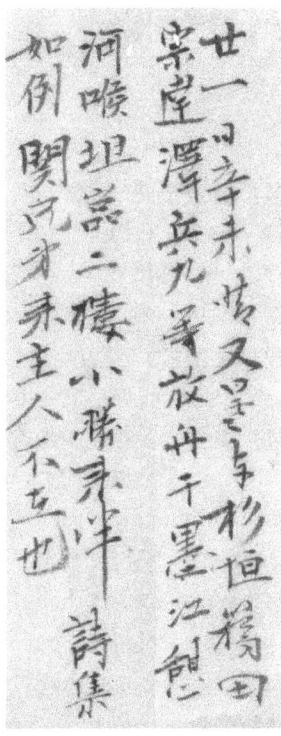

Figure 4. Diary entry for 05.21 of Ansei 4 [June 12, 1857], from Narushima Ryūhoku's *Kenhoku nichiroku*, vol. 4. Courtesy of Cornell University Library. After describing the outing on the Sumida, Ryūhoku concludes the entry with: "My poetry gathering was held as usual. The Seki brothers came, but the master [i.e., Ryūhoku] was absent."

---

[14] *Kenhoku nichiroku* (315–316). On this excursion, Ryūhoku was in the company of two physicians, Sugimoto Kōseki and Tamura Sōtatsu, and a student of his, Izawa Heikyū (Inui, *Narushima Ryūhoku kenkyū*, 37). The term *kanoto-hitsuji* (lit. "metal junior sheep") is from the sexagenary cycle dating system, which combines the traditional five elements, the principles of *yin* and *yang*, and the twelve animals of the zodiac into a sixty-item repeating sequence used in East Asia to identify dates.

The geisha "Kokatsu" mentioned here was in fact one with whom Ryūhoku briefly became romantically involved later that year. From 1857 to 1859, Ryūhoku's trips to Yanagibashi grew increasingly frequent, and by mid-winter of 1859 he had written the bulk of the first volume of his *New Chronicles of Yanagibashi*, though he added some additional material the following year.[15]

As its foreword suggests, the text presumably circulated to some extent among Ryūhoku's friends and associates. Indeed, rumors about it, and the profligacy it implied about its author, may have been part of the reason Ryūhoku lost his job in the shogunate a few years later in 1863. One story, which appears in the afterword of the second volume, holds that Ryūhoku had written a satirical Chinese couplet on the walls of a shogunal office, mocking its shortsighted policy. Yet Ryūhoku himself was notoriously evasive about the reasons for his dismissal, which left him in domiciliary confinement and without an official post for three years. He offers only a series of tantalizing possibilities in his 1868 autobiographical essay "Bokujō inshi den" (Biography of the Sumida Recluse): "One morning Ryūhoku was purged and left without a position. Perhaps he was just too suave, perhaps it was because he offended people by being too blunt, or perhaps it was because he advocated study of the West" (*Ryūhoku zenshū*, 1). Whatever role his experiences in Yanagibashi and the work he wrote about the quarter may have played in his 1863 dismissal from office, Ryūhoku seems to have attempted to publish the first volume in 1869, but his request was apparently denied. The text nevertheless

---

[15] Ryūhoku's diary for 1859 is no longer extant, but Nagai Kafū had access to it before it was destroyed. According to Kafū, the entry for 09.01 of that year read, "I began writing *Shinshi*." Ryūhoku had basically finished the bulk of the work by the winter of 1859, but he subsequently edited and supplemented it through 07.05 of the following year, on which day his diary reads, "I completed *Ryūkyō shinshi*." ("Ryūkyō," 284, 288, 290; see also Narushima Ryūhoku, *Kenhoku nichiroku*, 595).

reached an audience through pirate editions that circulated in the early Meiji period, before permission to publish it was granted in 1874: at which point the text's second installment had already appeared.[16]

The text enjoyed immense popularity upon its publication. Two years later, when Ryūhoku's stinging newspaper editorials critical of the new regime's draconian Press Laws got him into trouble with the Meiji government, sale and distribution of the book were again prohibited. Nevertheless, it remained widely known; as Nagai Kafū recalled, "There probably wasn't a student around in the Meiji period who was unfamiliar with Ryūhoku's *New Chronicles of Yanagibashi*" ("Ryūkyō," 283). A few years after the publication of the first two volumes, Ryūhoku composed a third installment, but was again prevented from publishing it by the Meiji authorities. Today, the only parts of the third volume that are extant are the preface and the foreword, both of which appear in translation here; the text itself has unfortunately been lost.[17]

---

[16] Shioda Ryōhei has carried out an exhaustive bibliographic study of the various printed pirate editions of the first volume as well as a manuscript copy of it held by the Imperial Library; see his essay in the 1940 paperback edition of the text and his 1941 article. He rejects the prevalent assumption that there were pirate versions of *New Chronicles of Yanagibashi* circulating in the late Tokugawa period, and conjectures that the absence of a colophon in the pirate editions has led people to mistakenly date them on the basis of the dates of completion given in the body of the main text: 1859 and 1860. Furthermore, the published version of 1874 includes a preface dated 1869, suggesting that this is when Ryūhoku first tried to publish it and was denied the right; consistent with Shioda's hypothesis, Saitō Shōzō lists the first volume of *Ryūkyō shinshi* in his yearbook of censored books for 1869 (2). Shioda concludes that both of the known lines of pirate editions were produced after permission for publication was denied in 1869, and furthermore that the pirate versions must have been to some degree authorized by Ryūhoku. Not everyone agrees with Shioda's conclusion that the pirate editions were from the early Meiji period; used book dealers in Japan routinely offer for sale "pirate editions" of the work that are said to be "from the late Tokugawa."

[17] Imamura Eitarō's "Narushima Ryūhoku shōkō," however, quotes extensively from the main text of the third volume. Unfortunately, Imamura does not disclose his source for this material, and somewhat puzzlingly, he gives no suggestion that he is quoting something that is, so far as I can determine, universally believed to be no longer extant.

Ryūhoku was of course not the first to document the particular culture of the pleasure quarters, nor was he the first to do so in literary Chinese. In fact, Ryūhoku closely modeled *New Chronicles of Yanagibashi* on two earlier texts, both of which he repeatedly refers to in the course of the work: *Banqiao zaji* (Miscellaneous Records of the Wooden Bridge) by the Qing literatus Yu Huai (1616–1696); and *Edo hanjōki* (Account of the Prosperity of Edo) by the late Edo-period Confucian scholar Terakado Seiken (1796–1868). In the former work, Yu Huai combined a retrospective celebration of the culture of the Nanjing pleasure quarters during the height of its popularity with a lament for the area's destruction during the Manchu conquest of 1644. In a 1964 article comparing Ryūhoku's work with Yu Huai's, the eminent literary scholar Maeda Ai pointed out several similarities in their diction, structure, and content. More importantly, he argued that there was a key distinction between *New Chronicles of Yanagibashi*, especially its first volume, and *Miscellaneous Records of the Wooden Bridge*. Maeda emphasized the "cynical realism" of Ryūhoku's text and suggested that whereas Yu Huai sought to reconstruct an ideal world with his biographies of Nanjing's beautiful courtesans, Ryūhoku instead clearly saw through the shimmering façade to "the mechanism of the pleasure quarters world that manipulated and toyed with these women, the hollowness of a world of vanity and money" (*Bakumatsu*, 222).[18]

---

[18] Yu Huai's text was well known to writers of the Edo period, having been reprinted in Japan, and even translated into Japanese; Yamazaki Ransai's 1772 *Tōdo meigi den* (Biographies of famous courtesans of the East) features a Japanese translation written in between lines of the original text. Given the differences between the glosses for the same kanji compounds in Ransai's version and those in *New Chronicles of Yanagibashi*, Maeda argues that Ryūhoku was not reading Ransai's translated version but another edition. Maeda's original article, "*Hankyō zakki* to *Ryūkyō shinshi*," is from March 1964, but my references are to the reprinted version appearing in the 1972 anthology *Bakumatsu ishinki no bungaku* (215–235).

The second work Ryūhoku repeatedly invokes in *New Chronicles of Yanagibashi* is particularly important because it served as a key inspiration not only for the text's content and structure, but for its basic style. Ryūhoku's narrator in fact draws repeated analogies between himself and Seiken, asserting, for example, that *New Chronicles of Yanagibashi* will be a fresh update and continuation of Seiken's project, or claiming that the life circumstances of the narrators are comparable. Moreover, Ryūhoku's difficulties in getting his text published, and the penalties he bore when it eventually was, paralleled Seiken's experiences a generation earlier. As Ryūhoku notes in *New Chronicles of Yanagibashi*, just as Seiken was preparing to publish the third volume of *Account of the Prosperity of Edo* in the spring of 1835, government authorities ordered his publisher to stop selling the two volumes that had already come to their attention and to destroy the text's printing blocks.

It is worth looking at the official justification for censoring Seiken's *Account of the Prosperity of Edo* since its argument focuses specifically on the text's irreverent combination of a generally dignified style with "improper" subject matter, a feature that characterized Ryūhoku's work on Yanagibashi as well. Hayashi Jussai (1768–1841), a Confucian scholar who directed the shogunate's official academy, was asked by the local authorities to render his judgment on Seiken's work, which was unambiguous:

> I have read *Account of the Prosperity of Edo*, and I believe that inasmuch as it is a book that is harmful to the public, weaving the manners and vulgar words of the contemporary city into a *kanbun* narrative, its publication should be ceased in accordance with your orders.[19]

---

[19] Maeda Ai quotes Tsutsui's letter and Hayashi's response in a 1965 article reprinted in his *Bakumatsu ishinki no bungaku* (120). Nagai Hiroo also quotes a slightly different

Jussai did not elaborate on what precisely made Seiken's text "harmful to the public," and though he did not frame the matter in unmistakably causal terms, it is suggestive that the single feature of the text that he points out for criticism is its use of elevated *kanbun* to report "vulgar" words and manners.[20] In any case, Seiken and his publisher were apparently undeterred by Jussai's admonition, and additional volumes continued to appear in coming years. As Mizuno Tadakuni's Tenpō Reforms gathered ground, however, the climate grew decidedly less tolerant, and in 1842, Seiken was summoned by the authorities.[21] Again, they called upon a top Confucian scholar, Jussai's son Hayashi Teiu (1793–1846), to evaluate the work. As had his father, Teiu focused on the style of *Account of the Prosperity of Edo*, faulting the text for recording its vulgarities in *kanbun* and reserving his most acute scorn for the author's misappropriation of the words of the Confucian Sages. Seiken was initially ordered confined for one hundred days, but his punishment was later changed to a permanent prohibition on official service.

Perhaps aided by this notoriety, Seiken's *Account of the Prosperity of Edo* went on to prompt a series of successors to publish *hanjōkimono* focused on other locales. These "chronicles of urban life" are, along with Ryūhoku's *New Chronicles of Yanagibashi*, part of a genre called *kanbun fūzokushi* ("*kanbun* chronicles of customs"), which played an important role in the future development of modern Japanese literature. As the name suggests, *kanbun fūzokushi* employed literary

---

account of the event by Takizawa Bakin (70–71).
[20] Endō Shizuo sees Seiken's punishment as evidence of "a tacit rule inevitably requiring those who use *kanbun* orthography to be self-restrained, to produce proper writing that fits the Confucian order" (*Kanbun*, 101).
[21] For a discussion of the Tenpō Reforms and their impact on publishing, see Kornicki's *The Book in Japan*, which mentions Seiken briefly (344–345); see also Bolitho's "The Tenpō Crisis" (esp. 143–146).

Chinese, often including *gikun* (playful glosses), to record the local conditions, customs, and manners that were typically overlooked in orthodox gazetteers or histories.[22] Such topics had of course long been addressed in other forms of writing, but to use *kanbun* to chronicle the humble or unseemly sides of contemporary life was to stake a claim for such material as a legitimate concern of literary expression at a time when the category of texts that we now regard as "literature" was still inchoate. The appearance of the *kanbun fūzokushi* genre thus anticipates an important development in Japanese letters that took place several decades later, when Tsubouchi Shōyō's 1885 treatise, *The Essence of the Novel*, established "customs, manners, and emotions" as the defining foci of modern prose literature. Part of the project Shōyō undertook in theorizing the novel was to create a space for a new autonomous literary domain that would endeavor to "fill in gaps," offering a "detailed portrayal of customs and manners that are not included in official history," a process that Atsuko Ueda has recently shown occurred through a negation of orthodox categories of discourse (56). This is an aim we can see clearly adumbrated in the closing lines of the preface to Ryūhoku's first volume, where the "foolish and empty-headed student" narrator writes: "There are some things that an upright Confucian gentleman would be unable to write, and that is precisely what someone like me ought to record."

Set in the "flower and willow world" and focused on amorous matters, the content of Ryūhoku's *New Chronicles of Yanagibashi*

---

[22] I have borrowed the formal and content-based criteria from the four-part definition proposed by Niina Noriko in her study of the slightly more narrowly circumscribed category of *hanjōkimono*: "They record the familiar circumstances and manners of various locales that are not depicted in proper gazetteers; almost all were written between 1832 and the fourth decade of Meiji [1907–1916]; in principle, the title is composed of a geographic name followed by *hanjōki* or *hanjōshi* (where the *shi* can be one of: 'chronicle' 誌, 'account' 志, or 'poems' 詩); they are composed in *kanbun* to which *gikun* (playful glosses) are appended in katakana" (5–38).

was thus in tension with the author's position as a Confucian scholar and editor of official histories. For this reason, it is not at all surprising that we see the narrator assume the guise of a "foolish student" who contrasts himself to "an upright Confucian gentleman"; nor is it surprising that the named author identifies the work as a "frivolous composition" (*gicho*) on the work's title page (Figure 5). Like the synonymous *gesaku* ("playful" or "frivolous writings"), the term *gicho* was a sort of disclaimer often used by scholars who wished to experiment with lighter fare while simultaneously maintaining a safe

Figure 5. Title page of Volume I of *Ryūkyō shinshi*. Ryūhoku's name and "frivolous composition" (*gicho*) are visible at right. Keishōkaku, one of the text's distributors appears at left. The date is given in the imperial calendar as April 2534, i.e., April 1874.

and respectable distance from it.[23] Nevertheless, within the text's preface and toward the end of both the first and second volumes, Ryūhoku repeatedly engages in extended efforts to justify the worth and legitimacy of his work's subject, defending the text from imagined interlocutors who would impugn its preoccupation with amorous matters.

In addition to the role *New Chronicles of Yanagibashi* played in mounting this defense of such content, the text was also significant for its distinctive style, which combined *kanbun* with colloquial Japanese *gikun*, or "playful glosses." Here again, the work had an important connection to future literary developments. In a wide variety of texts, Japanese glosses are frequently appended to the right side of Chinese characters to serve as a rather straightforward guide to pronunciation or sometimes as an explanation of meaning.[24] Yet as Chieko Ariga has observed about the glosses that often appeared to the left of some characters in works of *kanbun gesaku* (playful *kanbun* writings), such *rubi* (glosses) departed from simple correspondences and created "a more complex semantic space ... Unlike the texts in which *rubi* functioned as a reading aid, these genres were for readers who could appreciate fine literary nuances created by the varied combination of *kanji* and *rubi*" ("The Playful Gloss," 321). Playful glosses achieved their effects by foregrounding the discrepancy between the elegant *kanbun* style and the

---

[23] See Atsuko Ueda's useful discussion of Nakamura Yukihiko and others' work on *gesaku* in the context of early Meiji Japan (esp. 33–37).
[24] When Japanese is written horizontally, these glosses appear above the characters. The explanatory function can of course work both ways. For example, the contemporary Chinese word for "computer," *diannao* 電脳 (J. *dennō*; lit. "electric brain"), might be glossed in a Japanese text as *konpyūta*, in which case the gloss would be the more familiar term that served to explain the meaning of the characters—which would be readily intelligible to a Japanese reader individually but would perhaps be unfamiliar in combination. Alternatively, a potentially unfamiliar term such as *toposu* (topos) might be introduced as a gloss and simultaneously explained with the familiar character for "place" 場.

humble subject matter. While such disjunctions could be exploited for amusement, Kamei Hideo has identified another productive potential that was engendered by the very difficulty of capturing a contemporary Japanese scene using the language of *kanbun*:

> Out of the stratagems writers concocted to overcome this distance from their object there emerged a reflexivity about their own situatedness. For the first time, writers became self-conscious about how they positioned themselves. It was out of these efforts that the so-called "techniques of description" of the modern novel emerged. (28–29; trans. 21)

The playful glosses thus underscored the gaps between form and content that were inherent in the *kanbun fūzokushi* genre, and according to this view, the defamiliarization they permitted fostered the development of a new awareness of perspective.[25]

Another function of these playful glosses, which are usually written in colloquial Japanese, is to represent direct speech, thereby allowing for a more realistic portrayal of a particular character's diction than the *kanbun* prose alone would allow. Take, for example, the following scene from the first volume of *New Chronicles of Yanagibashi*, which narrates the interaction between a customer and a Yanagibashi boathouse Madam eager to act as his intermediary (Figure 6):

---

[25] Kamei's larger point about how such gaps created new opportunities for authorial reflection can be applied to Ryūhoku's work, but I should note that in his brief consideration of Ryūhoku's text, Kamei contends that Ryūhoku's narrator continually looks down upon the puppet-like figures who populate *New Chronicles of Yanagibashi*, never sharing the same space that they do. While this is true for many of the scenes in the text, there are also several scenes in which the tables turn and the narrator's smugness or short-sightedness, his specious reasoning or his naïvete, instead become the targets of the text's mockery. Moreover, if the "poor student" narrator of *New Chronicles of Yanagibashi* views a world from which he is usually excluded, Ryūhoku's authorial persona is nevertheless repeatedly made part of that world through the analogies drawn between geisha and Confucian scholars.

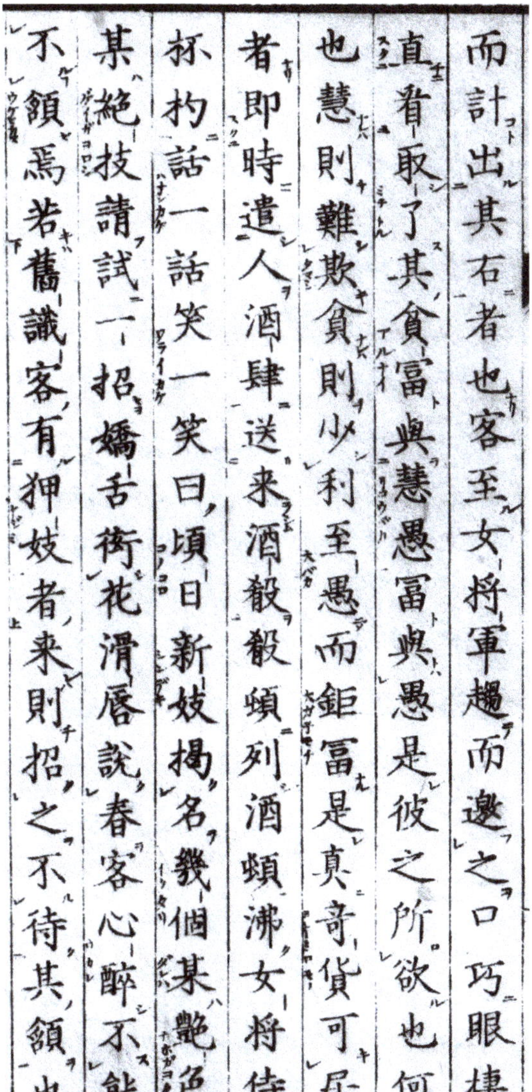

而計出其右者也客至女将軍趨而邀之口巧眼棲
直者取了其貧富與慧愚冨與愚是彼之所欲也何
也慧則難欺貪則少利至愚而鉅富是真奇貨可居
者即時遣人酒肆送来酒殽殽頻列酒頻沸女将侍
杯杓話一話笑一笑曰頃日新妓揭名幾個某艷色
其絶技請試一招嬌舌街花滑唇說春客心醉不能
不領焉若舊識客有狎妓者来則招之不待其領也

Figure 6. Sample of text from *Ryūkyō shinshi*. I: 5 verso. The passage discussed here begins with the eighth character in the rightmost column: 客.

客至。女将軍趣而邀之。口巧眼捷。直_{スグニ}看取_{ミテトル}了其貧富與_{アルナイ}慧愚_{リコウバカ}。富與愚、是彼之所欲也。何也。慧則難欺_{ダマシ}。貧則少利。至愚而鉅_{オホバカ}富_{オホカネモチ}、是真奇貨_{ヨキシロモノ}可居者。即時遣人酒肆、送來酒殽。殽頓列、酒頓沸。女将侍杯杓、話一話_{ハナシカケ}、笑一笑_{ワライカケ}、曰、「頃日_{コノゴロ}、新妓_{シンデキ}揭名幾個_{イクタリ}。某艷色_{ダレカホガヨク}、某絶技_{ダレゲイガヨクテ}。請、試一招」。嬌舌衒花、滑唇説春。客、心醉_{ウカレ}、不能不領_{ウケヒカヌ}焉。若舊識客有狎妓_{ナジミ}者、來則招之。不待其領也。

A customer arrives. The Madam runs to greet him, her words beguiling and her eyes quick. Straight away she has taken _{him up} stock, seeing whether he's wealthy or destitute, intelligent or _{stupid} foolish. Wealthy and foolish is what she seeks. Why? If he is intelligent, then he will be hard to deceive; if he is destitute, then there is no profit to be made. An absolute imbecile who _{a big spender} is also exceptionally wealthy — now *that* is a rare _{prize catch} piece of goods to put in the warehouse. Without hesitation, she sends someone off to the tavern to bring over some wine and food. The food is soon laid out, the wine is soon heated. The Madam attends on the customer, pouring his drinks. She _{chats him up flirts with him Recently a few fresh faces} talks a bit and smiles a bit: "Of late, several new girls _{So and so nice} have made their debuts. A certain one has a charming _{face so and so has many} countenance, and a certain one is exceptionally _{talents} accomplished. Why don't you invite one over and see for yourself?" Her charming tongue bespeaks flowers; her smooth _{gets carried away} lips tell of spring. The customer's mind grows intoxicated and _{accept the offer} he finds he cannot but nod his assent. When a regular _{steady} customer who has a particular favorite geisha arrives at the boathouse, the Madam will immediately invite her over without even waiting for him to nod.

This passage provides one of the earliest examples of the extensive use of *gikun* in the text and shows the multiple effects of such glosses, which are rendered here in smaller type above the main text line, much as they are in the original. In this passage, the *gikun* do not function simply as explanations or reading aids: there is no sense in which it is unclear that the straightforward term *hinpu* (貧富) refers to the relative wealth or poverty of the patron and that the similarly toned *keigu* (慧愚) refers to his intelligence or lack thereof. By glossing these terms as *arunai* ("got it or not?") and *rikō baka* ("sharp or stupid?"), however, the narrator brings us closer to the thought process of the Madam, who presumably neither thinks nor speaks in such abstractions of written discourse as *hinpu* or *keigu*. The technique furthermore allows the author to exploit the rhetorical and allusive possibilities of *kanbun* while at the same time allowing a degree of representational realism. In describing the "absolute imbecile who is also exceptionally wealthy" with the phrase "a rare piece of goods to put in the warehouse," for example, the *kanbun* narrative makes use of a classical allusion to the biography of Lü Buwei in Sima Qian's *Records of the Grand Historian*. The phrase refers to how the calculating merchant Lü Buwei perceived the potential profits he could obtain by supporting Zichu, a scheme that ultimately led to substantial material rewards and also enabled him to father the first Qin Emperor.[26] The colloquial gloss on this phrase,

---

[26] The *Shi ji* biography of Lü Buwei states that he uttered this phrase upon discerning the potential of Zichu: "Being merely a grandson of the king of Qin and the son of a concubine, and having been sent as hostage to one of the other feudal states, Zichu was poorly provided with carriages and other equipment and had to live in straitened circumstances, unable to do as he pleased. Lü Buwei, visiting Handan, the capital of Zhao, on business, saw him and was moved to pity. 'Here is a rare piece of goods to put in my warehouse!' he exclaimed." (Watson, *Records of the Grand Historian: Qin Dynasty*, 159) 子楚，秦諸庶孼孫，質於諸侯，車乘進用不饒，居處困，不得意．呂不韋賈邯鄲，見而憐之，曰「此奇貨可居」. While the basic sense of the term is a neutral expression of far-sighted planfulness, Ryūhoku's use of it here in reference to the cunning of the boathouse proprietress resonates with the craftiness of Lü Buwei in the

yoki shiromono ("a real prize catch") aims at a more representational account of the thought or speech of the boathouse proprietress. While the effect of the juxtaposition here is humorous, there are also many instances of colloquial glosses in the text that have neither a discernible humorous effect nor an explanatory function. For example, in glossing the term *jiko* 自己 (Ch. *ziji*), which functions in colloquial Chinese as a first person pronoun, with the virtually synonymous and equally toned Japanese term *jibun*, the narrator aims not at any humorous clash of registers but at phonocentric verisimilitude in depicting colloquial speech.[27]

As an exemplar of the *kanbun fūzokushi* genre, *New Chronicles of Yanagibashi* allows us to appreciate how *kanbun* texts continued to serve nineteenth-century Japanese writers as a site for stylistic innovation and rather daring experimentation. The passage of time has perhaps given *kanbun* an undeserved reputation as forbidding, bland, ponderous, and stodgy, but this text shows just how much fun late Edo and early Meiji literary figures could have with the medium. Moreover, in addition to achieving humorous effects by adding jarring "playful glosses," by willfully misquoting or misappropriating lines from the Confucian classics, or by exploiting the disjunction between form and

---

original story. There, Lü Buwei's plan is to convince Lady Huayang, the childless concubine of the crown prince Lord Anguo, to have Zichu designated as his heir in order to reap great future rewards. In the process, Lü Buwei deceives even Zichu, who asks his patron for the hand of a dancing girl with whom he is smitten, not suspecting that the woman is already carrying Lü Buwei's child. Eventually Zichu becomes the crown prince and shortly thereafter King Zhuangxiang of Qin. Zheng, the biological son of Lü Buwei whom Zichu's wife bears, later became the infamous Qin Shihuang.

[27] While *New Chronicles of Yanagibashi* is largely written in literary Chinese, there are many instances that show the influence of vernacular Chinese fiction on the text, especially in sequences of dialogue. Occasionally, the influence of vernacular Chinese fiction is also apparent on narrative prose, as in the structure 話一話、笑一笑 appearing in this passage. For a detailed discussion of the influence of vernacular Chinese fiction on Japanese and Korean literature, see Pastreich, "Reception."

content, the authors of *kanbun fūzokushi* texts used the medium to write some of the most trenchant critiques of contemporary society that were published at the time, and Ryūhoku's *New Chronicles of Yanagibashi* is no exception in this regard. Though he drew heavily upon the defining precedents in the genre, Ryūhoku also developed their possibilities further, demonstrating the continuing vitality and relevance of the form into the Meiji period.

Diary of a Journey to the West

If Ryūhoku's discovery of Yanagibashi's geisha culture in the late 1850s proved transformative for his development as a writer, another important encounter occurring at the same time set in motion a sequence of events that ultimately enabled him to travel abroad and to later publish the diary he kept about the experience. While still in his early twenties, Ryūhoku befriended Katsuragawa Hoshū (1826–1881), a scholar of Dutch whose family had served the shogunate for generations as physicians. Ryūhoku's encounter with Katsuragawa and the young Western scholars who gathered in his salon had a decisive influence on his future. In addition to his dalliances in Yanagibashi, one of the other reasons Ryūhoku suggested for his 1863 dismissal from the shogunate was his advocacy of Western learning, and it was in the company of the Katsuragawa salon members that this interest was first instilled. In the process of being exposed to Western learning, Ryūhoku had come to have serious doubts about the relevance of traditional Confucian studies to the crisis Japan faced from Western imperial powers.

For several years after he had been dismissed and confined to his home, Ryūhoku turned his attention to the study of Dutch and English. This effort bore fruit when Kurimoto Joun, one of his former colleagues in the shogunate, recommended him for a position in the modern military units that the shogunate was planning to create and to staff with French advisors. In his new role as cavalry commander, Ryūhoku befriended Charles Chanoine, the French officer who came to train the Japanese soldiers and with whom Ryūhoku would reunite a few years later in Paris. Yet in spite of its newly trained military, the days of the Tokugawa were numbered, and just before the Meiji Restoration, Ryūhoku resigned his post and went into temporary reclusion. He tried his hand in business for a time before landing a job in the eighth month of 1871 teaching *kanbun* and English in a school on the grounds of Higashi Honganji's branch temple in Asakusa.

It was the combination of his work with the French military officers and his connections to this Shin sect Buddhist temple that led to Ryūhoku being awarded the rare chance to travel to Europe in 1872. Ryūhoku was chosen to accompany the Reverend Gennyo,[28] Ishikawa Shuntai,[29] Matsumoto Hakka,[30] and Seki Shinzō[31] on their tour of the

---

[28] The Reverend Gennyo 現如 was also known as Ōtani Kōei 大谷光瑩 (1852–1923) and at the time of the Higashi Honganji group's departure, he was in line to become the twenty-second Head Priest of the temple. Gennyo had studied the Chinese classics under Ryūhoku and had served as a missionary in Hokkaido in early Meiji; on Honganji's activities in Hokkaido, see Ketelaar, 68–69.

[29] Born in Kanazawa, Ishikawa Shuntai 石川舜台 (1842–1931) studied at the Takakura Academy, an exegetical school run by Higashi Honganji before opening his own academy in early Meiji. After his return from Europe, Ishikawa participated in several reforms and instituted new programs at Higashi Honganji, chiefly involving the translation and compilation of religious and academic texts. He also was active in the propagation of Buddhism both inside Japan as well as in China, Taiwan, and Korea. Taya Raishun's article (esp. 156–161) and Kano's monograph provide detailed descriptions of Ishikawa Shuntai's major accomplishments; see also Takahata for a discussion of his intellectual development.

[30] Also from Kaga domain, Matsumoto Hakka 松本白華 (1838–1926) pursued Confucian studies under Hirose Kyokusō. After his return, he took part in various reforms in the Shin sect, including the encouragement of the study of Sanskrit. He was also active in the overseas missionary activities that Ishikawa Shuntai had planned and overseen. In 1877, for example, Hakka became one of the rotating supervisors of the Higashi Honganji annex in Shanghai, and he was also later involved in the plan to establish a school in Korea.

West, where he was to act as the group's treasurer and translator. This group of priests from Higashi Honganji had been motivated to plan a tour of the West because of Buddhism's embattled position during the 1870s. Its clergy were weakened and demoralized, and its traditional dominance of religious life was jeopardized by both the influx of Christianity and the new position that Shinto had been given as the national religion. Buddhist institutions found themselves under siege when the movement known as *haibutsu kishaku* (lit. "expel the Buddha and crush Shakyamuni") swept through Japan in the first years of Meiji.[32] This effort to exterminate Buddhism included forced closings of temples, the return of priests to secular life, the destruction of Buddhist images and relics, other forms of vandalism, and even violence. The movement understandably left contemporary Buddhist priests profoundly concerned about the future of their faith and prompted several to investigate religious traditions and institutions abroad.

Acting as the group's liaison, Ryūhoku and the four Shin Buddhist priests left Yokohama on October 16, 1872, aboard a French mail packet steamer bound for Hong Kong. The group transferred there to another French vessel for the journey to Marseille. Along the way, they called at the ports of Saigon, Singapore, Galle, and Aden, traversed the newly opened Suez Canal, and continued on to Marseille,

---

[31] Born in Mikawa, Seki Shinzō 関信三 (1843–1879) participated in the surveillance of Christian groups for Higashi Honganji during the last days of the shogunate: work that he continued in Yokohama on behalf of the Meiji government in the early 1870s. He became familiar with American missionaries such as James Hepburn and J. H. Ballagh, and was even baptized as a Christian several months prior to leaving for the West with the Higashi Honganji group (Kuniyoshi, esp. chapters 4–7; see also Oda Kenshin's article). After returning to Japan, he organized Japan's first kindergarten and remained a central figure in early education for the remainder of his life.

[32] For a concise discussion of the threat to Buddhism, see Martin Collcutt's essay and Notto Thelle's book (esp. chapters 2–4).

where they arrived in November 1872. Ryūhoku and the others from Higashi Honganji lodged in Marseille for two nights before traveling by rail to Paris, where they were based until late April 1873, aside from a three-week excursion to Italy.[33] Instead of returning to Japan by the route they had come, Ryūhoku and Ishikawa continued to England, crossed the Atlantic, and made their way to Japan via the United States. Hakka and Gennyo meanwhile visited Germany, then returned by the same route they had come.

Ten of the poems Ryūhoku had written while abroad were included in an 1875 *kanshi* anthology, but it was not until 1881 that he began to serialize *Diary of a Journey to the West* in his literary magazine *Kagetsu shinshi*. The text soon became one of the most widely read and influential overseas travel diaries of the early Meiji era. Mori Ōgai's novel *Gan* (The wild goose), for example, is a work that was published as the Meiji era ended and the Taishō era began, but is set three decades earlier, in the early 1880s. In it, two young men recall reading about Ryūhoku's departure for Europe:

> "I once read in *Kagetsu shinshi* that the idea of going abroad suddenly occurred to Narushima Ryūhoku in Yokohama, and that he immediately made up his mind and went aboard the ship."
>
> "Yes, I read that too. Ryūhoku apparently left without so much as a letter to his family...." (*Ōgai zenshū*, VIII: 597)

At this point in the novel, the two characters are discussing the impending departure of the second speaker to Germany, an opportunity that has come about unexpectedly and that will take place

---

[33] Donald Keene has written an essay focused on Ryūhoku's Italian tour in which he observes that Ryūhoku was both "the first Japanese tourist in Italy" and also "the first Japanese of literary ability to visit Italy" (220).

outside of the official scholarship support structures of the Japanese government. That the two instantly recall Ryūhoku's journey shows how Ryūhoku's travelogue lingered in the memories of students who came of age in the first decades of the Meiji period. Moreover, it suggests that readers of *Kagetsu shinshi* may have been led to identify with its narrator precisely because of the way *Diary of a Journey to the West* emphasizes Ryūhoku's individual autonomy: his lack of affiliation with any state mission and even his freedom from familial obligations. In these two Meiji students' shared recollections, Ryūhoku's departure takes on an even stronger degree of decisive spontaneity than the *Diary* itself records.[34]

As this passage from *The Wild Goose* illustrates, Ryūhoku's account was likely popular among readers of *Kagetsu shinshi* because it facilitated imaginative armchair traveling at a time when opportunities to make overseas journeys were limited. Yet *Diary of a Journey to the West* was also important as a model for travelers who did in fact venture abroad, as Ōgai's own experience attests. Japanese scholars have identified several points of similarity between Ryūhoku's *Diary of a Journey to the West* and Ōgai's 1889 travel diary "Kōsei nikki" (Diary of a Western journey), starting with their titles. Maeda Ai notes the similarity between the two travelogues' descriptions of a few overseas sites and suggests that "Ōgai may well have re-read [Ryūhoku's] *Diary of a Journey to the West* … as a way to familiarize himself with the journey ahead of time … there are several passages in [Ōgai's] 'Diary of a Western Journey' that suggest *Diary of a Journey to the West* may have been the model for its narrative style as well."[35] Other literary scholars such as

---

[34] Ryūhoku's journey would of course have had this potential as an object of identification only for the highly educated readers of his magazine; for a discussion of readerly identification with the figures in more popular early Meiji fictional genres, see Mertz, 38–55.
[35] *Narushima*, 176; see also the English translation in *Text and the City*, esp. 277–279.

Taniguchi Iwao and Kojima Noriyuki have followed Maeda's lead, identifying additional points of similarity between Ōgai's travelogue and the predecessor by Ryūhoku. This project seems to have reached its culmination in an article by Ueda Masayuki providing an impressive catalogue of no fewer than forty-six points of similarity between Ōgai's travelogue and its predecessors ("Kōsei," esp. 20–32).

Ōgai's travelogue resembled Ryūhoku's not simply because they both traveled to Europe via similar routes, nor because Ryūhoku's was the only Japanese travelogue available. As the staggering number of Japanese personal names in his travelogue indicates, Ryūhoku made his journey during a period that saw a sudden surge in travel to Western countries by Japanese in a variety of different capacities, and many of these early overseas travelers left some sort of account of their journeys.[36] Several kept diaries, a few of which circulated, some compiled systematic reports on conditions in the West, intended either as official memorials or for more widespread publication, and several composed poetic collections, either in Chinese (*kanshi*) or in Japanese (*waka*), commemorating the journey and the sites they encountered. In addition to this diverse array of texts composed by Japanese travelers, a few reports by Chinese who were making their own journeys to the West around the same time were also re-published in Japan. Moreover, geographic treatises imported from China or translated directly from

---

[36] One of the most famous and important records of Western travel kept by nineteenth-century Japanese was the massive report compiled by Kume Kunitake, secretary of the Iwakura Mission, an entourage of government officials that toured the West in 1871–1873 and was in Paris at the same time as Ryūhoku. Maeda Ai has written an insightful comparison of the two accounts. Emphasizing Ryūhoku's assumption of the role of "useless man," Maeda concludes that, "On the side of the Iwakura mission was the Paris of fortresses and factories, while on Ryūhoku's side was the Paris of theaters and art galleries" (*Text and the City*, 288). While Maeda's juxtaposition has been very influential, more recent scholarship has emphasized ways in which Ryūhoku's account also reflects his continued interest in and engagement with more "useful" matters of public interest.

European sources provided not only information about Western countries but also a potential organizational framework for travelers' accounts.

At the time Ryūhoku departed to Europe in 1872, then, there already existed a wide variety of models for inscribing an overseas tour. One of the major characteristics that distinguishes *Diary of a Journey to the West* from Ryūhoku's Japanese precursors is the difference in its narrative style. Whereas the earlier texts often obscure the narrator's relationship to the material he reports or merge the narrator into an un-individuated traveling entourage, Ryūhoku's text is from start to finish the individual account of a single observer. Virtually everything that is reported in the text is actually witnessed or experienced by Ryūhoku, and unlike other texts of the time, both Chinese and Japanese, there is very little quotation or overt reference to extratextual sources, such as atlases, earlier travelers' reports, and geographic treatises. The point of the travelogue, in other words, is not so much to convey objective information about the countries visited as to foreground Ryūhoku's experience traveling there. This is not to say, however, that Ryūhoku ignored previous textual inscriptions of the sites he visited; he clearly read earlier materials during his trip and even made occasional reference to them in his own travelogue.[37] But what emerges most clearly from Ryūhoku's encounter with a given foreign site is not a more accurate description of it, newly supplemented with up-to-date first-hand information, but rather a lyrical tribute to the site that constructs it as the object of remembrance, often framed in terms drawn from Chinese antiquity.

---

[37] For a discussion of Ryūhoku's travelogue in relation to its predecessors that attributes its intertextual features to the particular compositional context in which such works took shape, see my "Kōsei no Tōdō shujin."

Perhaps the most concise statement of Ryūhoku's understanding of the overseas travelogue author's project comes not from his own travelogue, but from the comments he made about Nakai Ōshū's *Man'yū kitei* (Record of return from a leisurely journey). Ōshū was touring Europe at the same time as Ryūhoku, and the two had even met in France (see the April 19 entry). Upon his return Ōshū published his travelogue, for which Ryūhoku contributed the following afterword:

> Whether dawn or dusk, whether day or night, clutching letters and delivering missives, he travels hurriedly, crossing mountains and fording streams, and knows nothing of the beauties of these natural features. Who is he? A postal carrier. The gentlemen these days who make voyages of ten-thousand leagues across the sea, who see the splendid sites of the five continents, and yet who cannot produce a single prose account of it, or a single poetic depiction of it, are these not men of the same ilk? My friend Nakai has traveled abroad for years. Recently he has written *Man'yū kitei* and asked me to provide comments and an afterword. I took the volume and made it my repast; calling for some wine, I read and wrote my comments. Each time I would meet with some passage that suited my mind or agreed with my thoughts, I would raise my cup and call out "Splendid!" My wife and children sitting nearby all laughed. I also once traveled to foreign lands, and I wished to make a record of it, but I have not yet done so. And now dear Nakai has done it all. Chen Shiye once commented on [Fan Chengda's] *Wu chuan lu*, saying "If the famous scenes of Shu had not met with Shihu [i.e., Fan Chengda], then the marvelous craftsmanship and artistry of the Creator would be but skills and talents vainly deployed." I could say the same about this text. Those imitators who would venture abroad in the future ought to bring along this book as part of their luggage. I hope in this way they could escape the calumny of being called a postal carrier. (317)

On the one hand, Ryūhoku suggests the overseas travelogue's practical value: it provides a good model for future visitors to foreign sites, allowing them to appreciate and perhaps write about each site more successfully. Rather than being letter carriers, hurriedly rushing from one destination to the next, never stopping to appreciate their environs, he exhorts travelers to slow their pace, pausing to savor the surrounding scenic delights. But this metaphor of the letter carrier is an instructive one with a significance that goes beyond these immediately apparent meanings. A letter carrier is one whose chief duty is to take information (in the form of a letter) from one location and transmit it safely and reliably to another location, often far away. He is a good letter carrier if he can simply transmit this information quickly, consistently, and without corruption. Merely the handler of discrete packages of information originating externally, the ideal letter carrier's own thoughts, responses, and feelings are all beside the point; he is not the source of the information so much as its conduit. In drawing an analogy between the letter carrier and the authors of earlier overseas diaries and travelogues, Ryūhoku is suggesting not only that they rushed through foreign landscapes too quickly to appreciate them fully, but also that part of the reason for this is that they saw their role too much in terms of the rapid and impersonal transfer of information. It is this role that Ryūhoku is implicitly rejecting. Rather than new data speedily delivered, Ryūhoku emphasizes instead the importance of the author's lyrical response to the scenery he sees.

Ryūhoku's afterword is also important for the literary lineage it invokes. In *Inscribed Landscapes*, a study of Chinese *youji* (游記; travelogues), Richard Strassberg singles out the text Ryūhoku mentions above, Fan Chengda's *Wu chuan lu* (Diary of a boat trip to Wu), as marking an important advance in the development of the genre, for this text included "subjective, poetic responses to the landscape … as well as the observations of quotidian life" (49). These are precisely the factors Ryūhoku found lacking in earlier travelogues that sought only the expedient imparting of information. He offered praise for Ōshū's 1874 travelogue because its author had successfully produced a text that integrated these elements and was in the esteemed tradition of Chinese *youji* travel writers. Ryūhoku's *Diary of a Journey to the West* and other Japanese travelogues that in this way included Chinese poetry were part of a body of texts that Saitō Mareshi discusses as forming an emerging genre that might be called *yūki* (Ch. *youji*), based upon the long tradition of such writings composed by literati in China. This genre of travelogues proliferated in the late Tokugawa period and throughout Meiji, and includes records of both domestic and foreign travels. In Saitō's words, *yūki* are "in general, texts that are written in *kanbun*, interspersed with *kanshi*, and while not being 'daily logs,' arrange their topics in roughly chronological order."[38] Aspiring authors of *yūki* were aided not only by the availability of travelogues composed by their contemporaries but also by the inclusion of model travelogues in various anthologies and guides to writing *kanbun* published in the Meiji period, a factor that likely contributed to the similarities that can be observed among them.

This might seem to us an antiquarian, pedantic, or Sinocentric lineage to claim, but for Japanese literary figures like Ryūhoku, the choice of *kanshibun* for an overseas travelogue, while not necessarily a foregone conclusion, would certainly have required no special

---

[38] Saitō, *Kanbunmyaku no kindai*, 189. It is worth noting that the term *yūki*, while generally indicating travelogues composed in Chinese, was also sometimes used more or less interchangeably with other terms for "travelogue" like *kikō*. For example, Ryūhoku refers to his own 1869 domestic travelogue *Kōbi nikki*, which is written in Japanese and includes both *waka* and *kanshi*, as a *yūki*, though it is anthologized in his posthumous collected works under the heading *kikō*.

justification.³⁹ Classical Chinese discourse still functioned for many early Japanese overseas travelers as something of a transcendent linguistic medium. Not only did it have a long history as a bridge between different linguistic communities in East Asia and as the language through which foreign cultures were first introduced to Japan, but it also had none of the particularity of Japanese-language poetic discourse. One of the major organizing principles of the long tradition of lyrical travelogues written in Japanese is their invocation of *utamakura* (literally, "poetic pillows") that had been inscribed in the poetry of earlier travelers. Whether actually visited or merely remembered, these geographic sites and their associated images served as the inspirations for lyrical expression, creating over the centuries a densely inscribed web of intertextuality.⁴⁰ In her study of Japanese overseas travelogues from the late Tokugawa and early Meiji periods, Susanna Fessler notes the difficulty that early Japanese travelers abroad encountered in fashioning poetry from lands lacking such codified *utamakura*: "They faced the daunting task of venturing into an unknown world, bereft of familiar poetic images. If a writer were to employ *uta makura*-style imagery in this new type of travelogue, he would have to make it or borrow it from the Western tradition" (118).

This was one area in which Chinese-language poetry proved a more amenable form to the Japanese poet. Though the term *utamakura* is specific to the Japanese-language poetic tradition, the analogous mode of *huaigu* (懷古; J. *kaiko*) in Chinese poetic practice, in which poets view (or imagine viewing) sites of literary or historical renown

---

³⁹ The hefty tome of overseas Chinese poetry by Japanese authors compiled by Kawaguchi Hisao gives some indication of how prevalent the *kanshi* form was for nineteenth-century Japanese overseas travelers.
⁴⁰ The definitive study of *utamakura* in English is *Utamakura, Allusion, and Intertextuality in Traditional Japanese Poetry* by Edward Kamens; for a consideration of Japanese intertextuality in general, see also Haruo Shirane's "Lyricism and Intertextuality."

and compose poems on them to express their "feelings on the past," provided Ryūhoku with an important model in *Diary of a Journey to the West*. Especially during his period of confinement in the early 1860s, and during his tenure at the Yokohama military training camp, Ryūhoku had read extensively in Western history and was thus well equipped to express his appreciation of a given site's historical resonances by weaving such knowledge into the prose and poetry of *Diary of a Journey to the West*. In a related technique, Ryūhoku occasionally summoned famed figures and episodes from the annals of Chinese history into the poetic spaces he fashioned in his overseas *kanshi*. Just as the style of *kanbun fūzokushi* like *New Chronicles of Yanagibashi* allowed for a type of superimposition wherein contemporary Japanese scenes and customs could be simultaneously depicted and viewed through the lens of comparable Chinese referents, the *kanshi* form afforded the Japanese traveler the means to inscribe the foreign scene with reference to Chinese analogues. Strictures in form, language, and codified imagery made this sort of technique challenging for poets composing *waka* overseas, and many of their poems featured not a juxtaposed or doubled vision but some sort of cognitive gesture toward Japan. It was thus not simply the prestige attached to *kanshibun* composition as a privileged form of discourse that made it the medium of choice for many overseas travelogues, but rather the ways in which specific features of Chinese poetic practice made it more amenable at this stage to the Japanese traveler abroad.

    Ryūhoku initially wrote his diary in *kanbun*, but in the process of serializing *Diary of a Journey to the West* in his literary journal *Kagetsu shinshi* nearly a decade after his return to Japan, he made some revisions to the original text of his diary, the most significant of which was to transform the original *kanbun* to *kundoku*, or Sino-Japanese. Though Ryūhoku's original diary does not survive, a partial transcription made by his traveling companion Matsumoto Hakka is extant (Figure 7).[41] To see what sort of changes Ryūhoku made to the diary upon publication, consider the following excerpt from the 09.29 entry in *Diary of a Journal to the West*, describing Ryūhoku's entry into the port of Singapore:

> 港内ノ兒童皆裸體ニテ瓜片樣ノ小舟ニ乘リ來タッテ文具ノ類ヲ賣ル客小銀錢ヲ水中ニ投ズレバ跳テ水ニ没シ之ヲ攫シテ浮ブ蛙兒卜也タ似タリ土人皆黒面跣足ニシテ紅花布ヲ纏ヒ半身ヲ露ハス畫圖ノ羅漢ニ同ジ其中少シク財産有ル者ノ如キハ皆回教ノ徒ト見エ桶樣ノ帽ヲ戴ケリ女子亦袒シテ跣ス鼻ヲ穿ッテ金環ヲ垂レシ者アリ奇怪極マレリ

> Naked children from the harbor-side approached us in little boats shaped like half-melons, selling patterned shells and other sundries. When a passenger from the ship tossed a small silver coin into the water, they dove in, snatched it, and floated back up, rather like frogs. The locals have sun-darkened faces and walk around in bare feet. They drape printed cloth garments around themselves, leaving half of their bodies exposed, just like Arhats in a painting. Those who are a little wealthier all appear to be Muslims, and they wear hats shaped like little buckets. Even the women were barefoot and exposed their shoulders. Some had pierced their noses and hung golden hoops from them. It was all quite bizarre!

According to Hakka's transcription, the original version of this portion of Ryūhoku's diary read:

---

[41] For discussion of the original form of Ryūhoku's travelogue and consideration of the relationship between it and Hakka's own travelogue, entitled *Kōkairoku*, see Maeda Ai, "Ryūhoku *Kōsei nichijō* no genkei;" Ueda Masayuki, "Matsumoto;" and my own "*Kōsei nichijō* no sho kontekusuto" (esp. 15–21).

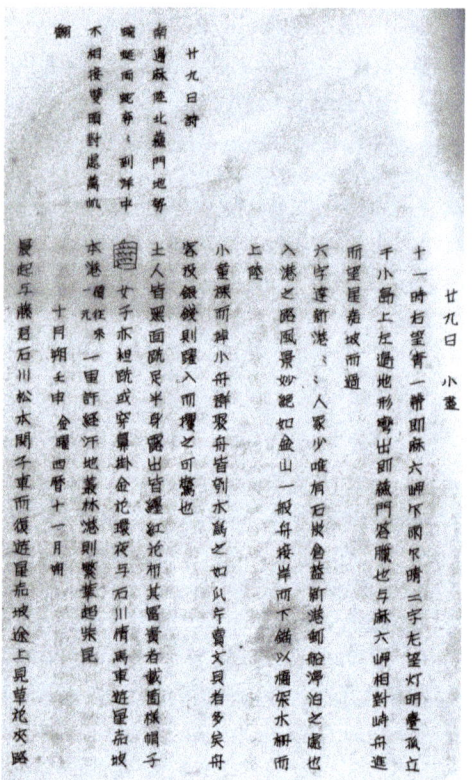

Figure 7. Entry for 09.29 in the handwritten copy of Matsumoto Hakka's partial transcription of Ryūhoku's original *kanbun* diary. The passage about the children in the Singapore harbor begins midway through with the column headed 小童.

> Naked children rowing little boats thronged us. Their boats were made from hollowed out trees and were shaped like half-melons. Many of them sold patterned shells. When a passenger from the ship tossed a silver coin into the water, they leaped in and snatched it. How surprising! The locals have sun-darkened faces and go barefoot. They leave half of their bodies exposed, and all wear printed cloth. Those who are a little wealthier wear this kind of hat [see sketch]. The women also went barefoot and some had pierced their noses and wore golden patterned hoops from them.

These passages show that while Ryūhoku preserved the basic content of his original diary and much of its diction when he started publishing *Diary of a Journey to the West* in 1881, he also made many additions, deletions, and rearrangements: inserting the comparisons of the diving children to frogs, for example, or likening the local men to the Arhats featured in Buddhist iconography. The major difference, of course, is the transformation of its style, which reflects the increasing prevalence of *kundoku* as a general-purpose style of written discourse during the second decade of Meiji. The precision and clarity, lexical richness, and neutrality of *kundoku* led to its widespread adoption at this time, when it came to be referred to as *futsūbun* (regular writing) and *kintaibun* (writing in the contemporary style).[42] We can therefore see Ryūhoku's transformation of his text into *kundoku* as symptomatic of this consolidation of the *kundoku* style as the default mode of discourse in a variety of modern media during the second decade of Meiji.

When Ryūhoku left for Europe, these developments lay in the future, and Ryūhoku probably had no precise picture of how his life would unfold upon his return to Japan. Yet it is clear that a concern for inscribing the journey was uppermost in his mind when he departed from Yokohama in 1872. In the opening of *Diary of a Journey to the West*, Ryūhoku foregrounds this will to produce literary prose in one of the two quatrains he composes to commemorate the beginning of his journey. In the published travelogue, the poem is said to have been composed in Yokohama harbor on the eve of his departure, but in the partial copy of Ryūhoku's original diary that Matsumoto Hakka made, it appears at the very head of the text:

---

[42] Saitō Mareshi has detailed the process by which the *kundoku* style gained independence of *kanbun*, becoming an increasingly widespread mode of discourse while *kanbun* became progressively provincialized (*Kanbunmyaku to kindai Nihon*, ch. 2).

右望巴黎城上月　左瞻龍動埠頭雲　快哉萬里風濤上　要作人間得意文

> I will gaze right at the moon above the city of Paris;
> I will look left at the clouds over the pier in London.
> What a thrill to journey ten thousand leagues through wind and waves!
> I shall write a journal to capture these feelings.

In this way, the composition of a travelogue is fixed as one of the journey's paramount objectives. Not only will Ryūhoku gaze on the sights of Paris and London, but he will produce a literary prose account that "captures" his "feelings." As the inclusion of this quatrain itself suggests, poetic expression would be an integral part of that project. The articulation of this goal in the quatrain's final line has an important double meaning, for not only does 得意文 suggest "prose writing that captures my feelings," but also "prose writing that I am good at." Ryūhoku's *Diary of a Journey to the West* succeeds in both senses, for in it Ryūhoku displays his skill in adapting the forms that he had mastered to the new situation of overseas travel, yielding a text that foregrounds his personal experience and response.

For Ryūhoku's fellow travelers from the Higashi Honganji temple, such activities as meeting with various Western scholars and translators, perusing ancient texts, visiting ruins from antiquity, touring newspaper offices, and inspecting printing facilities were preparations for the establishment of the temple's Translation Office, which was itself part of their larger strategy of defending and modernizing Japanese Buddhism. But for Ryūhoku, we can see here an early indication of his future career path as a journalist and publisher. The eight months spanning the years 1872 and 1873 that are the subject of *Diary of a Journey to the West* preceded his debut as a full-fledged newspaper man, but Ryūhoku clearly had a longstanding interest in the emerging domain of modern print journalism, as the final episode of the second volume of *New Chronicles of Yanagibashi*, in which he explicitly compares the work to the "newspapers printed in the various countries of the West," suggests. In the course of his travelogue, Ryūhoku comments extensively on the translators, scholars, publishers, and newspaper men he meets, tracing the path by which his incipient interest in journalism became more concrete.

A Note on the Translations

Perhaps the most challenging element of translating *New Chronicles of Yanagibashi* was negotiating the *gikun* (playful glosses).[43] I experimented with various strategies over the years and even produced a complete version of the translation that incorporated the playful glosses into a single smooth narrative. Ultimately, however, I concluded that while this approach might offer greater accessibility and readability, such benefits did not justify the sacrifice of an important textual feature: its polyphonic playfulness. The fragmentary nature of the glosses may seem at first distracting to the English reader unaccustomed to such an orthographic practice, yet it is important to bear in mind that in the original, the interplay between the two linguistic registers that the *gikun* permits also occurs in brief bursts, the intermittent nature of which heightens the effect.[44] Indeed, the appreciation of the text hinges on the silent reader's ability to perceive the occasional *gikun* at the same time as the character it glosses. A

---

[43] Of course, even without the additional wrinkle of *gikun*, the text's *kanbun* style presents its own vexing dilemma. In the spring of 2001, I commented to a Japanese scholar that a German translation of *New Chronicles of Yanagibashi* had recently been published. At the time, we were within earshot of Hino Tatsuo, the annotator of the standard Japanese editions of both *Account of the Prosperity of Edo* and *New Chronicles of Yanagibashi*; he soon approached me in disbelief, saying, "The charm of the text is that it is written in *kanbun*. If you translated it into German, it wouldn't be interesting." In spite of Hino-sensei's cautionary comment, I ultimately decided to translate the text; hopefully not all of its charm has been lost.

[44] In an article on *New Chronicles of Yanagibashi*, Emanuel Pastreich adopted an innovative alternative strategy to translate the passage quoted earlier involving the boathouse proprietress. Pastreich endeavored to capture the multilingual interplay between the *kanbun* and the *gikun* by using French for the *kanbun* text and English for the *gikun* glosses ("Pleasure," 211). While this is an illuminating heuristic device, we must bear in mind that even in this section with relatively dense *gikun*, there are not in fact two continuous linguistic threads in the text, as the scattered nature of the Japanese glosses shows.

reader who wished to vocalize the text would be forced to choose between reading the characters according to their traditional pronunciation or according to the *gikun* gloss. The silent reader is able to enjoy both possibilities, a feature that Andrew Markus has noted about the *gikun* in *Account of the Prosperity of Edo*: "The eye grasps simultaneously the exalted and mundane designations, and savors in concentrated form the genius of the entire work—a sardonic wit behind a half-donned mask of high solemnity" (Terakado, "Blossoms," 12). As Markus suggests here, one important component of the *hanjōkimono* text was its visual impact on the reader, a dimension that Chieko Ariga has stressed as well (*Reading*, 51–57). Ryūhoku exploited the pairing of Chinese text and Japanese glosses for a wide range of explanatory, comic, and representational effects, but readers of the original text were also free to ignore the glosses entirely, and I have tried to arrange them in such a way as to make that mode of engagement possible here as well.

While Ryūhoku's pairings of Japanese glosses and Chinese text in *New Chronicles of Yanagibashi* frequently aim at the sort of humorous disjunction that Markus describes, there are more than a few instances where little ironic juxtaposition seems intended. These cases often occur when some particular local practice, occupation, or custom is described and when the term given in the Japanese gloss would, if written in Chinese characters, be confusing or even unintelligible as Chinese. For example, the Japanese term *sendō* 船頭 indicates a "boatman" who piloted small skiffs and ferries along the Sumida and other Japanese rivers, but the same characters in Chinese (read *chuantou*) typically mean the prow of a ship or, in an archaic usage, an officer in charge of a ship's cargo. The direct use of these characters in the Chinese text would thus be unnatural, but Ryūhoku is nevertheless able to incorporate the local term *sendō* into the text by employing it as a gloss on the colloquial Chinese term for "boatman," 舟子 (Ch. *zhouzi*). Far from emphasizing disconnection, this pairing can be seen as an attempt to suggest comparability and functional equivalence between the Chinese term and the Japanese gloss. In such cases where the interest seems to lie less in a humorous clash of registers than in how Ryūhoku translates a given Japanese term into Chinese, I have translated the Chinese characters but retained the Japanese gloss. I hope that those readers familiar with the Japanese terms will find their presence useful and invite those unfamiliar with the Japanese terms to consult the explanations provided in the glossary.

For *Diary of a Journey to the West*, I have attempted to render the terms that Ryūhoku used for the sites he visited in Europe as accurately as possible without compromising intelligibility. Because his guides in Italy spoke French, Ryūhoku records the names of some Italian sites using French pronunciation, but I have in general used the terms most familiar to an English audience (writing, for example, "Vesuvius" instead of "Vésuve"). In identifying the people whom Ryūhoku met and the sites he visited during his world tour, my goal has been to be informative without burdening the text with excessive annotation. Several of the individuals mentioned do not appear in standard Japanese reference works, so I have noted what I have been able to discover about their identities in such cases. For readings of individual Japanese names, I have chosen what I deemed to be the most common pronunciation. It is worth bearing in mind that a single individual might well read his name in multiple ways, which makes assigning a definitive reading impossible. Irie Fumio's name, for example, appropriately appears in Léon de Rosny's *Cours Pratique de Langue Japonaise* as an example of the difficulty of reading Japanese names; Rosny, who knew Irie well, notes that while Irie's name appears to be pronounced Bunrō, he actually read it "Fumio," and would inevitably correct those who mistakenly called him Bunrō (222). Yet extant French letters also demonstrate that Irie signed his name "Iryé Bounrau" on some occasions (Tomita, *Yokohama Furansu*, 102). Finally, I should note that I use square brackets to indicate places where I have added clarifying phrases into quoted text; parentheses indicate interlinear and other notes that are part of the original text.

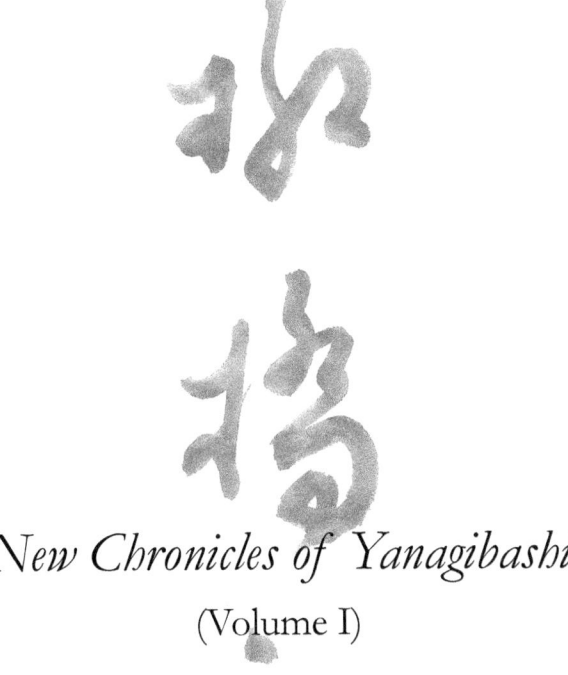

New Chronicles of Yanagibashi
(Volume I)

Preface

Some time ago, the Immortal What-of-it was kind enough to show this volume to me.[1] I took it in hand and read it straight away, but found it obscure and beyond my comprehension. I assumed that the reason for this lay in the fact that I had yet to make sufficiently wide-ranging tracks in the world of play. I accepted this easily enough, and did not regard it as peculiar in the slightest. Yet now I have been enjoying the cherry blossoms along the Sumida River, the moon at Ryōgoku Bridge, the evening breeze at Ayase, and the snow at Mount Matsuchi for a good seven or eight years; when I go on boating excursions, I invite geisha without fail, and when dining at a boathouse, I inevitably call for wine.[2] And so it was that I assumed I had more or less come to understand the charms described herein. Yet when I perused the volume again, it was every bit as incoherent and obscure as before. I was left bewildered and overwhelmed.

---

[1] Ryūhoku used the sobriquet "Immortal What-of-it" (Kayū senshi 何有仙史) not only in both volumes of *New Chronicles of Yanagibashi*, but in "A glimpse of the capital's cats" (*Keibyō ippan*), a piece he wrote in 1874 about the geisha districts of Kyoto. The idiom 何有 (J. *kayū*; Ch. *he you*), translated here as "What-of-it," occurs multiple times in the *Analects*, where it tends to be read rhetorically as "What difficulties will there be?" (IV.13 or XIII.13). The phrase can also imply "What does it have to do with me?"
[2] See Figure 2, where Mount Matsuchi appears as number 11 and Ryōgoku Bridge as number 5.

Ah! I suspect that the Immortal What-of-it must indeed be a true immortal. How vast and all-encompassing is his talent! How marvelously manifold and inexhaustible is his prose! It is as though he lures the reader five leagues out into the fog, leaving the pier completely out of sight. I suppose someone made of such undistinguished stuff as I can never hope to fathom the realm of a true immortal. My profound laments know no end. I cannot but fear that those who attempt to follow on this ferry will also become lost in its passages.[3] And so I will offer them just one piece of advice: unless you are possessed of immortal stuff, read no further!

Signed,
Tipsy Fisherman, Friend of the Gulls
The *tsuchinoto-mi* hour, of the *tsuchinoto-mi* day, of the *tsuchinoto-mi* month, of the *tsuchinoto-mi* year[4]

Authorial Preface

In the past, there was a man called the Retired Scholar Seiken.[5] He wrote *Account of the Prosperity of Edo*. He described the scenery and

---

[3] The preface author plays on the multiple senses of the term *shinbatsu* 津筏 (Ch. *jinfa*), meaning a ferry as well as a textual guide.
[4] The date, given here somewhat incredibly as a sequence of four identical points in the sexagenary cycle, works out to 04.27 of Meiji 2 (June 7, 1869). Maeda Ai suggests that the preface was written by Nakajima Suidō 中島翠堂, a calligrapher who lived on Mukōjima with Ryūhoku at this time. As the preface writer suggests, Ryūhoku had written the main text of the work some ten years earlier.
[5] As Ryūhoku goes on to explain, Terakado Seiken (1796–1868) was best known for his *Account of the Prosperity of Edo* (Edo hanjōki), a satirical text in five volumes that landed its author in serious trouble with the authorities when it was published serially in the 1830s. Written in the same style of *kanbun*, Seiken's text purported to document the flourishing of Edo while at the same time leveling harsh criticisms at various elements in the urban spectacle. Seiken used the suffix *koji* (居士; Ch. *jushi*) on his literary name, to indicate that he was a "retired scholar" and had renounced the ambition of serving in a government post.

circumstances of the 808 districts of the city in complete detail. Not a single famous site or hotspot was omitted, and there was no place left unmentioned. His writing was extremely funny, and his account clear and detailed. The text allowed the reader to know what these famous places offered without having to leave his bed. Even a person who had completely mastered the manners of Edo would have been unable to add anything to supplement the work. Now, however, over twenty years have passed since that time; things have shifted, customs have changed. More than a few former bustling hotspots have become deserted and cold, and vice versa. Shinchi and Fukagawa, where the geisha in their houses once made a forest of their silken finery, lie desolate now, their erstwhile glory having disappeared without a trace.[6] The houses of the pretty *kagema* boys in Yoshichō and Shinmei once vied with the brothels, but they are vacant now, their former visage vanished.[7] The splendor of various other places declined by the day and dwindled by the month, such that there are few today that attain the heights of past glory. If we compare places like Yoshiwara and Shinagawa with what Seiken said about them, then it seems they have diminished by fifty or sixty percent. Ah! If he could only see how these places look today, he would surely be agape with astonishment, and sigh with dismay. I do not know whether he is still alive or not.

Yet, how could the splendor of this great metropolis be swept from the earth into oblivion? There are, in fact, places so minor as to have been only barely discernible in the past that are now coming into full flower.

---

[6] Geisha houses flourished in the Shinchi district along the banks of the Sumida and in the Fukagawa area until they were closed during the Tenpō Reforms of the 1840s.
[7] The *kagema* 陰間 were boys and young men employed by teahouses to entertain their customers, often sexually. Here Ryūhoku uses a Chinese term for male prostitute, *luantong* 孌童 (lit. "attractive youth") with the vernacular gloss *kagema*. On the decline of *kagema* teahouses in the wake of the Tenpō Reforms, see Pflugfelder, esp. 155–159.

Yanagibashi is just such a place. What accounts for this rise of Yanagibashi? It is due to the decline of Fukagawa. Generally speaking, when something is grandly flourishing and then suddenly subsides, it does not simply fade away. To take an example from the samurai families, perhaps it would be something like the house of Nitta.[8] In other words, the Yanagibashi of today is the dead embers of Fukagawa burst into flame anew, with a flourishing vigor following fast on old Fukagawa's heels. Ah! Unless someone records its splendor now, then after five or ten years, who is to say that it will not have withered to an unrecognizable vestige of its present state?

I am a foolish and empty-headed student. With my worn-down inkstone and my bald brush, I am just barely able to get enough to eat. I have none of Seiken's talent and none of his learning. On top of that, I am cleaned out and utterly penniless. I have never spent so much as a single day playing in the quarter to investigate the actual conditions there. How could I possibly be qualified to write about it? I have, however, eagerly listened to the tales told by the playboys and have looked at the maps of the city, and these have given me a general glimpse of the quarter's workings. And now, I have taken advantage of a tranquil evening to write it all down. If an upright Confucian gentleman were to read this book, with its vulgar language and obscene contents, he would spit upon it and discard it at once. But on the other hand, it is not as though anyone is waiting for me to write something that an upright Confucian gentleman could write. There are some things that an upright Confucian gentleman would be unable to write,

---

[8] The Nitta house faded from prominence in the mid-fourteenth century with the demise of Yoshisada (1301–1338) and his son Yoshioki (1331–1358). Ryūhoku here asserts that looked at in the long term, however, the family's decline might be seen as only temporary since the Tokugawa house, which had ruled as shoguns since 1603, traced its ancestry to one of their descendants.

and that is precisely what someone like me ought to record. I shall only write of those things I know. As for those things I don't know about, I imagine that there will be someone foolish and empty-headed like me out there who will be able to fill in the gaps.

Signed,
The *tsuchinoto-hitsuji* year of the Ansei era, in the month where the early plum blossoms are just about to bloom, written under the southern eaves of the Immortal What-of-it's Mansion of Enclosing Spring.⁹

New Chronicles of Yanagibashi Volume I

The Yanagibashi, or "Willow Bridge," is named for willows, and yet there is not a single willow growing there. An old gazetteer says that it was so named because it is located at the end of Yanagiwara, or "Willowfield."¹⁰ However, to the southeast of the bridge is another bridge, and to its side stands an old willow. People call this second bridge "Old Willow Bridge." (Moto Yanagi Bashi) Some would say that since this bridge has a willow tree, it must be the Yanagibashi of antiquity (old), and that

---

⁹ Ryūhoku uses esoteric variants of the sexagenary cycle to give a date that works out to the twelfth month of Ansei 6; this corresponds to the last eight days of 1859 and most of January 1860. The "Mansion of Enclosing Spring" was one name for Ryūhoku's study in Neribei, the Sashunrō 鎖春樓, also known as the Shunseirō 春聲樓 (Mansion of Spring Voices).

¹⁰ The old gazetteer presumably referred to here is *Edo meisho zue* (An illustrated guide to the famous sites of Edo; published 1834–1836), which attributes the origin of the name Yanagibashi to the bridge's proximity to Yanagiwara. As for the theory about Moto-Yanagibashi that follows, Maeda Ai and Hino Tatsuo both cite the 1751 *Edo Sōganoko meisho taizen* 江戸惣鹿子名所大全, which notes that there were originally two willows, said to represent a man and woman, standing to the left and right of the north side of Naniwabashi (the original name of Moto-Yanagibashi). By the late Tokugawa period, there was just one left standing.

what is now called Yanagibashi was in fact built later and stole the name. But this theory contradicts^(doesn't) that^(square) of^(with) the old gazetteer. It is my considered opinion that the proper name of "Old Willow Bridge" is Naniwa Bridge, though there are few who are privy to this knowledge. When one ponders the pros and contemplates the cons of these two theories, it seems that the account in the old gazetteer is correct.

Yanagibashi is located at the mouth of the Kanda River. It is just a few dozen *ken* from Ryōgoku Bridge.[11] Therefore, it is the place in Edo most advantageously situated for waterborne traffic, and it is where pleasure boats^(yanebune) and lighters^(choki) are most numerous.[12] Anyone venturing southward to Nihonbashi, Hatchōbori, Shibaura, or Shinagawa; and anyone going northward to Asakusa, Senju, Mukōjima, or Hashiba; all eastward traffic coming to or going from Honjo, Fukagawa, Yanagishima, or Kameido; and all westward travelers entering or leaving Shitaya, Hongō, Ushigome, or Banchō—no one fails to pass this place. Everyone takes his watercourse through here, whether he is on his way to the brothels in the Five Streets of Yoshiwara, or departing to see a dramatic production^(play) at the Three Theaters; whether he is going to seek out^(gaze at) blossoms^(flowers), view the moon from a pleasure boat, enjoy the evening cool, or appreciate the snowy scenery. For this reason, the boathouses^(funayado) and boatmen^(sendō) are as numerous as a brocade of stars or a clustering of clouds in the sky: something no other place can equal. And floating in the mix are fishing boats, trawlers, et cetera^(and the like).

---

[11] The word "bow" 弓 is used for the distance measure *ken* 間. According to Maeda, the distance between Yanagibashi and Ryōgoku Bridge was about eighty *ken* or 145 meters around Ryūhoku's time; in the early twentieth century, Ryōgoku Bridge was rebuilt slightly upstream, decreasing the distance to about 54 meters.

[12] Japanese glosses identify the two river vessels as *yanebune*, "roofed boats," and *choki*, long thin "boar's tusk boats" used for ferrying passengers. Rather than employing the characters typically used in Japan to write these local terms, Ryūhoku here gives characters that are more readily intelligible as Chinese: 遊舫 and 飛舸.

To the east and west of the Yanagibashi Bridge, and to the north and south of Ryōgoku Bridge, the boats of each establishment are packed in so that the bow of one directly abuts the stern of the next, the oar of one collides with the pole of another. Who can guess how many thousand boats there might be? And in the height of summer, the revelers descend like a herd of giant deer, jostling and floating away, leaving not a single vessel vacant on the shore day or night. Truly it is thriving. What's more, the grand and beautiful roof tiles of the drinking establishments complement each other, and the chic curtains of the teahouses flap together. The aroma of the roasted eel shop assaults one's nose, and the bright blood from the butcher shop stains one's sandals.[13] The *mochi* from the confection shops would be enough to dam up the Yellow River, and the fruit from the green grocer would be enough to strike down all the birds in Qi's garden.[14] With sushi shops, soba vendors, this and that, no one leaves without his appetite sated. The inventory brought in each morning is completely liquidated by evening. One can thus easily imagine how many travel to these parts for food and drink.

Yet the real reason this area now surpasses its erstwhile splendor lies not in such gustatory matters but rather in something else altogether.

---

[13] Ryūhoku uses the word *momonjii* as a gloss for "butcher shop." Originally a term for some sort of fantastic monster, *momonjii* was also used as a pejorative term for tailed or hairy creatures, and from this meaning came to be used to refer to pork and venison.

[14] The reference here is to Ikuyomochi 幾代餅, a famous confection made of *mochi* and sweet bean paste, sold by the Wakamatsuya shop at the western end of Ryōgoku Bridge. It is memorialized in the 1836 Chinese poetry collection *Edo meibutsushi* (Poems on famous products of Edo). The reference to "Qi's garden" is to a story in *Mencius* (1B.2), where Mencius faults King Xuan of Qi for imposing harsh penalties on hunting instead of sharing his spacious garden with the people as did King Wen of Zhou. The idea is that the prohibition on hunting within the garden would have led to an abundance of birds, but as Ryūhoku notes, even this great number of birds could all be brought down by the plentiful fruit of Yanagibashi.

What is this something else? In a word, geisha. This quarter takes the ^(first) ^(place) crown in all of Edo for both the number and the loveliness of its geisha. To be sure, Yoshiwara and Shinagawa also have their geisha, but the main attraction there is prostitution, and geisha are something ^(thrown in on the side) secondary. True, the theater district also has some geisha, but they are employed merely for the benefit of its spectators and not because they themselves are highly prized. Herein lies the reason that these other places ultimately cannot compare to Yanagibashi. In addition, areas such as Shinbashi, Yoshichō, Kōjimachi, Nakachō, and Matsuichō have only two or three geisha for every ten here. The geisha of Yanagibashi wear their makeup with subtlety and adorn themselves with taste. They are refreshingly frank and not obsequious. Raised on the water of Kanda, they have what is commonly termed the temperament of the Edokko, and they retain the manner of Fukagawa.[15] Isn't this the reason that Yanagibashi exceeds the other places?

I hear that ten years ago, the complement of geisha here was not very ^(number) high. In recent years, they have increased by the month and grown more numerous with every passing day. First thirty, then fifty, and then by the spring or summer of this year, they had reached 130 or 140. Even the locals say that "Things have never been so prosperous." The geisha are invited each morning to the drinking halls and each evening to the boathouses, so much so that on especially flourishing days, not ^(lively) a single geisha sits empty-handed in her house. I suspect that the

---

[15] The "water of Kanda" mentioned here was the drinking water derived from the Inokashira Pond that served central Edo; Edokko, or "children of Edo," were said to take pride in having grown up drinking from this major water source. In saying that the geisha of Yanagibashi "retain the manner of Fukagawa," Ryūhoku reiterates the idea expressed earlier that Yanagibashi's success originated in Fukagawa's collapse, but more specifically he is referring to the fact that geisha and prostitutes of Fukagawa were known for their light makeup.

busiest months out of the year for geisha peddling their wares are the second, third, fifth, sixth, and seventh, with the first, fourth, and eighth coming in next. And yet for a geisha of great renown,^(who is famous) even the lonely desolate three months of winter leave her not a single^(idle) unengaged day.

The prevailing practice in the city these days is for everyone, whether samurai or merchant, to complain, "I'm poor. I'm destitute.^(strapped)" And so it remains unclear: just what sort of person can afford to divert himself in this quarter and bring about such flourishing? Gaozi once said: "Appetite for food and sex are human nature." This place is rich in both of these. No surprise then that the visitors keep endlessly^(coming) streaming ^(in) in^(droves), losing themselves before they know what is happening.[16] Confucius once praised water, saying "Water! Oh, water!" And *The Classic of Changes* says: "The benefit of boats and paddles was such that one could cross over to where it had been impossible to pass." This place also abounds in water, boats, and paddles. No surprise then that the visitors who come and immerse themselves in Yanagibashi offer praise for the place! No wonder that uncouth men who would never have passed muster cross over into a quite passable connoisseurship.[17] How could it be anything but splendid?!

---

[16] Indulging in preposterously specious reasoning while maintaining a deadpan tone was a favorite comic technique of *kanbun gesaku* writers. Ryūhoku here marshals classical Confucian authority to support his explanation of Yanagibashi's flourishing as a manifestation of eternal principles. He first refers to Mencius's dialogue with Gaozi (VIA.4), which he then supplements with the "endlessly streaming" phrase drawn from Mencius's dialogue with Wan Zhang (VA.3).

[17] The cryptic reference to *The Classic of Changes* comes from a fourth-century commentary known as the *Xi ci zhuan* (Commentary on the appended phrases). I have used Richard Lynn's translation with a tiny modification to hint at how Ryūhoku deliberately misconstrues the word *tsū* 通 (Ch. *tong*), which not only means to "pass" but also indicates a "connoisseur" of customs in the pleasure quarters; the figure of the *tsū* was important in the illustrated *kibyōshi* fiction of the eighteenth century. The exclamatory quotation from Confucius is recorded in Mencius (IVB.18).

The houses of the boat companies are known as *funayado* in the vernacular. These boathouses are divided into four districts. The first lies on the east bank of the bridge and along the south road: Tanbaya, Kazusa, Hino, Izu, Masuda, Nakamura, Omoto, Yoshikawa, Fujimoto, Iimura, Wakatake, Shinkazusa, Yamada, and Takeya. These are what are called the "Front Street" (Omote chō) of Yanagibashi. A second division lies on the Western bank of the bridge: Shinano, Sakitama, Miura, Sagami, Fukuyoshi, and Shinwakatake. These are called the "Rear Bank" (Ura gashi) of Yanagibashi. A third division lies to the southeast of the bridge in Yonezawachō: Fukuyoshi, Miura, Harima, Sagami, and Nagashima. These are called the Front Street of Yonezawa. A fourth division lies to the south, on the Old Yanagibashi side: Ise, Suzuki, Ebi, Yoshino, Kikyō, Futami, Owari, and Kashiwaya. These are called the Rear Bank of Yonezawa, or the Old Yanagibashi bank. These four areas are called the "four banks" in the local parlance. All told, there are thirty-three houses. It is traditionally said that in bygone days (times now past), there used to be ferry services operating along the Front Street of Yonezawa. The boathouses of today are all former ferry operations from back then that have been continuing their business for many years. Not so long ago, the two houses of Matsuyoshiya and Daikokuya fell upon financial hardship and left, creating a gap in the original membership for the first time. It is said that Fukuyoshiya from the Rear Bank of Yanagibashi opened its offices as a replacement for Matsuyoshiya. The four banks are bonded together like family; they help each other out in times of crisis and disaster, and they all make inquiries as to how others are getting along. If two banks are having some sort of conflict, then the other two banks step in to resolve it. If fault lies with one bank, then the other three banks remonstrate with it. When a boatman is expelled from one bank for some act of villainy, the other three banks will shun him as well. The boathouses to the north of the bridge, such as Fujiokaya, Yawataya, and Kiriya, are not, however, part of this league.

As for the fortunes of the boathouses, there are some discrepancies in wealth, some variances in popularity, but by and large, they are comparable.^(alike) Each house inevitably has a second floor, and this upstairs space has both outer^(front room) and inner^(back room) areas. In smaller places, there may be only a front area upstairs. The members of the proprietor's family all live downstairs, and customers are entertained on the second floor. Depending on its means, each house can support several boatmen, ranging from four or five at the upper^(in the good houses) end, to one or two at the lower end of the scale. They all have two or three *yanebune* and *choki* tied up in the dock.

There are also some samurai^(military) houses^(families) that construct a boat and entrust it to a boathouse. These are known as *yashiki*, and they are identified^(marked) by a strip of metal embedded in the vessel's prow. On each boat is raised an^(a) ensign^(banner) with the house's crest on it; furthermore, they are permitted to outfit the boat with paper^(shōji) dividers just like an official boat. This feature is not only convenient but also makes the vessels look more impressive. For this reason, there are also some boathouses that borrow the name of a samurai house in order to build their own *yashiki* boat.

The largest of the pleasure boats is commonly called a *yakata*; those that are slightly smaller are called *shirukoboshi*. Each has a placard identifying its name as so-and-so *maru*. The construction of these boats is not permitted unless one is a member of the designated boathouse guild. The *yakata* include such vessels as the Koide-maru of the Komatsuya, or the Iwato-maru of the Akashiya, but in the whole of

13

this great metropolis, they number only seven. Now when it comes to leisure, what should be most esteemed are convenience and a relaxed and un-fussy refinement. For moon-viewing or for cooling-off, for trips with geisha or for drinking parties, a single *yanebune* will suffice. Who needs one of those pointlessly imposing and extremely lethargic [sluggish] *yakata*? That sort of boat is only good for those heavily made-up, thick-thighed court matrons to use on their aquatic wanderings, or for elderly [old] people [codgers] to use as they ingratiate themselves to the Buddha and curry favor with the priests at the Segaki rite.[18]

Only two other craft are indispensable supplements to the *yanebune*: the *choki*, which can take the place of a palanquin [yotsude] for travelers seized with the sudden urge to hurry in the height of evening to San'yabori; and the hired [nitari] boat, good for gathering clams in the Shinagawa River in the late spring when the tide goes out.[19]

In each of the boathouses, the one who assumes responsibility for running the house and for receiving guests is the proprietor's wife. She is commonly referred to as empress of her domestic domain, but I shall call her the Madam.[20] The Madam of every boathouse is astute [shrewd] and articulate [smooth]; not a single one is dull or mindless. Did the proprietor choose her as a wife because she already possessed the requisite

---

[18] The Segaki 施餓鬼 was a service held annually on the fourth day of the eighth month to placate the spirits of the deceased who lacked descendants. In one particularly famous *segaki* sponsored by Kamakura's Myōhōji, the participants (who might be members of a cooperative organization known as a *kō*) would recite the *daimoku* (Namu myōhō rengekyō), and do a dance with fans.
[19] San'yabori was the name of the pier at which customers bound for the Yoshiwara pleasure quarter would alight.
[20] Ryūhoku here uses the term 女将軍 (lit. "female general" or "Generalissima") for the boathouse proprietress; even in present-day Japanese the characters 女将 are used to write *okami*, the hostess of a traditional inn or restaurant.

qualities? Or did she just naturally learn them over time? As for the proprietor, he goes out every day to try his luck at dice,^(gambling) or to listen to a rustic recitation^(kōshaku telling a story) or a *rakugo* performance.^(with a twist) If an altercation^(a fight) breaks out, he will race to resolve the matter. Otherwise, all he does is snooze beside the tea furnace and the cashbox.

The customers who visit the boathouses are not uniform in their tastes. Some hire a boat to attend to some business. Some board a boat for an evening of dalliance in the pleasure quarter or the theater district. Some want to rent out a room to play *go* or to gamble, to sleep or to chat. Some invite geisha and order wine. But the customers treated most regally by the boathouses are those who are there for geisha.

Though the prices of a *yanebune* vary somewhat depending on the distance of the journey, they never exceed three or four *shu*.[21] And even if a *choki* takes flight with a flash of its tusks, or a *nitari* exhausts its legs for a speedy journey, the extra charges would not be more than a scant four or five hundred *mon*.[22] Even if a boathouse sent out several boats every day, it would still not allow them to yield^(be) sufficient^(in the) revenue.^(black) And we need not even mention the paltry take from the firefighters^(workmen) and superintendents^(landlords) who come to gamble, play *go*, sleep, or chat, leaving after paying just a seating charge and the price of their tea. This is the reason that the customers who call for geisha are treated so well. The highest of the high are called "rice pots," perhaps because

---

[21] Four *shu* 銖 were equal to one *bu* 分, thus the gloss for "three or four *shu*" 三四銖 (J. *san shi shu*) reads "three *shu* or one *bu*" (*san shu ichi bu*).

[22] These sentences contain wordplay based upon the unusual characters used to write the names of the two vessels: *choki* is written with the characters "boar's tusk" 猪牙, and *nitari* with the characters "load legs" 荷足. This is a good example of what might be called "visual punning," for the terms *choki* and *nitari* are etymologically unrelated to "tusk" and "legs"; the puns Ryūhoku employs are predicated solely on the terms' peculiar orthography.

they are able to keep the boathouse family well fed. What I fear is that those big-spenders who serve as the "rice pots" of the boathouses will sooner or later completely ^(scrape the) exhaust ^(bottom of) their own house's rice pot!

There are some establishments that are boathouses in name, but in fact make their living off of geisha, permitting their customers to sleep with the geisha. We could just as well call these businesses "geisha houses." I hear that back when Fukagawa was at its height, a boathouse would lure its customers using the same method that the so-called *hikitejaya* of Yoshiwara use.[23] Yet while the Yanagibashi boathouses have inherited their basic style from Fukagawa, they have taken it one step further.

A customer arrives. The Madam runs to greet him, her words beguiling and her eyes quick. Straight ^(In no) away ^(time) she has taken ^(sized) stock, ^(him up) seeing whether he's ^(got it) wealthy or ^(not) destitute, intelligent ^(sharp) or foolish. ^(stupid) Wealthy and foolish is what she seeks. Why? If he is intelligent, then he will be hard to deceive; ^(cheat) if he is destitute, then there is no profit to be made. An absolute ^(outright) imbecile ^(fool) who is also exceptionally ^(a big) wealthy—now ^(spender) *that* is a rare ^(real) piece ^(prize catch) of goods to put in the warehouse. Without ^(Just) hesitation, ^(then) she sends someone off to the tavern to bring over some wine and food. The food is soon laid out, the wine is soon heated. The Madam attends on the customer, pouring his drinks. She ^(chats) talks ^(him) a ^(up) bit and ^(flirts) smiles ^(with) a bit: ^(him) "Of ^(Recently) late, several ^(a few) new ^(fresh) girls ^(faces) have made their debuts. A ^(So) certain ^(and) one ^(so) has ^(nice) a charming ^(face) countenance, and a ^(so) certain ^(and) one ^(so) is ^(has) exceptionally ^(many) accomplished. ^(talents) Why don't you invite one over and see for yourself?" Her charming tongue bespeaks flowers; her smooth lips tell of spring. The customer's mind grows ^(gets) intoxicated ^(carried away) and he finds he cannot but nod ^(accept) his ^(the) assent. ^(offer) When a regular customer who has a

---

[23] The *hikitejaya* 引手茶屋 were teahouses that acted as intermediaries to arrange meetings between customers and courtesans; some also served as places of assignation.

particular favorite [steady] geisha arrives at the boathouse, the Madam will immediately invite her over without even waiting for him to nod.

A geisha arrives. She opens the partition [shōji] and invariably says, "Excusez -moi," [me] and when she assumes [takes a seat] her place she always says, "Grateful [Thanks] for the invitation this evening." [for having me over tonight] She first bows to the customer and then bows to the Madam. With her beautiful face she seduces [flatters] him coyly; with her lovely music, she expresses her sentiments [feelings]. The Madam sits beside, guiding the rudder on a steady course. Stimulating [Raising it up] and steering, [bringing it down] she drives their interaction with a deftness that is simply ineffable. She does the boathouse profession proud. The customer finds his spirit [mood] soaring [buoyed] and his soul lifted; he is unaware that his own hands have begun to dance and his feet have begun to tap.[24] In the end, he searches his bosom, throwing down a few coins for the geisha and the Madam. And thereupon the strains of her shamisen grow all the more lovely; the rudder is guided ever more expertly. If the man is a profligate [big spender] patron, perhaps the geisha's attendants [companions] and the maidservants of the house might likewise be rewarded with a gratuity. [tip]

When a customer and a geisha attain a familiarity surpassing mere strings and song, drinking and dining, their new intimacy is the result of Madam's services as an intermediary. In this sort of case, when the customer gives a present to the geisha on each of the five holidays and the two seasons of gift exchange, the boathouse will inevitably get

---

[24] This passage makes amusingly irreverent use of the classical definition of poetry in the Great Preface to the *Book of Songs*: "The poem is that to which what is intently on the mind goes ... The affections are stirred within and take on form in words. If words alone are inadequate, we speak it out in sighs. If sighing is inadequate, we sing it. If singing is inadequate, unconsciously our hands dance it and our feet tap it" (Owen, *Anthology*, 65).

something too.²⁵ Those having the wherewithal will also provide the geisha with new clothing or pay to have the boathouse outfitted with new tatami mats on occasions like the Ten'ō and Ebisu festivals. Such clients are the so-called rice pots [sugar daddies], and there is never more than just one in any boathouse. In addition, the boathouse may urge the customer to go on a boat excursion with the geisha to see the pyrotechnics [fireworks], or to take part in the first-rabbit pilgrimage.²⁶ Casting their nets wide at such times, they can pull in a great deal of profit on top of the regular boat fare.

In general, when a geisha is called to a bar or boathouse, her commission [fee] is paid by the customer, but she must also give the venue a gratuity of 200 *sen* for every *bu*, 400 *sen* for 2 *bu*, and 600 *sen* for 3 *bu*. When the boathouse orders refreshments from a bar, they plunder [tack on] about 300 *sen* for every couple *shu*. Now then, if the boathouse is already taking from the customer, and on top of that taking from the geisha, and furthermore taking from the restaurant, then how much profit are they taking in altogether? And the only reason they are able to bring in such profits is thanks to the eloquence [smooth tip] of the Madam's three-inch tongue.

I once heard from a Buddhist priest that "In the Hell of Screams, there are hot iron pincers that are used to rip out the tongues of

---

²⁵ The "five holidays" are the New Year (01.01, i.e. the first day of the first month), the Peach Festival (03.03), the Iris Festival (05.05), Tanabata (07.07), and the Chrysanthemum Festival (09.09); the "two seasons" of gift exchange are Chūgen and Seibo. The Ten'ō Festival referred to in the next sentence is another name for the Gion Festival, which occurs in the sixth month of the lunar calendar; the Ebisu festival, associated with commercial success, occurs in the first and tenth months.
²⁶ The fireworks mentioned here are those set off on summer evenings in Ryōgoku beginning with the opening of the river on 05.28. The "first-rabbit pilgrimage" or *hatsuu* 上卯 took place on the first day of the rabbit in the New Year.

prevaricators." But I am not altogether certain whether they would be able to extract the Madam's slick tongue. I have also heard it said that "In ancient times, Lady Tomoe was able to wield her halberd to cut down the enemy general though surrounded by an army of ten thousand."[27] But I do not know whether or not the blade of our Lady Tomoe's sword would be a match for the tip of the Madam's tongue. In the *Doctrine of the Mean*, it says, "One can tread upon a gleaming naked blade."[28] Ah! Even though it would certainly be sharp, I think I could tread on Lady Tomoe's halberd.[29] Yet with just one step on the tip of the Madam's tongue, my legs would turn to jelly and my arms would go numb. De-boned and de-brained, I would be left flaccid and atrophied as a sea cucumber. What a terrifying thought!

There are regions "where the nearest wine shop is three miles away and the closest tofu store is two miles away," but such places exist only out in the desolate periphery.[30] In the great metropolis these days, even in dilapidated districts and cramped alleyways, you will find a shop every ten paces, a tavern every hundred. If you can sit down and feast

---

[27] Tomoe was a favorite concubine of Kiso (also known as Minamoto no) Yoshinaka (1154–1184) who was famous for her bravery and martial skills. Tomoe's dance with the pole-shaped *naginata* (sometimes translated "partisan" or "Japanese halberd") is a highlight of the eponymous Noh play.

[28] This quotation comes from the ninth section of the *Doctrine of the Mean*, which states that achieving the mean is more difficult than treading on a naked blade.

[29] Ryūhoku uses the somewhat unusual character 銛 (Ch. *xian*; J. *surudoshi*) for "sharp" here, explaining its meaning with the Japanese gloss *kireru* (lit. "can cut"). Coming as it does within the extended discussion of the sharpness of the Madam's "tongue," there is an added visual pun here, since the character is written with components meaning "metal" and "tongue."

[30] This sentence incorporates a translation of a *kyōka* ("wild poetry") lyric by the Tenmei period (1781–1789) poet Tsuburi no Hikaru: *hototogisu jiyū jizai ni kiku sato wa sakaya e sanri tōfuya e niri*: "In the village / where one can always / hear the cuckoo sing / the liquor store is three miles away / and the tofu store two," a comment on how the delights of rural areas also come with practical consequences.

yourself on sea bass from Songjiang or wine from Hangzhou at one of these establishments, just think what a place as splendid as Yanagibashi can offer. The number of drinking houses is the crown of the whole city. Kawachō and Manpachi,[31] for example, lie to the north of the bridge. Umegawa, Kamesei, Kawachiya, and Yanagiya, for example, lie to the south of the bridge. Hirasan, Fukagawatei, and Sōkaya all fly their banners on the Yonezawa street side. Kashiwaya, Nakamura, and Aoyagi are just a slight distance across the water. In addition, the small shops and food stalls like Marutake, Wakamatsu, Izusa, and Komatsutei are too numerous to count.

Notable among these, the most delicious food and wine can be found at Kawachō, with Kashiwaya next best. Places such as Manpachi, Kawachiya, and Nakamura are popularly called "rented rooms." [kashizashiki] Clients reserve the banquet room, line it with straw mats, and hope to draw a large crowd; latter-day Youjuns [calligraphers] and Daozis [painters] rent space for their calligraphy and painting parties, while Tao Zhu and Yi Dun [rich men] rent rooms for their money-lending clubs.[32] Instructors of dance, shamisen, or flower arranging use the space for displaying their talents and trying their skills. I hear that when domain samurai first come to Edo on their

---

[31] The famous restaurant Manpachi was in business from the early nineteenth century; a common location for calligraphy parties, it was featured in *Edo meibutsushi* and was also the place where Takizawa Bakin had his seventieth birthday party.

[32] In this passage, Ryūhoku uses allusions to famous historical figures in the Chinese text as general categories of individuals; "Youjun" 右軍 refers to the famous calligrapher Wang Xizhi 王羲之 (307?–365?), and the explanatory gloss "calligrapher" (*shoka* 書家) appears above his name. "Daozi" 道子 refers to "sage of painting" Wu Daoxuan 呉道玄 (c. 680–750), and a reading of "painter" (*ekaki* 絵画) appears above his name. The next two names are given a shared gloss of "rich men" (*kanemochi* 金持) and refer to famously wealthy men from the Spring and Autumn period: Tao Zhu 陶朱 is the name Fan Li 范蠡 took after retiring as official of Yue, and Yi Dun 猗頓 was a successful salt trader in Lu. For a discussion of the "painting and calligraphy parties" (*shogakai*) mentioned here, see Campbell, "Tenpōki," and Markus, "Shogakai."

alternate attendance service, they always go for a drink at Umegawa or Aoyagi. Perhaps it is because the names of these establishments have been renowned in the world for some time now. Yet business at both Umegawa and Aoyagi has gradually stagnated[cooled] in recent years; their wine's bouquet and their food's flavor cannot compete with places like Kamesei. As for sushi shops, there are Atake, Yohei, and Nakagawa. For restaurants specializing in roasted eel, there are Tamajin, Yamaguchi, and Funaji. A customer has but to raise his hand and a rare feast of tasty morsels will be arrayed in abundant mounds before him.

In the various drinking establishments, they get up early in the morning and send their shop clerks[young fellows] over to Nihonbashi to buy fish.³³ Only when the clerk returns can they entertain customers. If a customer unknowingly comes early, they turn him away, saying "He is still[has not come] at the docks[back yet]." For this reason, the customers begin to come at the hour of the snake[of four bells sound].³⁴ There are samurai, merchants, rich farmers, and skilled craftsmen. A bunch of physicians, their bald heads like so many watermelons, pile up on the mats; a pack of palace maidens[ladies-in-waiting], their rear-ends looking like giant stone mortars, climb the ladder. The men with kite-like[sternly squared] shoulders and shrike[babbling] tongues[voices] who drink with long swords at their sides are newly arrived domain samurai from the Western Sea.³⁵ Those who occupy a vacant back room, casting glances[tucked away quivering nervously] like foxes or mice, are priests from the Eastern Mountain duly upholding the precepts.³⁶ There is a single established procedure in

---

³³ The term "shop clerk" 店丁 is here glossed *wakaimono* "young fellow," a term used in the pleasure quarters for any low-ranking male employee, regardless of age.
³⁴ "The hour of the snake" was around 10:00 a.m., when a bell was struck four times, hence the gloss of *yotsu* (four).
³⁵ The term "shrike tongue" (Ch. *jushe* 鴃舌; J. *gekizetsu*) occurs in *Mencius* (IIIA.4) and refers to the unintelligible speech of foreigners; here it probably implies the rural dialect of the Saikai Region (Kyushu).
³⁶ The Eastern Mountain is Kan'eiji 寛永寺 Temple in Ueno, the counterpart of

providing meals to guests that all the restaurants use. First, tea and an appetizer are served, then soup and sashimi, then broiled fish are brought out in sequence. The bowl of stew [chawanmori] is the last to come. It is left up to the customer to decide whether or not to eat rice. Though there are some variations in the flavor and fineness of the food, the price for one person ranges from one *shu* on the low end to just four *shu* on the high.

When a customer comes in the summer months, he cannot enjoy his meal without a proper bath beforehand. For this reason, the restaurants have installed baths, all of which are elegant [neat] and immaculate [clean], a far cry from the clamor [noise] and filth of the public bath. They make *yukata* bathing robes for the customers, dyeing them with the restaurant's insignia [crest] or name. To drink in a *yukata* is a refreshingly cool delight for the skin, and one can dry off the sweat on one's underclothes. Perhaps the most wonderful bathing room is at the Kashiwaya. And what's more, they run the bath all year round. So on snowy and windy days, one can thaw out his frigid [cold] body, and on those nights when one has imbibed [drunk] excessively [too much], he can dispel his hangover. It is not like those other restaurants that only have installed baths for the sultry [hot] summer.

Now then, our customer has already had his bath. And he has already had something to drink. It would not be right for him not to have any geisha. Inviting a geisha to the restaurant is the same sort of affair as inviting her to a boathouse. The only difference is that the provisions do not extend so far as letting the customer spend the night and sleep with the geisha. I heard from a friend that "Both Umegawa and

---

Kyoto's Hieizan. The irony here is that the priests are not eating the prescribed vegetarian fare, and thus their selection of the isolated room for their furtive foraging. The temple is identified as number 10 in Figure 2.

Kamesei have very similar practices to the boathouses. It seems that the proprietor [master] feigns ignorance and has his maid act the part of intermediary." Perhaps it is so. But the fact remains: these restaurants just cannot compare to the convenience and discretion of the boathouse.

It is the rule in the restaurants that when a customer brings a geisha with him, the restaurant serves her a meal. When the restaurant itself invites the geisha, it does not serve her food. Yet when a geisha is in a restaurant, she dares [will] not sate [not stuff] herself, but rather consciously conducts herself with polite restraint. She must exert [take great pains] herself in relating to the proprietress and serving girls even more than she needs to in relation to the customer. Otherwise, they will say, "How conceited she is!" [That girl is so stuck up] or, "What an egocentric crone!" [That old hag is selfish] They will call her "The gluttoness" [Miss chowhound] and ridicule her also for affecting [expecting to be treated as a guest] the part of the customer. Finding fault with her mouth and critiquing her nose, they will liken her to a cow or horse, and it might reach the point that they never invite her back. Even if her regular customer comes and requests her by name, they might reply, "She is unavailable." [not in] For this reason, the geisha will often ask the customer to reward the serving girls with an extra two *shu* in cash. If she does this, then the serving girls will show respect to the customer and cozy up to the geisha; the one whom they yesterday berated as a cow or horse is now [today] like a sister, someone whose wisdom they praise to the proprietress [hostess] and whose beauty they proclaim [speak of] to the other customers.

Ah, how the vicissitudes [twists and turns] of human feeling all depend on money. Money can transform idiocy into sagacity, change ugliness into beauty. And thus the sage wrote in *The Classic of Changes*: "Pure Yang is metal" and "The Dao of Pure Yang changes and transforms."[37] Remarkable how aptly these phrases grasp the nature of metallic manifestation! Indeed, how great are the profitable applications of metal! A samurai has his stipend, a merchant has his business. Of course they do not lack for millet [rice] to eat and wine to drink. And yet they trouble themselves to go out to the restaurants downtown, spend their money on banquets, spend it on geisha, and spend it on tips for the serving girls. That this comes to a handsome sum is not hard to imagine. Now there is nothing wrong with eating the things one fancies. And it is permissible [only natural] to lose oneself in the things one loves. Yet when a man abandons himself to indulgence, it reaches the point that his affections for the one he loves compel him to extend generosity to those he does not love at all. All one can do is laugh.

Nevertheless, this sort of laughable situation is not the sort of thing a destitute student such as I could ever manage to indulge in. Mencius once said, "Their tables, laden with food, measure ten feet across, and their female attendants are counted in the hundreds. Were I to meet with success, I would not indulge in such things."[38] Now, Mencius's Way was never put into practice, and no one ever paid attention to what he said. Even if he had wished to avail himself of these delights, he would not have been able to. And that is the only reason he could say something like this. But suppose for a moment that Mencius actually had attained such a high position. For all we know, he might very well have become sleepless with sheer delight. I know that if I were in a position to enjoy the laughable situations of which I just spoke, I would

---

[37] Needless to say, these lines from *The Classic of Changes* have been selectively quoted and rather boldly ripped from their contexts; my translation is based upon Lynn, pp. 123 and 129.
[38] Mencius is here discussing his circumspection in dealing with men of high status (VIIB. 34; D. C. Lau, *Mencius*, 201).

dance around like a sparrow, deluded and deranged; I would have nothing to regret until the day I died. How could I waste my time worrying that others might laugh? My only motivation in taking up my brush now and wasting all of this paper to record the laughable situations of others is that I pity myself and envy them—for my purse is empty. And that too is a laughable plight. That too is a laughable plight.

These women are collectively known as *shōgi*.[39] Those who sell their bodies but do not sell their talents are called *jorō*; those who sell their talents but do not sell their bodies are called *geisha*. In the old days, the courtesans of Fukagawa plied their trade with a dual certificate, and were permitted to sell both their bodies and their talents.[40] Such women could probably be called *jorō-geisha*. The courtesans of Yanagibashi sell their talents and are not *jorō*. Nevertheless, there are more than a few who do sell their bodies. Why is this? Is it because Yanagibashi has inherited the ways of Fukagawa? And yet, at Fukagawa, the women peddled their wares openly, whereas here, they sell privately. Selling openly is the typical manner of prostitution and is easy to do, selling privately is a variation from it and is hard to do. This is how the two districts differ.

---

[39] By *shōgi* 娼妓, Ryūhoku apparently refers to female entertainers (including geisha and prostitutes) as a collective. In early Meiji, however, the term sometimes referred specifically to prostitutes, and was occasionally used in distinction with *geigi* 藝妓 (referring to geisha and other artistic entertainers), as in the 1872 Prostitute Emancipation Act: "The release of all prostitutes, singing girls, and other persons bound to serve for any term of years, is hereby ordered" 娼妓・藝妓等年季奉公人一切解放可致 (Yoshimi, 19; DeBecker, 91).

[40] The "dual certificate" consisted of an official contract detailing the woman's term of service, and an unofficial certificate covering prostitution; see Tanaka Yūko, 41, 60. As Ryūhoku goes on to explain, prostitution was something of an open secret in Fukagawa, but the courtesans in Yanagibashi were ostensibly not engaged in prostitution.

By and large, when a customer procures a *jorō*, he does so in order to
^(buys)
sleep with her. But when he calls for a geisha, it is to listen to her
performance, not to sleep with her. When a customer sleeps with a
woman with whom he is not supposed to sleep, when he causes her to
sell the body she does not dare sell, it is called "rolling" her.[41] Upon
consideration, I believe that the term derives from the fact that the
customer is "rolling" her into another line of work, much as though he
were shifting the position of a deep-seated, immovable boulder.
Alternatively, perhaps "roll" means to "push over;" the one who has
stalwartly preserved her chastity falls forward, losing what she has been
protecting all along. I am still not certain which theory is correct, and
am left with no choice but to await the illuminating council of
evidentiary scholars for a definitive conclusion.

Now then, "rolling" a geisha seems simple but is actually hard, and yet
it appears difficult but is in fact easy. Why might this be? It is
something she does not dare to sell, and the customer is causing her to
sell it. To do so not only violates an official prohibition but amounts to
engaging in illicit private sex.[42] This is the first principle of difficulty.
The customer may be pleased with her looks and accomplishments, but
she too selects men for their talents and appearance. Her situation is
thus quite different from that of a *jorō* who serves solely in bed, unable
^(the sack)
to choose between handsome and hideous men. This is the second

---

[41] The term used here is 轉 (Ch. *zhuan*), glossed *korobasu*, a transitive verb meaning "to roll"; the intransitive verb *korobu* has the additional senses of "to fall" or "to stumble," as well as referring specifically to a geisha's illicit practice of prostitution. Masuda Sayo notes the related term *mizuten* 不見転, meaning a geisha who would "fall into bed without looking" or is a "sleep-around" (see G. G. Rowley's translation, 52–54). As a noun, *korobi* also described lower class prostitutes, who might be dismissively called "rollovers" (Dalby in Swinton, 59).

[42] Regulations prohibiting certain kinds of prostitution and quasi-prostitution activities were promulgated repeatedly; Ryūhoku may have in mind one enacted in 1848.

principle of difficulty. The customer cannot carry out by force what she will not countenance.^accept If he tries to force her, she will simply leave, just as in the case of the master of a house who makes advances on the maid. Indeed, how much more is this true in the case of geisha: women who drift along like floating waterweeds with no particular place where they must come to rest. This is the third principle of difficulty. How apt the verse by the haiku poet that goes:

> *ukikusa ya*   Drifting waterweeds
> *kyō wa mukō no*   today you bloom
> *kishi ni saku*   on the far bank[43]

The poem can serve as evidence of what I have said. These three are what is known as seeming easy but in fact being difficult.

Yet she is also a human being, so how can she lack emotion? The customer lavishes her with his affections and woos her with his feelings; she cannot fail to be moved. This is the first principle of simplicity. She was raised amid the sounds of sensual strings and bawdy ballads^songs and she has grown accustomed to amorous diversions in the world of "wind and moon, mist and flowers."[44] She is not like some rich family's daughter protecting herself so adamantly. This is the second principle of simplicity. And in our present age, it is true for all the people between^in heaven^the and^whole earth^world, whether men or women, that

---

[43] In the Chinese text, Ryūhoku paraphrases this haiku by Nakagawa Otsuyū 中川乙由 (1675–1739), giving the original version (with one insignificant variation) in the Japanese gloss. Hino Tatsuo notes one tradition surrounding this well-known haiku: that Otsuyū was inspired to write it when he went to the theater and saw the courtesan whom he had gone out with the previous day in the company of another man.

[44] The elegant phrase "wind and moon, mist and flowers" (J. *fūgetsu enka*; Ch. *fengyue yanhua* 風月煙花) refers to lovemaking, and often to the world of the courtesan.

the sole thing they enjoy, the only thing they covet, is money. Money is the warp and weft running through every single affair. If one is not chary with his money, then what woman could he fail to obtain? Excluding of course royal consorts^(empresses) and faithful^(chaste) women^(ladies) from consideration, that is. And how much more does this principle hold for women of the courtesan's ilk, who are so poor that they are selling their bodies? This is the third principle of simplicity. A *senryū* poet once wrote:

> *imori yori*   What works even better
> *motto kiku no wa*   than the newt potion
> *Sado no tsuchi*   lies in the earth of Sado[45]

The newt is popularly thought to be an aphrodisiac, while the earth of Sado refers to gold. This poem can also serve as evidence of what I have said. These three are what is known as seeming difficult but in fact being easy.

It is only with a man who knows these three principles of difficulty and three principles of simplicity that one can talk meaningfully about the techniques of "rolling" geisha.[46] Nevertheless, to merely know these principles and comprehend the techniques is pointless. Unless one has

---

[45] The island of Sado had been the site of silver and gold mining from the beginning of the Edo period. A similar poem comparing the newt's putative potency as an aphrodisiac with the efficacy of gold can be found in the *senryū* collection *Haifū Yanagidaru*, vol. 38: "Imori yori / Sado kara deru ga / itsuchi yoshi" (More than the newt / What comes out of the ground at Sado / works the best).

[46] This passage mischievously invokes the praise Confucius offered to a disciple for perceptively marshalling a relevant passage in the *Book of Songs* to illustrate the unstated implications of his teaching: "Ci, it is only with a man like you that one can discuss the *Book of Songs*" 賜也、始可與言詩已矣 (I.15). Ryūhoku's text reads 知此三難三易之理者、始可與語轉妓之法已矣.

the proper provisions [tools] it is impossible to really accomplish anything. There are three tools for "rolling" geisha. To wit: talent, looks [handsomeness], and money. But the greatest of these is money. For a man with lots of talent and looks but without any money, his plans are hard to carry out. To use a metaphor, it is like trying to fight a battle without any weapons. He certainly will not win. Nevertheless, for a man with money who is not blessed with good looks, then clearly if the woman allows herself to be "rolled" it is because she covets the money: not because she covets the man. When the man has money, she is friendly and familiar, but when the money runs out, she keeps her distance. To use a metaphor, it is like a fisherman; the fish disperse as soon as the bait is gone. Then there is the man who has money but no talent. He falls prey to an onslaught [one lie after another] of mendacity, her avariciousness [all she does] unbounded [is take]. Dazed and confused, he wishes only to fulfill her whims. Before long, he simply exhausts his funds and taps out his resources. To use a metaphor, it is like an opium smoker; he indulges his taste without recognizing the poison, and it ends up killing him.

And thus we can conclude: even if one understands the principles and has mastered the techniques, unless he is equipped with the three tools, then it will be difficult for him to accomplish anything. But suppose there were a man who possessed these three tools and had also been able to master the principles of the three difficulties and three simplicities. Such a man would be able to make the hundred-plus geisha of Yanagibashi line up their pillows and die in the height of passion. He surely would not stop at one or two "rolls." We could call this man the "Flying General" [gladiator] of the arena d'amour, the Buddha incarnate of the rouge and powder demimonde.[47] He would be a man the likes of

---

[47] The term "Flying general" 飛将軍 refers specifically to the Han general Li Guang 李廣, but in general to any exceptionally gifted fighting man. The term translated as

whom are few in this world. Now let us evaluate how the rest may be ranked. The man with money and talent, even though he lacks good looks, is still able to have a great exhilarating romp. The man with money and looks but no talent can also obtain her love and be regarded as a prized customer. The good-looking man with neither money nor talent and the talented man with neither money nor good looks are at the low end of the scale, and their situations are beyond remedy. [lost / causes]

If, for the sake of argument, we were to evaluate [weigh] these two situations, there is still something that can be done with just talent. But there really is nothing to be done with just looks. Why? The answer is this: looks are dead; talent is alive. A dead thing cannot change, but a living thing can. Now then, if one goes into battle without any weapons, then his defeat is guaranteed. But even so, Chen She and his followers rose up in the periphery [countryside], and wielding only the handles of their hoes and spades managed to crush the thirty-six commanderies of mighty Qin in a single day.[48] Nurhachi, the founder of the Qing dynasty, arose in Tartary with just thirteen inherited suits of armor, and in the end took control of the four-hundred-odd prefectures of China. How can this be anything but a case of taking action to fit a changing situation, seizing the right moment, and ultimately realizing one's aspiration? How apt are the words of Mencius: "They can be made to inflict defeat on the strong armor and sharp weapons of Qin and Chu, armed with

---

"amour" is *fūryū*, which often connotes a refined and artistic sense of style or panache, but here refers to an elegant sophistication about the ways of love.

[48] On this day in 209 BCE, inclement weather prevented two Qin dynasty officers, Chen She 陳涉 and Wu Guang 吳廣, from reporting to their intended destination at the appointed time. Knowing that the authorities would be unforgiving of their tardiness, even though it was unavoidable, the two officers decided to foment a rebellion, which quickly spread among the disaffected peasantry.

nothing but staves."⁴⁹ It follows then, that even if one has no weapons there are still things he can do.

It is as though the few *shu* in the customer's coin-purse are the hand-me-down armor of Nurhachi or the rough farming implements of Chen She. If he is able to plot his actions by adapting to change and grasping the moment, then who knows? Perhaps a *soupçon* ^(little bit) of money will cause this geisha to not tell so many false^(lies)hoods and instead ^(treat) attend him ^(well) sincerely; perhaps at some point she will "roll" for him, and he will not need to imitate the Minor Captain of Fukakusa, venturing to her door on ninety-nine successive nights to press his suit.⁵⁰ And later on, if he polishes his skill and hones his linguistic skills more and more, getting her to ^(offer) remit to him what she has ^(snatched) seized from others, then he will be able to store up a great deal of materiel. This can be called a success. In this way, even if the events differ significantly from the "crushing of thirty-six commanderies" and the "seizing of four-hundred-odd prefectures," nevertheless, their essence is the same. We would be wholly justified in calling this man the "Flying General"; we would have every right to name him the "Living Buddha." And this would be due to one reason and no other: his talent. And thus, it is demonstrated: a talented man lacking both money and looks nevertheless has some potential.

---

⁴⁹ The passage appears in section IA.5, in which Mencius tells King Hui of Liang that benevolent government and moral behavior will enable his people to triumph over the strong militaries of neighboring states; the translation here is modified from Lau, *Mencius*, 53.

⁵⁰ The Noh play "Kayoi Komachi" tells of how the Minor Captain of Fukakusa was instructed by the beautiful Heian period female poet Ono no Komachi that if he came to her quarters on successive nights she would reward him on the hundredth visit. He died on the ninety-ninth visit.

The discourse I have elaborated above was only intended to apply to geisha of some renown.⁵¹ When it comes to those trifling^(petty) servile geisha who will bend over for anyone, then all the customer has to do is raise his hand and she rolls like a ball and sticks to him like candy. What need is there to expound upon principles and discuss techniques? Alas, there are a great many reasons that a customer might call for a geisha. There are some who wish to listen to her musical talents. There are some who want to make a show of their extravagance. There are some who want to enjoy a drink. There are some who want to treat another to a great meal. How can it be that men only find pleasure in "rolling" her? In discussing these points, I have turned them over again and again, but I was not motivated by any intention to inculcate depravity or incite decadence. It was simply that I suspect Yanagibashi owes its present degree of splendor to this single word: "roll." Therefore, in order to record its flourishing, I was inexorably compelled to make explicit the theory of "rolling." May it please the reader not to ridicule me.

If people can be ranked by their seniority or youth, so too can geisha be distinguished by whether they are "big" or "little." A "big geisha" is a "geisha" proper, whereas a "little geisha" is what is known in the vernacular as an *oshaku*.⁵² The *oshaku* is so named because she does not play the shamisen but instead spends her time exclusively in attendance, serving drinks. The fixed^(going) price^(rate) for a "big geisha" is eight *shu* for an

---

⁵¹ Here the phrase translated "geisha of some renown" is 有名校書, glossed *na no aru geisha*. The use of the term 校書, which literally means "to collate texts," for *geisha* is based upon the figure of Xue Tao 薛濤, a famous courtesan of the Tang who was also skilled in literary arts and worked at comparing variant versions and editions of texts to determine the proper reading.
⁵² The term *oshaku* 御酌 refers to young women who poured drinks, danced, and provided other entertainment at banquets.

afternoon-to-evening course, and perhaps costs an extra four *shu* for the "dragon-to-rat" course of morning to midnight. It is also four *shu* to call a geisha out for even just a tick of the clepsydra. A "little geisha" costs one half of these prices. It is therefore acceptable to call her a "half geisha." In addition to the set price, the customer has another expense, and this is called the *hana* or "flower." The term "flower" suggests "floral." It means that the "flower" makes the banquet "flourish" splendidly. Typically the "flower" is four *shu* for the "big geisha" and two *shu* for the "little geisha."

The clothes the geisha wear also have distinctions. The big geisha's garments drag upon the ground and so when she walks she draws in the hem of her kimono with her left hand; hence the term *hidarizuma* or "left hem."[53] Her obi sash is made entirely of silk, and so is commonly known as a full obi. As for her undergarments, they always show white at the collar. The little geisha, on the other hand, gathers her dress in at the waist and does not drag it along the ground. The inside and outside of her obi have different silk on them, and the obi is called a *hara-awase*. Her undergarments are red at the collar.

The job of the big geisha is to play the shamisen and sing. Her talents include performing *nagauta*, *Tomimoto*, and *Tokiwazu* ballads, but the most common song style is *Kiyomoto*.[54] When these women entertain at

---

[53] One theory explains this distinctive behavior of the geisha in terms of a contrast to the courtesan, who uses her right hand for the same purpose, noting that the geisha's principal responsibility is entertainment and thus she needs to keep her right hand free for her shamisen plectrum (Chinpunkan Shujin, 211–213). Even today, the term *hidari-zuma* is a synecdoche for geisha (Downer, *Women of the Pleasure Quarters*, 182).

[54] The *nagauta* originated as the accompaniment to theatrical works but it came to be performed independently. The Tomimoto, Tokiwazu, and Kiyomoto are three forms of narrative recitation that flourished in Edo in the eighteenth century and are collectively called *Bungo jōruri*. According to Foreman, the *Tokiwazu*, which is held to be more

a banquet, however, they perform nothing more than short *hauta* songs [zashiki] and new lyrics [popular tunes]. Although there are some little geisha who are talented on the shamisen, they are not allowed to play it; this is because such a presumptuous incursion would deprive the big geisha of her work. For this reason, they all learn how to dance. It is a general rule that a little geisha must never fail to treat the big geisha with the respect she would accord an elder sister—no matter whether she is in fact older or younger in age.[55] And when it comes to the Madam of a boathouse, even a big geisha must call the Madam "elder sister." At a banquet, the big geisha strums her shamisen and the little geisha dances, thereby providing the guests with something to see. However, among the little geisha dancers and the big geisha players, there are those who are skilled and those who are inept. They cannot all be regarded as equivalent. Out of ten geisha, there are perhaps only three who are skilled, while the other seven are inept. Among the beautiful are many poor performers, and among the ugly are many skilled performers. The ugly seek to market themselves through their talents [arts], and this is thus the sole focus of their efforts. The beautiful seek to market themselves through their appearance [looks], and this is why they are remiss [lax] in acquiring polite accomplishments. For customers too, there may be seven men who prefer looks and only three who prefer accomplishments. Therefore, the untalented get more revenue and the talented get less.

Nevertheless, there are some girls whose looks and talents alike are on the low end, and yet who are quite successful. Indeed it is a curious state of affairs. I once asked a friend about this peculiarity, saying, "The

---

masculine, and the *Kiyomoto*, which is held to be more feminine, are the two forms still regularly performed today (*The Gei in Geisha*, 20–24).
[55] On the foregrounding of ritual ties of sisterhood between geisha in contemporary Japan, see Dalby, 39–40.

only reason you would call for a geisha is because she is talented or good-looking. If she is bereft of both of these qualities, then what does she have that's worthwhile? It would be better to stay home, fool around with the maid, and thereby save your money." My friend laughed and said, "Dear child, you are seeing only part of the picture and missing the rest.⁵⁶ Think how numerous the travelers are who visit this splendidly thriving metropolis. Their minds are all different. Some take delight in a woman's looks. Some appreciate her polite accomplishments. Some fall in love with her character. Some are fond of her disposition. Looks and talent are naturally what are most highly esteemed. However, the geisha's fondness for dashing chivalry [gallantry] and her lack of stinginess, her honorable [principled] fidelity [charity] and her refusal to embarrass her man—these are traits that one could not even dream of finding in a wife or average girl.⁵⁷ Her appearance is simple yet refined, her adornments subtle, her movement and comportment never lose sight of the situation, her diction and responses never mistake the moment. These too are simply not traits a concubine or maid could ever manage to attain. These are traits that the geisha alone possesses and no one else can master them. Surely the appeal of a woman who lacks both looks and talent lies here."

When I heard this explanation, my nagging doubt was instantly resolved. But just then another doubt took shape in my mind. Namely: "A *geisha* lacking *gei* [talent] is able to be one because she still has some worthwhile qualities. But what about the *jusha* [Confucian scholars], the *isha* [physicians], and the others of the world who have a *sha* in their

---

56 The narrator's interlocutor uses a phrase almost identical to one attributed to Confucius in *Zhuangzi* (識其一、不知其二); see Mair, *Wandering*, 112.
57 The gloss "principled charity" is *tatehiki*, or "proud insistence on honor or principle," but refers also to a courtesan picking up the tab for her client.

name? There is no shortage of Confucian scholars who haven't a clue about the Way expressed in the Four Books and the Six Classics, or physicians who don't have any idea what is contained in *The Yellow Emperor's Classic of Medicine*.[58] These two types are comparable^{just the same} to^{as} a *geisha* without any *gei*. Do they have any redeeming qualities?" He pondered, contemplated, reasoned, and considered, and then suddenly struck his thigh and exclaimed, "Nothing!^{No} Not^{No} one!^{No}"[59] Perhaps I do not need to ask others about this matter. If pronouncements^{lectures} on the "cultivation of the person" or the "regulation of the family" serve^{have} no^{no} function,^{use} then they are not as good as the geisha's short ditties and popular tunes, which at least please the ear.[60] The physician's spoon should supplement *yang* and adjust *yin*, but if he cannot^{does not} discern^{know} the^{how} proper^{to make} proportions,^{the medicine} then it cannot equal the geisha's ivory plectrum, which heightens the mood and encourages one to drink. What a laugh. Ah! These scholars are supposed to rescue the world by disseminating their teachings, these men are supposed to play God and save the afflicted young, and yet they are shown up by these graceful and delicate young ladies. How intolerably sad!

---

[58] The Four Books 四子 (also known as 四書) are *Lunyu* (The Analects), *Daxue* (The Great Learning), *Zhongyong* (The Doctrine of the Mean), and *Mengzi* (Mencius). The "Six Classics" 六經 refers to *Yi jing* (The Book of Changes), *Shu jing* (The Book of Documents), *Shi jing* (The Book of Songs), *Chun qiu* (The Spring and Autumn Annals), *Li ji* (The Rites), and *Yue jing* (a non-extant treatise on music). The extant texts are often called the "Five Classics" 五經. Ryūhoku mentions here the earliest Chinese medical text, *The Yellow Emperor's Classic of Medicine* (Huang di nei jing), with specific references to two of its sections.
[59] I have interpreted this sentence as a continuation of the narrator's dialogue with his friend, but the dialogue here may instead be internal. In other words, the unstated subject of this sentence could be the narrator: "I pondered ... struck my thigh and exclaimed."
[60] "Cultivation of the person" and "regulation of the family" are Confucian terms appearing in *The Great Learning*. They are two of the steps in a sequence that progresses outward from "investigating things" to the "administration of the realm."

I hear that geisha in the olden days were often accomplished in their various arts. There were some who played the flute and some who beat the drum; some were skilled at haiku and some were gifted *go* players; some used their legs to dance and some used their throats as flutes to sing. There was none who did not excel at pastimes such as *ken*.[61] Today, things are not so, and they are barely able to play the shamisen. They are all quite inexpert at *ken* too, and there are even some who are completely unfamiliar with it. Moreover, it is said that when it comes to the *ken* games of recent years, such as *tōhachi*, *koikoi*, and *mitsuuchi*, there is no geisha so skilled that the customer is no match for her. Alas, among Confucian scholars there is none who writes prose or composes poetry as well as those in the past; among physicians there is none who understands acupuncture or pharmacology as well as those in the past. When we consider people of the present day from the point of view of the past, we are truly driven to tears.[62] I have written this with a sigh, then a smile, and then a tear, not because I wish to condemn others, but only in order to condemn myself.

If one makes a right turn to the south of the bridge, he comes to Dōbōmachi, a nest (den) of geisha. From the Rear Bank toward the north, all the way to Hirokōji toward the south, the geisha houses are lined up as close together as the teeth of a comb. The houses along the street each have a front and back section. The bustling (popular) places are in the front, while the less popular are in back. The houses also diverge (vary) in

---

[61] *Ken* was a general term for parlor games played with the hands, similar to rock, scissors, paper; the three games mentioned later in the paragraph were variations on the theme.

[62] The referents of the pronouns in this line are ambiguous; it reads just: "When we consider the one from the perspective of the other …" Another interpretation would therefore be, "When we consider the Confucian scholars and physicians in comparison to the geisha, we are truly driven to tears."

their wealth and poverty. But they are not so different in their overall atmosphere. The exterior of each is covered with latticework doors, and in the interior each has a square hibachi stove. The stove is kept immaculate and dust-free, for "Where the kettle rests, the kettle is so sleek; With the warm cinders white and glistening."[63]

Beside the hibachi, the geisha wearily sighs and settles down for an afternoon nap. In general, geisha are conceited and indolent, and resolutely refrain from traditional feminine occupations. They practice their shamisen and their singing, and they apply their makeup and their powder; but aside from that, they do not do a single thing. Nevertheless, when it comes to praying to the gods and buddhas, they are all very diligent. They make a special altar upon which to enshrine sacred tablets. There might be tablets for Konpira, for Taishakuten, or for Fudōson, with the particular arrangement depending on the purposes of the geisha's prayers.[64] The shelf is invariably fitted with a golden phallus called an *ingi*. A small rope is suspended from the pillar at the side, onto which pieces of paper are twisted and tied. They bunch together and hang down haphazardly. These seem to be gratuity envelopes presented by her customers. The geisha returns with the envelopes tucked into her obi, strips them of their cash, twists the paper enclosures, and ties them here. She would say that doing this with the money-wrappers will enable her to summon more of them. But her intention it seems is simply to boast to others of her own popularity.

---

[63] This final line about the spotless kettle is a parodic transformation of a poem in *The Book of Songs* that Mencius discusses in his dialogue with King Hui of Liang; it depicts the "Marvelous Park" of King Wen, where "The doe lay down; the doe were sleek; the white birds glistened" (Lau, *Mencius* IA.2).

[64] The deities mentioned are protective deities of Hindu origin that were incorporated into Buddhism and became the subject of propitiation directed toward specific purposes, such as insuring safe travel.

The geisha's worship of Buddha is more than twice as intense as her worship of the Shinto gods. She always makes the patriarch of her sect the focus of her piety. And nine out of ten geisha households are of the Nichiren sect. They have unshakable devotion, their piety one degree more extreme than the average person's. I imagine that because their daily conduct is a grave, sinful litany of deception and avarice, they are merely seeking to borrow the power of the sect patriarch to insure that they do not fall into Hell after they die. But I believe that their position itself is Hell, and I am dubious about whether there is a separate Hell beyond this.[65] In spite of the fact that they are Nichiren sect members, their nefarious deceptions are practices to which even a Christian would not stoop.

In most geisha houses, those with a father are only one in ten and those with a husband are only one in a hundred. By and large, the geisha lives alone with her mother. They may keep a cat or a *chin* dog as a pet, making a group of three all told. With the obsequious geisha who is as wily as a fox, and her mother little more than a badger in human clothing, the cat or dog must wonder, "Mother and daughter are part of our pack. Why are *we* singled out as beasts?" And as for the one who enters this bestial lair and becomes intimate with its beastly denizens, would we not be justified in calling him a beast too? And how many there are in that category!

A customer arrives. The old badger hurriedly calls for food and drink. She ingratiates herself with smiles and flattery, perhaps praising the

---

[65] The sentence puns on the double meaning of *jigoku*, referring to both "Hell" and to the lowest class of unlicensed prostitutes. One somewhat fanciful theory holds that this term derives not from *jigoku* 地獄 "Hell," but rather as a contraction of *chijō* 地上 "earthly" and *gokuraku* 極楽 "paradise" (Chinpunkan Shujin, 105).

39

customer for his dress and his manner, perhaps saying, "She's been passionately yearning for your arrival." Never forgetting to intersperse a few comments about how down-and-out they are, she prattles on and on. When the mood is ripe, and the sake has run dry, she will urge him to venture upstairs and go to bed. The second floor is where her daughter applies her toilette, and there her various cosmetics are arrayed. Houses without a second floor are quite lacking in convenience. In that situation, when the time comes that the customer wants to go to bed, the old badger claims she has some errand to run and excuses herself. When a special *najimi* customer visits a geisha's house, even if invitations for her come in from other establishments, such requests are refused with the claim that she is sick or unavailable.

waiting *for* *you* *to* *come* (above "passionately yearning for your arrival")
turned down (above "refused")
she is out (above "unavailable")

My friend The Bamboo Lover once told me, "Going to a geisha's house for diversion is far and away better than going to a boathouse or to a restaurant where there are many expenses and many watching eyes. But on the other hand, there is one exception. While the avarice of the geisha can at least be endured, the avarice of her mother is intolerable. How much more is this true in the case of those mothers who are envious of their daughters—these are the most fearsome type."[66] Still, it is difficult to make any generalizations. Among those geisha who bring customers to their houses, some try to use him for his money; they try to maximize their own take by denying the boathouse a chance to skim off the top. Some other geisha really love the man; they are hoping to create bonds for the long term, and do not want to let him

bad point (above "exception")
a little green *toward* (above "envious of")

---

[66] "The Bamboo Lover," Aikōshi 愛篁子, is a whimsical reference to the Dutch scholar and lexicographer Katsuragawa Hoshū 桂川甫周 (i.e., Kunioki 国興, 1826–1881), a companion of Ryūhoku's who was particularly fond of the geisha named Otake (Bamboo).

squander his resources on the boathouse. In comparison with other places, the geisha's own house offers lower expenses, more discreet affairs, deeper passions, and longer affections. It is a good bet, we might say. For this reason, unless a geisha has for her part observed the customer's position and how he carries himself, she will not invite him to her house.

There is some variation among the geishas' mothers too. Some are greedy, others are not; some are crafty, others are not. Clearly we cannot see them all in the same light. The greedy and crafty ones are for the most part foster^(fake) mothers.[67] Those who are not like this are the girls' birth^(real) mothers. Why are there so many foster mothers and not very many real ones? The geisha's mother must make her own child attend upon men when they drink; she must make her flatter and curry favor with them; and in extreme cases, she must make her do things no different than a prostitute. This is truly unendurable. One simply would not do this unless one was poor beyond redemption. In general, those who become prostitutes when they are still lovely young girls cannot become wives who serve their husbands when they get older. This is why such women buy a girl from a poor family and turn^(make her) her^(do) to^(what) their^(they) former^(once) trade^(did). In addition, there are many who support themselves by buying girls and turning them into geisha. This is why there are more foster mothers than real mothers. How does a foster mother regard the customer? As she might track a bird to be captured. She plots out how she can obtain her prey by using the girl as a decoy. How does a real

---

[67] According to regulations promulgated in 1848, being a geisha was permitted for women who needed to support their parents. A similar concession had been made in 1824 (Chinpunkan Shujin, 144, 201) but this had been temporarily rescinded during the Tenpō Reforms. In any event, some women exploited the loophole by adopting girls to be their "daughters" merely in order to use them as geisha; these are the "foster mothers" 假母 referred to here with the gloss "uso no" (fake; false; not real).

41

mother regard the customer? Perhaps she sees him as a son-in-law, such that she is true to her feelings and discards any thoughts of profit. Therefore, the geisha of a foster mother "roll" ^(all over) quite ^(the place) loosely, and those of a true mother do not. There is a vast difference in the relative merits of the two.

In general, the Yanagibashi district is unlike the ^(licensed) flower ^(quarter) town in that buying a girl with the aim of marketing her as a prostitute is prohibited in the first place. For this reason, the foster mothers proclaim that "My daughter has been ^(hired) employed by a drinking house in order to support her mother." They are all alleged to be bar-girls. When several girls are lodged in the same house, it is claimed that they are sisters, or it is claimed that they are from different houses.[68] The age of the "big" senior geisha may be anywhere from seventeen or eighteen to thirty, whereas the "little" junior geisha range from twelve or thirteen to twenty. Yet when they state their ages, they always ^(shave off) deduct two or three years, or sometimes even seven or eight. Can they be unaware that a single ^(feel) grope of that fragrant grass growing luxuriantly beneath their obi will reveal if spring is gradually coming into full flower? Or that no matter how she tries to iron them away, the ^(wrinkles) delicate waves rippling her forehead will confirm the winds of autumn? All one can do is laugh.

Imagine that a foster mother buys a girl and turns her into a geisha. If the foster mother plans to raise the girl from the time she is very young, then her price will be inexpensive but the time period required will be

---

[68] It seems that depending on the situation, the madam of the house might portray her relationship to the various geisha working under her and their relationship to one another differently. She might claim that they were her daughters and therefore allowed to help support their mother by working as geisha. Or, since the regulation that allowed this only permitted one daughter from each family to do so, she might instead say that they were allowed to work as geisha since each was from a different house.

long. She will thus instruct the girl in singing and dancing, make clothing for her, and then when the girl comes of age, the mother can reap great profits. A girl who has already nearly mastered her talents and is precisely^(just about) the right age, on the other hand, cannot be had for a price of less than twenty or thirty *ryō* and a contract limited to one or two years. In another kind of arrangement, known as *tataki-wake* or "going halvsies," the girl can be purchased at half the going rate, under the condition that as a geisha, she will share her profits with the madam. In such circumstances, the madam regards the girl as a guest, and the girl likewise does not regard the madam as her mother.

When a customer purchases redemption^(the debts) for^(of) a geisha and makes her his wife or his concubine, the price he pays can fluctuate^(go up or down) according to her appearance, her talents, and her degree of popularity. At the high end, it might be one hundred *ryō*, and at the low end, twenty or thirty. When it comes to a wealthy and influential customer, money is no object. And while the foster mother is insatiably avaricious, the real mother is not since she has feelings. Yu Huai wrote in his *Miscellaneous Records of the Wooden Bridge*, "It is not often that the biological mother will try to take a lot of money. But a foster mother will insist upon a high price."[69] This shows us that human feelings are the same whether in East^(Japan) or West^(China). The biological mother may well send the girl's clothing and personal effects along with her, but as for the step-mother, she will skin her and sell her off naked. Thus, the true mother is still to be loved, while the foster mother is the most despised.

---

[69] *Banqiao zaji* (Miscellaneous records of the wooden bridge) was a melancholic reminiscence about the pleasure quarters in Nanjing written by Yu Huai 余懷 (1616–1696) that was a major influence on Japanese writing about courtesan culture. This passage appears in Yu Huai, 13; see the translation by Levy, 42.

How much the more is this true since the foster mother does not even know whose daughter the girl is—she might be a beggar's kid, or perhaps she is of royal stock. As for the man, what intention motivates him to redeem such a girl and make her his wife or concubine? It is written in the *Zuo Tradition*, "When purchasing a concubine, if one does not know her surname, then one should perform an augury about the matter."[70] But I wonder, alas, if men of this ilk really perform an augury about the matter. It is the proper ritual to perform an augury in front of the ancestral graves only once one has already purified the mind and cleansed the body. But clutching twenty-four *mon* in your pocket as you race to consult with Yan Junping on the banks of Yanagiwara is also a form of augury.[71] I once saw a diviner using bamboo lots to augur for a customer concerning the purchase of a geisha. The man got the *mō* hexagram ䷃, or "juvenile ignorance," followed by the *ko* hexagram ䷑, or "ills to be cured." The diviner intoned: "*It will not do to marry this woman. Here she sees a man strong as metal and discards her self-possession, so there is nothing at all fitting here.*[72] Perhaps this means that she will run off with someone else in no time at all. *Mō* means dim and lacking brightness. *Ko* means that things will collapse and there will be a mishap. If you are not very bright and believe her deceptions, then as soon as things collapse, a great transformation will occur. How much more does this hold in the case of this woman, who sees only profit. Is she really going to be able to live out her days just sitting around minding the house?" From my position on the sidelines, I asked the diviner, "How about this woman's

---

[70] The quotation comes from *Zuo zhuan* (Zhao, year 1), which in turn is quoting from the *Book of Rites*. The purpose of the augury was to prevent the accidental union of two individuals from the same clan.
[71] Yan Junping 嚴君平 was a famous fortune-teller of Han times.
[72] The italicized portion is the diviner's quotation from *The Classic of Changes* (translation from Lynn, 161).

stock? Is she high or base?" The diviner responded, "*Kan* becomes horse, *son* becomes smell, *kon* becomes collapse. She is a rotten old horse bone from god knows where!"[73] After a while, he turned his head and said, "*Kan* is the trigram for due north. She can only be a horse bone from Kozukappara."[74]

<small>How in the hell should
I know where she is from</small>

I heard this and had a good laugh. When I withdrew, I wondered to myself. This sort of man is racing out to spend his money and buy these horse bones. Who knows what he plans to use them for? I once read in a natural history almanac that "Horse bones can be used to avoid the vapors causing acute disease. They are placed in a red cloth bag and hung at the waist: men on the left, women on the right."[75] For the first time, I realized that even horse bones have some sort of use. In ancient times, Guo Kui told King Zhao of Yan, "A ruler in the past once had one of his palace eunuchs buy a dead horse's bones for five hundred gold pieces."[76] If that is the case, then even if the horse bones

---

[73] The diviner now divides the hexagrams that have been drawn into their constituent trigrams, *gen* (J. *kon* 艮 ☶) and *kan* (J. *kan* 坎 ☵), and *gen* ☶ and *xun* (J. *son* 巽 ☴), offering a far-fetched interpretation that culminates in a play on a common Japanese expression (*doko no uma no hone to mo shirenai*—lit. "a horse bone from who knows where") for a person of suspicious or unknown origins.
[74] Kozukappara was the site of a well-known prison execution ground. Because of its proximity, the Senju pleasure quarter was called "Kotsu," and the phonetic similarity with *kotsu* meaning "bone" is the source of this joke.
[75] Ryūhoku quotes here from the late Ming *Bencao gangmu*, a comprehensive treatise on *materia medica* that was extremely influential on the founding of Edo period *honzōgaku* (herbology, nature studies).
[76] The quotation is from the *Zhan guo ce* (Strategies of the Warring States); Guo Kui's argument is that the King of Zhao, who is looking for capable men to serve him, should start with Guo Kui himself—he may not be the best, but he is a good place to start. To illustrate his point, Guo Kui introduces the story of the ruler who sought a strong horse for one thousand gold pieces; he sought it for three years without success when a eunuch asked to help the ruler seek the horse. In just three months, the eunuch obtained a horse, but it was already dead. The eunuch bought it anyway for five hundred gold pieces. The ruler was infuriated at the waste but the eunuch explained that people would start coming to the king with horses to sell once word got out that

that this lot of men redeem cost them one hundred *ryō* each, how could it be considered expensive?

When a drinking house or a boathouse calls for a geisha, they do not contact the geisha's house directly to arrange her visit. There are two places that can place orders for geisha: Okazakiya and Tachibanaya, and both are on Dōbōmachi. These geisha dispatchers are known as *kenban* in the precincts of Yoshiwara. I hear that the houses in Yoshiwara that dispatch geisha write her name on a small placard and hang it up outside. When a brothel calls for a geisha, the *kenban* looks at the placards and sends one along. This is why the geisha dispatch is called a *kenban* or "board watcher."[77] Yet Yanagibashi is distinct from the pleasure quarter of Yoshiwara. Under its old traditional conventions,^rules officially there were *shakujin*, or "drink-servers," and *okyūji*, or "waitresses": the so-called "big geisha" and "little geisha." For the last three or four years, however, when a "little geisha" has made her debut, she has rather brazenly done so as a "drink-server." The term "waitress" has thus become extinct. Nevertheless, the title "geisha" proper is still something that the women of Yanagibashi cannot presumptuously claim for themselves. For this reason, one cannot refer to either establishment, the Okazakiya or the Tachibanaya, as a "geisha dispatch." Although they must use a different name, in fact they are the same in content.

These businesses have hired men in their employ: they are known in the urban vernacular as *hitoyado*, or "intermediary agents." Because of the

---

the king would pay five hundred gold pieces for a dead horse. Sure enough, they did.

[77] The *kenban* were intermediaries that sent geisha out in response to requests from teahouses and other establishments; the characters are typically written 見番 (suggesting "lookout"), but Ryūhoku bases his etymological explanation on the homophonous alternative form 見板: "board watcher."

services they provide, they are also known by the name *hikyakuya* or "fleet-footed messenger."[78] It seems that they employ men whom they can send to accompany the geisha. Okazakiya and Tachibanaya together have around thirty men. There are some other places who are in this line of work too, but they are very few in number. Drinking houses such as Kawachō and Kashiwaya may also employ their own servant men. But there are just two businesses that specialize in performing this service. The geisha and the drinking establishments and boathouses all call these two businesses "box^(hako) houses^(ya)," and they call the men themselves "box^(hako) carriers^(mawashi)" or just plain "boxes^(hako)." They are called "box houses" or "box carriers" because the singing girls of the Northern Quarter in Yoshiwara have these men carry their shamisens in a box on their backs. The geisha around here in Yanagibashi, on the other hand, are not officially permitted to carry a shamisen box. All of them wrap their shamisen up in a cloth *furoshiki* and have the man carry it on his back with a set^(change of) of garments^(clothes). This is why the shamisen is always the type with the detachable neck. Nevertheless, the "box" name continues to be used idly.

When a box boy accompanies a geisha, he receives 150 *mon* for every banquet fee^(one bu) she gets—about ten percent of the take. If he is accompanying a "little geisha," then he will get 100 *mon* for her two *shu*. When he alone is accompanying three or four geisha, then the work is the same and yet his profits are great. For this reason, the box boy takes no pleasure in accompanying just a few, preferring instead to go along with a large group. When a drinking establishment or a boathouse calls for a geisha, some of them will call Okazakiya and some will call

---

[78] The term *hikyakuya* 飛脚屋, or more commonly *machi-hikyaku* 町飛脚, referred to a messenger service that would speedily deliver letters within the city. The intermediary *hitoyado* 人宿 sometimes accepted these delivery responsibilities as well.

Tachibanaya. Each of them has a contracted provider [set] [place] upon which it always relies. Likewise, they have their likes and dislikes about the individual box boys. So-and-so's boys are agreeable [gentle], so-and-so's boys are garrulous [too chatty]—in this way they make their evaluations and decide whom to hire. The geisha are the same way, and each has a different box boy to favor with her patronage.

When a box boy accompanies a geisha, just when the geisha is getting ready to play the shamisen, he will fit together the instrument's neck for her and string it. When she is ready to change her clothes, he will iron her skirts, fold up her obi, and put it away. He is just like a nursemaid [nanny]. If it starts to rain, he will return to fetch an umbrella, and when it gets to be late at night, he races to ready a lantern. Scurrying east and hurrying west, he is solely at her command. If the geisha has a favorite regular customer, the boy certainly knows this. In this case, the customer takes good care of the box boy too, giving him a little something [bribe] on the side. Similarly, the geisha also treats the boy twice as intimately as she does the others. Unless she does this, there will be no stopping him from divulging [spreading] their intimacies [secrets] and uttering [talking] imprecations [trash] about them. This may well be the reason why the geisha all have their particular favorites.

Alas, agriculture is the foundation of the state.[79] The artisans and merchants may be of base status, but they at least have their occupations. Cattle and horses help in transportation, shouldering the burdensome and crossing great distances. They all are useful to man. A dog barks at a thief, a cat captures a rat—each has its proper

---

[79] Similar statements about the importance of agriculture to the state can be found in *Di fan* (Model for emperors), a seventh-century text by the Tang emperor Taizong, as well as in the eighth-century *Nihon shoki* (Chronicles of Japan).

occupation. But what about this lot?^(these guys) These are full-grown men with bushy^(unkempt) beards, and yet they readily accept their lot as these low women's lackeys. By stooping to tie the woman's *tabi* socks and line up^(fix) her shoes, they curry favor with her, perhaps getting a few hundred *mon* for their trouble if they are lucky. How shameful and humiliating! To be a man and yet almost no better than a cat or dog! I think that when men of their sort die and go to Hell, they shall find it difficult to become bucentaur^(ox head) or centaur^(horse head) spirits who torment the dead even should they desire such a lowly fate.⁸⁰ What a pity!

When a regular *najimi* customer comes directly to the home of his favorite geisha, then there is no way for the box boys to make any money. They therefore all hate this situation. Similarly, it is said that if a *najimi* customer takes a geisha with him on a boat cruise, he may sometimes not hire a box boy. When a drinking house or a boathouse calls for a geisha, if they specify the geisha by name, then the box boy simply races to the appointed house. Otherwise, the box boy selects a geisha at his own discretion^(fancy) and brings her. And thus it is simply not the case that the box boy has no way to subjugate^(lord) the^(at) geisha^(least) through^(some) coercion^(power) and^(over) benevolence^(her). From my readings of unofficial^(kusa) histories,^(zōshi) I understand that in former times, intimate^(affairs) matters often occurred between certain well-known geisha and their box boys. Now however, there are no such affairs. There are just some desperate^(down on) faded^(their luck) geisha who enlist the box boys' help to drum up business; and when such a geisha has intimate relations with her box boy, the other geisha ridicule her as an eccentric "tea-freak." A geisha nevertheless content to

---

⁸⁰ The *gozumezu* were demons of the underworld in Buddhist cosmology. The *gozu* had the head of an ox and the body of a man (i.e., the bucentaur), and the *mezu* had the head of a horse and the body of a man; together, they tormented the condemned.

become a fancier of such bizarre brews is willing to do so because she wishes to avoid being placed on permanent "tea-pounding" detail.[81]

When a geisha does not get any calls and sits at home, she is said to be "pounding tealeaves." I am not sure what the *locus classicus* of this phrase is. I suspect the meaning might be that an idle geisha can use her leisure time to clutch a pestle and pound tea. In a poem by Liu Zongyuan is the couplet "I awake alone at noon, hearing no other sounds / Across the bamboo grove, the boy pounds the tea-leaves."[82] Even though the situation described is not exactly identical, the elegant feeling of refined grace is the same. For the popular geisha, in the busy spring and summer seasons, they may have fifty or sixty banquets in a given month. Even in the three months of winter, it is extremely rare for them to be pounding tea.

---

[81] The term *chajin* 茶人 refers to an aficionado of the tea ceremony, but also came to mean someone with strange tastes. Continuing the tea association, *cha o hiku* (to pound or grind tea leaves) is a colloquial expression for a geisha spending time without a customer, whereas *chatate-onna* was literally a woman who served tea in a teahouse but also functioned as a euphemism for women who provided additional sexual services. On a literal level, then, the geisha accepts the role of a "tea aficionado" (one who drinks tea in the tea ceremony) or "tea server" to avoid being in the complementary role of "tea grinder" (one who prepares the requisite tea powder). In a more important sense, however, the reason she acts as a "tea aficionado" (one with strange tastes; i.e., a geisha who inexplicably consorts with a box boy) is to drum up business and thus avoid being left to "grind tea" (pass time without a customer). Even today, the phrase "ocha o hiku" is used for "those times when a geiko has to dress up with nowhere to go" (Iwasaki, 183) or when a hostesses (or host) is without a paying customer; see Hikawa, *Monogatari*, 126; and Hikawa, *Bōizu*, 40. For theories on how "ocha o hiku" came to have this meaning for idle geisha and courtesans, see Nakamura Shikaku, 36, and DeBecker, 118–119.

[82] Liu Zongyuan 柳宗元 (773–819) was a famous Tang poet and celebrated essayist. The quoted lines are the closing couplet of his quatrain "Spontaneous summer composition." For the full poem see Barnstone and Chou, 183. Needless to say, the statement that follows about the refined "feeling" being the same in these two situations is facetious.

The geisha's fee for a banquet is called her "jewel." The term is rooted in the Northern Quarter of Yoshiwara. The prostitutes of the Northern Quarter call the record of their customers the "jeweled ledger." The term "jewel" has thus been passed down from this practice. The geisha all ask each other, "How many jewels did you get this month?" "Thirty," or "Fifty," they say, vying to boast the largest number. They all seek jewels and shun tea. A vernacular expression that means "to ridicule" someone is "to *tea*se" him; perhaps herein lies the origin of that term as well.[83]

The unpopular geisha worry about being on tea-pounding detail even during the peak season. Needless to say, in the desolate^(cheerless) months of the year, it gets so bad that they are unable to keep from going hungry. For this reason, when the autumn wind starts to blow, they all board up their doors and cover their traces. Only when spring has come, when flowers bloom and the languid willow droops, do they come back to peddle their wares again. The locals refer to this group of girls as "overgarment^(haori) geisha." A *haori* can be taken off if it is too hot, and put on if too cold. These girls are the precise opposite. Thus the name.[84]

The number of geisha in this area exceeds one hundred during the spring and summer, but shrinks to half of that during the autumn and winter. It is because of the *haori*. In addition to the *haori* are the "grebe geisha."[85] These are geisha who peddle their wares without making a

---

[83] This false etymology (*kojitsuke*) of the idiom *cha ni su* (to tease) parodies the approach of evidentiary scholarship.
[84] The term *haori geisha* also referred to a particular cross-dressing custom practiced especially by Fukagawa geisha, who sometimes wore men's *haori* jackets (Chinpunkan Shujin, 121–122). For discussion of additional meanings, see Tanaka Yūko, 35.
[85] The name *muguri*, grebe, apparently derives from the similar sounding *moguri* (diver), here meaning women who "evade" or "dive under" the nets of prohibition on private prostitution.

formal debut. The geisha do not count [include] them among their number. The grebe is an aquatic bird, one that surfaces above and vanishes beneath the waves feeding on fish. The "grebe geisha" takes her name from the fact that she makes her livelihood by surfacing and vanishing among genuine [real] geisha. When a geisha makes a formal debut, she must offer a bit of banquet [payment] money to the likes of the municipal officials, and she must also make presents to the drinking house, the boathouse, and the box house. On top of that, she also has to pay for her garments [clothes]. When one totals it up, it cannot be done for less than about thirty *ryō*. For this reason, there are many who work as "grebe geisha."

The most renowned geisha may make more than one hundred *ryō* in a year. It would seem that they ought to be rich, and yet they are all impoverished. Why? Even though they have their income, they also have their expenses. For every *bu* they earn, they only get to keep three *shu*, or three-fourths of their gross fees. Moreover, they also are deprived of some of their earnings during the five holidays and the two gift-exchange seasons. Their expenses for food and drink are also much more lavish than those of the ordinary person, to say nothing of their expenditures on clothing, or on hairpins and other accessories. They spend on *geta*, on handkerchiefs, on cosmetics [rouge and powder]. It reaches the point that their expenditures exceed their income, and so there are few geisha houses that do not have to borrow from others.

In general there are set times at which a geisha changes into a new style of dress: the beginning of the year, the first snake day of the third month, the first of the fourth month, the day of the Tango festival, the twenty-eighth day of the fifth month, the Ten'ō festival, Tanabata, the first of the ninth month, the Double-Nine day, the Ebisu festival days. But geisha of mid-rank and below cannot necessarily afford to change their dress for each occasion [every single time]. The custom is to wear an unlined *hitoe* kimono on Tango, or the fifth day of the fifth month. On the night of the twenty-eighth that month, the fireworks festival is held to the south of Ryōgoku Bridge. This is called *kawabiraki*, or "the opening of the river," and it is the first day on which they wear a thin silk crêpe kimono. This custom is unlike the practice in the average home, where people are already wearing thin silk and cotton kimono by Tango. When a geisha orders new clothes, she orders a single kimono, a single obi, an outer sleeveless top, and long undergarments called *nagajuban*; for the last of these, a deep crimson is considered the finest. For that [the] slightly [geisha] wilting spring flower [who is a little older], white is regarded as the proper color. Those who wear secondary colors or patterned designs are thought not elegant and stylish but rather just the opposite. The "little geisha" have their own waist sash [koshiobi]. They all also bring along with them a separate set of garments. During a banquet, they will excuse themselves and change into them. And this is why it is impossible for a new set of clothes to be only five or seven yen. Even if they pawn their old clothes to buy new ones, or change front into back [turn their clothes inside out], it will nevertheless involve a substantial outlay of money.

For this reason, each geisha cultivates [maintains] her own favorite customer, by means of whom she can escape from this kind of hardship. The favorite customer cannot bear to stand by and watch her spend money without making a contribution himself. In *Miscellaneous Records of the Wood Bridge*, it is recorded that a courtesan's "clothing is all provided by her favorite customer. Stylish looks and new tailoring are left up to the courtesan's 'foster-mother.' The length of her clothes and the size of the sleeves follow the vicissitudes of the times; and those who view her call it the contemporary look."[86] This was written in the Chongzhen period [1628–1644], separated in time by over two hundred years from the present day, and in space by tens of thousands of leagues. It is truly peculiar that the customs and manners are nevertheless so similar.

In recent years, clothing has been getting more beautiful by the month, better by the year. This spring in particular was quite something. The costumes of the "big geisha" far and away exceeded those of even aristocratic ladies.{high-class} {wives} The "little geisha" strain against the proper limits of their station by brazenly emulating the ways of their elders. Adorning their heads are ornamental hair clips made of resplendent{sparkling} tortoiseshell. As for the senior geisha, they wear long *kōgai* bodkins of tortoiseshell. It seems that the wearing of these bodkins by geisha is the practice of the Northern Quarter in Yoshiwara; it is not something that geisha of other districts can do. But as fashions reach new heights, they are left with no choice but to do what they are actually forbidden from doing.

Moreover, when the geisha from other districts entertain customers, they can only sing and dance. They cannot add drums or flute to their performances as the Yoshiwara geisha of the Northern Quarter can. Yet in the spring or summer of this year, a dispute{tiff} arose at a certain establishment on the Rear Bank of Yanagibashi because a geisha played a drum{taiko} there. When the people of Yoshiwara heard this, they accused her of audaciously transgressing her proper place, faulted her ostentatious dress for good measure, and reported her to the authorities. The Yanagibashi district officials were frightened by this and ordered local women to be more restrained in their dress. For obi, they could not use gold thread. They had to eliminate{take off} their *kōgai* bodkins, and the

---

[86] For the full passage from *Banqiao zaji*, see Yu Huai, 13; or the translation by Howard Levy, 42.

number of allowable hairpins was reduced. As for the junior geisha, they were only permitted to wear a single silver hairpin. Moreover, the officials ordered that geisha would henceforth be forbidden from responding to the invitations of customers after the first watch of night. This was, one suspects, in order to prevent "illicit affairs." [first watch = eight in the evening]

Among those men who visit Yoshiwara, there were many who first came to Yanagibashi for a drink, took a geisha with them to the Northern Quarter and then returned to Yanagibashi to spend the night. The people of the Northern Quarter grew angry at the personal losses they were suffering because of the steadily [bit by bit] increasing frequency with which Yanagibashi geisha engaged in "illicit affairs." In addition to their grievance about Yanagibashi geisha playing drums or dressing themselves inappropriately, they ended up establishing a set of rules that prohibited the entry of Yanagibashi women into the Quarter. They permit geisha traveling by boat or seeing off their customers to go no further than just the San'ya moat. In recent years, the Northern Quarter grows ever more cold and desolate, while Yanagibashi gets hotter by the day. That rancor and jealousy have accumulated and brought matters to this pass is completely understandable. However, it was just twenty or thirty days after these prohibitions on the showiness of the Yanagibashi geisha's clothing and her invitations to late-night assignations had been issued before things were back to normal again. This is not because the geisha are wanton and willful, fearlessly doing as they please because they do not fear authority [the man]. Rather, it is the momentum of prosperity in this great metropolis that makes it so. How could it be impeded [stopped]?

There is a folk-saying that goes, "A prostitute's pure heart [sincerity] is every bit as common as a square egg. When you see it, you can be sure the full moon will appear on the last day of the month."[87] Ah, but the courtesan is also human; how can she lack sincerity? It is only that, being steeped in the music of Zheng and Wei,^(wayward states) she has become adept at mendacious^(clever) deception^(lies) and avaricious^(wily) craftiness.^(greed)[88] She has reached this point simply because she acquired her habits along with her wits, and their pervasive influence has become set in her heart.

And yet there is naturally a difference between a singing courtesan or geisha and a prostitute. There are many geisha who are spirited and who do not enjoy coquetry,^(flattery) who are graceful^(mild) and do not countenance depravity. How can we neglect to investigate their true circumstances and instead compare them to a full moon at month's end or a square egg? Nevertheless, it must be conceded that there are of course a decent number of depraved and shiftless geisha who waste all their money because they are in love with a kabuki actor, or yield their bodies to the firefighter they have fallen for, who run off to elope and end up making a disaster^(mess) of their whole lives. It is little wonder that people in the world should only see these types and fail to perceive that there are graceful and talented ones who dwell among them: those who tower triumphantly over jealous wives and fierce^(shameless) concubines.^(hussies)

I suspect that creating the charm of shamisen songs and the mirth of sake serving is something of which only the senior geisha is capable. Turning our discussion to a geisha's temperament, however, if one wishes to find a geisha who is gracefully demure, then he had better choose a junior geisha. There are a few junior geisha with lovely

---

[87] The full moon occurs on the fifteenth day of the lunar month; on the last day of the month, therefore, the moon would not be visible. Various versions of this proverb have been recorded, such as in the preface to the 1746 *Yoshiwara saiken*.

[88] The *Book of Rites* identifies the music of the states of Zheng and Wei as being that of a disordered realm.

dispositions, aged fifteen years or thereabouts, who have not been so deeply stained by the baleful customs of their trade, who are not yet so adept in the arts of deception and trickery, and who are still unpierced.^innocent [89] If an amorous customer is able to deflower her, then he can be said to have enjoyed the ultimate pleasure of the flower-willow world. If he uses human emotion to become familiar with her, if he encourages her with a sense of duty, then it is guaranteed^a sure bet that she will never develop any avaricious schemes or plans to betray^turn against him. The reason that senior geisha are easy to "roll" is because they are greedy. Junior geisha are hard to "roll" because they are not greedy. Some people hold that "Junior geisha lack the charms of their senior sisters." This assessment is thoroughly apposite^sound. Nevertheless, if we are talking only about manufacturing that subtle charm of the drinking party, then what need is there to debate the presence or absence of sincerity? It is sufficient to simply evaluate the lively mood and the thoroughly festive atmosphere. When people of the world debate sincerity, what they have in mind lies in^at matters^a of the^deeper bedchamber^level. If that is the case, then unless she is gracefully demure she does not^is no qualify^good. And for graceful demureness, one must look to the junior geisha. You cannot find such qualities among the senior geisha. Moreover, we need not even mention that once you already have a junior geisha in the palm of your hand, it will not be more than three or four years before she is a senior geisha herself, and then how could you fail to have the best of both the barroom and the bedchamber at once?

---

[89] The original phrase 未破瓜 literally means that the girl's "melon is not yet pierced." In addition to suggesting her virginity, this specifically indicates that she is not yet sixteen, for the character for "melon" 瓜 is said to resemble two Chinese numeral eights 八. The Japanese gloss *mada ubu* suggests both "still innocent" and "still virginal."

Out of pity for the sort of suave [young] dandy [playboy] who gets involved with a woman without considering what kind of person she is first, the type who suffers [loses] a [all] crushing [he] defeat [has], tasting ephemeral [brief] ecstasy [pleasure] then protracted [lasting] perdition [woe], his resources gone and his name ruined, I write the following as a light-hearted warning to the [those] amorously [who like] inclined [to play]. It is nothing more than my nanny's [meddlesome] heart. As Yu Huai tells it, the famous courtesan of Nanjing Li Shiniang once said, "Though I may be of base status, I am not given to depravity like Songstress Xia or Madame He Jian. If you really are one whom I love from the heart, then even if I relate to you with respectful deference as I would a distinguished guest, nevertheless I still admire you from the bottom of my heart. If you are someone whom I do not love from my heart, then even if I force myself to go to bed with you, our hearts will still be far apart."[90] Ah! How numerous are the geisha of Yanagibashi! If one were to make a thorough search of them, how could there not be a single one who recalled Shiniang?

Since the shogunate was [start] inaugurated [of], there [Edo] have been countless famous geisha in the metropolis, whose appearance is incomparable, who are skilled in various accomplishments, whose names are transmitted in unofficial [kusa] histories [zōshi] and whose traces are preserved in theatrical [kabuki] works [plays]. But now it is so no longer. They are all essentially [more or less] comparable [the same], and there is none among them who genuinely exceeds the rest, none who is [has emerged] truly distinguished [to stand out] from the crowd. Nevertheless, there is one woman at present who is still worth mentioning—Okiku of east Ryōgoku Bridge.[91] Her looks will not be bringing any states

---

[90] Xia-ji 夏姬 (sometimes translated as "Songstress Xia" or "The Summer Maid") and Madame He Jian 河間婦 are both held to have been lascivious women of antiquity. The original passage is in Yu Huai, 24; for another translation, see Levy, 52.

[91] Several photographs of Okiku and the Yūmeirō teahouse were collected by Charles Longfellow during his stay in Japan in the early 1870s; see Figures 8 and 9.

Figure 8. Photograph of Okiku, proprietress of the Yūmeirō Teahouse, circa 1872. From the collection of Charles Longfellow, whose album gives the caption: "Okiko san, keeper of the Eumero." Courtesy of National Park Service, Longfellow National Historic Site.

to the brink of collapse and her talents are not exactly peerless. And yet with nothing more than the power lying in her delicate female hands, she deftly manages a grand dining hall on the west side of the Sumida

River with a placard outside identifying it as the Yūmeirō, or "House of the Dawn." The name Yūmei was soon spread throughout the city. Among the grand gentlemen and playboys, there is not a single one who has not been drunk here at least once. Restaurants like the Kawaguchi and the Hiraiwa would rank somewhat below it. Moreover, the master of the Yūmeirō is a woman. It must be that her gallant spirit and talents are worthwhile. Even though she has been able to succeed in these plans because she has some benefactors upon whom to rely, nevertheless this is not an enterprise that a run-of-the-mill typical geisha who bows down for anyone could come close to realizing. Other than Okiku, I

Figure 9. Photograph of the Yūmeirō Teahouse, circa 1872. From the collection of Charles Longfellow. Courtesy of National Park Service, Longfellow National Historic Site.

have never heard of another woman being able to attain such levels of success.

The splendor of Yanagibashi has now reached its peak. How can it be that there is not a single person whose talents surpass all the others and whose name resounds throughout the metropolis? Yu Huai listed the names of the famous courtesans of Jinling and Zhushi and wrote short biographies for them so that the traces these lovely ladies had left in the world would not fade away, but endure for one hundred generations. Now, I seek to follow his example and make a record of Yanagibashi's red skirts.^(geisha) But I still am not certain if there is any one of these women who has accomplished anything worth recording. I will just list below those geisha whose names I have heard, or most of them anyway. Perhaps some future fellows, fools for love like me, may seek out the facts concerning these girls, compose their biographies, and thereby continue the work of Yu Huai. If they did this, then they would first of all be preventing the color of these girls' makeup from fading, and second of all be making a record of the flourishing of this place for later days. Those listed below are recorded as I have heard them, with regard neither to the beauty or ugliness of their appearance, nor to the deftness or incompetence of their polite accomplishments.

Ohito, Osan, Okin, Oei, Okō, Oyumi, Otoyo, Okane, Ofumi, Okon, Ohana, Otake, Osato, Oyama, Oroku, Ohayku, Oman, Ohisa, Oshio, Oume, Odai, Ohama, Omon, Otama, Ochō, Okoto, Otoku, Otsune, Oryū, Otsuna, Omaki, Oai, Okinu, Onui, Otsuru, Ofude, Omino, Outa, Oyoshi, Otoki, Oito, Ohan, Oren, Omoto, Omitsu, Okuni, Otaki, Onami, Oyuki, Oiro, Kokatsu, Koharu, Koshige, Kotsuru, Koman, Kochō, Kohana, Koteru, Kotoku, Kotetsu, Kinhachi, Kumehachi, Yonehachi, Tamahachi, Tomihachi, Takeji, Kikuji, Komakichi, Eikichi,

Tsunekichi, Chōkichi, Yonekichi, Sankichi, Jinkichi, Kamekichi, Kurakichi, Harukichi, Asakichi, Onokichi, Umekichi, Miyo, Kiku, Kisa, Sano, Ika, Towa, Nobutama, Iroha, Toyomisa, etc., are the senior geisha.

Onaka, Osei, Oaka, Ohana, Osato, Ofuji, Oyakko, Outa, Okame, Ofuki, Ofusa, Omame, Koito, Koyoshi, Kotama, Kokin, Komichi, Koina, Komatsu, Kofuji, Kojima, Masakichi, Hisakichi, Sankichi, Senkichi, Tanekichi, Satokichi, Komakichi, Yae, Kanpachi, Gonsuke, Kintarō, etc., are the junior geisha.

I imagine that one would assign relative ranks of superiority and inferiority to these women according to his own perceptions, and that these would differ from person to person. How could I unilaterally$^{\text{decide alone}}$ issue^{on} an evaluation? In the future, if someone prepares these geishas' biographies and sheds light upon their histories, then their relative merits will naturally be settled.

> Because this record was initially compiled in the mid-winter of the year of the sheep [1859], those listed in it are all women active around the year of the horse [1858] and the year of the sheep. However, in the present year of the monkey [1860], Okane, Kikuji, Koteru, Umekichi, and several others who were junior geisha, have now become senior geisha. And others such as Yonehachi and Nobutama have newly made their debuts this year. I have appended the names of these women to the rolls in the early autumn of this year of the monkey. Furthermore, geisha such as Kanehachi and Tsunekichi were redeemed from the geisha rolls during the horse and sheep years. Otoyo and

Eikichi were also redeemed this year. I have elected not to elide their names and have left them as they are.

Alas! In recording the flourishing of Yanagibashi, I have written of the diverting charms of the singing geisha. And in so doing I have ended up pointlessly rooting out their secrets and exposing some ugly features. What a drab and cheerless exercise! What an insensitive sort I must be, unparalleled in times ancient or modern! I have surely given offense to the talented young men and beautiful women. But after all, I am not a man utterly bereft of feeling. I am rather a supremely sensitive and passionate soul. If such a sensitive and passionate soul nevertheless makes cruel and heartless statements, then he must have a reason why. It must be because he has something on his mind.

How can one discuss sensitive and passionate matters with those ignorant squirms? How can one enjoy elegant amorousness with those fussy and small-minded folks? The only sorts of people with whom one can discourse on these subjects and savor elegant diversions are the world's first-rate connoisseurs and the top-flight talented men of this and earlier ages. But surely there are not so many of these connoisseurs and talents. It is for this reason alone that I have written these cruel and insensitive words, endeavoring to enlighten those ignorant squirms about the principle that a woman may from the outside seem like a Bodhisattva, but inside beats the heart of a demon; to make them realize that what they perceive as a paradisiacal world is in fact a limitless Hell; and to turn them away from their deluded state of abandonment and thereby help them to make themselves whole and preserve their houses.

And yet, how can there not be a single connoisseur or talented man in this vast universe? [*vast* = whole; *universe* = wide world] If this work were to accidentally find its way into the hands of such a man, then he might well be inclined to regard me as one of the foolish lot too. And if that were to happen, what words could I offer in reply? Now then, these intimate matters of the wind and the moon, these diverting charms of the flowers and willows, they seem foolish but are not foolish; they verge on the vulgar and yet are not vulgar. Can a man apprehend their innermost secrets by himself? When it comes to plucking fragrant blossoms from this grove of orchids and chrysanthemums, or pilfering pearls from this pool of beautiful jewels, it is true that these are not the teachings of the Duke of Zhou or Confucius. But how can the proper Confucian gentleman manage to shun such amorous matters with a look of horror in the same way that he avoids "violence and heedlessness, lowness and impropriety"?[92]

Let us take the case of a vassal. Is it not sufficient for him to be like Xie Anshi, who could subdue a million strong enemy soldiers with a smile on his face and thereby save the state? What right do we have to pass judgment on his happy diversions at the Eastern Mountain?[93] Or, let us look at the case of a literatus. If he has the broad knowledge and vast vocabulary of Bo Juyi, if he can have his name illuminate the annals of history and make his poetry known overseas, that would also be enough. What fault would lie in his inability to suppress his passions? The

---

[92] The reference here is to *Analects* (VIII.4): "There are three principles of conduct which the man of high rank should consider specially important: that in his deportment and manner he keep from violence and heedlessness; that in regulating his countenance he keep near to sincerity; and that in his words and tones he keep far from lowness and impropriety" (Legge).
[93] Xie Anshi 謝安石 (320–385) was said to enjoy consorting with courtesans during a period of reclusion on the Eastern Mountain outside Guiji, but he subsequently served as Prime Minister of Jin, defending it against the attacking Former Qin army.

gentlemen of today with their exceedingly minuscule[cramped] disputations and their extremely suffocating codes of conduct have never had a clue what the feel and charm of refined style and tasteful elegance are all about. They do not perceive the fact that a haughty wife or an arrogant concubine causes much more harm than a sensual chanteuse or a lovely dancing girl. And thus we see a surfeit of these men who have failed to become masters of their curtained[inner] bedchambers[sanctum], and instead earn the scornful sneers of the playboys.

Playing among the flowers and willows has a long history. For this reason, there are needless to say hundreds of renowned courtesans and charming dancing girls whose deeds have been transmitted down to us over thousands of years just like heroic generals and loyal vassals. Is it not the case that these records have been preserved because passionate souls took the time to record them? They spoke of the heart of Su Xiaoxiao, who manifested her honor at the pine and cypress of West Mound.[94] They wrote of the fidelity of Mao Xixi, which vies in its purity with the waves of Huai Lake.[95] Lü Zhu never turned her back on her obligation to Shi Chong.[96] Hongfu saw where she should run in Li Jing.[97] Wherever Chu Lianxiang would sit or lie down, bees and butterflies would flutter about to steep in her fragrant breezes.[98] As befit her name, whenever Gao Linglong composed poetry, it would

---

[94] Su Xiaoxiao was a famed Six Dynasties courtesan; the reference here is to her poem "Where?" which ends with the couplet "Where will sweethearts become one? / At West Mound 'neath pine and cypress" (Birrell, 272).
[95] Mao Xixi was a Song Dynasty courtesan who was martyred in 1235 for refusing to serve the rebel general Rong Quan.
[96] Lü Zhu was the beloved concubine of Shi Chong (249–300); she committed suicide when Sun Xiu destroyed Shi Chong in order to seize her.
[97] Hongfu was a famed courtesan of the Sui who discerned the general Li Jing's promise and ran away with him.
[98] Chu Lianxiang was a noted courtesan of the Tang.

always sound like the clinking of precious stones.⁹⁹ Gu Mei artfully enraptured poets in her labyrinthine Milou.¹⁰⁰ Xue Tao's iridescent texts added color to one's study.¹⁰¹ Ge Ruifang's fierce sense of integrity [chastity] and Li Shiniang's refined elegance [fūryū] were completely unlike those of a woman.¹⁰² In our country, the so-called *shirabyōshi* of antiquity were also geisha. Senju played the *biwa* lute at the inn where Shigehira was held captive and soothed him.¹⁰³ Lady Shizuka did not bend before Yoritomo but performed a dance at his encampment.¹⁰⁴ These are passionate tales for the ages, elegant stories of a hundred generations that have dazzled and captivated listeners, making their spirits take flight and their souls soar, drooling over their beauty and crying over their pathos. But our age has become frivolous [shallow], people have become petty [stingy], and now individuals graced with such a manner are nowhere to be found. Nevertheless, human nature admits no "old" and "new"; for it is not the nature of wood or stone. The talented young men and beautiful women of the present are no different from their counterparts in the past. And when it comes to excursions with the wind and moon, when we speak of diversions amid the flowers and

---

⁹⁹ According to a Song text entitled *Bi ji man zhi*, Gao Linglong was a Tang courtesan whom Bo Juyi sent to sing some poems for his close friend Yuan Weizhi. Weizhi responded with a poem stating that he did not want to hear his own compositions sung in this manner, since many of them were parting poems addressed to Bo Juyi.
¹⁰⁰ Gu Mei was a Ming courtesan whose biography appears in Yu Huai's *Banqiao zaji*.
¹⁰¹ As mentioned earlier, Xue Tao was a courtesan of the Tang period who was particularly accomplished in writing poetry.
¹⁰² Ge Ruifang was a Ming courtesan of Jingling whose story appears in Yu Huai's *Banqiao zaji*. She was martyred when she resisted a general from the Qing army.
¹⁰³ As told in *Tale of the Heike*, Senju 千手 (1165–1188) was the lover of Taira no Shigehira 平重衡 (1156–1185).
¹⁰⁴ As told in *Tale of the Heike*, Lady Shizuka 静御前 (1165–1211) was Minamoto no Yoshitsune's lover. After Yoshitsune fled to the north to escape his brother, the new shogun Yoritomo, Shizuka was captured and ordered to dance for him. She sang of her continuing love for Yoshitsune, angering Yoritomo; fortunately his wife Masako felt pity and had her spared.

willows, how can there be nothing about these realms that evokes old times?

And when the spring breeze melts the chill and the weather gradually becomes fine, the plum trees blossom in front of the houses along the east of the river, both the northern and southern branches blooming at the same time. One can lead a lovely lady through the fragrance of plums wafting in the darkness, or embrace a beauty beside a thin branch. The tips of her red skirt flutter, captivating the soul of the flower god; her red lacquered clogs [glazed] [geta] resound in harmony with the song of the warbler. Drinks can be purchased at Yanagishima and amusements enjoyed on the Sumida jetty. And how much more can these pleasures be had when a riot of red peach and white apricot blossoms fills the sky; when clusters of cherry-blossom clouds appear; when the river flows ever more sapphire, and the whitefish sparkles silver. With a golden cask one gets drunk in the evenings, with magnolia oars one paddles upstream at dawn. Five or six senior geisha and six or seven junior geisha, some led on one's left, others escorted on the right, all vie to have the newest spring clothing. Add to this the pleasures of competing to pick the most distinctive flowers and grasses to adorn the hair. Enjoying the breeze and composing poetry, one loses oneself and forgets to return. I do not know whether the Master would permit [be] it [in] or not, [favor] but this is even superior to Dian's way.[105]

---

[105] This section is a reworking of a story in the *Analects* in which Confucius asks several disciples what they would do if their abilities were recognized. After several disciples enumerate their aspirations, Zeng Xi (Dian) is asked to sketch his thoughts: "'In late spring, after the spring clothes have been newly made, I should like, together with five or six adults and six or seven boys, to go bathing in the River Yi and enjoy the breeze on the Rain Altar, and then to go home chanting poetry.' The Master sighed and said, 'I am all in favour of Dian'" (Lau, *Analects*, XI.26).

Crow^(Days) and rabbit^(months) race by fleetingly, and when the enjoyments of the spring season have suddenly become like something glimpsed only in a dream, verdant trees fill the gardens, and cuckoos chirp in the rain. One talks of former adventures by the beautifully curtained windows, speaks of welling feelings under the quiet eaves. After weeks of charming frustration at not being able to venture out have passed, the rainy season is over. Just then comes the night of the river opening and the fireworks. At the head of Ryōgoku Bridge, ten thousand teashops and a thousand taverns raise their new curtains in unison, their colorful lanterns illuminating each other. Boats run east and west, their paddles colliding and poles brushing against each other. They are so packed together that for several leagues on the great river, one cannot even catch a glimpse of the sapphire waves. Some float their *yakata* boats in midstream, like Emperor Wu of the Han enjoying a trip on the canal. Others take lighter *choki* boats out in search of shamisen and song, faintly recalling Bo Juyi's sorrows on the Xunyang River.[106] The wind and string music continues to the dawn, the conversations and laughter have no end. Beneath the bridge and off the midstream islands, the cool breeze pierces to the bone, and one forgets what the oppressive heat of summer months in the city even feels like. One's body purified and heart refreshed, it is just as though one has followed the goddess Chang'e to the cave^(her palace on the moon) of the toad. With such terrestrial delights, Zhang Qian's immortal raft need not depart Bowang for the Milky Way.[107]

---

[106] The allusion here is to Bo Juyi's "Song of the Lute"; for a translation, see Minford and Lau, *Classical Chinese Literature*, I: 890–893.
[107] The reference is to Zhang Qian, the marquis of Bowang, who is said to have followed the Yellow River to its source, reaching the Milky Way. In the previous sentence, the "cave of the toad" refers to the Chinese legend of a toad (a manifestation of the lunar goddess Chang'e) dwelling in the moon.

On the evening of Tanabata, when the Ox Herder and Weaver Girl stars meet, it is Yanagibashi that is the magpie bridge of the human realm.[108] And here the Weaver Girl plays the shamisen well, having no time to weave clouds into silk. The Ox Herder, meanwhile, has sold his ox for drink, spending the night in pleasant intoxication. The couplings^(encounters) happening here night after night are quite a far cry from their celestial counterpart, which only occurs once a year. And still more is this true in mid-autumn, when the skies are clear and the weather fine. Then, there are Yu Liangs who climb the second floor to enhance their pleasure.[109] There are Yuan Hongs who float on their boats and sing songs.[110] The moon is ever brighter and the wind ever more refreshingly clear, and what's more, there are fragrant^(good) wine and fine^(sake) fish, sensuous strings and melancholy flutes. Beneath the Deer-tail^(How'd-you-fare) Pine, people tie up their mooring ropes and share drink.[111] Toward the

---

[108] The Ox Herder and the Weaver Girl are figures associated with the two stars Altair and Vega. According to a legend popular throughout East Asia, the lovers were condemned to be separated by a river of stars (the Milky Way), except for one night each year (07.07, Ch. Qixi; J. Tanabata), when magpies would form a bridge that allowed them to meet.

[109] A story from *A New Account of Tales of the World* tells how the underlings of Yu Liang 庾亮 (289–340) were once enjoying themselves in the Southern Tower when they heard his footsteps. Expecting his stern disapproval, they were "on the point of getting up and making way for him, but Yu said amiably, 'Gentlemen, stay awhile. The old chap's pleasure in this spot is by no means light.' So saying, he sat down on a folding chair … chanted poems and joked with the company" (Mather, 336).

[110] The *Jin shu* (History of the Jin) records how Yuan Hong 袁宏 floated his boat one autumn evening and chanted poetry. He was overheard by Xie Shang 謝尚, who was impressed and felt a connection with him.

[111] The *shubi no matsu* 首尾の松 was a pine (or set of pines) growing near the shogunate's granaries along the Sumida River. Located halfway between San'yabori and Yanagibashi, the site was often featured in woodcut scenes of Edo. The term *shubi* suggests "outcome," and the site served as a place where leisure boat passengers might pray for success at Yoshiwara, where returnees might discuss how everything had turned out, and where other passengers might tie up their boats and seek their own outcomes (Nakamura Shikaku, 124–133). Ryūhoku uses the characters 麈尾 (lit. "deer-tail") for *shubi*, which refers to a tufted staff used in Buddhist rites. Timon Screech translates the place name as "topsy-turvy pine"; it appears as item 7 in Figure 2.

vicinity of Hundred-Pegs, they beat their paddles and go. When the autumn light gradually fades and a sharply chill frost comes, one visits chrysanthemums in the gardens to the east of the river, and sees maples in the inns on Matsusaki. Gazing upon the chrysanthemum flowers of reclusion, they seem like the peony flowers of fortune. A palanquin has come to a stop, but within its curtains one sees a face like an ephemeral hedge-tree tree blossom.[112]

When the season turns to the three months of desolate winter, when the vulgar lot and rustic sorts no longer make tracks, then it is time to have truly satisfying excursions. The low-class geisha and second-rate girls have stopped plying their trade, and the time is ripe for the ultimate passions. On nights when the wind is frigid and the sleet pours down, it is still spring inside the curtained chambers. Passionate reveries are warming up and the sake's bouquet is always fragrant. No one realizes that the moon over Ryōgoku Bridge outside is enough to freeze one to death. I suspect that this is just the sort of time when Sun Lin felt the enjoyment of confirming his passions, or when Han Xiang experienced the intimacy that led her to refuse any other customer.[113] When the dawn has broken, when all the roof-tiles are a dazzling white, one pours sake into the bottles, outfits the boat with a *kotatsu* stove, and goes on an excursion to view the snow along the Sumida River jetty. Surely no one will be hurrying back home because the mood has worn off.[114]

---

[112] In this sentence, Ryūhoku combines language from "A Mountain Walk," a famous quatrain by the Tang poet Du Mu on stopping a carriage to view fall foliage (for a translation see Burton, 60) with another poem involving a carriage from the *Book of Songs*, which contains the lines "There is the lady in the carriage [with him], With the countenance like the flower of the ephemeral hedge-tree" (Legge, Mao 83).
[113] The references are to courtesans of Yu Huai's Nanjing and their lovers.
[114] The story referenced here appears in the *Shi shuo xin yu* and tells of how late one winter night, Wang Huizhi 王徽之 was seized with the desire to go visit his friend Dai Kui 戴逵. As soon as Wang arrived at his friend's gate, however, he turned around and

Not only that, but when the year is just drawing to an end, and people are feeling a little frantic, they have "forget-the-year parties," at which time they pledge^(promise) in advance to have their spring merriments. Ah, what a delight it is!

I put myself in the position of the talented young men and beautiful women of antiquity, imagining^(bringing to mind) the fulfilling and satisfying diverting excursions of the past. How can there possibly be a heaven-and-earth difference between these and the situation today? The seasonal variations of wind and flowers, clouds and moon, the subtle delights of strings, flutes, and the human voice, the intertwining of sorrow and joy, the entanglements of frowns and smiles—this is the very stuff of poetry and painting. And yet how can one speak of such things with those foolish philistines who just want to throw their money around, who make a showy display of their grandeur, who are indifferent^(do not care about) to subtle charms and who only drool over physical beauty?

Oh, will the talented young men and beautiful women of the future think that I am an insensitive soul? Or, on the other hand, will they take me for an overly sensitive soul? Just for fun, I have written these silly words with the aim of posing this question. If the mountains and rivers, wind and moon, the delights of silks, strings, and songs are such that they get better the more you have of them, then how could I possibly exhaust the topic here? To say nothing of the subtle plots and novel schemes that lurk only within^(in the mind) people's hearts! It is truly something that the inked brush fails to describe. Ah!

---

left. When later asked to explain his puzzling behavior, he responded that he had returned once the mood had left him.

Appendix

Included in the second fascicle of *Rare Book of Calculating Methods*, written by the Immortal Ryū.[115]

The Immortal What-of-it wrote *New Chronicles of Yanagibashi*. The entire volume consists of 6720 characters. These characters are so many pieces of gold and precious gems. The amount of money that our Immortal spent in compiling this volume can surely be no less than two thousand *ryō*. Suppose there were someone who purchased this volume for two thousand *ryō*. I wonder how much money each character would be worth. The methodology for solving this query appears below.

One piece of gold is equal to one *ryō*. This is equivalent to sixty *monme* of silver.
We shall take his recording of 6720 characters as the first term.
We shall take two thousand *ryō*, or 120,000 *monme*, as the second term.
We shall take one character as the third term.
Having done this, we are able to calculate the fourth term.
Let us respond to the question.

The answer: the value of one character is 17.862 *monme* and change.

---

[115] "The Immortal Ryū" was Yanagawa Shunsan 柳河春三 (1832–1870), a friend of Ryūhoku's and fellow member of the salon that centered on Dutch studies scholar Katsuragawa Hoshū. His name is also read Shunzō. Among Yanagawa's many accomplishments was the 1857 publication of an early primer on Western arithmetic, entitled *Yōsan yōhō* (The method of Western arithmetic). The title mentioned here, *Yōsan chinsho*, was a genuine text that was published in 1869, though this appendix does not seem to have been included in it.

New Chronicles of Yanagibashi
Volume II

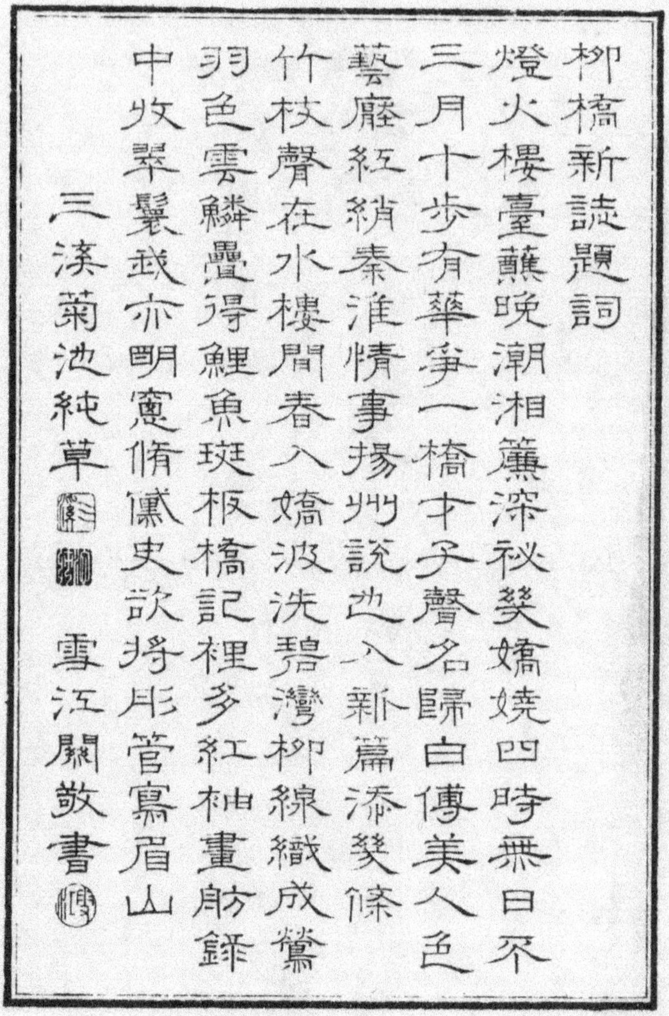

柳橋新誌題詞

燈火樓臺簾晚潮湘簾深祕獎嬌嬈四時無日不

三月十步有華爭一橋才子聲名歸白傳美人色

藝廳紅綃泰淮情事揚州說也入新篇添獎條

竹杖聲在水樓間春入嬌波洗碧灣柳線織成鶯

羽色雲鱗疊得鯉魚斑板橋記裡多紅袖畫舫鑼

中牧翠鬘或亦明窻修儻史欵將彤管寫眉山

三溪菊池純草

雪江關敬書

Figure 10. Poetic inscription to the second volume of *New Chronicles of Yanagibashi*. Kikuchi Sankei wrote the two heptasyllabic regulated verses appearing here, which are translated on the facing page. The calligraphy, in the *reisho* (Ch. *lishu*) clerical style, was done by Seki Sekkō.

Lantern flames and tall buildings play on the evening current;
How many charming ladies do the bamboo curtains conceal?
In all four seasons, not a day unlike the three months of spring;
A lovely flower every ten paces, all vying near one bridge.
The fame of this talented young man recalls Bo Juyi,
The looks and arts of the beautiful women exceed Hong Xiao.[1]
Amorous tales of the Qinhuai River and anecdotes of Yangzhou
Will surely fill out a few lines of this new volume.

"Bamboo branch" ballads resound from the waterside inns;
Spring pervades the charming ripples, bathing the emerald bay.[2]
Sinuous streams of willow interwoven like the warbler's feathers,
Cloud-stippled roof-tiles recall the scales of spotted carp.
Many red-sleeved beauties grace *Miscellaneous Records of Wooden Bridge*;
Emerald-coiffured ladies adorn *Painted-boat Records*.[3]
Beside my clear window, I too will write a sensual history;
With my colorful brush, I will depict their beautiful brows.

Sankei Kikuchi Jun (text). Sekkō Seki Kei (calligraphy).[4]

---

[1] In this poem, Sankei compares Ryūhoku ("this talented young man") to the Tang poet Bo Juyi, pointedly using the latter's title of "Junior Mentor to the Heir Apparent" for its similarity to Ryūhoku's former position as tutor to the Tokugawa shoguns. Hong Xiao was a famous courtesan who appears in the Tang *chuanqi* story of "The Kunlun Slave." The subsequent references to Yangzhou and Qinhuai are to favorite haunts of Tang poet Du Mu and Qing literatus Yu Huai, respectively.

[2] "Bamboo branch" (竹枝; J. *chikushi*; Ch. *zhuzhi*) ballads constitute a genre of *yuefu* ("music bureau") poetry focused on local customs that was developed by Tang poet Liu Yuxi (772–842). In Japan, the genre became especially popular in the late Edo period, where poets often used the form to address romantic subjects or depict life within the pleasure quarters.

[3] *Painted-boat Records* refers to *Wumen huafanglu* 呉門畫舫録, a mid-Qing record of famous Suzhou courtesans written by Xixi Shanren 西溪山人. Along with Yu Huai's *Miscellaneous Records of the Wooden Bridge*, it was widely read in late Tokugawa and Meiji Japan.

Preface

I parted company with the Immortal What-of-it after we had shared a drink at Tomoe in Yanagibashi. Counting back now, I find that already three years have passed since then. Recently, the Immortal sent me the second volume of his *New Chronicles of Yanagibashi* in the mail, saying, "I have become a useless person now, and merely wish to write useless books for my own pleasure. You, after all, are also one who enjoys useless words. Won't you write something for me?"

I received the text and read it. The prose is amusing and brings an irrepressible smile to the reader's lips. However, a more discerning appreciation of its flavor shows that there are satirical comments lodged within, that deep emotions are incorporated into it. Not only does it allow the reader to understand the charms of Yanagibashi, but it also informs him of the prevailing circumstances in today's Tokyo. Not

---

[4] Originally from Wakayama, Kikuchi Sankei 菊池三溪 (1819–1891) was a Sinologist who served as a tutor to the fourteenth shogun, Tokugawa Iemochi (1846–1866, shogun 1858–1866). He served briefly in the Meiji government for the Police Agency, before quitting his post and moving to Kyoto. He was an active member of Ryūhoku's circle, contributing to his literary magazine *Kagetsu shinshi* and providing comments on the poems in the posthumous collection *Ryūhoku shishō*; for recent research into this important figure's biography, see Fukui Tatsuhiko's article. Seki Sekkō 關雪江 (1828–1878) was a calligrapher from Tsuchiura domain who was also one of Ryūhoku's associates (see Robert Campbell's essay in Seki, esp. II:101–103; Nagai Kafū, *Shitaya*, 268).

only does he learn the current state of today's Tokyo, but he can also infer from it the future conditions of the realm. How can we not call this One Marvelous Tome? However, inasmuch as the Immortal himself calls this a useless book, those in the world who read it will likewise certainly regard it as a useless book. That being the case, one supposes that there would also be nothing preventing us from calling it One Useless Tome.

The Immortal's talent is sharp, his learning broad, and he does not accept the restraints of decorum or propriety. He acts in accordance with the dictates of his feelings and convictions. Many in the world recognize the Immortal's talent and learning, but do not yet recognize the grandeur of his aspirations or the fact that he has many worthwhile accomplishments. In the past, the Immortal lost his position in the Confucian academy and was confined to his home. At the time, everyone looked down upon him. Minister Kigai alone believed his talents to be distinguished and recommended him for a position.[5] The Immortal's service as a general in the army was characterized by his dual qualities of compassionate benevolence and dignified authority. Even a fierce and unruly hawk of a soldier would submit to his control. And the Immortal's role was considerable when it came to matters such as the tripartite armed forces, in which the cavalry, infantry, and artillery of Western countries were studied and practices updated. As the end of the shogunate drew near, the government's treasury was utterly empty. At this moment, the Immortal assumed control of the finances, making payments for expenses domestic and foreign. Officers of sea and land depended upon him and did not go hungry. Perhaps the

---

[5] "Minister Kigai" 龜崖相公 refers to Matsudaira Norikata 松平乗謨 (1839–1910), head of Tatsuoka domain in Shinshū. In 1865, he recommended Ryūhoku for the position of cavalry head.

Immortal also knows "the great principle for the production of wealth."[6] After the Boshin War, the Immortal resigned his post and became an urban recluse. With wild abandon, he went into decline. However, when one saw him in his constricted and straitened circumstances, his spirits were high and his mood refreshing; never could one detect even a hint of depression. Is it not the case that he has some qualities that exceed the common man?

Ah, Immortal What-of-it! You are possessed of useful abilities, and yet you choose to squander them. Surely it is sad indeed for such a man to write useless books just to please himself! That being said, it is nevertheless the case that the Immortal What-of-it's discarding of usefulness to enjoy uselessness is the very factor that makes him the Immortal What-of-it. I cannot help but add these comments for the benefit of those who would read this book. But when the Immortal sees my inscription, he will certainly spit upon it, saying, "You loquacious lout! You have cheapened my book with your useless words." And I will then graciously accept this spit.

Late spring, in the fourth year of Meiji [1871], recorded by Hekiun Sanjin, the Recluse of the Azure Clouds, in his temporary lodgings beneath the peak of Mount Fuji.[7]

[Original] Calligraphy by sexagenarian Gyōden Ōshima Shin.[8]

---

[6] The author of the preface alludes here to a line from the Confucian classic *The Great Learning*. 生財有大道 "There is a great principle for the production of wealth" (see the translation in Chan, 94).

[7] The identity of Hekiun Sanjin 碧雲山人 is uncertain, but Iwamura Eitarō argues that it was another sobriquet used by Tanabe Taichi (Renshū), who served as a key diplomat under both the Tokugawa and the Meiji government (Imamura, part 2, p. 8).

[8] Ōshima Shin 大島信 (1805–1885) was a calligrapher who used the sobriquet Gyōden 尭田.

New Chronicles of Yanagibashi Volume II

> I once wrote a book called *New Chronicles of Yanagibashi*.[9] Already a dozen years have passed since then. At the time, I believed I had skillfully captured the "new" elements of the place. And for their part, readers likewise perhaps took pleasure in the text's "new"-ness. But since then, the times have changed and things have shifted; the pleasures of Yanagibashi have been transformed and these "New Chronicles" are now quite stale.^(old) After the Tokugawa clan went west, it has not been unusual for daimyo compounds, with their vermilion gates and white plaster walls, to be transformed into mulberry and tea fields.[10]

And yet, the geisha of Yanagibashi have not lost their livelihood. They keep on, employed as before playing the flute or plucking the strings while they cavort about in places of elegant diversion. Surely their lot is superior to that of the former shogunal officials, who cling to life by fleeing like rabbits or hiding like mice.[11] Since the monarchical government has been completely

---

[9] This indented section is an authorial preface. It is unlabeled as such in the original, but indented to mark it off from the main body text.

[10] The Tokugawa clan's move to the west refers to their relocation to Shizuoka. This sentence draws upon a common literary idiom about the world's vicissitudes—"the azure sea transforms into a mulberry field" 滄海桑田—but here it also refers to actual government policy from 1869 to 1871, which encouraged the use of former daimyo compounds for mulberry and tea cultivation.

[11] Hino Tatsuo offers a convincing reading of this metaphor, arguing that the "fleeing rabbits" are those former shogunal officials who fled to Shizuoka with the Tokugawa and the "hiding mice" are those like Ryūhoku who remained in Tokyo without serving the Meiji state. Hino's reading suggests a self-deprecatory dimension lacking in the more embittered tone of Maeda Ai's reading that the rabbits and mice collectively refer

renovated, it only makes sense that Yanagibashi would also have been completely renovated. But there still has not appeared a connoisseur of the curious to document these new changes. I hear that in recent times someone has stolen and printed my *New Chronicles of Yanagibashi*, and that many young stylish and sophisticated lads purchase and read it. I lament the fact that they are reading a book that has already gone stale in these days of renewal and Restoration.[12] Thus, I have produced this second volume of *New Chronicles of Yanagibashi*.

Subsequent ^(Ever) to ^(since) the Keiō period [1865–1868], the department stores have depleted ^(cut) their stock by half and only the restaurants can command enough wealth to make their houses shine.[13] Why is this? It is because whereas the population of the city has decreased by half, the number of pleasure seekers has doubled.[14] Why has the population decreased and the number of pleasure seekers doubled? It is because people are so in awe of the majestic beauty of the imperial government that they do not make plans for their descendants in future generations. As soon as a coin falls into their hands, they buy something to eat; as soon as they get a banknote, they go have a drink. The drinking

---

to the former shogunal officials who agreed to serve the new Meiji government.

[12] Among the many "new" things defining the early Meiji moment were reforms, reconfigurations, and reworkings of earlier practices; the term for the 1868 Meiji "Restoration" 維新 (J. *ishin*; Ch. *weixin*) itself derives from a phrase in *The Book of Songs*. 周雖舊邦、其命維新 "Although Zhou is an old country, its [heavenly] mandate is new."

[13] The allusion is to a line in *The Great Learning* 富潤屋、德潤身—"Wealth makes a house shine; virtue makes a person shine." This maxim is variously interpreted as "Wealth only makes a house shine, but virtue makes one's person shine" or "Just as wealth makes a house shine, so too can virtue make a person shine."

[14] The population of Edo is estimated to have been in excess of one million in the 1840s and 1850s, but the population of the Tokyo urban wards had fallen to around 570,000 in 1872. It was not until 1886 that the population in the wards of Tokyo city grew above one million (Hino, 385).

establishments of Yanagibashi all are flourishing unlike they ever did in
the past. Kawachō and Umekawa compete [face off] against each other for control of the league from their respective positions along the north and south of the bridge. Manpachi is also rallying back and seems poised to shake off its recent decline. Kamesei and Yanagiya have developed the new quarters in Shin-Yanagimachi, and there is a vibrant color in their banners.[15] With the land reclamation at Shin-Yanagimachi, the prosperity of Yanagibashi has increased all the more. After the conflagration, Great Nakamura (Note: there is also a boathouse called Nakamura. Therefore, the locals refer to this drinking house as Great Nakamura) raised up a giant new building, and now it can be called the hegemon of the eastern bank. Kashiwaya and Aoyanagi have also remodeled themselves and now compete for supremacy. Establishments such as Fukagawa, Ryūkō, Ikuine, and Taikyō have gotten the edge on the competition by dint of their modest [low] prices. Renowned as especially unusual items are Yūshintei's *tomoshiraga*, or "growing gray together," a confection made of dried gourd strips, and Shōchūan's *odamakimushi*, a steamed egg custard with noodles. The reason Ryūshō plies its customers with such saccharine fare is in order to disguise the food's bitter taste with sweetness. I can discern the flavor, and therefore do not wish to "swill their lees."[16] Each hall vies for grandeur and competes for exquisiteness; hot-spots become not-so-hot-spots and vice versa. Amid this confusion, Tomoeya has started to thrive. In recent years, the various dining halls have vainly

---

[15] Both Kameseirō and Yanagiya are mentioned, along with Nakamurarō, in Tsukioka Yoshitoshi's series of prints from the 1880s, *The Twenty-Four Hours at Shinbashi and Yanagibashi*; see the commentary by Harue M. Summersgill and Alfred H. Marks in Seigle, *A Courtesan's Day*, 104.

[16] The narrator here adopts words that recall the righteous figure of Qu Yuan; in the *Songs of the South*, a "Fisherman" recommends to Qu Yuan: "And if all men are drunk, why not sup their dregs and swill their lees?" (Hawkes, 206).

stoked their fires to an ostentatious roar. More than a few tend to make their décor splendid, but do not make their dishes savory; they raise their prices and yet give little thought to their customers. If you want to raise your spirits by making a dazzling display of wealth, then you should have a drink at Nakamura, Kawachō, Kamesei, Kashiwaya, Umegawa, or Aoyanagi. But if you want to discourse on the true flavor of fine cuisine, then there is no place around Ryōgoku that outdoes Tomoeya. The master of Tomoeya could be called, quite simply, a latter-day Yi Ya.[17]

During those lovely times when the spring breezes blow, or the autumn moon shines, it has been my custom for years to drink in the restaurants at Ryōgoku. But I have never seen it as popular with customers as it is today, nor has the appearance of new construction [building] ever been as beautiful as it is today. It stands to reason that the only way it could possibly be flourishing like this is that there are in fact people out there who are causing the place to be so prosperous. To my way of thinking, it is almost as though the high-and-mighty these days are all like the Lord of Mengchang, and the customers are like Feng Xuan.[18] How they demand excellence in their food! Not only do the retainers of Lord Chunshen and Lord Pingyuan arrive at the various establishments of Yanagibashi sporting jeweled shoes and precious

---

[17] Yi Ya 易牙 was a eunuch serving Duke Huan of Qi; his culinary skills were so legendary that it was said: "... in taste the whole world looks to Yi Ya" (VIA.7; Lau, *Mencius*, 164).
[18] Among the numerous retainers of the Warring States era Lord of Mengchang was Feng Xuan, who attracted his Lord's attention immediately after he had entered service by loudly lamenting the absence of fish from his rations, along with a string of other complaints about his treatment. The Lord of Mengchang promptly responded to his demands and Feng Xuan eventually proved himself worthy of the special attention. Here the reference seems to be to Feng Xuan's unexpected demands for lavish material comforts.

swords, but in fact the place causes even the feudal lords of Qi, Chu, Yan, and Zhao to personally direct their palanquins to make a special stop there. Ah, what splendor![19]

The boathouses of the four banks have also experienced vicissitudes^(changes) of their own. On Front Street, Omotoya and Takeya have closed their doors, with Mikawaya and Itonakamura taking their place. Shinkazusa has also changed its name to Matsuba. On the Rear Bank, Fukuyoshi has departed and Maruya has appeared. Shinwakatake has moved its location to "Old Willow Bridge," and Harima in Yonezawachō has become the Okinaya. There have also been various shifts in the wealth and popularity of the establishments, but aside from these changes, things basically remain in their original state^(as they always were)—the bustling success of the three houses of Masuda, Izu, and Suzuki still takes the crown for the four districts. Even though the charms of the alehouses and boathouses have not changed since the old days, the menu prices and the boating rates are now four or five times what they were ten years ago. This state of affairs, however, is simply due to the use of paper currency in the place of a bad flood of gold coins. It is, after all, not something worth puzzling over in the slightest.

A certain person asked me, "These days there are more than two hundred geisha in Yanagibashi if we count both junior and senior. This is nearly twice the number there were in the past, and yet the numbers of boathouses and alehouses have not increased. And if you look up in

---

[19] Along with Lord Mengchang and Lord Xinling, Lord Chunshen and Lord Pingyuan are sometimes called the "Four Heroes." These third century BCE men were noted for their ability to attract large numbers of retainers. The phrase about "jeweled shoes and precious swords" refers to a passage from the biography of Lord Chunshen in *The Records of the Grand Historian*; Chunshen's top retainers were said to be rewarded with such splendor.

the old ledger-books how many invitations of geisha there were from the various houses, you find that the number now is comparable [more or less the same as] to the number back then. Why is this?"

I answered him saying, "In former days, if a Yanagibashi geisha did not have good looks, then she had some artistic talents. If she did not have artistic talents, then she was witty and knowledgeable. It was an extraordinarily rare girl indeed who lacked any of these three traits and had the sensibility [appeal] of a menial maid. But now it is not so. Out of ten girls, those who have neither looks, nor talent, nor wit, who vainly powder their faces, drape themselves in brocade, and call themselves geisha number about seven or eight. It is not just the discerning customer who looks down on this type and avoids her. Even a yokel [hick] or a dimwit [fool] would still doubt whether these geisha were really geisha. For this reason, there are many girls who have still not been favored with even a single invitation for more than a month after their debuts. Therefore, although the number of geisha on the register increases by the day, nevertheless the individual houses have been unable to increase their profits. I think that in recent years business has stagnated [fallen off] and there are innumerable [many] places in the city that have lost their income. All try a hundred schemes to eke out their livelihood. Thus, young girls with a decent nose and a fair pair of eyes who can pluck their way through 'I waited at night, resenting the dawn' race to get on the geisha rolls.[20] This is the root cause of the daily increase in geisha who are not like geisha.

---

[20] The reference is to a simple *nagauta* piece entitled "The dawn bell" ("Ake no kane" 明の鐘), which goes, "I waited at night, resenting the dawn; pillowing my head on my elbow, I thought at least I might meet him in my dreams."

"Of course, a geisha with neither looks nor talent naturally knows that she has no basis for getting customers. She will therefore recklessly tumble,^(drop of a hat) beguilingly increasing her appeal and having only profit in mind. Once such practices take root, then even a midrange or better geisha of considerable repute gradually becomes stained by them. Ah, the ways of the singing geisha of Yanagibashi have disintegrated^(crumbled) and words are inadequate to express how repugnant the decline has been! Bearing that in mind, we may wonder that even though it is true that Yanagibashi is more prosperous now than it was in the past, perhaps we should say that in fact it has declined greatly? But of course the customer is also to blame. Far too common is the man who does not know that there is a Way of playful diversion; who does not comprehend what *fūryū*, or 'stylish elegance,' is; who abandons himself to indulgence without even considering whether or not the girl is a geisha; who takes delight in an easy 'roll,' misconstruing it as a sign of special fondness for him; who trusts her beguiling appeals and thinks she loves him. If perchance there happened to be an elegant and graceful geisha not at all given to promiscuity, one who maintained well the venerable ways of old Yanagibashi, then he would berate her as a foolish and stubborn old hag who did not understand how things work. Now then, I ask, if this is how the customers are, then how can the geishas' headlong slide into depravity be stanched?"

In former times, even though the Northern Quarter in Yoshiwara was bustling, even though Yanagibashi was hot, one never heard of famous^(people) lords^(of) or^(a) great^(certain) ministers^(station) coming here to play and savor the flavor of passion. During the Bunsei and Tenpō periods [1818–1844], the shogunate's net of legal prohibitions was made so extremely strict that even bannermen^(hatamoto) would be penalized if they strayed into the quarters. The imperial government of Meiji has corrected these baleful excesses, forgiving minor infractions to promote wise and talented men, rectifying the great principles and revising the grand legal codes so that "caressing the flowers, embracing the willows" and other such trifling peccadilloes would be passed over and not prosecuted. This is why it is not infrequent that a high official directs his high-canopied coach-and-four to stop three times at Su Xiaoxiao's house.[21] The scions of daimyo houses and the young nobles who were once cosseted deep within the women's chambers, never allowed to venture into the pleasure quarter's narrow lanes, have all of a sudden been unleashed to go wherever their spirits might take them. Like wild cranes flying out of their cages or floodwaters surging over an embankment, their exuberant delight is something anyone can imagine! The geisha and male entertainers come to offer their coquetry, waiting with their jaws hanging open.[22] One hundred pieces of gold for every drink, a thousand pieces for every song on the shamisen. Truly this is a case where "One selection won her she knew not how many red silks!"[23] To

（realm of above "narrow"; play above "lanes"; freed above "unleashed"）

---

[21] Su Xiaoxiao 蘇小小 was a famous courtesan of the Six Dynasties period. The phrase about "stopping three times" at her house transforms the famous anecdote of Liu Bei (160–223), the ruler of Shu, seeking out talented men to serve under him. Having heard that Zhuge Liang (181–234) was a "sleeping dragon," Liu Bei visited his house three times before he was able to finally meet him. Zhuge Liang went on to become his chancellor.

[22] The "male entertainers" referred to here are the *taikomochi*, also known as *hōkan*, and sometimes called "male geisha." These men's services were generally non-sexual, and resembled those of a jester; for a brief discussion, see Downer, 95–100. The kanji for *hōkan* appear here with a gloss of *taiko*, indicating the drum that was part of the entertainment they provided. As Ryūhoku occasionally did in the first volume, he uses the term *kōsho* (Ch. *jiaoshu* 校書) or "editing clerk" for "geisha" here, a usage deriving from the fact that famous Tang courtesan Xue Tao 薛濤 held this title. The metaphor of the jaws hanging open implies a covetous or avaricious expectant expression and derives from a passage in *The Classic of Changes*: "'You ... watch me move my jaw': such a one certainly is not worth esteem" (Lynn, 306).

[23] Ryūhoku here quotes Bo Juyi's "Song of the Lute," in which the poet records his encounter with an old lutenist who recounts her popularity as a young singing girl: "Young men from the five tomb towns vied to give her presents / one selection won her she knew not how many red silks" (Burton Watson's translation in Minford and Lau,

grasp the true conditions of society and to really understand human affairs, there is nothing better to consider than the world of amusement. If the high and mighty standardbearers^(officials) invested their most profound intentions in the world of play and thereby attempted to monitor conditions within the city, it would not be without merit. In this way, it would be like the various Western countries, where the sovereign shares the same diversions as the masses. In countries such as the United States of America, there is no distinction between the classes.[24] This is what should truly be called "civilization and enlightenment." Recently in this country, baleful old customs are being eliminated every day, and there is an effort to institute new forms of government and education. How we can say this is anything other than a splendid thing? Even so, I do not dare declare my solidarity with those who fecklessly regard their alehouse merriments and brothel dalliances as the Way of Civilization and Enlightenment.

A certain lord loved his geisha to the utmost. His feelings were bonded to her with a fixity to rival glue or lacquer.[25] I knew the two of them, but have forgotten both of their names. When the lord was about to return to his home province, he could not bear his feelings of longing. On the day his palanquin departed, he secretly ordered a vassal to present the girl with a letter. The geisha read the letter and nearly perished.^(died) She tucked the letter into her bosom and did not relinquish^(let go of)

Classical Chinese Literature, I: 892).

[24] Ryūhoku uses here a colloquial Chinese term for the United States, the "Federation of the Flower Flag" 花旗聯邦, with the "flowers" referring of course to the flag's stars.

[25] Several scholars have suggested that the identity of this "certain lord" was Tosa daimyo Yamauchi Yōdō 山内容堂 (1827–1872) who had played a key role in urging the Tokugawa shogun Yoshinobu to cede power to the Emperor in 1867. After the Restoration, he went on to serve very briefly in the Meiji government, but was better known for his drunken dissipation in Yanagibashi.

it day or night, treasuring it as though it were a giant jade disk. One day I stole the letter and read it. It said:

My darling, how have you been managing after our parting? Ever since the day I took leave of you, my feelings and thoughts have been in a rapturous haze, with your figure constantly floating before my eyes and your whispered sweet-nothings forever going through my mind. This pain of ours will continue, knowing no final end.[26] You must try to understand my feelings, dear. By day I raise up your photograph, by night I read out your letters. Even though my body has taken leave of you, my spirit remains at your side. Looking back on the trips we took on the Sumida, the banquets we enjoyed at Ryōgoku, they are now just a pitifully heartrending dream! Please try to understand, my dear. A set of undergarments is, according to the rules of my house, not something that can be cavalierly awarded even should the recipient be an important vassal. Yet because of my relationship to you, my dear, I have forsaken these rules and presented one to you. I entreat you guard it well and do not tell a soul. I beseech [am counting on] you.

Moreover, there is something that weighs on my mind. Secretly I worry that our clouds-and-rain lovemaking may have left its mark for good; that bears and snakes may enter our dreams.[27] If that is so, then please give a letter to my vassal and apprise [let me know] me at once. When I come to the

---

[26] Hino Tatsuo points out that Ryūhoku uses several terms in this letter that closely recall the diction of Bo Juyi's "Song of Lasting Pain," which records the ill-fated affair between Tang Emperor Xuanzong and Yang Guifei. For example, this line is a close paraphrase of the famous poem's closing line 此恨綿綿無絶期: "This pain of ours will continue and never finally end" (Owen, *Anthology of Chinese Literature*, 447).

[27] "Clouds-and-rain" (J. *un'u*; Ch. *yunyu*) is a euphemism for sexual relations based on the story of King Huai of Chu having a dream encounter with the goddess of Mt. Wu (told in Song Yu's "Rhapsody on Gaotang"). Dreaming of bears was said to foretell the birth of sons, dreaming of snakes the birth of daughters (Waley, *Book of Songs*, 162).

East next year, I will without fail purchase you. I will build a detached palace for you where we can grow old together. You can play your charming strings in the tall halls, and float pleasure boats on the crooked ponds. Wouldn't this be splendidly delightful? I swear that I shall not forsake our bond, and you must please try to understand that. I cannot express my feelings in their entirety, but will close here.

Signed,
Prudence demands anonymity _(You know who)

When I finished reading, I found that tears were streaming down my face in spite of myself. According to the account transmitted down to us in a musical score, when Councilor Yukihira was exiled to the bay of Suma, he fell in love with two young women named Matsukaze and Murasame. The affair was elegant _(courtly) and refined, their feelings for each other touching and poignant. A thousand years later, when one hears the music or sees the dances from this Noh, it still makes one shed mournful tears. In recent years, the customs of the age have become as superficial and thin as watery liquor, and people's hearts have become corrupted, crafty, and conniving to the point that in matters of love, it seems there is none who maintains the old ways. But when I read this letter now, it recalled the manner of those people in ancient times who became fools for love. How sincere and sad their thoughts! I enjoy going to see the _a theater, _{play} and I always lament the tale of Yorikane and Takao. With a single sword-feint at Mitsumata, the Wei River flowed with blood.[28] How oppressively bleak! Truly we cannot discuss such an incident alongside the amorous affairs of this lord.

---

[28] Takao was a famous courtesan, and one of the many kabuki plays about her was the eighteenth century *Meiboku sendai hagi*, in which Ashikaga Yorikane mistakenly kills his courtesan Takao while the two are aboard the boat he has named for her, just as they

There is a new popular song that goes, "On the ones and sixes it's a holiday; we will have a great party." On the days of the month that have ones and sixes in them, the various government ministries all shut their doors and the officials take the day off, a system that seems to have been copied from the Western practice of having Sunday be a holiday. Some hold lavish banquets and some float on pleasure boats; they relieve the toil of their burdensome labor by drinking to their heart's content. Geisha always come to attend on the officials and pour drinks for them. Not only do they know the full names and residences of these men, but they also know the ranks of their positions and the sizes of their salaries. They have completely memorized the contents of the staff directories and official rosters. One day, I was drinking upstairs in a certain establishment. In the room adjacent to mine, there were two geisha waiting for clients. Geisha A said to Geisha B, "You ought to offer up an oblation!"[29] Geisha B replied saying, "Why should I?" Geisha A said, "I hear that your paramour has been awarded a certain official post. Namely, a top-ranking position granted with imperial approval. The salary is over three hundred. This calls for celebration! Now the brocade embroidery of Daimaru, the coral hair ornaments of Maruri—you have only to ask for what your heart desires. So, let's have your oblation! A great feast! You ought to share the wealth." Geisha B hung her head and said, "No, it is otherwise. Even though his worldly success has allowed him to tread on the clouds, in fact he obtained his position by being a sycophantic toady. His shrinking

---

are nearing Mitsumata ("Three Forks") of the Sumida River at Nakazu. This play, in turn, was based upon rumors surrounding Date Tsunamasa (1640–1711). Ryūhoku here uses the "Wei River" as a *mitate* (metaphoric substitution) for the Sumida, imagining the city of Tokyo as the Tang capital Chang'an. Mark Ōshima has written about the figure of Takao in kabuki dance (Swinton, 99–100).

[29] Part of the humor here is that in the Chinese text, the first geisha uses the esoteric word *dairō* (大牢; Ch. *dalao*), an ancient Chinese offering of an ox, sheep, and pig, for the meal she entreats her friend to provide.

shoulders and servile smiles even make me ashamed. And what's more, he is frugal [a natural-born] by temperament [tightwad]. On those days when we go out, he does not give even one [two] banknote [shu] to the boatman [sendō] or the box boy [hakoya]. Sometimes he even makes me foot the bill out of my own pocket; the man can't even wipe his ass by himself. To make matters worse, his comportment [every] is [move is] most imperious [cocky] and he is always treating me like his maidservant. Truly it is intolerable. Even if he plans to celebrate for himself, he certainly isn't going to give me anything to celebrate! He wouldn't even buy me a skewer of cured sardines! Sister, please try to understand [see it my way]. And haven't you heard? That crafty [little] wench [minx] from the Rear Bank captured the Generalissimo of Yamanote alive. She amused [toyed] herself [around] with him for three months, and managed to make complete [clear the] restitution [books] of her three-hundred-yen arrearage [loan]. She's a real smooth operator: just the type of girl Confucius had in mind when he said, 'It is fitting that we should hold the young in awe.'[30] I always say that when it comes to genuine [your] passion [true love], what you seek are the feelings, but when it comes to phony [your] passion [patron], what you are after is profit. If your goal is profit, then you should select someone with an imperial appointment—fourth rank or higher. Barring that, a prefectural governor or a member of the nobility will do. Those fifth-, sixth-, and seventh-rankers may be high, but they still cannot keep us from going hungry." Before she had finished speaking, a loud voice could be heard from outside the hall, calling out: "Chart [Ranking] of Actors' Salaries in the Three Theaters!" The geisha hurriedly called out to the box boy, "Ei-don, would you please go buy me that Chart of the Officials' Salaries?"

---

[30] Ryūhoku here quotes a famous statement by Confucius in the *Analects* completely out of context: "It is fitting that we should hold the young in awe. How do we know that the generations to come will not be the equal of the present?" (Lau, IX.23).

There was a student who went to school and became extremely fluent in English. One evening, he went drinking at Ryūkōtei, but when he spoke to the geisha, half of his words were in English. The geisha said, "Only you, my dear, understand English. We don't comprehend^(have a clue) what you're saying, and that's no fun at all.³¹ Won't you teach us some English?" Delighted^(Pleased with himself) to oblige, the student said, "You're a genius, I tell you, a genius! If you study for a few months, I guarantee you'll become a master. I know everything there is to know about English. But I'm not sure where you would like to commence your studies." The geisha replied, "When we women address each other, it's so boring to use the usual terms. Why don't you first teach us how to say our names?" "A novel idea!" replied the student. The geisha asked how to say "Otake," and the student answered "Bamboo." She asked, "Oume?" "Plum," came the reply. She asked, "Otori?" "Bird," said the student. She asked, "Ochō?" "*Chaple*," he replied.³² The answers came back instantly like an echo. Then she asked, "Misakichi?" The student lowered his head and thought intently, but could not think of what to say. Then, "Ochara?" The student grew even more perplexed. Wiping the sweat from his brow, he said, "Today I haven't brought my dictionary. Next time I'll come with a copy of *English Vocabulary Notes* in my breast pocket, and I shall answer your myriad queries."

---

31 The geisha uses *langjun* 郎君, a term commonly used in Chinese vernacular fiction by women to address male intimates; it is glossed *danna*. To refer to herself and the other geisha, she uses the first-personal plural form *nubei* 奴輩, humbly implying "your servants," which is glossed *wachikitachi* "us girls"; the first person pronoun *wachiki* was a specifically feminine word associated with the speech of Yoshiwara courtesans (Nakamura Shikaku, 200).

32 The 1861 *Eigosen* (English vocabulary notes), which the student in this episode soon mentions, gives "chaple" as the equivalent of butterfly. It is thought that this derives from the Dutch word for butterfly, *Kapel*.

The amount of copper alloyed^(mixed) into gold and silver coins is great, which means prices skyrocket. When gold and silver currency gave way to mulberry^(paper)-bark notes, prices shot up even higher. But the price of a geisha's "jewel" is the same as in the old days. For this reason, gratuities^(tips) are inevitably twice what they were in the past. These days, when a customer has a senior geisha, the fee will range from two *bu* on the low side to one yen on the high. Even a junior geisha would be between one and two *bu*. If someone tried to act in accordance with the old practices, giving one *bu* to the geisha and two *shu* to the box boy, then everyone would chastise him for his stinginess. All in all, the prices of various and sundry things have risen four- or five-fold. Since the clothing a geisha wears and the food she eats have not been spared this fate, surely it would be illogical for the gratuity alone to remain the same as in the old days. If one regards frugality as a wise virtue, then one had better not go out to play at all. When a geisha receives a gratuity from a customer, if she deposits it all into the hands of her sponsoring^(foster) madam^(mother), then she will never see it again. For this reason, she purloins^(skims off) some to supplement her own finances, snatching one for every three, seizing two for every five. Even in the case of an^(a) actual^(real) mother and daughter, it is a rare girl who does not take anything.

There was a young geisha, still not familiar with the ways of crafty^(sly) conniving^(trickery). She first attained her enlightenment in the wonders of purloining when she overheard her^(the) seniors^(older girls) talking one day. At the next possible opportunity, she purloined a banknote before returning home. Her foster mother, the madam, was by nature a perspicacious^(shrewd) woman, and there was nowhere in the house to conceal the banknote. After much consideration and contemplation, the girl suddenly hit upon a plan: she found a place in the upstairs eaves that was a little rotten, and she surreptitiously inserted the banknote between the planks. She believed that this clever scheme, the product of her own inspired stroke of genius, would be foolproof. One day there was a sudden squall,^(rainstorm) but it cleared up soon after it began. The young girl stayed in the house while the madam departed to take^(for the public) her ablutions.^(bath) The geisha wanted to retrieve the banknote and buy some sweets. She pried the boards up and pulled out the bill. The note was wet and severed^(torn) in half.^(pieces) The geisha was confounded^(shocked) and turned pale. She stealthily took one of the severed halves and went to ask the elderly woman next door: "My one-*bu* note has been severed in two. Might it retain^(be) the^(used) value^(now) of two *shu*?^(as)"³³ Those who heard her question laughed and felt pity for her.

Several warriors^(samurai) from a certain domain held a banquet^(boozed it up) in a certain establishment. Numerous side-dishes were laid out, shamisen music and song flowed freely. The mood was very lively, and spirits quite robust. One of the revelers, a public safety squadron captain, issued a special command to summon the geisha whom he particularly adored. But she did not come. Repeatedly he made inquiries and urgings to the barmaid. The barmaid said, "Your treasured^(favorite) one^(girl) has accompanied a customer on a boating excursion today. Her return will perhaps be rather leisurely.^(late) You ought to choose another, Sir." The squadron captain was incensed.^(miffed) He clutched his iron fan and said, "If a geisha in the Western capital of Kyoto gets an invitation from her regular *najimi* customer, she will decline^(turn down) other banquet invitations and come attend on him immediately. How is it that Yanagibashi alone has no standards like this?" The barmaid replied, "Customs vary East and West, and the people differ too. Moreover, when the geisha of Yanagibashi engage in some private^(secret) affairs,^(matters) they are unlike the girls in the Western capital

---

³³ A *bu* was equivalent to four *shu*.

because they do not shamelessly make it public." The squadron captain's indignation exploded forth and he shouted, "Vile^You maid!^bitch How loquacious you are! Such impertinence! Such impertinence!" (This is a contemporary turn of phrase.³⁴) He seized a large wine-cup and threw it at the barmaid's face, but it mistakenly struck the lamp stand. With a single sonorous clash^clink, the cup was shattered and the lamp extinguished. The barmaid was astonished and fled. The squadron chief drew his sword and was about to chase after her. The others there were all astounded^surprised, and strapping young arms blocked the path forward while delicate hands enfolded him from behind.³⁵ They comforted him and apologized to him by turns, reining in his thunderous temblor and calming his angry waves. The barmaid fled and reached the kitchen, where she said to the chef, "Most of the customers these days are mad with violence. They use alcohol and spout nonsensical arguments; some throw bowls and plates, others unsheathe their swords and stab the pillars. They are always making me unbearably^ticked off angry. Even if I raised^jacked up the prices for the drinks and the side-dishes by twenty or thirty percent and pocketed the difference, it still wouldn't be enough to make me happy. These barbarians^Chinamen with their disheveled^cropped coiffures^hair should^are be^no expelled^good! They should^are be^no expelled^good!"³⁶

---

³⁴ This interlinear note appears in the original and apparently refers to the use of the phrase *shikkei* or *shikkei kiwamaru* ("Such impertinence!") by indignant rural samurai.
³⁵ The "strapping young arms" are those of the male servants, while the "delicate hands" are those of the female servants.
³⁶ Ryūhoku uses the term *tōjin* 唐人 (literally, "man of Tang") here; it was a slightly pejorative term for foreigners in general, not just Chinese. The maid's final exclamation is "*Peke! Peke!*," a pidgin term apparently used during the late Tokugawa and early Meiji period in the foreign quarter to communicate "no good." It is said to derive from Mandarin *buke* 不可 or Malay *pergi*. The reference to "cropped hair" indicates the new short-haired coiffures that were still confined to Western scholars and the soldiers of various domains who had received training in Western style military techniques in the first years of the Meiji period. In 1871, this closely cropped hairstyle became more common when the Meiji government issued an edict making the wearing of swords and the dressing of the hair in a *chonmage* topknot optional for samurai men.

I, the Immortal What-of-it, declare, "When peace prevails in the realm for a long time, the way of the warrior lapses into lethargy. But after a skirmish,^battle^ martial spirits are naturally reinvigorated. The murderous air has not yet been quelled since the eruption of the 1868 Boshin War. Under the right conditions, men like Xiang Zhuang and Xiang Bo might find themselves carrying out a sword dance in a brothel. And even though decrepit, a man like Fan Zeng might very well become so infuriated that he smashes some jade dippers.³⁷ Such momentum is difficult to resist. In recent years, there is a new code for banquets. When you present a person with a wine-cup, you often throw it into his palm. In Li Bo's preface to the 'Peach and Apricot Garden,' he writes of 'letting fly the winged wine-cups and becoming intoxicated with the moon.'³⁸ Among today's samurai are many with a special fondness for the past. Perhaps the so-called new ways find their legitimating precedent in this word 'fly.' I imagine it means 'to let fly the wine-cups' or 'let fly the goblets.' In a certain sense then, this practice is old, and in a certain sense it is new. Marvelous and novel? Perhaps. Carefree and uninhibited? Sure. But, all things considered, a transformation has occurred so that now people are injuring their foreheads and wounding their eyes. (Such behavior is what might be called far-flung). These

---

³⁷ This passage refers to the "Banquet at Hongmen," a famous meeting that took place in 206 BCE between Xiang Yu and Liu Bang, two generals of Chu and Han respectively, who had just toppled the Qin. Recorded in "The Basic Annals of Xiang Yu" chapter of *Records of the Grand Historian* (and later retold and embroidered in various forms down to the present), the episode tells of how Xiang Yu's councilor Fan Zeng hoped to have Liu Bang killed by using the subterfuge of urging Xiang Zhuang to perform a sword dance with him; contrary to his expectations, however, Xiang Bo interceded to protect Liu Bang. Liu Bang then excused himself to use the toilet, and summoned his carriage attendant Fan Kuai to go with him. Liu Bang ordered Zhang Liang to stay behind and make excuses to delay the others from discovering that he had escaped; he gave Zhang Liang the pair of jade discs and the pair of jade wine dippers originally intended as gifts for Xiang Yu and Fan Zeng respectively. When presented with the jade dippers, Fan Zeng smashed them with his sword (Watson, *Records*, Han I: 30–33).
³⁸ See the full translation in Lau and Minford's *Classical Chinese Literature*, I: 723.

vessels are easily broken; wouldn't we be better off if we followed traditional etiquette and used them to pour sake for one another? I heard this from a venerable geisha."

A geisha strummed her shamisen strings and sang out, "The insignia[crests] of paulownia and chrysanthemum, these are the noble insignia[crests] of the Council of State." A customer listening to her song sighed, saying, "Such breadth! Such gentle harmony! Circuitous, yet there is a certain directness in it. They must represent the virtue of the imperial government.[39] In its magnificence[grandeur] it can be compared to that of Duke Wen of Zhou, and it has the timbre of the Greater Odes." The geisha began singing again, "The insignia[crest] of the Luoyang[lavender] flower[pink], this is the insignia[crest] of Gonrō[Gonchan]."[40] The customer was not amused and said, "This man Gonjūrō is an actor! Actors are nothing but beggars. You are singing about some menial beggar in the same breath as the Emperor. What sort of preposterous[unreasonable] talk is this?!" The geisha replied in a gentle tone, "Perhaps you do not understand much about singing. I hear that 'Zhen and Wei' and 'Sang Zhong' are poems about salacious abandon among the common people.[41] The Sage Confucius took these and included them in *The Book of Songs*, placing them before the 'Odes'

---

[39] Ryūhoku here adapts Prince Ji Zha of Wu's evaluation of the Greater Odes from the *Book of Songs*, as told in the *Zuo Tradition* (Xiang Year 29). In 544 BCE, the Prince was sent on a diplomatic mission to Lu, and while there, he was treated to a performance of songs from the *Book of Songs*, offering his judgment of each in turn. In the original, the Prince concludes, "They must represent the virtue of King Wen" (Watson, *The Tso Chuan*, 151), but here the attribution is to the Meiji government.

[40] "Gonchan" refers to kabuki actor Kawarazaki Gonjūrō, the name Ichikawa Danjūrō IX (1838–1903) used prior to taking the latter name in 1874. Gonrō is a Sinicized abbreviation of his name. The "alternative crest" (*kaemon*, sometimes translated "sub-crest") he used was actually a *gyoyō botan*, a peony surrounded by apricot leaves.

[41] The two pieces mentioned here are from the "Guofeng" (Airs of the states) section of the *Book of Songs* and tell of romantic encounters between men and women, frolicking while gathering plants in "Sang zhong" (Waley, 40–41) and cavorting by the riverside in "Zhen and Wei" (Waley, 95).

and the 'Praise-songs.' And now instead of condemning the Sage you condemn me. What sort of preposterous [unreasonable] talk is that?! Moreover, have you never seen the insignia [crest] of Ōtomo?⁴² It is the same as the Lord of Satsuma. The Lord of Satsuma is the head of the Three Domains and the object of fear and awe throughout the realm.⁴³ And yet I have never heard of the Lord of Satsuma commanding Ōtomo to desist and change his crest. The Lord of Satsuma does not get angry with actors and yet you persist in getting angry with me. What sort of preposterous talk is that?!" His face flushing crimson, the customer beat his retreat.

I, the Immortal What-of-it, declare, "In recent years, many of the Yanagibashi geisha have become personally involved with actors [kabuki players], and more than a few with sumo wrestlers. They have all achieved their aspirations: Miyokichi with Tosshō, Kohana with Tanosuke, Osue with Takamiyama.⁴⁴ Senkichi died after surrendering herself to Aioi, and Aioi cried for ten days because of this.⁴⁵ Now then, actors adorn and paint themselves, and in their alluring figures and attractive appearances, they are just like women. It is of course little wonder that geisha would come to desire and long for them. But what about those powerful wrestlers with their imposing [great] miens, with their muscles and bones made of iron [like metal rods]? There are some who are like Thunder incarnate, some like demonic Yaksa. And yet just like the actors they become the passionate clients [lovers] of these geisha. I find this very peculiar. I wonder if it is because the geisha, as masters of the so-called forty-eight

---

⁴² Ōtomo refers to Ōya Tomoemon V 大谷友右衛門 (1833–1873), an actor who took the name Ōtomo Hirotsugi 大友広次 in 1870. His family crest was a cross inside a circle.
⁴³ The three domains are Satsuma, Chōshū, and Tosa.
⁴⁴ Tosshō refers to the actor Sawamura Tosshō II, Tanosuke refers to his younger brother Sawamura Tanosuke III (1845–1878), and Takamiyama refers to the sumo wrestler Takasago Uragorō (1838–1900).
⁴⁵ Aioi was a name used by the sumo wrestler Ayasegawa Sanzaemon (1835–1877).

techniques, have become skilled at capturing^(taking) their^(them) quarry^(alive).⁴⁶ Or is it rather because the geisha have some sort of adhesiveness like sumo wrestler ointment? I will have to pursue this question further with some men learned in the Western physics."

Two junior geisha returned from the bath house, carrying a bag of roasted beans in hand, which they munched on as they walked. Geisha A said to Geisha B, "Yesterday I encountered something intimidating^(scary)." Geisha B asked, "What?" Geisha A responded, "Yesterday, I was accompanying a customer from Okinaya for an excursion along the Sumida River to Mukōjima. We were enjoying ourselves, gathering^(picking) greenery^(herbs). Suddenly we saw two samurai with cropped^(rough) coiffures^(cuts), each astride a large horse, riding toward us as fast as the wind.⁴⁷ Those around scattered^(got out of the way) to the four directions. I was in a bewildered flurry and nearly got trampled, but with the help of Old Kisuke I narrowly escaped. It was terrifying! Terrifying!" Geisha B said, "How terrifying indeed! The other day I heard that someone riding a horse trampled an old woman to death on the river bank near Ten'ōbashi. Her eyeball even popped out. The rider vanished^(faded) into^(away) thin^(like) air^(smoke) and has not been apprehended. How awful!" She then rubbed her own eye and recited a prayer^(spell): "Cranes and turtles, cranes and turtles." (This is an incantation used by girls).⁴⁸ Geisha A said, "Why have horse riders been so lawless^(unruly) lately? Some ride barefoot, while others ride in *geta* clogs. There are even some who ride while clutching umbrellas, and some who ride with

---

⁴⁶ The *shijūhatte* (lit. "forty-eight hands") are the winning moves codified in sumo wrestling; from this, the term also came to mean forty-eight techniques of lovemaking.
⁴⁷ The new "rough-cut" or "cropped-coif" (*zangiri*) hairstyle became popular for men in early Meiji and was considered a marker of the *bunmei-kaika* era; for a discussion of its significance, see O'Brien.
⁴⁸ The crane and turtle are both symbols of longevity and their invocation was therefore thought to serve as a means of neutralizing the inauspicious. Again, the parenthetical note is that of Ryūhoku's narrator; it appears in the original.

their hands in their breast pockets. It's just too bizarre! Like the circus or something. Moreover, they surge like tornadoes and charge like lightning, passing through thronging multitudes without even shouting ahead. How reckless they are! In former times, I remember seeing princes riding their horses, properly caparisoned and solemn in manner. They were what you could call true samurai. But the cropped-coif men these days have an appearance just like barbarians. How loathsome! How loathsome!"

<small>drive their horses faster than they</small>
<small>need to crowds of people</small>
<small>calling out</small>
<small>lords</small>
<small>rough-cut</small>

Geisha B said, "In my house there are three books of *shunga* erotic prints. My elder sister has sequestered them away and won't show them to me. Yesterday, she happened to be out and so I stole a glimpse at them. Inside there were some fine specimens as handsome as Tosshō, and others as repulsive as Nakazō.⁴⁹ Some of the men had topknots like rat-tails, others fat like a night-soil boat's straw scrubber.⁵⁰ However, uniformly and consistently, I never did see a cropped-coif man sleep with a girl. My personal suspicion is that cropped-coif men never do the deed."⁵¹ Geisha A said, "Cease your ludicrous chatter! Don't you remember? During the pleasant holiday season of *sekku*, there was a customer with a cropped-coif head; he was quite a lascivious guy and all the sisters despised him. I think that cropped-coif men are, when compared to average men, rather more

<small>hid</small>
<small>had</small>
<small>look good- looking men</small>
<small>hateful</small>
<small>shit</small>
<small>from the first page to the last</small>
<small>rough- cut</small>
<small>Don't be</small>
<small>so silly Did forget</small>
<small>rough- cut</small>
<small>lusty hated</small>

---

⁴⁹ Tosshō was the name of the attractive kabuki actor Sawamura Tosshō II, mentioned earlier. Nakazō refers to Nakamura Nakazō III (1809–1886), a kabuki actor who specialized in playing villains.

⁵⁰ This pejorative description of a bushy topknot as resembling the bamboo and straw broom-like tool used to clean the night-soil boat is referenced in earlier Edo period sources such as Terakado Seiken's *Edo hanjōki*.

⁵¹ There is wordplay here on 好事, glossed *irokoto*, meaning both "good deeds" and "amorous matters"; in addition, Ryūhoku puns on two senses of the verb 幹 (Ch. *gan*), "to do," a word with the same sexual double meaning as the English term, only slightly more crass.

amorously inclined. They are just like the Priest Hōkai depicted in that kabuki play.[52] And there's that cropped-coif customer at Minatoya; he's also loathsome [a creepy guy]. Given the chance, he will force himself on you and lift up your skirt. How detestable! I can't stand him!" Letting their soft tongues play, they chattered on endlessly. Suddenly they saw that the bottom of the sack had been perforated [torn] and the roasted beans were bursting [scattering] forth [down in] like [twos] hailstones [and threes]. Geisha A exclaimed with surprise, "Cursed [Oh] mess [no]!" Geisha B said, "This must be the penance we pay for insulting the cropped-coifs [rough-cuts]."

When a geisha has a husband, she is like watered-down wine. Her flavor is thin and not full-bodied. A geisha with a child is like wine with sugar added. Her flavor is heavy and impure. In the old days, all pregnant geisha harbored feelings of ignominy [shame]. There were some who would seek out medicines by which to eliminate the fetus. Others would make good by being redeemed [withdrawing], and their names would be removed from the register. In recent years, customs have changed, and now geisha bear children just like everyone [ordinary people] else. Many of them hire a wet-nurse to raise the child. Even when entertaining guests at a banquet they talk about such matters, insouciant [casual] and unabashed. What a peculiar situation! There was one geisha who had gotten pregnant. She had ten regular customers with whom she had "special circumstances." It could not be determined who the father was. She then summoned a customer and informed him she was pregnant. The customer said, "You have several customers. How can you look at me alone?" She called another customer. He too responded, "You have several customers. How can you look at me alone?" She asked all ten

---

[52] In the play *Sumidagawa Gonichi no omokage* (Latter-day memories of the Sumida River), by Nakawa Shimesuke (1754–1814), a roguish mendicant priest named Hōkaibō falls in love with the courtesan Okumi and attempts to rape her.

customers, and their answers came as though issuing from a single mouth. The geisha was quite dismayed. She then went to pray at the Kiyomasa shrine. She said, "I am pregnant [with child], but I do not know who the father is. I beseech the deity of the shrine to reveal the man to me." The deity Kiyomasa appeared to her in a dream, and said, "You have ten men, all of whom share equally of your pillow. Even a deity like me cannot ascertain who the principal one is. The child within your womb will naturally know the identity of his father. You should ask him."

The geisha woke up and realized what she had to do. Deep in the night, when no one was around, she conducted ritual ablutions [washed her hands and gargled], and then lighted some incense. Sitting down, she caressed her abdomen, and bending over, she examined her privates. In a relaxed and composed tone, she said, "The deity has commanded you to reveal to me the name of your father. Now tell me the facts." Immediately a voice issued from within her belly: "Mother, how can there be any doubt? You have ten men, Mother. My body is therefore made from the combined efforts of these ten men. One man made my head, and one man made my belly. There was one who made my chest, and one who made my back. Two men made my two hands, and two men made my two legs. My buttocks and my penis were also each made separately. Therefore, I have ten fathers. How can you attribute all of this to one man? My ten fingers, however, were made separately. Mother, have you forgotten? There are often men who vainly stain their fingers on your vessel without entering your chamber. These are the fathers of my fingers."

One geisha was long on wind and short on talent. Everyone called her Ms. Garrulous [Chatterbox] or the Eyeless [Oblivious] Girl [One].[53] One day, she went with several

---

[53] Perhaps the girl was "eyeless" in the sense of being blind to common sense, or oblivious to her effect on others.

other geisha to a banquet for a certain lord. When they were far into their cups, the geisha nonchalantly asked the Lord, "I hear that those aristocratic families living in the Western Capital are all in the business of manufacturing *hanafuda* flower pairing cards. Tell me, did your Lordship ever make any of these?" The Lord was left dumbfounded and unable to speak. After a while, he replied, "In the old days, everyone had a good deal of leisure hours.^(time to spare) I am not certain, but perhaps some people made such cards as a diversion. Even if we suppose that there were such individuals, they would only be those with an office and rank far inferior to that of myself. In recent years, the nation has been busy with many matters, and there certainly cannot be a single man who would persist in such trifling^(worthless) pursuits." The geisha struck her knee and said, "It^(Oh) all^(I) makes^(get) sense.^(it) Lately, flower cards have been extremely scarce around^(on the) town.^(street) Accordingly, their price has been quite high. My old man is always lamenting this. I never knew the reason, but on this day I have been so fortunate as to receive^(hear) Your Lordship's explanation, and my^(now) longstanding^(long) doubts^(last) have^(I) fallen away^(know) like^(the) melting^(reason) ice.^(why) You see, those who make these cards are few, and those who use them are numerous. Consequently, the supply of cards is perpetually insufficient, and their high price is only to be expected." Everyone in the room nervously clutched their sweaty palms.

Two samurai wearing brocade *hakama* trousers and with golden swords at their side were having a drink together in a certain establishment. After they had enjoyed several rounds, their conversation drifted to the trajectory of developments in the realm. Eventually, they debated the advantages^(pros) and disadvantages^(cons) of the federal versus the feudal systems of government. Their debate went on for several hours without reaching a conclusion; their mouths spit fire and their tongues spurted blood. Their sake grew cold and their food turned to mush, but they paid no heed. Several geisha were sitting in attendance on them, listening in on their conversation and growing listless.^(bored) One geisha stood up to go the restroom. A second geisha followed her, and they met up with each other in the hallway. Geisha A said, "Today's customers are such imbeciles!^(dopes) They don't drink the wine. They don't eat the food. They just drone^(jabber) on for half a day, talking about such^(who) abstruse^(knows what) matters. I am by nature not fond of what is called 'debate.' Whenever I hear one, I feel^(space) dreary^(out) and my head starts to spin." Geisha B was filled with vigor, and said, "Sister, don't be so glum!^(blue) I am about to go trounce those two fools." They then returned to the banquet hand in hand. The two men were still engaged in their fierce verbal battle. Geisha B advanced and sat in between the two, lifted up a large chalice^(drinking cup) and asked them, "What exactly is it that you two are arguing about?" One of the customers responded, "We are debating the benefits^(pros) and detriments^(cons) of the federal and feudal systems as structures of government for the realm. A topic that can be of little concern to the likes of you!" Geisha B offered a cup and said, "How mistaken you are! This debate about the merits and demerits of the feudal and federal systems has been exhaustively argued by eminent earlier philosophers from the Qin^(a long long time ago) and Han dynasties. What need is there for you two to prattle^(chatter) on about it now? I hear that in the United States, they have a *kyōwa*, or 'republican' form of government, and *kyōwa* means 'collective harmony.' So fair, so enlightened, so just, so grand, even the governance of those sage kings of antiquity could not surpass it.⁵⁴ You two would do well to cease your ruminations over

---

⁵⁴ The translation *kyōwa* (Ch. *gonghe* 共和) for "republic" was suggested to Mitsukuri Gyokkai as a term to use in his *Kon'yo zushiki* 坤輿圖識 (1845) by Ryūhoku's friend Ōtsuki Bankei (Umezawa Hideo, 24). The term's appearance in Fukuzawa Yukichi's 1866 *Conditions in the West* (Seiyō jijō) codified it as the equivalent of "republic."

these residual lees [dregs] of the ancients, abandon your debate on feudalism versus federalism, and promulgate the beauty of collective harmony. After all, when you have fun, more than anything you need to collectively harmonize in order to enjoy yourself. Here you are in a drinking house, and yet you leave your food and drink untouched, you eschew the flute and shamisen, relegating them to silence, and you leave us in the corner while you pursue these empty arguments and absurd assertions that only put us to sleep! Is this what you call the pleasure of 'collective harmony?' You two really don't know the first thing about having fun. Now I'll become your president, and do my best to invigorate [repair] this ruinously [tediously] decrepit [argumentative] mood. So please, first have a sip from this chalice as your punishment!" At this, the two customers were greatly embarrassed, and both of them lowered their heads contritely, saying, "We will reverentially attend on Your Royal Highness's commands."

I hear that lately there was a customer who purchased [redeemed] a geisha. I do not know the customer, but I do know the geisha. The geisha's name is Otatsu, and she is about seventeen or eighteen years old. From my perspective, her appearance and looks are above average, while her talents and accomplishments are below average. I asked the price of her purchase, and was told seven hundred yen. I was so surprised that I nearly fell down. Now then, in the past ten or more years, there has not been a single geisha in Yanagibashi who has received seven hundred yen and left the registry. This Otatsu is a late arrival, and yet before even one full year had passed since her debut on the registry, she encountered a bigwig customer like that. Truly this can be called the ultimate good fortune. This is not, moreover, merely Otatsu's personal fortune, for it will perhaps also burnish [give a bit of a boost to] the shine of Yanagibashi.

105

In the past, Okō (now known as Ōsaka) declined [turned down] an offer of five hundred in gold from Mr. Hon'ami.[55] Mr. Hon'ami was insulted by this and so he selected someone who was even more renowned than Okō, obtaining Okin. At the time, people all praised the lavishness of Hon'ami and were similarly impressed by the principled resolve of Okō; the story became something of a charming anecdote. But looking at this episode from today's perspective, how can an offer of five hundred and a refusal of five hundred qualify as lavish or principled? I imagine that it is not the case that there exists any sort of qualitative [better or worse] disparity in the merits of the women, but rather that there has been a shift in social trends. These days, those occupying the upper tier of singing geisha take in about fifty or sixty pieces of gold in one month. If we compare this to the situation in previous years, the disparity [difference] is one of heaven and earth. The complement [number] of geisha has also proliferated [gone up], reaching more than two hundred names. However, if we select out the cream of the crop, then the bulk are no more than chaff [dregs]. In the summer of the second year of Bunkyū [1862], Yanagawa Shunsan and I made up an *Evaluation of the Twenty-Four Flowers of Yanagibashi* for fun.[56] We compared Okin with the Japanese apricot blossom, Okō with the cherry blossom, Ohisa with the Japanese plum, Kokatsu with the apricot blossom, Miyo with the globeflower, Okon with the peach blossom, Okane with the chrysanthemum, Okiyo with

---

[55] The Hon'ami household was known for appraisal of swords from the time of Hon'ami Kōetsu 本阿弥光悦 (1558–1637), an early Edo cultural figure, skilled in calligraphy, pottery, and other arts. The geisha Okō married the aforementioned kabuki actor Sawamura Tanosuke, but later became the wife of San'yūtei Enchō. The characters of her new name (大幸) can be read either Daikō or Ōsaka.

[56] The contributor of an appendix to the first volume of *New Chronicles of Yanagibashi*, Yanagawa Shunsan was a close friend of Ryūhoku's. He is here identified as "Ryū Shunsan" 柳春三, for it was the custom of many literary men at the time to use only the first character of their surnames when referring to themselves in *kanbun* texts, an effect that made the name sound more Chinese.

the peony, Koshige with the cotton rose, Otake with the lotus blossom, Kikuju with the crepe myrtle, Umekichi with the wisteria blossom, Masakichi with the iris, Senkichi with the small peony, Oren with the narcissus, and Koteru with the azalea. In addition to these, we also compared Masukichi, Koito, Otsune, Miyokichi, Okaru, Hisakichi, Osumi, and Onao each with a flower. But those that remain today are just the following four: Okō, Kikuju, Masakichi (who now is known as Oiku), and Oren. The three known as Okiyo, Senkichi, and Hisakichi have already entered their attractive names in the register of spirits.[Book of the Dead] The rest have all scattered to the four directions, and for most their whereabouts cannot be determined. Ah! Over the span of these ten long years, one has risen while another has sunk, one has withered while another has flourished; but how can this be only the story of geisha?

It resembles a handcart, but is not a handcart; it resembles a palanquin, but is not a palanquin. Its passenger looks up while crouching down, its pusher looks down while running forward. It comes along with its iron wheels and wooden handles making a rumbling[clattering] sound. What is this thing? A rickshaw.[57] Upstairs at a drinking house, several geisha leaned on the railing and gazed out at one. One of the geisha turned to look at those to her left and right and said, "What a miserable[chintzy] cart! Lately these carts have become ubiquitous on every street and lane, squeaking their way east, roaring their way west. 'Oh! Oh! Strange business!'[What a funny thing][58] In the old days, the pleasure quarter customers all hired a *yotsude*

---

[57] The English term *rickshaw* is a shortening of the Japanese *jinrikisha* (lit. "man-powered vehicle"); the vehicles rapidly came into use in Japanese cities during the very first years of Meiji.
[58] Ryūhoku here uses the phrase 咄咄怪事, words that Yin Hao (d. 356) is said to have insouciantly traced in the air in response to his removal from office as military commander; the story appears in his biography in the *Jin shu*.

four-strut palanquin, which is a convenient and pleasant form of transport. The palanquin men were agile^(fleet) and nimble,^(of foot) and they used their rhythmic calls^(chant) of 'heave-ho' to give themselves a boost. Their voices were clear and bright, putting one in the mood for play. Truly the *yotsude* palanquin befitted the temperament of a child of Edo. It was quite a far cry from the unsightly^(shabby) crudeness of this rickshaw cart, which almost falls into the same rut as the wheeled dolly of a crippled mendicant.^(beggar) The fact that so many customers in recent years have discarded their palanquins and taken up these carts is because they consider the price only. How boorish^(stingy) is that?" An old geisha was standing beside her and laughed, saying, "You^(My) are^(dear you are) at^( ) a^(just a young) delicate^(girl) age, and you do not yet understand the vicissitudes of the world. In the olden days, whenever we would see counts^(the) and marquises^(daimyo lords) coming and going in the city, their retainers and attendants were as numerous as clouds. Two with swords walked in front, and a saddled horse brought up the rear. They struck an imposing air and competed for grandeur. Now, it is no longer this way. A lone rider races around, his style is simplicity itself, and frugality is the revered criterion; indeed, such austerity is regarded as beautiful. I hear that the government^(powers) officials^(that be) are throwing away prodigious sums of money lately in order to construct a road of iron rails, on which they are planning to run steam locomotives. The locomotives are so fast that they travel ten leagues in the blink of an eye, and a hundred leagues in a minute. Something like a round trip to Yokohama would only require the time it takes to eat a meal. One could get to Osaka or Nagasaki in a single day, or one could get to China or India in three days. That must really be what they mean by a 'Most Marvelous Carriage.'"[59] One geisha hurriedly asked, "Would

---

[59] Hino Tatsuo speculates that the reference here may be to a *gōkan* (extended illustrated fiction) by Ryūkatei Tanekazu (1807–1893) written between 1855 and 1874 and called *Warabeuta myōmyōguruma* (Nursery song: the most marvelous carriage).

you really be able to get to India?" "Indeed you could." "If that is the case, then I would like to get aboard that carriage and take a trip to the banks of the Milky Way [River of Heaven] so that I could see the encounter [meeting] of the Ox Herder and the Weaver Girl. How would that be?" Another geisha clapped her on the back and said, "Don't say such things. If a beautiful woman like you went, then the Ox Herder would be smitten [fall in love] with just one glimpse [at first sight]. The Weaver Girl, I fear, would turn green [become jealous].[60] She would certainly build fences at the Magpie Bridge to keep the carriages out, just like those at Ryōgoku Bridge." And with that, the geisha let out a broad and raucous laugh.

With the moon high in the heart of the heavens, the bar-boy [young fellow] locked up the tavern. The wind blew cool across the surface of the water and the boatman slept in his boat. The ringing [tinkling] bell of the nighttime soba noodle stand was already far off, the tenebrous [dim] lanterns of the tea-rice and tofu sellers were totally extinguished, and the streets in all four directions were deserted. Even the dogs were silent. In one small alehouse, a drunken customer lay in bed; he tried to sleep but could not sleep, he tried to talk, but could not talk; he seemed to be in anguish. A dejected geisha sat upright [stiffly] beside his pillow. The customer faced the wall, smoking tobacco and rapping the spittoon [ashpot]. He rapped once and started to speak: "It should be obvious to you how much consideration I have made for you recently [of late], how much money I have spent on you, and the extent to which I have unreservedly poured out my innermost [heart of] feelings [hearts] in elaborate detail. Yesterday, I entrusted my request to the

---

[60] This is a good example of Ryūhoku's occasional use of colloquial Chinese phrases in the text, a practice particularly common in sections of dialogue. Here, he playfully inverts his typical practice of glossing somber literary Chinese terms with lighter colloquial Japanese equivalents; a vernacular Chinese phrase meaning "to be jealous," *chi cu* 吃醋 (lit. "to ingest vinegar"), appears with a more literary-sounding Japanese gloss of *rinki*, a term derived from the Chinese *linqi* 悋気.

good offices of the ^(Madam) proprietress of this establishment, and she earnestly admonished you. Yet you ^(will) do ^(hear) not ^(none of it) consent. You don't seem to understand how things work. How exceedingly ^(stubborn) obstinate you are! There is not a single person in the entire world who clings ^(is so) to ^(proper) ^(to a fault) foolishness and who venerates ^(old) ancient ^(manners) ways as you do. If you make a ^(sudden) complete ^(change) turnaround ^(of) in your ^(heart) thinking, then not only will you reap ^(come) ^(out) the ^(ahead) benefits, but your mother who dwells beside the forgetting-grass will also be comfortable in her twilight years.61 Why don't you consider these matters?" The geisha lowered her head and remained silent. Tears spilled from both her eyes, and with her bright white teeth, she bit at her sleeve. After some ^(a good) time, ^(while) she spoke: "Master, why do you lavish your affections on a woman as ugly as I, often favoring me with such ^(heartfelt) sincere ^(words) guidance? How can I be unmoved, like a piece of wood or stone? Truly I am touched by your sentiments and appreciate your kindnesses. I simply have no words with which to express my gratitude. But there is after all a reason that I have not dared to comply with your wishes. I will explain it to you in full. Although I have consigned myself to this ^(muddy) bitter ^(marsh) world of harlotry, I knew from the start that I did not wish to perform the same services as prostitutes.62 I sought only to sell the entertainments of shamisen and song, and thereby care for my mother. My father was a former ^(samurai) warrior, his stipend ^(pay) some five hundred. When my father died, my elder brother succeeded him to the headship of our house. As a young man, my brother assiduously pursued both literary and military arts, and had nearly mastered the

---

61 The term used for "mother" is *jiken* (Ch. *cixuan* 慈萱), given a colloquial Japanese explanatory gloss *ofukuro*; the Chinese term comes from the custom of planting daylilies (also known as "forgetting grass" *wasuregusa*) beside the northern rooms of a home, where mothers traditionally lived.

62 The term *odei* (Ch. *yuni* 淤泥) is here given the gloss *doromizu*, which in addition to the primary meaning of "sludge," also indicates the bitter world of prostitution as a survival strategy.

Ways of loyalty and filial piety. In the disturbances [troubles] of recent years, the whole metropolitan area was heaved into turbulence, and several hundred of his confreres were dumbstruck and disoriented. It was only my brother who became so furious that he forgot even to eat. He went to petition those in control of the government three times, but his words were not taken into consideration. Overflowing with righteous indignation, he took his leave, giving me parting instructions and entrusting to me the care of our aging mother. He raced off to join his comrade samurai at the Eastern periphery, where they fought a hundred battles without caving in. In the end, he died with honor, slain [killed] among [in the course of] spears and arrows [battle]. Subsequently [After that], my relatives fled and hid themselves away. I do not know where they are. My friends have also fled and have not paid me any heed. I alone live with my mother, downcast and with no one to rely upon. Our estate [house] was confiscated [seized] by the officials, and we were stripped of all our possessions [belongings] by bandits. Hunger and cold grew more pressing by the day, and we had no plans to support ourselves. Fortunately, I had taken singing and dancing lessons when I was young, and drawing on this experience, I came here, and registered myself. Enduring the shame, I sold my ugliness. Relying [Thanks to] on the kindness [help that all have given] of my customers, I am barely able to feed and clothe my mother. Now, if I were to comply with your request, I would be certain to enjoy boundless fortune, and my aging mother would for her part surely be able to live out her days in peace. And yet, one problem remains: what could I do about the stain that would besmirch [sully] my father and brother's names? What could I do about the insult I would bring to my ancestors' spirits? Master, please be so kind as to understand this." As she finished speaking, the tears of anguish pooling in her hands dribbled onto her lap and she brushed them away. Just

111

then, the cat next door could be heard capturing a mouse. The mouse cried out pathetically: *Chū! Chū!*[63]

滄溟暗處白帆懸　知是載柑南紀船

Though the offing is dark a white sail can be seen emerging
On a dark patch of the blue ocean depths hangs a white
there
sail;

It is the tangerine boat from the province of
That must be the boat from southern Kii, loaded with
Kii
tangerines.[64]

These are the words to an old song, which in recent years has been sung with different lyrics and in a new style, accompanied by shamisen and dancing. The melody is choked yet graceful, and the sound is
halting　　　　　gentle
frivolous yet elegant. When people perform it moving both hands in a
coarse
circle, and dancing with one leg held up, it is quite an unusual sight. Now it is often performed as a popular piece at banquets. It is said that Kinokuniya Bunzaemon made a handsome profit when he braved
the　　　　storms
tempestuous weather to cross the sea and sell tangerines from Southern Kii.[65] His wealth grew gradually over time, and like a
bit by bit

---

[63] The word *chū* is both the squeaking sound that mice make, as well as the word for "loyalty" 忠. Furthermore, Ryūhoku writes it here with the character 忡 (J. *chū*; Ch. *chong*) meaning "sad and affecting." In other words, the last sentence means "The mouse made a *chū chū* sound," "The mouse cried out 'loyalty, loyalty,'" and "The mouse made a sad and affecting cry." A similar pun on the first two of these senses of "*chū*" occurs in the famous play *Kanadehon Chūshingura*.

[64] Rewritten here as a rhymed heptasyllabic Chinese couplet, the gloss gives the original form of this popular Edo song known as a *dodoitsu*, in which the lines are in a 7-7-7-5 pattern: "Oki no kurai no ni / shiraho ga miyuru / Are wa Kinokuni / mikan bune."

[65] Kinokuniya Bunzaemon 紀国屋文左衛門 (d. 1734) was an extraordinarily wealthy lumber merchant from Kii (modern Wakayama) who was also known for his lavish expenditures. Some of the many tales of his fabulous wealth are recounted in DeBecker, 282–288.

latter-day Tao Zhu, his riches became foremost in the entire city.⁶⁶ He enjoyed his dalliances in the demimonde [pleasure quarter], reaching the pinnacle of grandeur and the zenith of opulence; he exceeded his predecessors, overwhelming those of later generations. Even children these days know Kinokuniya Bunzaemon's name. Truly he can be called a happy man. In recent years, not a single one of the merchant houses of Tokyo has such energy and brio. One can see that their products are constantly expended [decreasing], and their resources are constantly deficient. Though they endeavor to embellish their outward appearance [thin veneer], when it comes to their internal circumstances [the inside story], they cannot escape exhaustion and hunger. Oh, how they have declined! And yet, ever since the opening of the port in Yokohama, businessmen have engaged in commerce [trade] with foreign countries. Though there have been some who lost their property through mislaid plans, nevertheless, there are also more than a few who have gone in empty-handed and in a few years greatly revived their houses. Among the merchants who are also skilled at leisure in Yanagibashi right now, those from Yokohama are most numerous. The up-and-coming geisha of highest renown, such as Oshun and Konaru, have all left the ranks after being redeemed by Yokohama men. I hear that last year there was a Yokohama merchant who had used up all of his resources, and was just about to close his doors and leave. But it so happened that this was precisely when paper currency [bills were] was being introduced. He borrowed one hundred in gold and bought *kōzo*, or "paper mulberry" trees, and in a single day made thirty thousand in profit. Subsequently [After that], when he bought rice, the price of rice skyrocketed, and when he bought oil, the price of oil shot up.

---

⁶⁶ As mentioned briefly in the first volume, Tao Zhu 陶朱 was the name Fan Li 范蠡 took after retiring as official of Yue in the Spring and Autumn period. Ryūhoku frequently makes use of such eponymy, with "Tao Zhu" functioning here as an equivalent for a wealthy man.

At present, the worth of his property is said to have exceeded one hundred thousand. I declare: "If the commerce at Yokohama becomes increasingly prosperous, then these partisans of opulent grandeur will increasingly compete as playboys. And when that happens, will Heaven produce another man like Kinokuniya Bunzaemon? But if an endless succession of ships comes from America, Prussia, England, and France loaded down with goods, then how will the tangerine boat of Southern Kii ever be worth singing about again? How will it be worth dancing about again?"

In his poem on "Guarding the Inkstone," Yuan Mei writes, "I caress it, cherish it, feel tenderly toward it—even more than to a fifteen-year-old girl's supple charms."[67] Generally speaking, one can use the words "feel tenderly" in regard to a young woman, and cannot apply them to a woman over twenty. Nevertheless, there are some steeped in diversion and practiced in affection who maintain that holding a tuft-hair$^{\text{young girl}}$ of fifteen or sixteen years is$^{\text{in short}}$ ultimately devoid of even a modicum^{bit} of interest,^{charm} like fondling a clay figurine.^{doll} Unless she has begun$^{\text{reached the age of}}$ to wear a hairpin^{twenty} and has to some extent tasted the sweetness and sourness of human feelings, then she can be no companion in conversation. Some men these days might well have their fun with a child and then blame her for not understanding such sweetness and sourness, or some might recklessly thrust the phrase "feel tenderly" on an old geisha, seeking it between her legs. We can say that both types of men have lost the Way. Now then, if you throw one hundred *mon* into a gully,^{ditch} at least it still makes a splish.^{plop} But what profit it a man to simply waste his money on courtesans, neither considering their flavor nor recognizing their feelings? Would he not be better off to take all of the money, valuables,

---

[67] The line comes from a poem entitled "A sketch of guarding the inkstone at Dongchang hermitage" 董暢庵守硯圖 by Yuan Mei 袁枚 (1716–1798).

possessions, and property in his house, throw the whole lot into the sea, and make a really impressive splash?^(plunk) There is a word for those who lose their money because of deceitful^(sham) words, for those who bankrupt themselves because of their own hedonistic hearts; these men are known as imbeciles.^(fools) ⁶⁸ But there are also those men who have cavorted in the flower and willow world for many years, and yet lacking even the slightest soupçon of stylish sensibility in their guts,^(hearts) they try their tricks and use their wiles to plunder money from the courtesans' pockets instead: these men are known as villains.^(bad guys) The imbeciles are certainly laughable, while the villains on the other hand are contemptible. Both the imbecile and the villain are in some way either excessive or deficient; surely neither man can be called one who has a talent for leisure. Yet if a man can strike a balance between imbecility and villainy, and thus neither lose his money nor besmirch his name, then he will be nothing less than the Captain^(Kingpin) of the Domain of Panache. With such a man, I can find no fault.⁶⁹

A certain geisha had two regular customers. One of them was a merchant, and the other was a samurai. The samurai had a wife but the merchant had not yet married. The geisha's affections lay with the merchant, but she was unable to sever her intimacies with the samurai. She had recently made up her mind to put^(have) things^(herself) right^(redeemed) with^(by) the merchant. One evening, she was drinking with the samurai; they were far into their cups, and were just about to go to bed. The geisha said, "I have long benefited from your devotion,^(patronage) and I shall not forget you until the day I die. I have long wished to take up a broom and dustpan

---

⁶⁸ As the gloss of *baka* suggests, Ryūhoku uses the word *chikan* 痴漢 here in its primary sense of "fool." Given the context however, we can perhaps see the incipient link to its meaning in contemporary Japanese (and thence to Chinese) as "pervert."
⁶⁹ The last line is 吾亦無間然矣, which echoes *Analects* VIII.21: "With Yu I can find no fault" 禹吾無間然矣.

and humbly serve as your wife. Yet my mother will not permit it. My mother grew up in a merchant house, and does not wish me to form ties of intimacy with the warrior^(samurai) class. What is more, you have a spouse^(wife) living back in your native^(home) province^(land). Even if you could realize your desires by having me learn^(run) from^(off) Hongfu^(with you), I personally fear that the well-dipper^(affair) will be^(come) severed^(to) from^(a) its^(worthless) tether^(end), and the jeweled hairpin will crack at its center.[70] It would, in fact, only cause problems for you. A certain merchant has loved me for a long time, and is always inviting me to pour drinks for him. Never^(Not once) has he attempted to cajole me into pillowed^(lewd) intimacies. Recently he sent a man to ask my mother to let him take me as his wife. My mother has already consented, and I cannot refuse^(say no). I could not bear to part without asking your leave, and now I have told you the truth. This is because I have no wish to deceive you. I pray that you will drink a cup in good spirits, sleep one night with me in good spirits, and we can make tonight our eternal^(final) farewell^(parting). If you are worried about lacking a good companion^(partner) for diversion, then fortunately there is a new geisha^(girl) who has just made her debut. She is charming, attractive, and quite lovable. I would like to act as an intermediary for you as a way of repaying my obligation; what do you think?" The samurai grew^(got) livid^(angry), and said with his face flushed, "You once promised me that we would be like the wings of a bird in heaven, and as intertwined branches on earth.[71] I also struck^(made a) my sword^(metal vow),

---

[70] As mentioned in Volume I, Hongfu 紅拂 (sometimes literally translated "the Red Feather-duster") was a famous courtesan of the Sui Dynasty who saw Li Jing's promise and ran off with him. Ryūhoku also incorporates in this passage imagery from one of Bo Juyi's "New Music Bureau poems" (*Xin yuefu*, number 40); the severing of the well-rope and the breaking of the hairpin both symbolize the parting of the lovers.
[71] The allusion is to the famous penultimate couplet from Bo Juyi's "Song of Everlasting Pain," which reads: "if in Heaven, may we become those birds that fly on shared wing; or on Earth, then may we become branches that twine together" (Owen, *Anthology*, 447).

solemnly presenting an earnest pledge to the gods.⁷² Now you turn your back on our agreement and eat your words, discarding me so that you can marry your [beau] lover. How can I bear to remain silent and send you off? Moreover, even if I could tolerate [permit] this in my heart, what about these two swords? What about those gods? If you do indeed leave, then I have a plan of my own! In my domain, there are ten large battalions of crack soldiers, and I will lead them to attack your house. What do you say to that?" The geisha replied, "You are being impossible! Now I am peddling my wares in order to survive. I sell and you buy. In other words I offer my merchandise and you pay for services rendered. I simply follow your command. But if one day I am withdrawn [taken] from [off] the geisha register, even though I may still be low in station, I will nevertheless be the young lady [daughter] of the house. Whether to wear a hairpin [come of age] or get married will be entirely my decision [up to me]. I will have perfect freedom, and what business [concern] will it be of yours? No matter how many dozens of troops you have in your honorable domain, what can you do to me? Moreover, surely you are not suggesting that the purpose of keeping troops in the various domains is to employ them for fulfilling the private desires of a Councilor or making personal threats on his behalf! If the troops come and attack me, then I will just race on over to make a fuss [lodge an appeal] with the authorities. Though your domain be large, though your troops be strong, I wonder how they will fare against the imperial house! Once the brocade flag is raised, they will just be crushed!" She laughed a loud guffaw, and left down the stairs.

---

⁷² The phrase 鼓刀 "struck my sword" is glossed *kinchō* 金打, which refers to a samurai custom of solemnizing a vow by striking the blades or shells of two swords together; the practice was adapted by those lacking swords to include other metal objects.

The lyrics of a popular song go:

> 吹分水風颺分箔　多情要見舫裏客
>
> B l o w   -   r i v e r   w i n d s   R i s e   u p   -   r e e d   b l i n d
> Let the river winds blow! Let the breeze raise the blind!
>
> O h   l e t   m e   g l i m p s e
> In my passion I want to see   the   face   of   that   passenger
>   inside
> onboard.[73]

One day in the height of summer, the red sun was just about to set; the shade of the water grew progressively green, and a far-off wind gusted in across the "southern depths." (open) (sea) Several hundred pleasure boats formed into lines, dashing (charging) right toward the very heart (center) of the waters at Ryōgoku. The blue curtains fluttered in the crisp and cool breeze; sounds of golden shamisen strings resounded in the skies and red damask was reflected on the waves. It gave one a refreshing (crisp) feeling, resurrecting (bringing him back to life) his energies and making him think that he had left behind the scorching heat of Hell and entered into a brisk and cool world. It seems that in the past, according to the regulations (rules) for pleasure boats, the samurai boats could have screens (shōji), and the merchant boats were only permitted to install curtains. Nowadays (In recent years), this system has disintegrated (fallen apart), so that each and every boat has abandoned curtains and installed *shōji* screens. The screens lock in warmth on snowy mornings and shield amorous springtime moments from view on windy evenings. True, these features of the screens both seem advantageous (convenient), but the pleasure of the blue curtains fluttering in the crisp and cool breeze is now gone for good. Last year, I went aboard a large boat that

---

[73] There are various versions of this song in different lyrical forms; here Ryūhoku gives a *dodoitsu* in the Japanese gloss: *fukeyo kawakaze / agareyo sudare / naka no okyaku no / kao mitaya*. It is the basis for the slant-rhymed heptasyllabic Chinese couplet.

was mooring in front of Old Yanagibashi. The anchor had been dropped to fix the boat in place, and they had set up a banquet on board, cooking inside the cabin, just like in an alehouse. The pleasure-seekers all tied up their boats and came aboard, calling for sake and ordering food. The sake was pure and the food delicious. On the boat was mounted a plaque with its name: the Willow Boat. The name "Willow Boat" was for a time quite famous in the city. Nevertheless, boats are busy when it is hot and idle in the cold, and when the autumn winds began to blow, the Willow Boat was also abandoned. In the past when the Yellow Emperor made boats and paddles, he probably got the inspiration from the hexagram *huan*.[74] Nowadays when people make boats, they do not just get their inspiration from one place; they take it from flowers, from the moon, from food and drink, and from courtesans. Who knows what other kinds of marvelous boats will be built in the future as an aid for such diversions. I cannot divine in advance what form they might take.

One customer sat down to wait, then he lay down and waited some more. The light from the lantern was just about out but then it grew bright again. The flavor of the sake seemed sour and bitter. In solitude, he turned to face his shadow in lament, discontent and dispirited. A maid came to comfort him, saying "Today is a one-six holiday, so the various bars are sure to be bustling, and the myriad geisha will all be busy. Yet the watchman's sticks have already

---

[74] This references a passage from a commentary on *The Classic of Changes* that is also mentioned in Volume I; the passage focuses on the hexagram *huan* 渙, which is connected to the image of floating wood: "The Yellow Emperor, Yao, and Shun … hollowed out some tree trunks to make boats and whittled down others to make paddles. The benefit of boats and paddles was such that one could cross over to where it had been impossible to go. This allowed faraway places to be reached and so benefited the entire world. They probably got the idea for this from the hexagram Huan [Dispersion]" (Lynn, 78).

119

announced the dog^(watch) hour [of eight o'clock]. I imagine that your treasured one^(favorite girl) will come back sooner^(before) or later^(long now). I ask that you endure it just a little longer." The customer said, "I have waited a long time. My blood has congealed and stiffened my shoulders! Have a masseuse come, will you?" The maid agreed and left. Presently, a blind masseuse arrived at the steps. The customer said, "So-and-so is here."[75] The masseuse sat at the customer's back and pounded away, clapping him on the shoulders and softly kneading his arms. The blind woman said, "Sir, your tendons^(muscles) are rather^(have gone) rigid^(stiff). It must be that you are sensitive to the changes of the seasons. It would be good to gradually^(little by little) work the knots out." The customer said, "Doctor,^(Madam Masseuse) is there any news lately?" The blind woman responded, "No, there isn't. But even Edo has declined quite a bit." The customer said, "How do you know this?" The blind woman responded, "People these days all say that Edo has really gone downhill. But my eyes cannot see the deterioration. Nevertheless, there is something by which even I can verify its decline." The customer asked, "What sort of proof do you have?" The blind woman responded, "Every day I go out and earn a living by using my hands. And every time I return home, I sniff my shoes^(geta). Without exception they have always had the smell of excrement on them, and so I would immediately wash off their teeth. Recently, however, when I sniff my shoes, it is exceedingly rare for me to perceive any odor. This makes me think that the amount of canine^(dog) droppings^(shit) in the city's streets has decreased. Inasmuch as the canine population has declined, we can

---

[75] Befitting the arrival of the blind masseuse, Ryūhoku makes the customer's diction closely echo the words Confucius used to help orient the blind music-master Mian in *The Analects* (XV.41): "When he reached the mat, the Master said, Here is the mat. When everyone was seated the Master informed him saying So-and-so is here, So-and-so is there" (Waley, *The Analects*, 190). Massage was one profession open to people in traditional Japan (and China) with visual impairments; money-lending was another, as indicated later in this passage when the masseuse shares the financial advice of her mentor.

surmise the human population's decline also. Now if that is not a sign of Edo's decline then what is it?"⁷⁶ The customer replied, "You have a point there." The blind woman continued, "In recent years, the feline population has mounted^(increased) day by day. (Note: In the city's vernacular it is customary to whimsically refer to geisha and singing girls as 'cats.' This is because their shamisens are all strung with cat skin.⁷⁷) I wonder if it is related to the canine decline. The buildings surrounding my house on all four sides are feline^(cathouses) dens. Mind you, I've heard that a certain Sajibei from the tenement house once went on a tour of Shikoku and turned into a monkey.⁷⁸ But nowadays all the girls in town are turning into cats—and they don't^(do) even^(it) have^(all) to^(without) go^(getting) anywhere!^(up) How agile^(quick) is their technique! I suspect that you, Sir, also love cats. I hear that recently the price of cats has veritably skyrocketed. To purchase just one of the critters, you must spend one yen. It seems the proverb is right: you just have to give 'a gold coin to a cat.'⁷⁹ These days, the prosperity of the cats is truly surprising. If one leaves aside the kittens and counts only the big cats, then there are one hundred fifty of them. And if for the sake of argument we simply figure at a rate of a yen for every one of them for each day, then the total for one month is four thousand five hundred yen. Oh, how prosperous! According to the injunctions bestowed upon me by my departed former teacher, the

---

⁷⁶ Contemporary readers would be familiar with a folk saying to the effect that "The things most numerous in Edo are shop merchants from Ise, Inari shrines, and dog shit"—each of which indicates, in its own way, the commercial prosperity of the metropolis.

⁷⁷ The etymology explained here for the term *neko* (cat) meaning "geisha" links the geisha to her role as an artist of the shamisen. At the same time, the term *neko*, especially when written 寝子 (suggesting "girl to sleep with"), was also used to mean "prostitute" (Swinton, 65).

⁷⁸ This seeming nonsense is from a mid-Edo counting song, where sequential numbers are incorporated into the lyrics.

⁷⁹ The proverb *neko ni koban* means something whose value is lost on one who cannot use it, like "pearls before swine."

high-ranking clerk Tightfist:[80] 'Thou shalt not believe in the Way of the gods or the Buddhas; Thou shalt not choose finery in food and clothing; Thou shalt not cherish thy relatives; Thou shalt not be too intimate with thy friends; Rise in the early morning and go to sleep in the evening; Fire^{Stoke} the lamp with your fingernail clippings and keep^{use} close^{an} track^{abacus} of^{for} your money. If you simply crave profit, then you can live out your whole life in comfort.' This is truly a profound^{wise} dictum.^{saying} But I have proven unworthy, unable to live according to these dying words of my teacher. And now I am so destitute that I do not have even half a *bu* to my name. I am a person and yet am no better than a cat. At mealtime, all I can do is sniff at the fragrance^{aroma} of roasted eel that comes wafting over when those felines next door feast upon it, making this my repast." Suddenly, the sound of the maid calling from downstairs was audible: "Your^{She} favorite^{is} has^{here} arrived.^{now}" The blind woman hurriedly said, "And with this, our badinage on cats must draw to a close. Your honorable tendons^{muscles} have become^{have} quite^{now} relaxed.^{loosened up a lot} I recommend you take to bed straight away."

Two juveniles^{young men} with dragon designs^{tattoos} all over their bodies^{carved} stood atop Ryōgoku Bridge. They each wore a long handkerchief in place of a fastened obi sash. Leaning over the railing, they surveyed^{looked down on} the scene below. Beneath the bridge, the pleasure boats swarmed like ants, music of strings and wind instruments rose up into the cool breeze, and people rinsed their cups and plates in the clear current. Truly it was a "sea of music and song."[81] Young Man A turned to look at Young

---

[80] The masseuse's teacher is surnamed Akanishi 赤西, a plausible surname but one that is used here because it is homophonous with a metaphoric term for "cheapskate." This other *akanishi* 赤螺 is literally a variety of gastropod known as a "rock shell" or "whelk," which has a tendency to tightly seal itself off; hence, the term's use in meaning "tightwad."

[81] The phrase 歌吹海 may have been familiar to Ryūhoku through the poem by Lu

Man B and said, "Damn it! What rough ${}^{\text{brutes}}$ beasts are making such an annoying commotion?! These days the singing girls are so popular. And it's all because those samurai with their dual swords are so fond of them.[82] The junior geisha around here are little more than ${}^{\text{babysitter}}$ dancing girls ${}^{\text{geisha}}$ ${}^{\text{still wet}}$ ${}^{\text{behind the}}$ ${}^{\text{ears}}$ who reek of piss, but they are so ${}^{\text{highfalutin}}$ haughty that you'd think they were fancy ${}^{\text{the Missus}}$ wives or ${}^{\text{the Mademoiselle}}$ princesses.[83] They are apt to not even ${}^{\text{regard}}$ treat a man like a human being. '${}^{\text{Geisha}}$ Singing girls, ${}^{\text{geisha}}$ singing girls'—or so they call themselves, but when they ${}^{\text{get back home}}$ return, they act like the ${}^{\text{prim and proper}}$ children of ${}^{\text{young daughters}}$ reputable ${}^{\text{You have}}$ houses. It is ${}^{\text{gotta}}$ appalling ${}^{\text{be kidding}}$ to hear! Pin one down and she'll say, '${}^{\text{Please do not say}}$ Refrain from referring to us ${}^{\text{we are}}$ as cats. This dyed yukata kimono was ${}^{\text{a gift}}$ presented ${}^{\text{from}}$ by my customer.'[84] No doubt she's boasting of her conquests!" Young Man B said, "Just ${}^{\text{let it}}$ drop ${}^{\text{be}}$ it. Recently, a lot more of them are making money. For this reason, it has become common for them to ${}^{\text{start to show}}$ affect an opulent ${}^{\text{off}}$ air: wearing their hair in curls, or jauntily sticking a pure gold hairpin in their forelocks.

You 陸游 (1125–1210) titled "A whimsical lyric composed while listening to the rain on a winter night" (冬夜聽雨戲作詞), which contains the couplet: "My memories go back to Jincheng, a sea of music and song; seven years of rainy nights, and I never realized it" 憶在錦城歌吹海 七年夜雨曾不知.

[82] The term 士人 (J. *shijin*; Ch. *shiren*), meaning gentry or samurai, appears with the gloss *ryanko*, which seems to be a corruption of 兩個 (Ch. *liangge*), meaning "two," and referring to the samurai's two swords (and metonymically to the samurai).

[83] The term 溺臭妓 literally means "urine-reeking courtesan," the first two characters of which pejoratively emphasize her immaturity. It is a good example of a hybrid neologism in the Chinese text, for the term presumably derives from the Japanese word *shōben kusai* 小便臭い, meaning "callow." Ryūhoku has presented this Japanese term in a plausible Chinese package, however, since the term 溺 (Ch. *niao*), which is most frequently encountered in Japanese as meaning "to drown," also means "to urinate" in colloquial Chinese and thus serves as a substitute for 小便, which means "urine" in both languages. Moreover, the phrase as a whole is glossed *komori geisha* or "geisha who (are made to) do childcare," an apparent reference to the responsibilities imposed on young geisha by the houses at which they served.

[84] The young man seems to be giving two alternative versions (shown here in italics) of a lyric popular in the late Edo and early Meiji period known as *otchokochoibushi*; the most common version goes "A cat, a cat, you say. But does a cat walk with a staff and come wearing a dyed *yukata*?" Kikuchi Sankei also alludes to this song in his preface to Ryūhoku's guide to Kyoto geisha culture, *Keibyō ippan*.

123

Such a shame! Such a shame! Sooner or later, they will encounter a
                                    Before   too   long
pickpocket and have their goods plucked; then we'll see the tears flow
                                 pilfered
on their hideous faces. A bee wouldn't even dare to sting those mugs.⁸⁵
Imagine how they'd look! It'd serve 'em right!" Young Man A
responded, "No, no. They're all a bunch of misers. When they go
                                                cheapskates
home at night, they always remove their hair ornaments, wrap them
                             take out
up with their paper currency and hide them in the folds of their
dresses.⁸⁶ How conniving is that!" Young Man B said, "But haven't you
heard? Last year that old dame Madam Fusahachi held a calligraphy and
painting party at Nakamuraya.⁸⁷ On the appointed day, various
distinguished persons all came; both the turnout of guests and the
copiousness of monetary gifts were unparalleled in recent years. People
all called it 'the wild party.'⁸⁸ Isn't that marvelous? I often go to her
                                                                    that
residence, and I have never once seen her grind the *sumi* ink, or lick her
chick's house
brush, or draw those so-called Chinese characters. And yet she is the
master of a calligraphy party. It surely is a mystery. From ancient times
down to the present, it has been unusual for a geisha to be the host of
a calligraphy party. How can we say for certain that we won't one day
see a geisha emerge to serve as a government official?" They looked at
each other and laughed out loud. Just then, they saw a well-formed line

---

⁸⁵ The second man alludes to the Japanese saying *nakitsura ni hachi* "a bee for a crying face" meaning "when it rains it pours"—one misfortune is followed by others.
⁸⁶ Ryūhoku incorporates a line from the *Analects* (XV.6), amusingly uprooted from its original context of describing the conduct of the gentleman who can "hide his jewel" (his talents and sterling character) when necessary: "A gentleman indeed is Qu Boyu. When the Way prevailed in his land, he served the State; but when the Way ceased to prevail, he knew how to 'wrap it up and hide it in the folds of his dress'" (Waley, *The Analects*, 183).
⁸⁷ In his article on the "calligraphy and painting parties" (*shogakai*) mounted in nineteenth-century Edo, Andrew Markus describes these gatherings as "celebrity banquets."
⁸⁸ The word *meppōkai* 滅法會 puns on the homophonous 滅法界, a term meaning something that is extreme or intense to a "wild," "crazy," or "out of control" degree.

of patrol^(police) officers^(men) come shouting toward them with their guns hoisted. Both men got down off the bridge hastily^(in a hurry) and left.

During China's Tianbao reign, among the three thousand ladies of the harem,^(rear palace) there was none who was not beautiful, none who was not lovely, and yet why was it that Emperor Xuanzong only had affection for Taizhen?^(Yang Guifei) In the course of one's life, just how often does one encounter^(meet with) such a fine specimen of womanhood: this state-toppler who not only had unparalleled beauty but literary gifts and talents to rival those of a gentleman? When I count up the red-skirted ladies of Yanagibashi that I have met in ten years, their looks and talents are all comparable.^(more or less the same) I have not yet seen one lovely lady whose "smiling glance exuded every charm" and who made those other lovely ladies "in the harem who wore powder and paint seem barren" of beauty.[89] Nevertheless, if I had to search among them for such a woman, there is one. Her name is Okiyo. Her lovely temperament was divinely made. Retiring and subdued, her words were few. To behold her was to gaze at a beautiful glimmering jade. To be in her presence was to encounter a warm spring breeze. When I first saw her at my friend Nagai Hōzan's house, she was fifteen years old.[90] I composed a poem that went:

夭桃花上露無聲 深鎖仙扃夢不驚 他日劉郎若相訪 丹唇一笑始相迎
  Dew stands silent atop the lithe peach blossoms;
  Deep within her immortal doors, she stirs not from her reveries.

---

[89] As indicated by the phrases enclosed here in quotation marks (marks that do not appear in the original), Ryūhoku closely mirrors lines from Bo Juyi's "Song of Lasting Pain," the famous poem on the romance between the Emperor Xuanzong and the palace lady Yang Guifei in the Tianbao era (742–755); see the complete translation in Owen, *Anthology*, 442–447.
[90] Nagai Hōzan 永井芳山 was a relative of Ryūhoku's first wife and one of his drinking companions.

125

If some day a gallant Liulang comes to visit her,
A smile will cross her red lips, welcoming him for the first time.[91]

There was once a time when Okiyo's name had taken the whole entertainment district by storm, but she was always prone to suffer from illness. In autumn of 1862, there was a fierce epidemic of measles, and Okiyo also became ill. She lay in her bed for several weeks, and in the end she didn't get up again. She was only seventeen. Hōzan composed a poem lamenting this:

國色古今相遇稀　多情淚盡血沾衣　夕陽人吊孤墳下　野菊香殘老蝶飛
Encountering a peerless beauty has always been rare,
Overcome with feeling, my tears are spent and blood stains my robe.
As the sun sets, I mourn her before the lonely mound;
In the lingering scent of a wild chrysanthemum flutters a late butterfly.

Using the same rhyme scheme, I also composed an elegy:

舊情欲說聽人稀　淚滴當年舊舞衣　借問嫦娥何處去　夢魂長向月中飛
I long to speak of past feelings, but there is no one to listen;
My teardrops fall down on your old dancing robes.
Where, I ask, has the lunar goddess Chang'e gone?
In my dreams, my spirit flies far off to the moon.

---

[91] Liulang is a generalized eponym for a playboy that originally referred to Liu Chen 劉晨, a character in the Tang *chuanqi* (tales of the marvelous) narrative *Youminglu* (Record of things seen and unseen) by Liu Yiqing. Along with his companion Ruan Zhao 阮肇, Liu Chen has a mysterious encounter with two lovely women while gathering herbs on Tiantai mountain. Returning after enjoying half a year with them, he finds that ten generations have passed in his absence; for a translation and discussion of the story see Rouzer, *Articulated Ladies*, 205–206.

Just one month later, Hōzan also passed away. Ah, how truly tragic it is that Heaven does not allot such talented young men and beauties more years. Among the older generation of geisha these days, there is only Osono. When she was young, Osono stood alongside Oei. For a long time, they shared the crown as the famed twin beauties of Ryōgoku. In the old days, the manner of geisha in Yanagibashi was not substantially different from places like Konparu and Shinbashi. Yet in recent years, there has been a change not only in appearance [style] and adornment [of dress], but in the kind of singing as well. Now noble purity and understated elegance are esteemed, and the divergence of Yanagibashi's atmosphere [mood] from the other districts probably got its start with these two geisha. It seems that Osono was impeccable in both looks and accomplishments, and on top of that, ever since her middle years, she consciously adopted a restrained [deferential] attitude and did not condescend to the customers. She was also good at instructing [promoting] the younger girls. Everyone regarded her as a wise worthy. One could say that she was the geisha equivalent of a proper Confucian gentleman. Among the up-and-coming generation, the one whose reputation enjoys the greatest renown is surely Otori. On the inside, Otori has amassed her talents without need for showy display; on the outside, she conducts herself with smooth equanimity. In attending upon her parents she is filial and obedient, in relating to others she is warm [mild] and graceful [gentle]. I have never once seen her give vent to anger in her voice or expression. She is also a good geisha. Osono has already been removed [withdrawn] from the geisha rolls at the end of last year, and Otori made [got] good [married] this spring. No one knows who will become the chief among this group of lovely flowers now. I still have not learned of the public's consensus. Long ago,

I drank with Takeuchi Seiha in a certain bar in Old Yanagibashi.[92] I wrote a poem for the wall:

嬌歌侑酒醉高秋　無限歡情卻惹愁　門柳蕭疎美人去　他年追感在此樓
    Listening to lovely songs, plied with sake, I get drunk in high autumn,
    Yet these boundless feelings of pleasure just bring on melancholy.
    The willow outside the gate lies barren; the beautiful girls have gone;
    In some future year, I will chase memories of coming to this hall.[93]

It was only seven or eight years ago that Seiha, old and ailing, wandered around in the North. At the time, the red-skirted geisha had declined in number, and were as scarce as early morning stars. I too decided that I would entrust the remainder of my life to the winds and dust. Every time I pass by Old Yanagibashi, I look up and see the old willow tree, finding myself stirred by painful memories of the past, and feeling the sorrows of Mr. Huan at Jincheng.[94] Ah, there are so many playboys in the world! But, who shares my feelings? Who shares my sorrows?

Ryōgoku is a flourishing place. Yanagibashi is the site of a pleasure quarter. Many writers and other literary types regard it as vulgar. However, when you take a boat out to midstream in the fullness^(depths) of a clear night, once people have settled^(gone to) down^(bed) for the evening; when you gaze south toward the river's mouth, and north toward the Sumida,

---

[92] Seiha 西坡 was the sobriquet of Takeuchi Gendō (竹内玄洞, 1805–1880), a physician and scholar of Dutch medicine who served the shogun Iemochi.
[93] I have followed Hino Tatsuo's interpretation of the final line given its congruity with the following paragraph. It is possible, however, that the reference to "another year" is in the past not the future, which would give: "Chasing after memories of another time, I come to this bar."
[94] This alludes to a story contained in *A New Account of Tales of the World* that tells of Huan Wen (312–373) returning to the willows he planted at Jincheng and being moved by how their growth marked the passage of time (Mather, 60).

then the bright silver moon pierces the waves, sending forth a rush of golden dragons over the waters; the cool breeze blows at one's robe as though to give him the wings of an immortal and carry him aloft. The points of several fishing lanterns can be seen flickering through the waterweeds on the islet. A single beam of light from a tavern lantern can dimly be made out within the curtains of a painted building. Such a place is lively but not vulgar; the scene is understated and not intimidating.^(harsh) Truly this area has the most panache among the three metropolitan centers. This is even more the case when the sake is delicious and the fish is fresh, when famous beauties and charming lovelies stroke their shamisen strings and perform their dances, fluttering and twisting as though moved by the winds. Such moments can make a man's mind dissolve^(melt) and set his spirits loose,^(free) washing him utterly clean of the myriad entangled sorrows lodged^(that) in^(lie in) his breast.^(his heart) If just once we could somehow bring men like Bo Juyi or Du Mu out for an evening to this district, then they would without a doubt compose long songs and new lyrics to celebrate^(praise) its splendor and proclaim its marvelousness. Those who regard the place as vulgar are viewing only the superficial^(outward) exterior,^(surface) and failing to understand its true nature. I once composed several miscellaneous poems about Ryōgoku. I submit two of them here as evidence.

絃歌惱殺幾多人　此地繁華世絶倫　簾影橫樓烟曖曖　櫓聲近岸水粼粼
梅薰羅袖梅川夕　柳映金絃柳屋春　姉妹新粧爭嫵媚　風流誰學李湘真

How many have fallen victim to the seductive strings and songs?
The prosperity of this place is in a class all by itself.
Shrouding the alehouse curtains hangs an uncertain mist;
The sound of oars drawing near the bank, the waters limpid.
Plum fragrance pervades light silk sleeves; it is evening at Umekawa;
Willows reflected on golden shamisen strings; it is spring at Yanagiya.

Junior and senior geisha freshly made up vie in their charms;
In the ways of elegant panache, who will follow Li Shiniang?[95]

秦淮山水未嘗遊 其勝想當輸二州 明月長臨才子宴 清風常滿美人舟
迸空煙火搖銀漢 倚閣凉衫映白鷗 此際好呼坡老帚 為君一掃十年愁

I have never traveled to see the mountains and rivers of Qinhuai,
But I imagine that their natural beauty would pale next to Ryōgoku.[96]
The bright moon shines long on the talented men's banquets;
A refreshing breeze always fills the beautiful ladies' boats.
Rocketing into the sky, fireworks shake the Milky Way;
Leaning on a banister, a cool *yukata* attractively sets off the white gulls.
It's times like these that call for Su Dongpo's "old broom";
Drinking with you lets me sweep away ten years of gloom.[97]

Long ago, I would always meet Seisai, Yōkō, and others for drinks in Ryōgoku.[98] The young girls that I saw then were all approximately ten years of age and they still knew nothing of painting in their moth-like eyebrows. With mucus dribbling to the corners of their mouths, they would clutch clay figures, squirming and wriggling around as they played. Now they have all grown up. They lift up the hems of their red

---

[95] As mentioned in Volume I, Li Shiniang (appearing here with the alternative name Li Xiangzhen) was the heroic Qinhuai courtesan whom Yu Huai praised in his *Miscellaneous Records of the Wooden Bridge*. Lines 5 and 6 play on the plant names "Willow" and "Plum" contained in Yanagiya (lit. "Willow House") and Umekawa ("Plum River").

[96] Robert Campbell uses the illuminating metaphor of the palimpsest to discuss how this poem superimposes the poet's present surroundings at Ryōgoku on to the unseen but textually familiar site of Qinhuai, allowing the latter to emerge into readerly consciousness ("Yomikaki," esp. 217–219).

[97] Su Dongpo's "jeweled broom" 玉帚 is an elegant term for wine. I have followed Hino Tatsuo's interpretation of the word "you" in the last line to mean a geisha, but it could be an apostrophe for the wine of the previous line, or a direct address of the reader.

[98] Seisai 晴簑 was a sobriquet of Katsuragawa Hoshū (Kunioki, 1826–1881). Yōkō 楊江 was a sobriquet of Yanagawa Shunsan.

skirts and caress the shamisen strings. Their comportment [manner] is impressive and their songs worth hearing. Because of this, I find myself touched by something sad and poignant. "Hard work will perfect your studies, which can be lost through play."[99] These are words that Han Yu wrote one thousand years ago. I suppose that courtesans are girls of low station, and singing and dancing are trifling accomplishments. Nevertheless, if a girl is assiduous in her study of them, then in a few years they will be sufficient to support her.

But what about those who now hold the reins of government? Receiving high titles and subsisting on large stipends, they have a robust sense of entitlement and a fierily imperious air. Yet in spite of this, the teachings of ceremony are still not upheld in the realm, and the blessings of virtue have yet to reach the people. Why is this? Surely it cannot be that they are lackluster [halfwit] mediocrities [good-for-nothings] not qualified to hold their positions. Rather, the reason is that people now enjoy the blessings of peace and cling only to the short-sighted hope of living another day of tranquility. The state is in such a hurry to promote the wise and use the talented that it ends up appointing sycophantic officials and unprincipled men. Can it be for any other reason than that they are not being diligent in the administration of government, and have instead made negligent [slipshod] abandonment [recklessness] itself the fashion? During the final days of the Tokugawa clan, it was not the case that men replete with talent and distinguished with discernment could not be found. And yet the flaw that caused the decline and decay of that government was precisely this "negligent abandonment." From antiquity to the present day, there has never been a government that did not achieve its success through diligent work and reap its destruction

---

[99] The source of the quotation is Han Yu's (768–824) "An Explication of 'Progress in Learning'"; see the translation by Charles Hartman in Mair, *Columbia*, 580–588.

through negligent abandonment. Whether we speak of negligence or abandonment, the gentlemen in power should heed my words. For I too am a reckless one who has yielded to wild abandon and neglected his career. Sooner or later I will be begging for food in the streets. And that will give me something to be most ashamed of in front of even these low-status girls.

During the period that I, the Immortal What-of-it, was drafting this volume, a certain person surreptitiously read it and said with a furrowed forehead and arched eyebrows, "Your book is devoid of any value for the world's improvement; you merely insult people. You produce this useless prose and thereby incite the world's anger. What possible reason do you have to carry out such crazy foolishness? Aren't you ashamed of yourself?" I laughed and replied, "I am, after all, a useless person. Where would I find the leisure to do useful things? Moreover, the targets of my insults are crimes of refinement and taste in amusements amorous and otherwise.[100] And the fact that I insult people is itself also a crime I commit because of my love for refined taste. If people in the world draw upon their scorn of refined taste to fault my refined and tasteful pen, then I will happily plead guilty as charged.[101] How could I refuse this? Moreover, who in the world is without crimes of taste? The only difference is between those who

---

[100] The term 風流罪過 (Ch. *fengliu zuiguo*; J. *fūryū zaika*) has a primary sense of minor transgressions that can be attributed to one's unconventional, suave, or stylish sensibilities. Ryūhoku here clearly draws upon the strong implication the term has of referring to indiscretions committed mainly in romantic matters, or to a dissolute character. As discussed in the Introduction to this volume, Ryūhoku used the same phrase in his autobiographical essay "Bokujō inshiden," suggesting that "being too suave" may have been one factor leading to his dismissal from the shogunate.

[101] Alternatively, perhaps this sentence contrastively anticipates the later encounter with the Confucian scholar; another interpretation might be "if people in the world use their personal sense of refined taste as the basis for a critique of mine …"

make them public and those who hide them away. Let us suppose that a Confucian scholar, riding around in his carriage of Shang, wearing his cap of Zhou, consulting the *Sixfold Statues of the Tang Dynasty* in his right hand and perusing the *Ming Legal Code* in his left came earnestly opining, criticizing me for my crimes against taste.[102] I would surely respond to him, "You are a scholar of the Confucian Way; I am a partisan of panache. We have not even a half *bu* of debt or credit between us. Your meddlesome intrusion into my affairs is unexpected; what is your reason?" Suppose then that he retorts, "The essays you write are no good. No reader can understand what you mean. I truly lament this. The annals you have recorded are wild distortions and untruths. I am dubious of them." Then I would certainly reply, "The reason my prose is no good is because I am uneducated. But how could I dare not ask you for some pointers? And as for the erroneousness of my annals, why don't you go to Yanagibashi and inquire about it yourself?" What do I have to fear? Long ago, Old Seiken wrote his *Chronicles of Flourishing Edo*. At the time, the shogunal officials were angered by his slanderous words and so they tied him up in jail, burned his book, proclaimed his crime, and ultimately banished him. The world scoffed at the petty intolerance of those officials and Seiken's book is still popular today. Moreover, haven't you heard? The newspapers printed in the various countries of the West carry libelous and insulting words, but the sovereigns do not fault them nor do the officials criticize them. Gentlemen do not become angered and petty men do not

---

[102] The "carriage of Shang" and "cap of Zhou" are emblems of proper ritual from earlier dynasties that Confucius identified in *Analects* XV.11 as important for state administration. The phrase 侃侃闇闇 refers to another passage in the *Analects* (X.2) that describes the manner of speech Confucius used in talking with councilors: affable toward the lower officials and frank toward the higher. In Ryūhoku's use, however, the Japanese gloss of *komuzukashiku* (peevish, querulous) places a less positive spin on such earnestness and circumspection.

begrudge them. Instead, they all vie to read them, thereby expanding their knowledge and vigilantly keeping abreast of conditions. Something like my book is nothing more than a kind of useless newspaper. How unwonted is your concern!" The visitor retreated in silence, but muttered as he walked out the door, "There is no medicine to cure stupidity."[103]

Postscript

This summer, I happened to be in Tokyo to carry out some work. One day, a friend came and showed me Volume II of *New Chronicles of Yanagibashi*, written by the Immortal What-of-it. He said, "The conditions in the Yanagibashi of ten years ago have all been exhaustively treated in the first volume. Of late, there have been some shifts in which spots are hot and which have cooled off, and this volume seeks to record these transformations. I ask that you open the book and apprise yourself of them." I was delighted and gave it a read. Its style is free and uninhibited, its prose is marvelously unique, and what is more, it adopts a tone of jaw-loosening levity to depict the mood of the moment. If people like Yue Guang or Pan Yue could read it, they would certainly cast aside their brushes and inkstones and be left to retreat, staring blankly at the carriage dust.[104] Now then, the Immortal is an old friend, and I am thoroughly familiar with what he is like as a person. And yet looking at this book now, he seems to be like a playboy who dallies in romance, or like a dandy who indulges his desires. As a young man, the Immortal grew up in a nest located within

---

[103] The Japanese saying *baka ni tsukeru kusuri ga nai* appears here as the gloss on a Chinese translation of the epigram: 療愚無藥.
[104] Yue Guang was a noted orator of the Jin, and his contemporary Pan Yue was a skilled poet.

the grove of Confucian learning, pecking on morsels from the garden of literature. In the mornings, he would soar in the domains of Han Yu and Liu Zongyuan; in the evenings, he would alight in the nests of Ouyang Xiu and Su Dongpo. His wings have already borne him aloft in the sky for ninety thousand leagues. I wonder if a work such as this presents us with no more than a single feather from the great Peng bird, a mere quill from the phoenix?

I am weak by nature, and on top of that, was admonished and warned by my strict father, so I have never ventured into the downtown area, and have only learned about these bustling places through hearsay. Now I can rely upon the Immortal's work to arrive at an understanding of the general conditions. Isn't this rather like borrowing the plumes of the Peng bird or the feathers of the phoenix to make a leisurely tour? In the past, the Immortal once wrote a poem on the walls of the hegemonic shogun's offices:

君看千載上	Behold! Over one thousand years ago,
二卵棄干城	For just two eggs, an officer was forsaken.[105]

His righteous indignation can be imagined. But midway along he switched the course of his life, and began to amuse himself by writing comical books such as this one. I wonder if this is the same as Sun Bin getting his legs mutilated, yet still teaching military tactics, or like Sima Qian being tied up in jail and yet writing his *Records of the Grand*

---

[105] The couplet references the story of Gou Bian of Wei, who demanded two eggs from the people he served, and was driven out of office for this minor indiscretion, in spite of the fact that he was a capable general. Ryūhoku was dismissed from his shogunal position in 1863 and is said to have written this on the walls of the government office. A variant version says, "Who would think that one thousand years later / two eggs would be enough to discard an officer" 誰知千載下 二卵捨干城.

Historian?[106] And thus, there is something here about the Immortal's mind that is moving. And you may wonder who is endlessly blathering on about him? That would be me, Crazy Keikakushi of the Eastern Boonies.[107]

The year *kanoto-hitsuji* [1871], the eighth day of planting season, written east of the river in the Cave of Dragon Drool. At the time, the peonies were in full bloom, and the wind filled my curtains with their fragrance.

Calligraphy by Seisen Hakuseki Sanjin In[108]

---

[106] Sun Bin 孫臏 was a military strategist from the Warring States period who had both of his feet amputated by Pang Juan, a fellow strategist who was envious of him. As noted here, he eventually went on to triumph over Pang Juan. The historian Sima Qian had been compiling his *Shi ji* for a decade when he was jailed (and castrated) for his defense of a disfavored official; he continued his work during his incarceration and while later serving as a eunuch, completing the project in 91 BCE.

[107] Both Maeda and Hino state that the identity of the postscript author, Keikakushi 桂閣子 (lit. Mr. Laurel Pavilion), is unknown. I suspect, however, that it might well be Ōkōchi Teruna (1848–1882), a former daimyo of Takasaki domain, who used the sobriquet Keikaku 桂閣. Ryūhoku would have been acquainted with Ōkōchi while the latter was training in Western style military tactics under Charles Chanoine in the mid-1860s. At the time the preface was written in the summer of 1871, Ōkōchi was nominally the governor of Takasaki in the province of Kōzuke, modern-day Gunma, but he was studying English at the Daigaku Nankō (which later became the University of Tokyo). A few months later he would be removed from office when the Meiji government abolished domains and established prefectures. Ōkōchi had deeply Sinological interests and he hosted a salon at his Asakusa residence where He Ruzhang, Huang Zunxian, and many other Qing diplomats who were posted to Japan came to engage in brush-talks with Japanese Sinophiles (Sanetō, esp. 5–7; Lynn, "Huang").

[108] The identity of Seisen Hakuseki Sanjin In 清泉白石山人筠, whose name means roughly "In, the mountain recluse of the clear streams and white stones," is unknown.

New Chronicles of Yanagibashi
Volume III

Preface by the Immortal What-Of-It

"If mere trees have changed like this, how can a man endure it?" These are the words that Huan Xuanwu spoke at Jincheng as he caressed the branch of a willow tree.[1] He was one of the craftiest men of his generation and yet he still had these laments. How much more so must this be true of someone like myself who is full of ardent loves and deep sorrows? When I first wrote *New Chronicles of Yanagibashi*, I was twenty-three years old. The shogunate had not yet lost its military power, and the flourishing of Yanagibashi was truly impressive. When I wrote the second volume, it was the time when the imperial house had established its capital in Tokyo, and everything was being "restored." I was thirty-four years old then. At the time, the women of Yanagibashi were vying in their silken splendor and the sounds of shamisen and flute competed in their charms. It was as though the high spirits of the place had grown even more intense. However, Yanigibashi was already pregnant with the seeds of its decay. Since that moment, already seven cycles of winter and summer have flown by. The scenery of the whole capital city has been shockingly transformed, and I myself have declined. On floral mornings and moonlit evenings, I summon a boat and call for sake, listening to the songs under the red glow of the lamp

---

[1] In the opening of the preface, Ryūhoku refers again to the story of Huan Wen being moved by the passage of time upon noticing how much the willow trees he had planted years earlier had grown (Mather, 60).

and on the azure waters. But the women of the pleasure quarter with whom I was acquainted and could talk about the past have all scattered to the four directions and vanished; none of the pleasures of former times remains. Even if there are one or two new geisha or young girls in training who are worth drinking with, they vanish as quickly as they come, leaving the place desolate. Recently the private *jigoku* prostitutes of Shimabara and Asakusa have been peddling their poison and have invited the misfortune of visits from the police in the middle of the night. The flower and willow world has been dragged in and made an unwitting victim of this new authority. The butterfly dreams of patrons in their fragrant bedchambers have been rudely disturbed, the amorous nests of lovebirds in the river houses have been violated, and the stories appear in the newspapers. Moreover, it seems that such incidents have been most numerous in Yanagibashi. It is no wonder that the district is now so lonely and forlorn, that the aroma of painted glamour has now completely declined. Perhaps the Buddha had the present state of Yanagibashi in mind when he said that "Form is emptiness." Alas, if the suavest place in all of Tokyo has already reached this sad state, then surely the fate of the rest can be surmised. Ah, if a man lacked any sentiment then that would be the end of it, but if he has any feeling, then how could he avoid being depressed at this?

Yesterday, I happened to pass by old Yanagibashi. The sun was just setting. There was a frosty chill in the air, and the cold moon hung in the trees. The willow branches had withered down to just thin threads. All that could be seen were a few remaining leaves sadly adorning the water. I hesitated and could not bring myself to leave. Just then, an old geisha appeared. Her face was wizened and her clothing thin. She bowed to me and asked, "Long ago there was one called the Immortal What-of-it and he wrote the *New Chronicles of Yanagibashi*. It was a record of the quarter's prosperity. But now its decline has reached this sad point. I do not know if the Immortal What-of-it is still alive, or if he is still writing wild words of fiction." Hearing this, I was dejected and the tears came streaming down. I write this as the preface to the third volume.

2 December, Meiji *hinoe-ne* [1876].

Kawada Ōkō says: "There are signs of desolation and decay in a district where the sounds of shamisen strings and bamboo flutes ought to thrive in vigor. How could someone as full of sentiment and passion as the Immortal Ryūhoku fail to be dejected at this? The final passage is splendid."

And: "He wields his brush with a light touch, with feeling and resonance. In sentiments expressed, he recalls Hou Fangyu, and in the style of his brush, he recalls Zhang Shanlai."[2]

---

[2] Kawada Ōkō (1830–1896) was a Sinologist from Okayama who was one of the major scholars involved in compiling national histories in the early Meiji period. He was an associate of Ryūhoku's and contributed poetry and commentary to his literary magazine *Kagetsu shinshi*. Hou Fangyu (1618–1655) was a literatus known for his dauntless and intrepid spirit; Zhang Shanlai refers to Zhang Chao, the author of *Yuchu xinzhi* (New tales of Yuchu), an early Qing collection of stories that was widely read in Japan.

Foreword to *New Chronicles of Yanagibashi Volume III*

Yoda, the Recluse of the Willow Shade[3]

The Immortal What-of-it's work *New Chronicles of Yanagibashi* has appeared, and with it the fame of the courtesans of Tokyo weighs heavy in the world. There are some who scorn these words, saying, "With powdered faces and green eye shadow, they present their charms and sell their favors / A song of the water melody makes the soul fly and the spirit soar. This is the nature of his talent.[4] The Immortal is nothing but a meager student who has fallen on hard times. And what's more, his works are written in the letters of China. How many people are there in this world who can understand them? How can he raise or lower their fame?" Alas, these are not the words of a sophisticated talent. The courtesans of Tokyo: they raise up their great sleeves and drag their long hems, with their coral adornments and tortoise-shell hair ornaments, their appearance is refreshing and their conversations spirited. But when one investigates their day-to-day lives, one finds that they are as avaricious as a wolf and as crafty as a cat. They are as bewitching as foxes and badgers. They are as wily as long-armed monkeys. If you search among them for one who is literarily refined, you shall not find any. If you seek out one among them who is graceful and subtly inviting, you shall be disappointed. Among the courtesans of China, there are those such as Hongfu who discerned Li Jing's potential though he was still impoverished and unknown. Or others like Li Qian who attended on Hu Dan'an while he was sent away in exile.[5]

---

[3] Yoda Gakkai (1833–1909) was an important Meiji period scholar and critic who was a frequent contributor to *Kagetsu shinshi*.
[4] Or perhaps "This is the nature of the courtesans' talents."
[5] The story of Hongfu and Li Jing is mentioned in both volumes of *New Chronicles of*

When it comes to Xue Tao, Su Xiaoxiao, or Li Yi-an, these are women who distinguished themselves as being literarily refined and adept in the ways of love.[6] How can their character be so far above that of the courtesans of our land? But it is not true. Tokyo is a vast place. Its courtesans are numerous. How can there be no such individuals? It is just that no talented literary man has broken away from the pack, seized his brush, and written an evaluation of them. The Immortal has something to contribute here. His spirited and marvelous talents with a brush leave no subtle point un-illuminated. He praises and extols their beauty, while chastising and punishing their faults. He meticulously evaluates their artistic talents, and precisely appraises their demeanors. Burning the rhinoceros horn to bring light to the darkness, he leaves nothing hidden. And so, when it comes to the avaricious wolves and crafty cats, the bewitching charms of foxes and badgers, and the guile of the long-armed monkeys, they cannot hide their tracks. And by the same token, the elegantly refined and graceful women of subtle charms who find themselves mixed up in this dusty world can achieve renown in the quarter. Thereby the appearance of these rouged and powdered ladies has been transformed. Thus, now that this work has appeared,

---

Yanagibashi. Li Qian 黎倩 was a courtesan and the lover of the Song literatus Hu Dan'an 胡澹庵, better known as Hu Quan 胡銓 (1102–1180). After spending ten years in exile, he returned and wrote a couplet praising her that referred to the "delicate whorls in her peach-like cheeks." The incident was made famous because Zhu Xi later wrote an admonitory quatrain that contrasted Hu's ability to transcend corporeal privation during his years of banishment only to reveal his attachment to Li Qian upon his return: 十年浮海一身輕　歸對梨渦卻有情　世上無如人欲險　幾人到此誤平生 "His body light after ten years of floating at sea / Yet on his return, he was moved by the whorls in her cheeks / In this world, there is no greater threat than human desire / How many ruin their lives because of it?" There is a brief discussion of the episode in Wang, 47.

[6] The literarily gifted courtesans Xue Tao and Su Xiaoxiao are mentioned multiple times in the first two volumes. Li Yi-an 李易安, perhaps better known as Li Qingzhao 李清照 (1084–1151), was of the gentry and is often identified as China's most famous female poet.

how can it be idle talk to say that the fame of the courtesans of Tokyo weighs heavy in the world? If there are, in this world of ours, heroic men like Li Jing, or men of integrity like Dan'an, then why shouldn't there also be women like Hongfu and Li Qian? The first and second volumes have already been released. Recently a third volume has been written. How can the rises and falls of the courtesans and the flourishing and withering of the narrow, slanted lanes of the quarter be connected to profit and loss? Upon reflection we shall see that when we consider the matter by applying this logic, there is something here we cannot dismiss entirely. And with that, I render my foreword.

Master Red-cloud says: "There is something significant in this conclusion."[7]

Ryūhoku says: "Mr. Gakkai has said what I wished to say but couldn't. Truly he has the long-nailed hand of Magu and has scratched my itch."[8]

---

[7] The identity of "Master Red-cloud" (Kōun gaishi 紅雲外史) is unknown.
[8] Magu 麻姑 (J. Mako) was a figure of Chinese legend with famously long fingernails. The phrase Ryūhoku uses here is a metaphor for things turning out just as one wishes. Magu's name is also the source of the term for a back-scratcher in Japanese: *magonote*, often assumed to derive from its homophonous sense of "grandchild's hand."

Diary of a Journey to the West

My Euro-American tour began when we cast off our mooring ropes in the ninth month of the fifth year of Meiji (*mizunoe-saru*) [1872],[1] and ended with our return in July of the following year. I saw and heard such a great many things during that time, but the pace of our travel was so hectic that I had no spare time to write them down. At today's late date, nothing can ease my regret that so many of these things passed before my eyes only to disappear like clouds or mist.[2]

---

[1] There are several calendrical systems used in *Diary of a Journey to the West*, but Ryūhoku was basically consistent in dating his entries according to the calendar currently in use in Japan. He started out by using the Japanese lunar calendar but when he learned while in Paris that Japan had announced plans to adopt the Western solar calendar, he immediately switched his entries accordingly, with 11.21 (the 21st day of the 11th month) becoming December 21 (actually, he made the change about ten days before it became official). The mid-journey calendrical switch means that Ryūhoku is referring in this first sentence to starting and ending dates given in two different systems. In other words, "the ninth month" refers to the traditional lunar calendar, and would correspond to roughly October by the Western calendar, whereas what in the original reads "the seventh month" is translated here as "July," for it was the seventh month by the newly adopted Western calendar. Finally, Ryūhoku offers the year using both the Meiji era name (the system of naming years based on the reigning emperor that is still in use today) as well as the corresponding year based upon the Chinese sexagenary cycle (壬 申 in this case, read *mizunoe-saru* or *jinshin*, "water–senior/monkey").

[2] The phrase "clouds and mist passing before one's eyes" 雲烟過眼 would likely have called to mind a passage in Su Dongpo's "Account of the Hall of Precious Artworks" 寶繪堂記: "Even though, when I came upon something that gave me pleasure, I would sometimes keep it, I no longer cared when such things were taken by someone else. Compare them to clouds and mist shapes passing before the eyes or to all the different

Nevertheless, I do have three volumes' worth of journals in which I jotted down a rough outline in pencil during the trip. I recently dug it out from the depths of my trunk, and now I am publishing it here, for my fellow comrades far and wide to see. Needless to say, the quality of the prose is crude, for I have merely described events exactly as they took place. In between, I have also inserted the poor poems I had occasion to compose, without editing or embellishing them in any way. I will certainly have difficulty escaping the dismissive laughter of discerning readers.

Diary of a Journey to the West   Bokujō Gyoshi[3]

It was in the middle of the eighth month of the *mizunoe-saru* year [1872] that Reverend Gennyo, the designated successor to the position of Head Priest for the Eastern branch of Honganji Temple, took it into his mind to sail to India and then on to Europe for a tour of the churches there, and urged me to accompany him. Needless to say, I was delighted with the offer. He had decided on three other men to accompany us on the trip: Ishikawa Shuntai, Matsumoto Hakka, and Seki Shinzō.[4] I was told to set out ahead for Yokohama to make the necessary arrangements:

---

birds that stir the listening ear—of course we rejoice when we encounter them; but when they are gone, our thoughts do not hang on them. Thus books and paintings always give me delight, yet they can do me no damage" (Owen, *Anthology*, 663–664).

[3] Bokujō Gyoshi 墨上漁史 was one of the pen-names under which Ryūhoku wrote. It literally means "fisherman on the Sumida," but *gyoshi* was a fairly common term appended to literary sobriquets at the time, and one that continued to be used by later Meiji literary figures. Mori Ōgai (1862–1922), for example, adopted the term when he first fashioned an identity for himself as a public literary critic, though he eventually distanced himself from the name; see William Tyler's translation of his 1900 essay "Ōgai Gyoshi to wa tarezo" ("Who is Ōgai Gyoshi?") in Rimer, 5–16.

[4] For information about Ryūhoku's fellow travelers, see the Introduction to this volume.

Twelfth day of the ninth month, *kinoe-uma* (14 October by the Western calendar). Fine weather.

I left Tokyo in the morning. For certain reasons, I departed without mentioning anything about the trip to my wife, nor to my friends and relatives, and thus there was no one to see me off. Just as I was setting out, however, I dropped in to visit Mr. Mitsukuri Shūhei,[5] and secretly revealed my plans to him before leaving. He was astonished, but enthusiastically congratulated me and wished me a great voyage. When I arrived in Yokohama, I stayed at the house of Tachibanaya Isobē and made the preparations necessary for travel. Hakka and Shinzō also arrived. We were busy with one thing or another through the night, and could not sleep at all.

09.13. Wednesday. Very fine.

At twelve o'clock, the Reverend came with Shuntai to Yokohama, and we went to the house of Nishimura Uhei to relax for a while.[6] After sharing a drink together, we said our goodbyes, and at seven o'clock took advantage of the light of the bright moon to board the French mail steamer *Godavéry*.[7] This evening is the auspicious night of the later moon.[8] I wrote two quatrains.

---

[5] Mitsukuri Shūhei 箕作秋坪 (1825–1886) was a scholar of Western subjects originally from Tsuyama domain. He had traveled abroad on two of the shogunal missions to Europe in the 1860s, and Ryūhoku had become friendly with him through their mutual contacts with the scholar of Dutch studies Katsuragawa Hoshū (Jiromaru, 34). After the Restoration, Mitsukuri opened the Sansha gakusha 三叉学舎, an academy that taught Western subjects and was (along with Fukuzawa Yukichi's Keiō gijuku) a significant center of learning in the first decade of Meiji. Mitsukuri continued his work as an educator for the rest of his life, and was also an active participant in the Meirokusha, an important early Meiji intellectual society. Two of Mitsukuri's sons had been sent to study in England in the 1860s and 1870s, and Ryūhoku met up with one of them, Kikuchi Dairoku, while visiting London.

[6] Nishimura Uhei was a Yokohama-based merchant who engaged in the silk trade.

[7] The 1875–1876 edition of *Lloyd's Register* lists the "Godavery" as a 280-horse-power, 1423-gross-ton screw steamer built in 1863 and owned by Compagnie des Messageries

149

誰知豪氣掣鯨鯢　一曲離歌酒到臍　好是橫濱明月夕　片帆直向仏蘭西

Who can fathom our bold spirits, harnessing the mighty whales?
We sing a song of farewell, sake warming our bellies.
How fine the bright moon over Yokohama Bay this evening!
Our little sail aloft, we head straight for France.

右望巴黎城上月　左瞻龍動埠頭雲　快哉萬里風濤上　要作人間得意文

I will gaze right at the moon above the city of Paris;
I will look left at the clouds over the pier in London.
What a thrill to journey ten thousand leagues through wind and waves!
I shall write a journal to capture these feelings.

There are many Japanese traveling with us on this journey. There is one member of the nobility, Anegakōji Kimitomo,[9] and eight public officials: Kōno Togama, Kishira Kaneyasu, Tsuruta Akira, Kawaji Toshiyoshi, Namura Taizō, Numa Morikazu, Masuda Katsunori, and Inoue Kowashi.[10] In addition, there are three other Japanese

---

Maritimes (which in its former incarnation, Messageries Impériales, had established regular service to Yokohama in 1865). Like the second ship Ryūhoku boards, the *Mei Kong*, the *Godavéry* was named after a great river: the Godavari that runs east–west across the Indian subcontinent. There is a photograph of the ship in Lanfant, 39; for further details on its trips between Hong Kong and Yokohama, see Sawa, 443.

[8] "The night of the later moon" (commonly called Jūsan'ya 十三夜, or Nochinotsuki 後の月) occurs on 09.13, a date that had been codified as an especially fine night for moon-viewing in Japan since the tenth century. Here, Ryūhoku uses the phrase *keika* 繼華 (literally meaning "succeeding splendor") to refer to the evening, the idea perhaps being that Jūsan'ya was successor to the more celebrated moon-viewing that took place annually on 08.15.

[9] A child of the nobility, Anegakōji Kimitomo 姉小路公義 (1859–1905) had been sent to study in Germany. He later served as a secretary in the Japanese embassy in the United States, and also as a consular officer in Germany. Some sources give the alternative reading Anenokōji Kintomo for his name.

[10] These eight men, Kōno Togama 河野敏鎌 (1844–1895), Kishira Kaneyasu 岸良兼養 (1837–1883), Tsuruta Akira 鶴田皓 (1836–1888), Kawaji Toshiyoshi 川路利良 (1834–1879), Namura Taizō 名村泰藏 (1840–1907), Numa Morikazu 沼間守一

passengers: Honma Kōsō of Ugo,[11] Matsuda Masahisa from Saga,[12] and Nitta Shizumaru of Myōdō prefecture.[13] Including our group of five, that makes for a total of seventeen.[14]

09.14. Wednesday. Very fine.
The sky had already started to become light when our mail steamer untied its mooring ropes. The wind and waves were quite strong today,

---

(1843–1890), Masuda Katsunori 益田克德 (1852–1903), and Inoue Kowashi 井上毅 (1843–1895), were all officials in the Ministry of Justice who were traveling to Europe to investigate its legal institutions. Many of them contributed to the development of Japan's legal infrastructure upon their return; for example, Tsuruta became a prominent legal scholar who, along with Namura, collaborated with French legal advisors to draft Japan's new legal codes (Tsuruta Tōru, esp. 123–170). Kawaji (who also read his name Toshinaga) was the creator of Japan's modern police system. Masuda, however, left civil service for a career in business, especially insurance. Ironically, the group also included Inoue Kowashi, who became the architect of the early Meiji state's draconian press laws, and whom Ryūhoku would specifically target in a satirical piece that landed him in jail. This group is sometimes viewed as a supplementary contingent of the Iwakura Mission. Most of its members were from Satsuma, Tosa, and Saga, but the group also included former shogunal official Numa Morikazu, who went on to become an important journalist and activist in the popular rights movement after retiring from public service.

[11] Honma Kōsō 本間耕曹 (1842–1909) later represented Yamagata in the Japanese Diet. An advocate of railroads and advisor for police agency modernization, Honma was apparently fond of making reference to his experiences and observations while abroad, a tendency that earned him the nickname "the Diet Member from Europe."

[12] Saga native Matsuda Masahisa 松田正久 (1845–1914) was encouraged to study in France by his teacher, Nishi Amane. Though urged by his army sponsors to pursue military studies, Matsuda became more interested in law and political science. Upon his return to Japan, he worked briefly as an army translator before becoming a journalist and participating in the popular rights movement. Beginning in the late 1890s and continuing into the Taishō period, he served in the cabinets of several prime ministers.

[13] According to Tomita Hitoshi, Nitta Shizumaru 新田静丸 (b. 1850) was a student from Myōdō (by which the former domain of Awa was temporarily known before becoming Tokushima) who had been sent to study military subjects in Paris. The editors of the *Shin Nihon koten bungaku taikei Meijihen* edition of Ryūhoku's *Kōsei nichijō* (hereafter abbreviated *Meijihen*) give a birth date of 1852, but also suggest that "Nitta Shizumaru" may be some sort of alias used by Nitta Tadazumi 新田忠純 (1856-1931), who was sent to France to study military subjects in 1872.

[14] I follow the editors of *Meijihen* in correcting what seems to be a typographical error here; in the published version of the *Diary*, Ryūhoku refers to the Higashi Honganji group as "our group of three."

and so Hakka and Shinzō both lay in bed and did not leave their rooms. In the afternoon, I gazed at Mount Fuji.

09.15. Thursday. Fine.
The wind grew increasingly violent, and hardly anyone ventured into the dining hall. I ate a Western apple, which was large and tasted quite delicious.

09.16. Friday. Fine.
The winds ceased. We navigated a course that brought us close to Hyūga and Satsuma. I gazed out at Kaimondake, and it reminded me of Mount Fuji.[15] When we lost sight of this mountain, it meant that we had completely left behind our homeland, a realization that made everyone gaze back downheartedly for a long time. At night, I composed a poem.

回頭故國在何邊　休唱賴翁天草篇　一髮青山看不見　半輪明月大於船
I wonder, as I crane my head around, where is my homeland?
I can't very well recite Rai San'yō's poem at Amakusa[16]—
Looking for that "single strand of blue" land, I don't see a thing!
Only the bright half moon, looming larger than our ship.

---

[15] Hyūga refers to modern-day Miyazaki prefecture, and Satsuma to modern-day Kagoshima. Kaimondake is a mountain rising 922 meters over the southeast tip of the Satsuma peninsula. Its resemblance to Mount Fuji has earned it the nickname "the Fuji of Satsuma."
[16] This is a reference to the celebrated poem "Anchored off the coast of Amakusa" 泊天草洋 by Rai San'yō 賴山陽 (1780–1832). One of the most popular Japanese *kanshi*, it begins dramatically with the poet's exuberant speculation that the coastline he glimpses faintly on the horizon might be the Chinese mainland: "Is it a cloud? Or land? Wu? Or Yue? / Where sea and sky meet, a single strand of blue" 雲耶山耶吳耶越 水天髣髴青一髮. For a full translation, see Shirane, *Early Modern Japanese Literature*, 919–920.

09.17. Saturday. Still clear.

At four o'clock, a squall arose suddenly, causing the whole ship to toss violently. I was not even able to stand up, and there was nothing to do but lie down in my room.

何物半宵掀我牀　乍天乍地奈飄颻　記他前夕雲容惡　也值陽侯一夜狂
  What is it that jerks my bed up in the middle of the night?
  Thrown skyward then down again, helplessly blown about!
  I remember the clouds last night looked ominous.
  Now I know we're in for an evening of Yang Hou's wrath.[17]

艙外雞鳴燭影殘　蠻奴捧水白陶盤　無端驚覺家山夢　撼枕濤聲客膽寒
  The cock crows outside the cabin, but the night lanterns are still lit;
  A native servant boy brings water in a porcelain basin.
  Without warning, I am torn away from dreams of home;
  The crash of waves jolts my pillow, bringing a chill to my soul.

09.18. Sunday. Overcast, rainy. Hazy and dark, fierce winds.

Most of us on board lay down in our rooms. At noon, the skies cleared, and the winds also ceased. This evening, the moon was bright. One of the ship's crew said that we were passing by Taiwan. I strained my eyes and look hard, but there was nothing to see. I have completed two quatrains since morning.

書在筐中酒在瓶　心安不覺度滄溟　艙窗眠足閑無事　坐聽朝餐第一鈴
  With my trunk full of books, and plenty of sake in the bottle,
  My mind is at ease, hardly aware that we are crossing the vast blue sea.

---

[17] Yang Hou 陽侯 (J. Yōkō) is the name of a sea deity, particularly associated with tempestuous waves.

I can sleep in the cabin to my heart's content; all is quiet, no distractions.
Sitting in stillness, I hear the first bell announce breakfast.

故山日夜望儂不　儂自出家多客愁　誰識風濤湃湃夕　夢飛三徑菊花秋
I wonder if those back home think about me day and night?
Since leaving, I have often felt a traveler's melancholy.
Can they imagine how it feels tonight as the wind and waves roil?
In dreams, I fly to the chrysanthemum paths of my fall hermitage.[18]

09.19. Monday. Pleasant, fine.
When I arose at dawn, I saw for the first time several Chinese fishing ships. As I gazed out to our right, I could see Xiamen lying off in the distance.

唯看漁舟數葉翻　茫々無際碧乾坤　按圖海客呼吾語　一抹雲山是厦門
All I can see are a few fishing boats: undulating leaves
on the limitless cerulean vastness of sea and sky.
Another passenger consults the map and calls to me:
"See the single stroke of land in the clouds over there?—that's Amoy."

At night, I could make out two islands rising to the right side of the ship. When I asked someone about them, he said: "Those are the Brother Islands."[19]

---

[18] The "chrysanthemum paths" of the poem serve as synecdoche for Ryūhoku's home in Tokyo, the Shōkikusō ("Pine and Chrysanthemum Cottage"). Ryūhoku was inspired to give his post-Restoration dwelling this name by phrases in "On returning home" and other works by Six Dynasties reclusive poet Tao Yuanming (372?–427).
[19] The editors of *Meijihen* identify the "Brother Islands" 兄弟島 (Ch. *Xiongdidao*) as Dadeng and Xiaodeng, islands in the Xiamen harbor (255). However, I suspect that Ryūhoku refers instead to the Xiongdidao islands located further offshore and slightly further along in his journey: south of Guleitou and northeast of Nan'ao Island (at +23° 32', +117° 41').

09.20. Tuesday. Fine.
I awoke this morning to find the tall mountain peaks of China at hand, right in front of my eyes. Everyone cried out in excitement. We reached Hong Kong at eleven o'clock. The mouth of the port is narrow, and so the ship had to twist along a crooked path as we entered. The harbor is indeed a splendid scene. In the afternoon, we boarded a lighter and went ashore. We gave the boat captain one shilling (British currency). We walked through the city streets, and strolled leisurely through a public park atop a mountain. The flowers and grasses, bamboo and trees were refreshingly pretty and lovely. After a drink at the Hotel d'Europe, we left and visited a streetside tavern called Santinwon, or "New Heavenly Harmony."[20] On the wall was a sign that read, "Our honorable customers are responsible for monitoring their personal belongings." We tried some of the tavern's noodles and fruits. The persimmons and tangerines are slightly different from those back home. In Hong Kong, one Western silver dollar is worth one thousand *wen* in Chinese money, but the funny thing is that they make no distinction between the Xianfeng and Tongzhi periods; large and small, the coins are all treated the same.[21] The locals ride around in palanquins. These have extremely long handles that strong young men carry on their shoulders. Though this is a remarkably lively and thriving place, I can't help but find the craftiness and noisiness of the commoners here rather

---

[20] The public park atop the mountain is surely Victoria Peak. Contemporary guidebooks to Hong Kong describe the Hotel d'Europe on Hollywood Road as offering the finest accommodations; a few years earlier, Tokugawa Akitake had visited the hotel and wrote about it twice in his French diary: "… nous sommes descendus à l'hotel de l'Europe …" (Miyachi, 42).

[21] Ryūhoku later published several numismatic treatises, and his attention to local currencies is apparent throughout the diary. Here, he refers to copper *wen* coins minted in China's Xianfeng (1851–1861) and Tongzhi (1862–1874) eras, the size of which had fluctuated widely during this period because of inflation caused by the Taiping Rebellion.

loathsome. The port's latitude is north 22°7' and I am surprised to find myself suddenly amid this burning heat.

枕水樓臺萬點燈　郵船估舶喚相譍　海南九月猶炎熱　爭買銀盤幾片氷
In the tall buildings along the waterfront, ten thousand lights;
The passenger and trade vessels call and answer one other.
Here in the southern seas, the ninth month is still fiery hot;
Everyone races to buy a few pieces of ice from a silver bowl.

層々鉅閣競繁華　百貨如邱人語譁　此際誰來賣秋色　幽蘭冷菊幾盆花
Climbing story after story, the great buildings vie for splendor;
A mountain of goods for sale amid the noisy welter of human voices.
Just then, someone comes by selling autumn flowers;
Elegant orchids and soothing chrysanthemums fill several trays.

Fearful of the great number of thieves in Hong Kong, everyone has returned to the ship and gone to sleep. Today I entrusted a letter home to the French physician Sabor.[22]

09.21. Wednesday. Fine.
When I got up this morning, I assembled my luggage and prepared to transfer to the next ship. I ventured ashore again with the group this

---

[22] Ryūhoku changes ships the following day, and the *Godavéry* returned to Yokohama, hence his decision to entrust the letter home to the French physician, whose identity is unknown. It is possible Ryūhoku encountered Paul Ludovic Savatier (1830–1891), who served as a military physician in Yokosuka from the 1860s and also carried out extensive research on Japanese flora, gathering several thousand plant samples for the Museum of Natural History in Paris (Nishino and Polak, 136–161). Savatier had taken a trip to France in February 1872 and would have been on his way back to Japan at roughly the same time Ryūhoku was headed toward France. On the other hand, some records suggest Savatier returned to Japan about two months after Ryūhoku's encounter with "Sabor" in Hong Kong.

morning. We went to the Taiping Shan Water and Moon Temple, which is dedicated to Kannon.[23] We met six Japanese who are lodging at Number 12 Aberdeen Street: Mizuno Jun from Aichi,[24] Komaki Masanari, Ijichi Suekata, and Takahashi Shin'ichi from Kagoshima,[25] Kuwabara Kaihei from Kōchi, and Igawa Totsurō from Shimane.[26] We

---

[23] The "Taiping Shan Water and Moon Temple" 太平山水月宮 is located in the Sheung Wan area, near the intersection of Taiping Shan Street and Pound Lane; it is adjacent to the Kwong Fuk Ancestral Hall 廣福義祠, one of Hong Kong's oldest temples.

[24] Originally from Nagoya, Mizuno Jun 水野遵 (1850–1900) was sent to Shanghai to study English in 05.1871 and subsequently entered a middle school in Hong Kong. He later served as a translator on multiple Japanese missions to Taiwan between 1873 and 1874. After returning to Japan, he spent several years as an official in the Ministry of Education and the Ministry of Justice. At the end of his career, he was the Civilian Head of Affairs under Japan's colonial administration in Taiwan.

[25] These three Satsuma men had all been sent to study English in Hong Kong. Komaki Masanari 小牧昌業 (1843–1922) had pursued Confucian studies under Shionoya Tōin (1809–1867) and poetry with Mukōyama Kōson (1826–1897) in Edo before being sent to Hong Kong in 1871. Upon his return, Komaki served in several high-level posts at home, including Cabinet Secretary and Secretary to the Prime Minister, as well as several appointments abroad. Little is known about Ijichi Suekata 伊地知季方. The third Satsuma man, Takahashi Shin'ichi 高橋新一, is identified in Tomita Hitoshi's dictionary of overseas Japanese travelers as the younger brother of English language scholar Takahashi Shinkichi 高橋新吉 (1843–1918). The elder Shinkichi studied English in Nagasaki and is best known for the part he played in editing an important early dictionary, the *Wayaku eijirin* 和訳英辞林, first published in 1869. He studied in the United States briefly and later received the support of the Japanese government to study in China. Upon his return to Japan, he took up a position in the Nagasaki customs office, later serving as Japanese Consul in New York, and then becoming president of the Kyushu Railroad. The editors of *Meijihen* make the plausible conjecture that Ryūhoku's "Shin'ichi" is actually a mistake for "Shinkichi." While information on "Shin'ichi" is sketchy, there is some reason to think that Ryūhoku did in fact meet Shin'ichi in Hong Kong, for this is the name recorded by another passenger on Ryūhoku's ship, Inoue Kowashi (338). Moreover, it seems that the elder Shinkichi was still studying in the United States; about nine months later, Takasaki Masakaze noted in his diary that Takahashi Shinkichi and Nakai Hiroshi had come from Boston to meet him in New York (355).

[26] Both Tosa native Kuwabara Kaihei 桑原戒平 (b. 1844) and Matsue-born Igawa Totsurō 井川訥郎 (b. 1847) had been sent by their domains to study English in Hong Kong in 1871. Kuwabara later served in the Imperial Ministry, was involved in the Shinpūren rebellion of 1876, and went on to work in Japan's colonial government on Taiwan.

stopped in at the Ying Wa College,[27] purchased some books and had a look at the typesetting department. As we were walking along the street, we came across a theatrical hall with a sign mounted overhead reading "Shing Ping Theatre." We ventured inside to have a look, and found the interior extremely magnificent and beautiful. The actors' voices were strikingly high pitched. The main piece that they were performing was entitled "Fervent Loyalty and Filial Piety," before which they performed "Fight Between a Fox and a Ghost"; these two were combined into a single program.[28] I found myself somewhere midway between being able to understand it and not. We also went to a restaurant called Fook Hing Kü, where we dined on a duck meat stew and a poached grouper, drank wine made from glutinous rice, and finished off our feast with fruit and rice.[29] The bill for all seven of us was four and a half dollars. It was quite a shock to discover that there was a toilet on the building's roof. This must be the kind of thing that marks the Chinese as unsanitary.[30] At the end of the day, I first returned to our original ship

---

[27] The Ying Wa College 英華書院 was initially founded in 1818 as the Anglo–Chinese College in Malacca by Rev. Robert Morrison (1782–1834) of the London Missionary Society. With the goal of spreading Christianity in China, the school trained students in both Chinese and Western subjects. The school came to Hong Kong in 1843 under the stewardship of Rev. James Legge, and there it continued as an educational institution while also serving as a center for translation and publishing. Ryūhoku would have known about the bookstore prior to his arrival, either from seeing Ying Wa publications or from reading earlier Japanese travelers' reports of their visits to Ying Wa in the 1860s and 1870s.

[28] In the Chinese popular theatre tradition at the time, it was customary to perform a short episode or excerpt prior to the main piece. I would like to thank Sun Chongtao for explaining this performance practice. Period maps show the Shing Ping Theatre as a large building located near Possession Point, at the intersection of Hollywood Road and Gap Street.

[29] The 1881 *Chronicle and Directory for China* includes the Fook Hing Kü in its list of "Eating House Keepers"; the restaurant was located at 74 Bonham strand (243).

[30] Descriptions of this sort are common in the overseas travelogues of Ryūhoku's contemporaries and immediate predecessors. In reference to Chinese people, Ryūhoku uses the word *Shinajin* 支那人. Based on a very old Sanskrit name for China, the term was becoming increasingly common in the nineteenth century. While sometimes

and then transferred to another packet vessel: the *Mei Kong*.³¹ Our new ship has nearly twice the size and splendor of the *Godavéry*, and the three meals they serve are very exquisite too.

09.22. Thursday. Clear skies, heavy winds.
We set sail at twelve o'clock. Since we heard that thieves are rampant in Hong Kong, we spent our two nights here on ship, without venturing to stay in a hotel on shore. Today, as the hour of our departure drew close, I was seized with a strong feeling of yearning for the place. After navigating our way around the hundreds of small islands off shore, we entered the open ocean. At dinner, we had ice cream, which was quite delicious. Moreover, since it is so swelteringly hot, the kitchen staff took turns pulling a rope to propel fan blades that blew a breeze over our seats. There aren't words to describe the refreshing pleasure. Today I was able to write two poems.

昌黎驅鱷已千秋　驚見巨魚波上浮　回首洋雲渺無際　天邊何處是潮州
  A thousand years since Han Yu drove out the crocodiles;³²
  Startled, I catch a glimpse of a giant fish rising to the waves' surface.
  Craning my head around, all I can see is endless sea and sky;
  Which place out there on the horizon, I wonder, is Chaozhou?

---

regarded as derogatory, it was also used by those who sought a neutral term for China as but one nation among others (Fogel, 66–76).

³¹ The *Mei Kong* was still quite a new ship, which might account for some of Ryūhoku's surprise at its splendor. *Lloyd's Register* for 1875–1876 lists it as a five-hundred-horsepower iron screw barque built in 1870 and owned by Messageries Maritimes.

³² Ryūhoku refers here to "Text for the Crocodiles," written by Tang literatus Han Yu (768–824) during his tenure as prefect of Chaozhou, when the area was tormented by crocodiles. In this amusing piece, Han Yu attempts to persuade the predatory reptiles with a high-toned and well-reasoned argument (not to mention the promise of military force) that they should return to their proper lodgings in the sea; for a translation, see Owen, *End*, 57–59.

亞剌羅山在那邊　風濤淼漫碧涵天　艙間併載牛羊豕　彷彿千秋諾亞船

In which direction does Mount Ararat lie?
Wind-blown waves stretch out forever, suffusing the sky with sapphire.
Aboard ship, we share space with cows, sheep, and pigs;
Just like Noah's ark from thousands of years ago.[33]

09.23. Friday.
I can't see even the slightest hairline hint of land. Today, I took a bath in cold water. In the afternoon, it began to rain only to clear up all of a sudden. The temperature at night is a scorching 87 degrees.

四邊無復一螺青　雲影濤聲數日程　巴里賈人龍動女　幾多生面已諳名

On all four sides, there is still not the faintest trace of blue mountains.
Days pass with just the sight of clouds and the sound of waves.
Among the passengers are Parisian merchants and women of London;
So many new faces, and I have already memorized their names.

午餐罷處水風徐　茶味可人微醉餘　浪靜行舟平似席　滿窓晴日寫郷書

When we finish with lunch, a gentle breeze comes over the water;
The flavor of tea is especially fine when one is slightly tipsy.
Waves calm, the ship glides as though across a mat;
Clear sunlight fills my window as I write a letter home.

---

[33] James Hepburn's translation of the Bible did not appear in Japan until after Ryūhoku's trip abroad; however, the story of Noah's ark was available in several other sources in the late Tokugawa period. Moreover, both the journal of Ryūhoku's traveling companion Matsumoto Hakka and Ryūhoku's own accounting record of their journey show that the Higashi Honganji group purchased copies of *Jiu yue quan shu* and *Xin yue quan shu*, Chinese translations of the Old and New Testament respectively, while touring the Ying Wa College in Hong Kong (Meiji gonen, 447).

天氣和時人快然 風濤起日只貪眠 誰知一笑一顰裏 經過南洋程幾千
> At times when the weather is pleasant, people are at ease;
> But on days when the wind and waves pick up, all one craves is sleep.
> Hard to believe that as we pass the hours, now a smile, now a frown,
> We are traveling through thousands of leagues on the Southern Seas.

09.24. Saturday. Very fine.
To the right, I spotted a range of mountain peaks, and one of the crew informed me that it is Annam. According to the Western calendar, today is October 26.

一鳥不翔雲水間 驚瀾吞吐碧屛顏 離家萬里安南海 無復風光似故山
> Not a single bird soars between the clouds and sea;
> The surging waves swallow up and spit out the blue mountain crags.
> I find myself in the Annam Sea, ten thousand miles away from home,
> With nothing about this scenery to recall the old mountains back there.

09.25. Sunday. Fine.
With neither wind nor waves, I have forgotten I'm on a ship. At eleven o'clock, I could make out a lighthouse and some houses in the distance, and I knew that we had drawn near to the port of Saigon. At noon, we entered the mouth of the port.[34] On both banks were green trees and dense, deep grasses. The landscape was just like a painting. Here and there grew giant fern palms. I also saw a group of gibbons playing together. Around the settled areas, the ground was lush green with rice seedlings, like Japan in the fourth or fifth month. Though the river is a

---

[34] When Ryūhoku writes about entering "the mouth of the port," he means entering the tributary of the Mekong that they follow upstream to the port of Saigon. The "Lancang River" mentioned later in the entry is the Chinese name for the upper reaches of the Mekong.

large one, the current is gentle and the water is murky. As we twisted and turned our way against the current, I asked the boatmen the river's name. One of them told me it is the Lancang River, and another said it is the lower tributary of the Cambodian River. I'm a little vague on the geography, so I will have to consult a map for the details some other day. At four o'clock, we reached Saigon, the capital of Annam, which has recently become French territory. The people here are racially related to the Chinese. The men and women all have blackened teeth. I wonder if perhaps it is because they eat betelnut. The roof tiles on their houses and huts are all red. For the first time in my life, I saw a grove of palm trees. Today, the thermometer read 94 degrees; apparently this port lies just 10°17' from the equator. At night, when I lay down to sleep on board the ship, the drone of insects on either side of the river filled my ears as I watched fireflies flitting about chaotically. They were immense! There were lots of mosquitoes and ticks, too.

針路縈回入港門　長流一帶不知源　夾舟雲樹奇於畫　誘得征人到塞昆
    We weave a winding course as our ship enters the port gates;
    A single long strip of flowing water, who knows its source?[35]
    The trees on either side of the ship rise to the clouds—more alluring
        than a painting;
    An enchanting scene to tempt the traveler as he arrives in Saigon.

夜熱侵人夢易醒　白沙青草滿前汀　故園應是霜降節　驚看蠻螢大似星
    Lingering heat invades my mind tonight, easily rousing me from dreams;
    White sands and green grasses spread across the waterfront.

---

[35] Ryūhoku may be playing here with the double meaning of "who knows its source" 不知源—saying that the Mekong is such a tremendous river that its origins are unfathomable, but also hinting at the earlier episode in which he asked the French pilots what the river's source was and they had two different answers.

Back home, it would be the season where frost settles on the ground;[36] I gaze in wonder at the exotic fireflies as big as stars.

09.26. Monday. Fine.
I got up early today and went ashore with Mr. Ishikawa and Mr. Seki. The city was noisy with the shouting of vendors selling meat and vegetables in the market. The earth of the city streets has a reddish color and is just like roofing tile. I imagine this is because the sunlight is so fierce here. However, there are also places where trees grow densely and luxuriantly, which is the perfect thing for a traveler trying to avoid the hot sun. Most of the trees planted along either side of the street are bean trees. Around peoples' houses, morning glory has been planted almost from the tips of the eaves to the foot of the fence, and dewdrops dribble down from the flowers. Their gardens are full of banana plants, all in full fruit, which grow one right after the next. I noticed that many of the stores sell pottery of the type known as Cochin ware, but even so, it looked like there were rather few truly exquisite pieces. There was a tavern called the Hall of Celestial Fragrance, where we stopped for a drink and a meal of noodles with strips of duck and boiled clams. After we left, I went to the post office to send a letter home. The cost for mailing a letter is one "franc." As the hour drew close to noon, we returned to the ship, fearing that we would be no match for the oppressive heat. Everyone was fatigued from the sweltering weather. Even though we raised anchor at nine o'clock tonight, we still haven't reached the mouth of the port. The tide has gone out, leaving the ship to stand still.

---

[36] Sōkōsetsu 霜降節, "the season when frost settles on the ground," typically begins during the middle of the ninth lunar month, or around October 23 in the Western calendar.

09.27. Tuesday. Fine.
At eleven o'clock, the tide came in and the ship began to move, and by two o'clock we entered the open sea. We enjoyed cool weather today, making us feel refreshed. The thermometer read 81 degrees. I gave a silver dollar to one of the ship's boys, and savored the great pleasure of bathing in warm water.

09.28. Wednesday. Fine.
We had neither wind nor waves today. The heat became extreme again, the thermometer climbing to 94 degrees. Clearly we are approaching the equator.

09.29. [Thursday.] Rainy.
At eleven o'clock, I made out a hairsbreadth of blue off to our right: the Malacca Peninsula. Today the weather was intermittently rainy and clear. At two o'clock, I gazed out to the left of the ship and saw a lighthouse standing atop a small island. The land jutting out in a line behind it is Sumatra, which lies across from the Malacca Peninsula. This strait is the port of Singapore.

南邊麻陸北蘇門　地勢蜿蜒兩蟒奔　奔到洋中不相接　雙頭對處萬帆翻
> The Malacca Peninsula to the south, and to the north, Sumatra;[37]
> The land contorts this way and that, like the writhing of twin serpents.
> They wriggle all the way down into the water, and yet they never touch;
> Where their two heads face off, ten thousand sails flutter.

At six o'clock, we reached the port. It lies only 1°17' from the equator, and is called "New Port." There are not so many houses, but there are

---

[37] The geography in this section is confused; the Malacca Peninsula is located north of Sumatra.

many coal storage buildings, facilities built to service the packet vessels that call here. As we entered the port, I surveyed the view on all four sides and found the scenery quite splendid. The ship can put in anchor right at the bank, which makes it very easy to go ashore. Naked children from the harbor-side approached us in little boats shaped like half-melons, selling patterned shells and other sundries. When a passenger from the ship tossed a small silver coin into the water, they dove in, snatched it, and floated back up, rather like frogs. The locals have sun-darkened faces and walk around in bare feet. They drape printed cloth garments around themselves, leaving half of their bodies exposed, just like Arhats in a painting. Those who are a little wealthier all appear to be Muslims, and they wear hats shaped like little buckets. Even the women were barefoot and exposed their shoulders. Some had pierced their noses and hung golden hoops from them. It was all quite bizarre! As the sun was setting, Mr. Ishikawa and I hired a horse-drawn carriage to take us to the city center of Singapore (that is, the Old Port). The distance was just one *ri*, and we paid one dollar for a round trip fare.[38] This city is clearly more bustling and prosperous than Saigon, but since it is difficult to go sightseeing at night, we had the carriage turn around.

10.01. Friday.
I got up at dawn, and again went to the Old Port downtown with several of my companions. The grasses and flowers lining the road were delicately charming and lovely, and the earth had a reddish color. The houses we passed along the streets were those of the natives and the Chinese, who live intermingled.[39] I understand that there are many

---

[38] Conventionally, one Japanese *ri* is 2.44 miles (much longer than a standard Chinese *li*), but Ryūhoku elsewhere uses the unit *ri* to mean Western nautical miles.
[39] Perhaps these references to Chinese and Malays living together were inspired by

immigrants from Guangdong and Fujian here. We went into a restaurant called New Lotus Fragrance, where we ate noodles with strips of chicken and drank rice wine. In front of one shop, there were *bonsai* trees lined up on display, most of them potted in Cochin ware. There was a sign reading, "Look with your eyes but do not touch with your hands. We ask for your understanding." After we returned to the ship, Mr. Seki was overcome with agony, having been stricken by the heat and seized with abdominal pains. Everybody was flustered and wanted to get some medicine for him, but after a little while, he recovered. Today, Mr. Numa Morikazu had his wallet stolen by a thief. Thieves are especially active when a mail steamer is anchored in the port, and so one must be on utmost alert. Some of the locals came down to the harbor-side to sell parrots, long-tailed monkeys, and the like. There was no shortage of exotic birds and curious beasts, and the prices for that matter did not seem to be terribly exorbitant either.[40]

幾個蠻奴聚港頭　排陳土産語啾々　巻毛黒面脚皆赤　笑殺賣猴人似猴

So many natives throng the harbor front;
As they spread out their handicrafts to sell, they chatter shrilly.
Curly hair, dark faces, and feet all bare;
I nearly die laughing at the monkey dealer with his simian air.

---

interest in the analogous domestic issue of whether foreigners should be allowed to live and travel outside of certain designated areas in Japan. This was a key point of contention in Japan's negotiations with foreign powers during the 1870s (see, e.g., Pyle, 101).

[40] Given Ryūhoku's background as a Confucian scholar, it is perhaps worth noting here his frequent use of the phrase "exotic birds and curious beasts" 珍禽奇獸 (J. *kinkin kijū*) as a marker of the alterity of his surroundings. The phrase comes from *The Book of Documents*: "If dogs and horses are not suited to the land's conditions, they cannot be raised; exotic birds and curious beasts cannot be kept within the state" 犬馬非其土性不畜珍禽奇獸不育于國.

We left the port at five o'clock, and by seven o'clock I could see a lighthouse to my right. At nine o'clock, we encountered great winds and a downpour of rain. Thunder roared, resounding across the water, but the ship itself hardly rocked at all. The Indian Ocean seems to be quite calm, with only gentle waves: truly it deserves to be called a paradise for the sea-borne traveler. This evening, I had a pleasant encounter with the Dutch official Mr. Kok; he is a warm and kind gentleman.

10.02. Saturday. Overcast skies.
The air had a slight coolness that felt pleasant on my skin. I could see the Malacca Peninsula off to our right. The terrain twisted around like a writhing snake, and I stared at it for a long time. It was only at one o'clock in the afternoon that it finally vanished into the clouds and mist. There is a passenger who has brought on board with him a small leopard from Singapore that he has locked inside a cage. He told me, "I'm delivering it to a museum in the French capital of Paris." At dinner, we ate "anana," which tasted truly delicious.[41] When night fell, a thunderstorm brought coolness to the air. It seems that in these equatorial regions, the perpetually heavy night rains wash away the heat of the afternoon. We must truly be grateful that the Creator so lovingly protects mankind. Today, I read *A Record of a Raft Voyage* (written by Bin Chun of the Qing), which I borrowed from one of my fellow passengers. This book is sufficient to serve as an expert guide.[42]

---

[41] The fruit Ryūhoku enjoys here is the pineapple. The term "ananas" (or "anana") entered English and French from the Peruvian "nanas." The term is still used in modern French and in the scientific name for the fruit: *Ananassa sativa*.
[42] The book mentioned here is *Chengcha biji* 乘槎筆記, written by Bin Chun 斌椿 and concerned with his 1866 voyage as part of one of the first Qing diplomatic missions to Europe. Ryūhoku was likely reading the edition that had just been published in Tokyo with *kunten* reading marks.

10.03. Sunday. The weather is unstable, alternatively overcast and clear. At 8:20 we encountered a sudden rain shower, but it passed us by. Today I could still see Sumatra to the left, which shows how big the island is. At the point of the cape is the city of Aceh. Today, we traveled 437 nautical miles, and I am told we are fifteen hundred nautical miles from Ceylon.

10.04. Monday. Clear.
We have left the strait completely behind, bringing us into the Indian Ocean. The appearance of the water was like oil. I looked around in all directions, but I could not see land anywhere. Though there was no wind, the ship moved along, and at twelve o'clock, we passed through the 5° northern latitude. We've come 268 nautical miles since noon yesterday. There is a Dutch officer on board who has spent three years in Java, and is now returning to his home country. He inspired me to compose the following poem:

拉兒拉婦太多情　試問移家何處行　印度三秋于役畢　今年歸向海牙城(ハアグ)
　Bringing child and wife in hand, he brims with sentiment;
　Where, I ask, will you move your family now?
　"Three autumns passed in the Indies, but now my term is up;
　This year, I am going back home to live in the Hague."

10.05. Tuesday. Clear.
It was intensely hot today, the thermometer registering 92 degrees. We've come 275 nautical miles since noon yesterday. We had a brief rain shower in the afternoon, but clear skies quickly returned. The moon was bright tonight, and when I gazed at Venus, it glowed a fiery red. With my fellow passengers, I wrote poetry expressing my nostalgic thoughts of home.

東望故山雲杳茫　濤聲欲裂遠人腸　怪他赤道炎燠地　添得吾儂鬢上霜
> I gaze eastward toward the mountains of home, but see only dim and distant clouds;
> The roar of the waves will surely tear this traveler's heart to pieces.
> How strange that even in this fiery equatorial land,
> A touch of frost should appear in my sidelocks.

10.06. Wednesday. Clear.
From morning, we have enjoyed a delightful coolness. Since yesterday afternoon, we have traveled 290 nautical miles. We are 1270 nautical miles from Singapore and 230 nautical miles from Ceylon. This afternoon, the temperature reached 93 degrees.

10.07. Thursday. Clear.
This morning I got up and could see Ceylon far off in the distance.

萬里來航印度洋　凄風吹盡客懷長　波瀾涵碧朝暾紫　報道行舟近錫狼
> Having sailed ten thousand miles, we come to the Indian Ocean;
> The fierce winds have ceased to blow, but the traveler's musings persist.
> On sapphire-infused waves, the purplish morning sun rises
> As someone reports that the ship approaches Ceylon.

At eight o'clock we reached the mouth of the port, which is called Point de Galle. It is located at the northern latitude of 6°1'. To the left of the harbor is a lighthouse, at the base of which waves collide against the rocks, sending forth an explosive spray like scattering snow. The natives have sharp eyes and prominent noses. They belong to the highest stratum of the Indian ethnic group. Their clothing is the same as that of the natives in Singapore. Because the waves in the harbor are unstable, they have built an unusual little boat with which to transport passengers ashore. The boat has a wooden plank attached to one side in order to maintain balanced weight distribution and prevent capsizing. The hull of the boat is extremely narrow, measuring little more than one foot across and twenty feet in length. Many natives approached our boat and begged to wash our clothing, tried to sell us their local delicacies, and suggested places for us to lodge. What a hateful commotion it was! I went ashore with my traveling companions. There was a gate to the city with the Dutch insignia still posted on it.[43] A Dutchman who came with us frowned with a look of melancholy when he saw it. I can truly imagine what his thoughts must have been. We went into the city and had breakfast at a hotel called the Oriental.[44]

After breakfast, my four fellow travelers and I hired a horse-drawn carriage. We rode along the shoreline and headed toward the mountains. There were many brothels along the road, where women with faces as black as *sumi* ink stood leaning in the doorways. Their savage looks were quite frightful. As we ascended into the mountains, we came to a gate, and the horse driver told us that it was the Bōgahā Temple.[45] We immediately got out of the carriage, entered the gate, and proceeded into the central temple hall. Inside the hall was a figure of a reclining Śākyamuni. It was of astonishingly large proportions and was constructed out of porcelain. On all four walls of the hall, there were

---

[43] Since the sixteenth century, Galle had been colonized successively by the Portuguese, Dutch, and British; among the insignia inscribed on the "Old Gate" of the Dutch Fort is the Dutch East India Company's VOC monogram.

[44] A contemporary guide such as William Morrison Bell's *Other Countries* confirms that this hotel was a common stopping point for travelers briefly calling in Galle: "In the piazza of the Oriental Hotel assemble all the different boats' passengers as they delay on their onward journey a few hours at Galle" (I: 325). Like Bell's narrator, Ryūhoku also hires a carriage and tours a nearby Buddhist temple.

[45] The temple is named for the Sinhalese *bogaha* ("bo tree"), sometimes translated as "god tree" or "bodhi tree." It was under this species of tree that the Buddha attained enlightenment.

images of hell. I was struck with how their antiquated and exotic style made them so different from the pictures my own countrymen draw. We climbed the mountain behind the temple hall, and found an old tomb there. It was ringed with stones, piled in two layers, one on top of the other, giving it a very sturdy structure. The temple priest said it was a tomb containing a portion of Śākyamuni's bones. There was no tombstone, but a single tree grew in the center of the stones: a bodhi tree, according to the priest. The priest gave us travelers several *pattra* leaves with holy scriptures written on them.[46] He also presented us with coconut milk, which has a sweet and delicious flavor.

古廟蕭條老蘚青　時看遠客敲幽扃　椰林深處山僧在　猶寫當年貝葉經
   The ancient temple stood in solemn silence, its old mosses green,
   When travelers from far away knocked upon its secluded door.
   In a place deep within the palm grove dwells the mountain priest;
   Still copying the sacred scriptures on the *pattra* leaves of antiquity.

As we climbed back down the mountain, we saw another temple. We went inside immediately, and asked to see the Buddha hall. The abbot was an old priest who claimed he could speak Japanese. We tried to see if he could understand our language, but he didn't have the slightest idea what we were saying. There were many statues among the figures enshrined in the Buddha hall the likes of which I had never seen. There was a great *dagoba* on the temple precincts, solemn and imposing. The old priest told us that this tower was built to pray for the repose of Māyā,[47] but I don't think the construction looked all that old. This temple must have been quite an impressive temple in former times, but

---

[46] *Pattra* (Skt. *pattra;* J. *baitara* 貝多羅) leaves are used in the Indian subcontinent for recording the Buddhist scriptures.
[47] Māyā was the mother of Śākyamuni.

now it has fallen into decay and the number of monks has dwindled to just two or three.

三千年古刹　一萬卷遺經　試問往時事　山風吹月青
 At this three-thousand-year-old temple
 Lies a heritage of a myriad sacred texts.
 I venture to inquire about bygone days;
 But there is only the mountain wind, blowing in the pale moonlight.

As we prepared to leave, the old priest forlornly lamented our departure. We boarded the carriage again and returned to the city center. There are a rich variety of grasses and flowers in this port, and their appearances have a rare charm that our seven autumn grasses cannot match.[48] The natives, however, are shamelessly crafty. They crowd in on you and try to sell you something, noisy as a swarm of mosquitoes—how truly loathsome it is! We bought several kinds of local products, and returned to the boat at dusk. At night, thunder roared and flashes of lightning dazzled us.

10.08. Friday. Fine.
At eight o'clock in the morning, we left the mouth of the port and headed west. We could see many fish jumping on the waves. The route our ship will traverse from Ceylon to Aden is 2432 nautical miles.

10.09. Saturday. Fine.
We traveled a distance of 325 nautical miles between yesterday morning and noon today. Today, a Dutch passenger presented me with an old

---

[48] The "seven autumn grasses," sometimes known collectively as *nanakusa* 七草, include bush clover, pampas grass, arrowroot, pink, maiden flower, thoroughwort, and morning glory (or bellflower).

silver coin he had brought with him; I returned his generosity by giving him a new gold Japanese coin.

10.10. Sunday. Clear.
There was a slight wind today, but the waves were calm, flat like a straw mat. We have traveled 288 nautical miles since noon yesterday. The moon was bright tonight.

10.11. Monday. Fine.
A wind arose and rocked the boat, sending many of the passengers into their cabins to lie down. We have traveled 300 nautical miles. Today, I watched some of the Indian passengers having a meal; they didn't use chopsticks at all, but instead snatched the food up with their hands.

10.12. Tuesday. Fine.
The wind has ceased, and the waves are calm. The heat is also not so oppressive. We traveled 308 nautical miles.

10.13. Wednesday. Fine.
During these last three or four days on board, we haven't seen even a hairsbreadth of land. The vastness of the Arabian Sea is staggering. Today we traveled 318 nautical miles in favorable winds. I've been feeling bored since yesterday, but today I played "quoits" with a Dutchman. The game is played by competing to throw a flattened disk on top of a dish, rather as in *dakyū*.[49] At dusk, I spotted something off

---

[49] Ryūhoku draws a comparison to the sport of *dakyū* or *uchimari* 打毬, which was imported to Japan from China during the Heian period. Popular as a courtly diversion in its original equestrian form, the game became popular again in the Edo period in a version played on foot.

to the right that vaguely resembled an island. Perhaps it is the Arabian subcontinent. Tonight, the moon looked just like the noonday sun.

10.14. Thursday. Clear skies.

We had a cool breeze today, and the thermometer read 84 degrees. Tonight, I caught a glimpse of a Brahmanist among the Indian passengers praying to his gods. As I watched the scene, it seemed to me that it was exactly the same as the way our Buddhist priests worship. There are two styles of prayer: standing and sitting. Today, our ship traveled 333 nautical miles.

10.15. Friday. Fine.

When I got up this morning, I could see mountains. It was the port of Aden, which we entered at 9:20. The coast of Arabia seems to be mostly covered with sand and pebbles, with little green vegetation in sight. The mountains and hills are all exposed bones with no surrounding flesh. Jutting up like swords or fangs, they give one a startling impression. I've never seen such scenery in Asia. The British have built artillery emplacements along these hills, which form a veritable natural Great Wall. In between, they have planted trees and constructed buildings. It must have required considerable effort. The harbor is vast, like someone has spread out a giant bag. The natives have curly hair and black faces, and they look much uglier, baser, and more fiendish than Indians. The children swim in the sea just like frogs, and it is hard to believe they are human. Many of my traveling companions went ashore, but since I could not stand the burning sun beating down on the rocky sands, to say nothing of the wind blowing dust in my face, I ended up not leaving the ship. Natives came to the boat to sell leopard skins and ostrich plumes. The currencies they use have names like "rupee" and "anna."[50] Those who went ashore reported that the city center of this port is desolate, that various regions have no wells, and that water is scarce. They said that on top of the mountains there were old pools, and that the locals collect rainwater in them to use for drinking. The pools were apparently originally constructed by the Romans and then fortified by the British.[51] The accomplishments of the British in this barren place—developing new land, building roads, and so on—are truly admirable. To transport their goods, the natives here all use camels. Other than that, there is nothing worth seeing, they say. The Indian passengers who were traveling on board the ship with us all disembarked here and are gone. At six o'clock, we left the port. Tonight, with the bright moon rising one thousand feet above the jagged crags, the scenery is splendid.[52] Since today is the fifteenth day of the tenth month, I imagine Master Su Shi's return to Red Cliff. Knowing that my own grand voyage is certainly not inferior to Su Shi's, I stay awake enjoying the moon until late into the night.

斷巖千尺海門開　大月晚從洋底來　萬里壯遊探絕勝　愧吾獨少老坡才
    Jagged crags jut a thousand feet above this open portal to the sea;
    The great moon rises from the water's depths at night.
    I have boldly ventured ten thousand leagues to find this striking scene;
    Yet shamed I am to find I have little of Old Su Shi's talent.

---

[50] The copper *anna* and silver *rupee* mentioned here were coins from British India that were imported to serve as legal currency in Aden at the time.
[51] This network of interconnected cisterns forms a reservoir system known as "Aden Tank" (*Meijihen*, 269).
[52] In this passage and in the *kanshi* that follows, Ryūhoku makes several references to lines from Su Shi's "Later Poetic Exposition on Red Cliff," a connection inspired by the fact that the latter piece had been composed on the very same night (10.15) 790 years earlier. Ryūhoku writes, for example, about the "moon rising one thousand feet above the jagged crags" 斷巖千尺, a close variant of Su Shi's 斷岸千尺; for a translation, see Watson, *Selected Poems*, 97–98.

四望難看寸草青　山容洞態赭而獰　知他大漠應非遠　満面炎風泊亞丁

I look around in all directions, but see no hint of grassy green;
The mountains appear reddish, and the shape of the caves is forbidding.
That great desert cannot be far away, I know;
For a hot wind meets me full in the face as we anchor in Aden.

10.16. Saturday. Fine.

Today, a wind came up and rocked the ship a bit. We advanced into the Red Sea. To the right, I gazed out at the mountains of Arabia, and to the left I could occasionally make out the mountain peaks of Africa off in the distance. I can tell that our ship's course is following the coastline of Arabia. The distance from the port of Aden to Suez is 1308 nautical miles. Since yesterday evening, we have come 215 nautical miles. Today, the thermometer read 84 degrees, and the heat was especially intense at night. According to Western historical annals, the ancient saint Moses crossed the sea to escape catastrophe. The King of Egypt pursued him but all of his army drowned, their blood making the waves roil red, and ever since that time the sea has been known by the name "Red Sea."[53] I wonder, however, if it might have been given its name because the water's color naturally becomes red when sunlight strikes the desert sands on both shores. In any case, for the time being I will follow the historical account to compose the following quatrain:

摩西仙去幾千秋　回首興亡事似漚　誰識當年紅海水　汪洋猶劃兩洲流

How many thousand autumns have passed since Moses left this world?
Looking back, the vicissitudes of history are but fleeting foam bubbles.

---

[53] Ryūhoku is of course alluding to the story of Moses parting the Red Sea in Exodus (14:15–31). The image of a bloody Red Sea does not appear in this passage, however, and it may be that Ryūhoku was confusing the Red Sea story with an earlier story also involving Moses in Exodus, where the water of the Nile turns to blood (7:20–21).

Who could imagine that the Red Sea waters that flowed back then
Would even today grandly divide two continents?

10.17. Sunday. Fine.
Today the ship traveled 282 nautical miles. At noon, the thermometer read 86 degrees. In the afternoon, we passed through a light rain. For another consecutive night, the moon shone brightly.

10.18. Monday. Fine.
The wind and waves are especially calm. Our ship traveled 277 nautical miles. The thermometer read 88 degrees. Since yesterday, I haven't seen the slightest hairsbreadth of land. The vastness of the Red Sea is striking. As evening approached, I saw a mountain crag off to the left that looked like the fang of a beast. This afternoon at three o'clock, sparks erupted in a spray from the smokestack, igniting a cloth canopy on the deck. The whole ship was thrown into frenzy, but in just a few moments the fire was extinguished and everyone was calmed. This evening, a British passenger got into a fight with one of the crew, which resulted in the crew member being confined as punishment. Apparently the problem arose because the Englishman was smoking. No one thought the Englishman was in the right.

10.19. Tuesday. Fine.
At twelve o'clock, I saw two rocks that looked like a cannon platform to our left. Today we traveled 275 nautical miles. Our position is at the northern latitude of 26°, and I am told we are 259 nautical miles from Suez. As evening drew near, I gazed at the mountain peaks of Africa to the left, and saw the islands of Arabia to our right. After night had fallen, we passed through a point in the strait with a width of just ten nautical miles. There was a lighthouse on the land just where the

passage was gradually becoming narrower. The orb of the moon had already come rising up, making for very lovely scenery. One of the boatmen told me that to the right you could see Mount Sinai, the place where Moses received the Ten Commandments. In the midst of the dark haze and mist, however, I was unable to make it out clearly. Today, I purchased several old Western coins from the Dutchman Rademaker.

電光夜掣萬重山　爛々碎紅波浪間　毒熱侵人烈於火　行舟正過鬼門關
At night, lightning lashes the terraced hills;
With a flash it shatters scarlet between the waves.[54]
The poisonous heat penetrates our bodies, searing more than fire;
As our ship passes right through the Demon's Gate.[55]

溽熱蒸空月亦紅　紫瀾萬頃夜無風　昨來艙裏人如醉　不識舟行埃及東
The sweltering heat steams the sky, reddening even the moon;
Purple waves spread out for miles on this windless night.
Since yesterday, it seems everyone on board is drunk,
Oblivious to the ship's progress toward the eastern coast of Egypt.

---

[54] It is possible that the lightning described in the first couplet refers to the light from the lighthouse (*Meijihen*, 272).
[55] The "Demon's Gate" (鬼門關; J. *kimonkan*; Ch. *guimenguan*) in the last line is a term that appears early in Chinese geographic treatises in reference to a particular area of southern China corresponding to present-day northeast Guangxi. Over time, the term became detached from its specific geographic referent and came to be used metaphorically for remote regions where tropical diseases were endemic. The term had an additional significance, however, in reference to Bab-el-Mandeb (which means "Gate of Sorrow" or "Gate of Tears"). Ryūhoku had just passed through this strait, which connects the Gulf of Aden with the Red Sea, and he would have been aware that nineteenth-century Europeans referred to it and the nearby area as the "Gate of Hell." Shibusawa Eiichi and Sugiura Yuzuru commented upon this term in *Kōsei nikki*, a travelogue Ryūhoku read during his journey (Fraleigh, "Kōsei no Tōdō Shujin," 69–70). In his 1881 Ceylon travelogue, Ernst Haeckel gives another demonic variant for the toponym for this area around Perim Island: "A residence in this scorching rock-settlement during the summer is the purgatory of the English garrison, and it is not without reason that the officers call it the 'Devil's Punch-bowl'" (40).

10.20. Wednesday. Fine.

The strait has become increasingly narrow. In the morning, I got up and sensed a slight coolness in the air. When I checked the thermometer, it read 77 degrees. It must be because we are at last approaching the Mediterranean Sea. The ship reached Suez at 9:30, anchoring at a place a little more than one nautical mile from the shore. Compared to Aden, this port seems to be much more bustling. The white sands of the many inlets make a pleasant sight to behold. Some natives came to the ship, selling red Turkish hats and photographs. At one o'clock in the afternoon, we left the port and entered the new canal. The banks are of reddish earth as far as one can see, and there isn't the slightest sprig of vegetation on them. I could catch an occasional glimpse of camels lying down on the sand. The desert heat closed in on us, pushing the thermometer up to 87 degrees. The width of this canal is about twenty or thirty *kyū*,[56] and it is eighty-seven nautical miles long. It must have taken considerable effort to dig this passageway. When night fell, the ship entered a lake to put down anchor and thereby forestall collision. I wondered if this lake might not be the Great Bitter Lake mentioned in the *Record of Things Heard and Seen in the West*, and when I asked the boatman, he replied that the lake is named "Mitsutsuru."[57] Today I composed two quatrains.

---

[56] The *kyū* 弓 is an archaic unit of measure, corresponding to eight *shaku*, though its length varied over time. Ryūhoku's estimate of the canal's breadth is somewhere between 120 and 240 feet.
[57] Great Bitter Lake is another name for Buheirat Murrat el Kubra, a very large lake north of the city of Suez. The curious pronunciation "Mitsutsuru" is an artifact of the revising process that took place in the 1880s when Ryūhoku serialized *Diary of a Journey to the West* in his magazine *Kagetsu shinshi*. From the partial copy Ryūhoku's traveling companion Matsumoto Hakka kept, we know that Ryūhoku originally wrote his diary in pure *kanbun* rather than Sino–Japanese. In Hakka's copy of Ryūhoku's original, the name of the lake is given as 美津都爾, characters which presumably represent the sounds "bi tsu to ru," i.e., *bittoru* or "bitter." When Ryūhoku transformed his original *kanbun* diary into Sino–Japanese for publication a decade later, however, he seems to

一道新渠兩海通　當知神禹讓其功　熱埃堆裏涼風迸　巨艦往來沙漠中

The new canal links two oceans together:
A feat before which even the great Yu would surely yield.[58]
A cool wind bursts forth through the layers of hot dust,
And mammoth ships make their way through the desert.

疏鑿黃沙幾萬重　風潮洗熱碧溶々　千帆直向歐洲去　閑却南洋喜望峰

How many thousands of layers of sand have been tunneled through?
Wind and current wash the heat away, leaving only emerald vastness.
A thousand sails head straight through for Europe,
Abandoned in the South Seas lies the Cape of Good Hope.

10.21. Thursday. Fine.
At 9:20, we left the lake and reentered the canal. The banks on either side spread out far into the distance, and all I could make out were the imprints of animal tracks. There were trees that looked like purple willows, and shrubs that looked like sedge grew in clusters here and there. Aside from that, all I could see were pampas grass flowers. There was a telegraph cable constructed along the bank, allowing for mutual communication to protect ships from collisions. Only rarely could I spot any houses, the residences of people who came to live here after the construction of the canal was finished. Before too long, we entered another lake, this one called Timsāh. It is extremely wide, and within it was a place that resembled a port. The place is called Ismaïlia, and there

---

have forgotten what sounds the characters represented, and guessed the equally plausible *mitsutsuru*. As his comment in this entry suggests, Ryūhoku had read of the lake in *Seiyō bunkenroku* 西洋聞見録, a lengthy report on conditions in the West published by Murata Fumio 村田文夫 (1836–1891) in 1869, and supplemented with a "Miscellany" in 1870. In the later publication, Murata recounts in extraordinary detail the history of the construction of the Suez Canal (471–480).

[58] Among the accomplishments of the great Yu, a legendary sage king of Chinese antiquity, was the canal system.

were many boats lodged here. On board the ship today, they took down the canopy from the top deck. One of the crewmembers said that the climate will abruptly change tomorrow, and that people will no longer need shelter from the hot sun. Everyone should change their clothing, he said, and make preparations to ward off the cold. As one who has relaxed for hours on end in the shade of the screen, I was quite saddened to see it removed today.

10.22. Friday. Fine.
Yesterday afternoon at three o'clock, we again entered a great lake, this one called Ballāh. At 4:20 we put in anchor. This morning, the thermometer read 67 degrees. I got up early, and as soon as I saw the banks on either side of us, I realized that we were no longer in the desert. Everywhere the land was muddy earth, which means that we are not far from the Mediterranean Sea. We entered another lake, this one called Manzāla. It is so vast that it reminds me of the sea. On the lake there were many waterfowl. At nine o'clock, we reached the new harbor at Port Said. The land is under the jurisdiction of Egypt, and there was an Egyptian garrison and Egyptian battleships in the port. The Dutchman Kok invited me to go ashore, and we strolled through the city center. It was remarkably clean everywhere, and many different goods were for sale. We dropped by the "Grand Hotel" for a drink. On the road I saw a tree called a "nisarupu."[59] Its leaves are like a bean tree

---

[59] The tree Ryūhoku describes here is likely the thorny "Egyptian mimosa" (*Acacia nilotica*). Unfortunately Matsumoto Hakka's partial copy of Ryūhoku's original *kanbun* diary terminates in the first lines of this entry, leaving the original *kanji* used to represent the name *nisarupu* unclear. Inoue Kowashi, who was on the same ship as Ryūhoku and Hakka as they passed through Port Said, observed in his diary that "the locals understand French" (341), which suggests that *arbre* may be the latter part of the name; perhaps *Nil* and *arbre* became concatenated to *nisarupu*. Somewhat more improbably, the *Acacia nilotica* species is known as *nkerebu* in Setswana, but this language is spoken more in Southern Africa.

and it has thorns. Its branches and trunk are like a willow. The natives lead travelers around by seating them on donkeys that they then pull.

新埔頭開海色妍　南來北去萬帆懸　千年砂磧無人地　築起樓臺數百椽
The new port city has opened and the seascape is charming;
Coming and going, north and south, the myriad boats hoist their sails.
A no-man's land of pebbles and sand for a thousand years,
But now stand hundreds of rafters as the raising of buildings has begun.

At 4:30, we left the port and entered the Mediterranean Sea. The winds picked up and the waves suddenly grew larger. I went to sleep without eating dinner. I am told that it is 1503 nautical miles from this new port to Marseille.

客舟忽入大濤間　凛々朔風吹裂顏　千古誰呼地中海　四邊杳渺不看山
Our passenger ship suddenly enters the great toss of waves;
The piercing north wind tears fiercely at our faces.
Thousands of years ago, who named it the "Sea Amid the Land?"
As far as I can see in all four directions, there aren't any mountains.[60]

10.23. Saturday. Fine.
The winds were strong today. Since yesterday, we have traveled 223 nautical miles. Our position is at the northern latitude of 32°. I was able to write one poem tonight while I lay in bed.

---

[60] The term "Mediterranean" was translated into Japanese and Chinese as 地中海, which Ryūhoku here interprets as "Sea Amid the Land." The original meaning of the toponym was apparently "sea at the center of the world."

人定連房燈影殘　汽機聲裏夜方闌　玻瓈窓底獨欹枕　星彩水光相映寒

    All have turned in, but along the row of cabins some lanterns are still lit;
    Amid the drone of the steam engine, we enter the depths of night.
    Beneath my glass window, I prop my head up on the pillow;
    Starlight reflects on the luminous sea water with a chilling brilliance.

10.24. Sunday. Fine and pleasant.
There was no wind today. I gazed out to our right at Candia, an island that is part of Turkey.[61] It lies to the south of Greece. Today, the boat traveled 286 nautical miles. At night it rained.

10.25. Monday. Fine.
Today, the southern winds blew in warm air, and at noon, the rains came. The thermometer read 76 degrees. The boat traveled 302 nautical miles today, and we are 692 nautical miles from Marseille. At four o'clock I could spot some mountains in the distance, but they were only vaguely visible, as though obscured in mist. These are Italian mountains, and what we could see to our left is the Strait of Sicily, the mouth of which is apparently just three miles wide. As night fell, we passed through Messina. In the rainy dimness, all I could make out were the lighthouse and the lanterns in people's houses.

江山咫尺水烟含　明滅簍燈一二三　凉雨凄風人不語　征帆夜過墨西南（メシナ）

    Rivers and mountains just inches away are swallowed in mist;
    Here and there I can see the flicker of lanterns: one, two, three.
    No one speaks amid these chilling rains and fierce winds,
    As our sail proceeds along tonight through the Messina Strait.

---

[61] Candia here refers to the island of Crete as a whole; it can also designate the capital, Iráklion.

10.26. Tuesday. Fine.

I got up this morning and all I could glimpse were the mountains of Italy off in the distance. At twelve o'clock, I could see a mountain peak to our right: this is Naples. Today, our ship traveled 250 nautical miles, and we passed through the northern latitude of 40°. How wonderful it is to have such clear and pleasant weather!

浴罷柁樓快欠伸　客中吾是一閑人　水容太静雲容暖　始識西溟亦小春

Freshly bathed, I ascend to the helm for a languid yawn and stretch;
As long as we are traveling, I am a man of leisure.
The water's surface looks quiet and the clouds seem warm;
I see the tenth month brings a "little spring" to these western seas too.

10.27. Wednesday. Unstable weather: first clear, then overcast, then clear again.

This morning, when I gazed out from the deck, I could see the island of Elba to the right and the island of Corsica to the left. Both islands have ports with people's houses crowded close together around them. Recalling the events of Napoleon I's life, I composed two poems.[62]

---

[62] Even before his death, Napoleon was in fact on his way to becoming something of a topos among Tokugawa *kanshi* poets. Rai San'yō, for example, wrote the lengthy "Song of the French King" 佛郎王歌 in 1818, three years before Napoleon's death in 1821. Later poets such as Ōtsuki Bankei and Saitō Chikudō wrote multiple poems on Napoleon's life in the 1840s, and Japanese overseas travelers frequently made reference to him. Ryūhoku's traveling companion Matsumoto Hakka, for example, made a lengthy entry in his diary on passing the two islands: "When I got up this morning, I could see lighthouses to our left and right. The one to the left was on the island of Corsica. There were many houses built one after another into the mountainside. This is where Napoleon was born. The scenery is beautiful. I guess it must be true what they say about places with superb natural scenery giving rise to people with marvelous talents. The island to the right is Elba. This is the land of exile where Napoleon went after his defeat in battle. Alas! How the heroes of the world rise and fall. A single glance fills one with boundless emotion" (391). For a survey of Edo treatments of Napoleon, see Iwashita.

想君韶齔伴漁郎　末路龍潛亦此鄉　夕日影沈雲影遠　雙巖相對立蒼洋

 I imagine you must have tagged along with the fishermen here as a boy;
 And at journey's end, the "dragon went into hiding" here too.
 Where the shadow of the evening sun sinks, amid the far-off clouds,
 Two great cliffs face off, jutting up from the azure sea.

兵威打破泰西天　屈指茫々七十年　島嶼空存當日景　英雄成敗付雲烟

 The awesome might of your soldiers rent the Western heavens;
 I count on my fingers: already seventy years gone by.
 The islands here still retain a hollow shadow of those former days;
 But the triumphs and defeats of the hero are consigned to the haze.

At one o'clock, we passed through the 43° latitude. The thermometer read 66°. It was windy, and suddenly it started to rain. Today, we traveled 307 nautical miles. I am told that we should reach Marseille tonight. All of the passengers on board are excited as we get ourselves dressed and ready our things. At dusk, we passed by Toulon and I could see a lighthouse. We are already in French territory!

10.28. Thursday. Fine.
At six o'clock in the morning we reached the port of Marseille. With the masts of ten thousand ships rising up like a forest of trees, the harbor seems somehow small in spite of its greatness. The ports of the Orient cannot measure up to its scale. We hired a boat to go ashore. A single glance at the city center—a vision of prosperity with its towering buildings soaring up into the sky—leaves a person astonished. We entered the customs office and had our luggage examined, but the inspection was only perfunctory. We then boarded a horse-drawn carriage, and at twelve o'clock entered the Grand Hôtel, where I

checked in to room forty-three.[63] This hotel's beauty and vastness are truly amazing. In front of the gate was a row of maple-like trees, and this subdued scene of fallen leaves was a world away from the luxuriant green vegetation of Indian climes. After lunch, we wandered around the city center, where I saw many young women selling flowers. At night, I went out again for a stroll with Tsuruta, Namura and Numa. Gas streetlamps illuminated the night, making it hardly any different from broad daylight. This is truly paradise!

望馬耳塞港作 *Composed while overlooking the Port of Marseille*
四旬經過怒濤間 報道今宵入海關 雲際遙看燈萬點 滿船無客不開顏
After forty days passed amid the wrathful waves,
They report that we will enter the harbor this evening.
Gazing off at ten thousand points of light on the clouded horizon,
Not a soul on board can keep a smile of eagerness from his face.

夜步街上口占 *Strolling the town at night—impromptu composition*
枕海樓臺十萬家 西來始是認豪華 氣燈照路明於月 佳麗爭馳幾輛車
Hundreds of thousands of buildings pillowed along the shore;
Since beginning our journey west, this is the first grandeur I have seen.
Brighter than the moon are the gas lamps that illuminate the streets,
Where many beautifully appointed carriages race each other along.

10.29. Friday. Fine and pleasant.
I went to a park with the others today. There was a waterfall, which was extremely refreshing. We also went to view a gallery with oil paintings

---

[63] The Grand Hôtel de Marseille was located on the busy Rue de Noailles, and as Ryūhoku's description suggests, it was quite an extravagant hotel. In the "Routes to Italy" section of Baedeker's *Northern Italy,* for example, the Grand Hôtel de Marseille is said to be "fitted up in the style of the great Parisian hotels" (16).

on display. They were executed with technical perfection. In the zoological gardens, there was a giraffe and an elephant; I cannot imagine how many different sorts of exotic birds and curious beasts they have.[64] We changed to a carriage and headed for the Burado Museum.[65] The physical setting was quiet and secluded. The building faces the sea and the view was quite gorgeous. The shade of the trees inside the garden was truly lovely. I hear that a wealthy businessman constructed this building as his residence, but it was entrusted to the government after his death. A statue of him is now on display inside the museum. Old Egyptian, Greek, and Roman vessels and relics made of both stone and metal were piled up on display, making the viewer positively drool with excitement. There was a sixteen-hundred-year-old stone sarcophagus; it is a good seven inches thick, and inside lay a skull. We also saw a Roman coffin used for the burial of bones remaining after cremation. It was square, measuring about three feet on each side, and the opening was about one foot and five inches deep. There were so many other objects in addition to these that it would be impossible to detail them all. We headed back by way of the road along the seaside, arriving at the hotel at five o'clock. We will leave for Paris tomorrow, and everyone began making preparations for this.

---

[64] Ryūhoku is describing the Musée des Beaux-Arts, located along with a botanical and zoological garden on the grounds of the Palais de Longchamp (Baedeker's *Northern Italy*, 18).

[65] The Musée des Antiques was part of the Château Borély, which lay at the end of the Promenade du Prado (presumably the source of Ryūhoku's "Burado" Museum). The Baedeker guide describes its location and holdings: "close to the sea, is the *Château Borély*, situated in an extensive park, and containing a valuable *Musée des Antiques* (Egyptian, Phoenician, Greek, and Roman inscriptions and antiquities, Christian sarcophagi, valuable glass, etc.)" (20). The *Dictionnaire de Biographie Française* notes how Louise-Jeanne-Marie de Panisse-Passis, the niece of Louis-Joseph-Denis Borelli (1731–1784), sold the house to the city of Marseille in 1856 (XVI:1100).

10.30. Saturday. Overcast.

At eleven o'clock in the morning we boarded a steam locomotive and left Marseille (the first-class fare to Paris is 110 francs). One compartment accommodates eight people. Inside, there was a foot warmer, which was exchanged from time to time. We encountered tunnels here and there along the way, the longest taking about twelve minutes to pass through. At two o'clock in the afternoon, it started raining. As I gazed out at the rural scenery from within the train, it seemed to me that it was not all that different from Japan.

坐看萬水又千山 數日行程轉瞬間 何事徃來如許急 火輪不似客身閑
I sit and gaze out at countless streams and myriad mountains;
A trip that should take several days passes by in just the blink of an eye.
How on earth can the journey be so rapid?
An odd pair: the racing locomotive and its idle passengers.

At seven o'clock, we reached Lyon. The sky was already dark, and I could see only the glow of the city lights. I relaxed for twenty minutes inside the train, and ate the meal that was provided. No sooner had I nodded off and begun to dream than we had already arrived in Paris. It was 4:20 a.m., and so the sky was still dark. From the station, we took a horse-drawn carriage to the Grand Hôtel on the Boulevard des Capucines.[66] Compared to that splendid hotel where we stayed in

---

[66] The Grand Hôtel had opened at 12 Boulevard des Capucines in 1862 and was one of the most elegant hotels in Paris. A decade before Ryūhoku's visit, the members of the 1862 shogunal mission to Europe, which included Fukuzawa Yukichi, Fukuchi Gen'ichirō, Mitsukuri Shūhei, and Matsuki Kōan, were able to stay in the "newly built hotel, the finest in the city" on their second stop through Paris (Fuchibe, 114; Haga, 192). Mission member Sugi Magoshichirō (1835–1920) even composed a *kanshi* to celebrate the hotel's completion. Marveling at the new hotel's scale, the poem contains this couplet: "In towers seven stories high, a thousand lanterns glow / Guests from countless countries in its eight hundred rooms" (17b–18a).

Marseille, it is like comparing Qin and Chu to Teng and Xue.⁶⁷ It truly is no wonder that they call it the finest hotel in the whole world.

11.01. Sunday (December 1 according to the Western calendar). Fine. We went for a leisurely stroll around the city center of Paris. The beauty and neatness of the buildings and the streets were astonishing to me. I dropped by the office of Commissioner Sameshima,⁶⁸ but he was not in. Osada Keitarō⁶⁹ was not in either, for he had been dispatched to Prussia, and so I left after meeting Secretary Gotō.⁷⁰ I then went to the Rue de la Paix to visit Kurimoto Teijirō,⁷¹ but he wasn't there either. In the dim dusk, I returned to the hotel. Today, I composed three poems.

---

⁶⁷ Qin and Chu were the names of expansive and powerful states during China's Zhou Dynasty; Teng and Xue were tiny states at the same time.
⁶⁸ Satsuma native Sameshima Naonobu 鮫島尚信 (1845–1880; also read Samejima Hisanobu), had learned French and English in Edo at an early age and had been secretly sent to study abroad in the 1860s. After the Restoration, he became one of Japan's most distinguished overseas diplomats. At the time he was serving in Paris as Chargé des Affaires, representing Japan to France and two other nations, but he soon became Resident Minister. The Japanese legation had been established only a year prior to Ryūhoku's visit and was located at 26 Avenue de La Reine Hortense.
⁶⁹ Osada Keitarō 長田銈太郎 (1849–1889) had studied French as a shogunal retainer and had served as a translator for French diplomat Léon Roches. In 1872, he began serving as "Attaché" in the French legation (Sameshima, 24). Osada was also the elder brother of Ryūhoku's adopted son Kenkichi. He went on to serve as a diplomat in Russia.
⁷⁰ Originally from Sendai, Gotō Tsune 後藤常, also known as Ichijō Jūjirō 一条十次郎, had traveled to America in 1867 to study English. After the Restoration, he joined the Ministry of Foreign Affairs in 1870, and was dispatched to Paris the following year to serve as an "Attaché" in the Japanese legation (Sameshima, 24, 481).
⁷¹ The adopted son of shogunal retainer and post-Restoration newspaper publisher Kurimoto Joun 栗本鋤雲 (1822–1897), Teijirō 貞次郎 (1839–1881) had studied French in the shogunate's Yokohama academy in the 1860s and had been put in charge of the academy students who went abroad to study in France in 1867. He went on to translate several French legal texts. Ryūhoku writes his name with a minor orthographic variant that I have not preserved here.

十載夢飛巴里城　城中今日試閑行　畫樓涵影淪漪水　士女如花簇晚晴

> In my dreams these past ten years, I have flown to the city of Paris;
> Today I seized the chance for a leisurely stroll through its streets.
> Picturesque buildings cast their shadows on the rippling water;
> Men and women in floral splendor gather in the clear evening air.

五洲富在一城中　石叟陶公比屋同　南海珊瑚北山玉　麈々排列衒奇工

> The riches of five continents are all to be found within this one city;
> Houses one after another, all with the riches of Old Shi and Tao.[72]
> Coral from southern seas and gems from northern mountains,
> Arrayed in the shops as a stunning display of rare craftsmanship.

晚餐圍案肘交肘　秦越相逢皆是友　醉臥誰能學謫仙　夜光盃注葡萄酒

> Sitting around the dinner table, our elbows brush against each other;
> When men of Qin and Yue meet, they all become friends.
> All lie down in their tipsiness—who will be the banished immortal?
> The light this evening shines in my cup, brimming with grape wine.[73]

11.02. Monday. Rainy.

Our hotel is one of the city's first-class inns, and the expenses are correspondingly great. Our budget will not permit us to stay for very long, and so in consultation with Mr. Gotō, we have decided to change our lodgings. This afternoon I left the hotel with Mr. Nitta and Mr.

---

[72] Both Shi Chong 石崇, from the third century, and Tao Zhu 陶朱 (better known as Fan Li 范蠡), from the Spring and Autumn Period, were men of great wealth.

[73] Qin and Yue were large states in Chinese antiquity that were located far apart. The reference to the "banished immortal" 謫仙 is presumably to Tang poet Li Bo, whose fondness for drink was legendary. Grain-based wines dominated East Asia at the time, and thus Ryūhoku emphasizes here that it is "grape wine" that fills his cup. Moreover, in this final line, he closely paraphrases a famous Tang poem by Wang Han entitled "Song of Liangzhou" that similarly celebrated the exotic beverage; for a translation, see Minford and Lau, I: 823.

Honma, but we got confused and lost our way. We then came back to the hotel and hired a carriage to take us to the new inn, which is called the "Hôtel de Lord Byron."[74] Satō Shizuo,[75] Ikeda Kanji,[76] Abe Hisomu,[77] Ōno Naosuke,[78] and Nagaoka Seisuke[79] are all guests at this hotel. It is encouraging to meet so many of my countrymen even though I am several thousand miles away from Japan. This evening, Ono Yaichi[80] and Kawazu Sukeyuki[81] came over for a chat.

---

[74] It seems that Ryūhoku stayed at the Hôtel de Lord Byron located at 20 Rue Laffitte, but contemporary Paris guidebooks also list a Villa Lord-Byron at 16 Rue Lord-Byron, near the Arc de Triomphe.

[75] Born in Yanagawa (in modern Fukuoka), Satō Shizuo 佐藤鎮雄 (1851–1897) was dispatched to study in England in 1869. After returning to Japan in 1876, he became a career naval officer.

[76] Ikeda Kanji 池田寛治 (1848–1881), also known as Masayoshi 政懋, studied French in the 1860s and went on to become an instructor of the language in his native Nagasaki after the Meiji Restoration. In 1871, he accompanied the Iwakura Mission to the United States and Europe, returning to Japan in May 1873. He continued his career as a civil servant in the Ministries of Education, Treasury and Internal Affairs, and also served for five years as a diplomat in Tianjin.

[77] Abe Hisomu 阿部潜 (1839–1895), also known as Abe Sen or Kuninosuke 邦之助, was a former shogunal retainer from Shizuoka who had served in the Army and at the Numazu Military academy from the very first years of Meiji. He had accompanied Yamada Akiyoshi to Paris a few weeks ahead of the rest of the Iwakura Mission to make preparations (Tomita, *Iwakura*, 121). After returning to Japan, he worked in coal mining and sericulture.

[78] Born in Suō (Yamaguchi), Ōno Naosuke 大野直輔 (1838–1921) had departed to England with Mōri Motoisa 毛利元巧 in 1868 to study economics. He subsequently entered the Ministry of the Treasury, and on this journey in 1872, he was accompanying Nagaoka Yoshiyuki on an investigation of import duties and customs; he returned to Japan in 1873 (Sameshima, 491).

[79] Nagaoka Seisuke 長岡精助 is presumably Nagaoka Yoshiyuki 長岡義之 (1840–1886), from Chōshū, who was investigating European import duties and customs along with Ōno Naosuke. Just a few days after Ryūhoku met these two, Minister Sameshima wrote a letter of introduction for them (Sameshima, 64–65, 491).

[80] Ono Yaichi 小野彌一 (1847–1893) was a former shogunal retainer from Shizuoka who learned French from Mermet de Cachon. He participated in the Yokohama military training program led by Charles Chanoine, where Ryūhoku would have met him. In the spring of 1871, he traveled to the United States, then Germany, and then Paris for study. He returned to Japan in 1876 and later became involved in the dispatching of Japanese workers to a nickel mine in French New Caledonia.

[81] Kawazu Sukeyuki 河津祐之 (1850–1894) was an early student of Western

11.03. Tuesday. Fine.
First thing today, I went by the old hotel to meet with Mr. Kurimoto and ask for his help on various matters. We had lunch at a restaurant downtown. The place was extremely crowded, and when I asked about it later, I learned that it was quite a low-class restaurant. I went to Bouché's tailor shop and arranged to have clothing made for our whole group.[82] All of the clothing we wore or brought with us from Japan is coarse and poor, and I don't think that even the carriage drivers or groomsmen here would be caught wearing such garments. It's rather amusing actually! Tonight I wrote several letters home and entrusted them to Mr. Abe.

11.04. Wednesday. Unstable weather—alternately overcast and fine.
Mr. Abe left early this morning; I believe he is returning home. At Mr. Ikeda's invitation, I went for the first time today to a bathhouse in the city. The price was one franc. Mr. Namura and Mr. Kurimoto came over and we had a chat. It rained in the evening.

---

languages who was sent to study in France by the Education Ministry in 1872. He worked as a legislative advisor, serving in several posts within the judicial system. He also translated texts widely read by those in the Popular Rights movement.

[82] Based on the diaries of Ryūhoku's contemporaries, it can be concluded that this tailor shop was Aux Galeries de Paris, located at 29 Boulevard des Italiens (the shop is listed in Baedeker's *Paris*, 35). As for Mr. Bouché, one of the Japanese living in Paris at the time returned to Japan with a business card for the tailor shop's proprietor; it reads "S. Bouché / Negociant / Expert en Douane / et de la Ville de Paris / 29, Boulevard des Italiens" (reprinted in Tanaka Ryūji, 79). Mr. Bouché's tailor shop was used by earlier Japanese travelers, especially those sent by the Tokugawa shogunate, including the Akitake mission of 1867. One traveler on this mission, scholar of zoology and botany Tanaka Yoshio 田中芳男 (1838–1916), placed a business card from the shop in his souvenir album, *Gaikoku kunshuchō* 外國捃拾帖 (an image of the card can be seen in Nishino and Polak, 126). In this connection, it is interesting to note that whereas Matsumoto Hakka's diary entry for 11.05 notes that the shop had the Tokugawa house hollyhock crest on its sign and a framed piece of calligraphy reading "In the service of Shimizu" 清水御用, Ryūhoku does not mention this fact at all.

11.05. Thursday. Fine and pleasant.
Bouché brought over the new clothing we had ordered. After dinner, I went out to walk around the city with my traveling companions.

11.06. Friday. Fine.
I visited Mr. Namura's hotel today, and we strolled along the Seine. We had a look at the antique shops, where there were a great many ancient vessels and coins.

11.07. Saturday. Fine. Rain in the afternoon.
Today I went to see a zoological park.[83] There were a great variety of exotic birds and curious beasts. This evening, my old friend Andō Tarō[84] came over and stayed the night. It was one of the most delightful times that I have had so far on this trip. He is traveling as an attendant to Ambassador Iwakura, and arrived today in Paris from London. He told me all about America, its physical features and its people's manners and customs. It was quite late in the night before we got to sleep.

11.08. Sunday. Very fine.
Shimaji Mokurai,[85] Umegami Kōen,[86] and Sakata Kan'ichi[87] also came over today. Today, I went to the Bois de Boulogne public park with

---

[83] According to Matsumoto Hakka's diary, the zoological park was located on the north bank of the Seine, which suggests the Jardin d'Acclimatation.
[84] Andō Tarō 安藤太郎 (1846–1924), or Tadatsune 忠経, was a former shogunal retainer who joined the Foreign Ministry after the Restoration and was traveling as a secretary with the Iwakura Mission when Ryūhoku met up with him in Paris. Andō went on to become a Christian and a leader in the Japanese temperance movement.
[85] The Nishi Honganji temple had dispatched Shimaji Mokurai 島地黙雷 (1838–1911) to Europe in early 1872. When the Higashi Honganji group arrived in Paris that winter, Matsumoto Hakka sent a letter to Shimaji in Germany, entrusting it to Honma Kōsō, whom the group had met aboard the *Godavéry*. Shimaji Mokurai's diary for 11.06 notes that he had already made plans to leave Germany for Rome, but upon

Andō and Ikeda. There is a waterfall there, and it is a lovely place, refreshing and secluded. We went for a drink at the Anglais, where the food was exquisite.[88] Buoyed by our tipsiness on the way back, we went to a brothel on the Rue d'Amboise. Yet we left only a wild swan's tracks in the mud.[89]

11.09. Monday. Fine.
I went out for a stroll with Shimaji and the others. We toured the royal palace[90] inside and out, and we also went to see the "Panorama." The "Panorama" portrays scenes from the Franco-Prussian War, and although it is done with paintings, one can hardly believe that they are paintings.[91] The show is a marvelous and enchanting spectacle; I have

---

receiving a letter informing him that the Higashi Honganji contingent had arrived in France, he immediately changed his plans and departed for Paris the following day (51). Shimaji was one of the most important figures in the modernization of Buddhism; in the early years of Meiji he had worked to foster ties between the Buddhist establishment and the new government, but during his time in Europe Shimaji came to believe strongly in the separation of religion and state. He was active in sponsoring proselytization efforts for the Shin sect both at home and abroad.

[86] Umegami Kōen 梅上廣延 (1835–1907), also known as Takuyū 澤融, was a Shin sect priest who had been dispatched by Nishi Honganji along with Shimaji Mokurai and three students to observe religious institutions in the West.

[87] Sakata Kan'ichi was more commonly known as Sakata Kan'ichirō 坂田乾一郎 (b. 1850), and he had traveled to France to pursue military studies in 1871. He was particularly close to Nakae Chōmin, and also served as a guide and translator to several visiting Japanese.

[88] Ryūhoku visited the Café Anglais, an elegant restaurant on Boulevard des Italiens.

[89] The phrase about "a wild swan's tracks in the mud" 鴻爪泥 was originally a metaphor for impermanence, but came to suggest the fleeting tracks of a traveler. It also seems to have been particularly common to use in reference to a momentary foray into a pleasure quarter, or a brief stay in a drinking house or other entertainment establishment: the idea perhaps being that like the swan's tracks, no sign of such escapades would endure.

[90] The "royal palace" 王宮 seems to refer to the Palais de l'Élysée, which served as the official residence of the President (*Meijihen*, 283). During his time in Paris, Ryūhoku would visit the bustling shops and cafés of the Palais-Royal frequently, but he referred to the latter site in his diary with an approximation of the French name.

[91] The Panorama was located next to the Palais de l'Industrie and was exhibiting *The*

never seen such splendid sights in all of my life. Mr. Osada Keitarō returned this evening from Prussia.

11.10. Tuesday. Windy and rainy.
I visited Mr. Osada Keitarō at the Japanese legation today. We talked about what events had been transpiring in Tokyo since he left, and I also asked him about the state of affairs in various European cities. Our fortuitous meeting today was thoroughly enjoyable. In the evening, too, he came over to my hotel and we talked more.

11.11. Wednesday. Overcast.
Today I visited Mr. Kurimoto with Shuntai. In the afternoon, there were powdery snow flurries. After dinner, I went to the Valentino dance hall[92] with Osada, Ikeda, and Andō. The majority of the hall's patrons were young playboys, and among the women too, there were many prostitutes. After I returned to the hotel, Satō and Gotō also came over for a chat.

11.12. Thursday. Fine.
Today I went with Osada and Andō to the Gare St. Lazare, where we boarded the 1:25 train. We crossed the Seine upstream (it was swollen

---

Siege of Paris by Henri Philippoteaux, a cycloramic portrayal of battle. Matsumoto Hakka reacted similiary to the Panorama: "I went to see some fine paintings of the Franco-Prussian war … it was impossible to separate the paintings from reality."
[92] Located at 251 Rue St. Honoré, the Valentino was a venue for concerts and balls held on alternating days. The 1876 Baedeker guide for *Paris and Its Environs* gives some indication of the type of venue the Valentino was in a crisp note stating that the concerts held there twice weekly were "of a lower class, particularly as regards the character of the audience" (52–53). An 1874 British handbook for Paris similarly notes the "Salle Valentino" is "a very gaily decorated ball-room, with good orchestra: the company more numerous than select" (Murray, 62). According to the schedule in the latter guide, Ryūhoku would have attended a concert on his first visit and balls on his three remaining visits to the Valentino on 11.19, February 1 and March 11.

from the recent rains and flowing quite forcefully). We passed through three tunnels along the way, and arrived in Versailles at two o'clock. This is the location of the national parliament, and it is also where the President, Mr. Thiers, lives.[93] We saw the Trianon villa; it was the residence of Louis XVI, and Napoleon I also lived here once. Inside the palace, there were portraits of Louis XIV and Louis XV. The most gorgeous items were the large malachite bowls, flower vase, and light stand presented to Emperor Napoleon by the country of Russia. There was also a study belonging to Napoleon, where the chaise-longue, desk, and other furnishings still retained their old appearance. In the room he used for meetings with his Empress, the brocade drapery and embroidered cushions sparkled with a vividness that made my mind imagine how things must have been in those former times. From clocks to tables, every furnishing in the palace was made from precious jewels, and their beauty was astonishing. We also saw the building where the carriages are stored. It housed a carriage that Napoleon had ridden in, the carriage used for the grand wedding of Napoleon III, as well as carriages that Louis XV and Louis XVI had used; even the equestrian gear was still intact. Not a single item there was anything less than magnificent. The villa's inner garden bore a striking resemblance to the Fukiage garden[94] of our old shogunate, and I found myself overcome with feelings of sorrow. Within the garden, there was a single thatched hut. Apparently it was built to look rustic because it was the custom of Louis XVI's queen to milk cows herself there.[95] If you cross through

---

[93] Louis Adolphe Thiers (1797–1877) had become President of the Third Republic in February 1871, just one month before he relocated his government to Versailles after the outbreak of the Paris Commune.
[94] Now a garden within the Imperial Palace in Tokyo, the Fukiage Gyoen 吹上御苑 was originally a garden northwest of the Nishinomaru in the Tokugawa shogunate's castle in Edo.
[95] The queen was Marie Antoinette (1755–1793).

the garden and exit through the gate, you come out on the imperial highway, that is, the Boulevard de la Reine. Both sides of the road are lined with trees: another spectacular scene. We had tea and left the palace, returning by train again to Paris at five o'clock.

<ruby>烏兒塞宮<rt>ウエルサイエ</rt></ruby>　　　*The Palace at Versailles*
想曾鳳輦幾回過　好與淑姬長晤歌　錦帳依然人不在　玻璃窓外夕陽多
　How many times, I wonder, did the august carriage pass through here?
　What splendid exchanges of verse he must have had with refined ladies!
　The brocade drapes remain untouched, but the people now are gone;
　Through the glass windows of the palace sets the evening sun.[96]

11.13. Friday. Rainy.
Today Reverend Gennyo wanted to go see the scenery at the Bois de Boulogne, and so I became his guide and escorted him there. Because of the rain, no one was visiting the park, and the quiet seclusion was quite lovely. This evening, Mr. Andō came over for a chat.

11.14. Saturday. Rainy.
I visited Mr. Kurimoto, but he was not in. I went by Bouché's shop and returned. Today, I was able to purchase two ancient Roman coins from an antique shop that I passed along the way.

---

[96] In this poem on Versailles, Ryūhoku makes use of antique terms idealizing the royal personage, such as *hōren* 鳳輦 (lit. "the phoenix cart"), the name typically used for the imperial carriage. Likewise, two of the terms from the quatrain's second line come from a poem (number 139) in the *Book of Songs*: "The pond outside the eastern gate / is perfect for soaking hemp; / That beautiful lovely princess / is perfect for sharing verse" 東門之池　可以漚麻　彼美淑姬　可與晤歌. The conventionality of such diction makes the novelty of the "glass windows" in the last line especially striking.

11.15. Sunday. Overcast.
Mr. Matsuda Masahisa transferred from this hotel to another. In the afternoon, I visited Mr. Numa Morikazu at his new hotel on the Rue de Monceau. Kawazu, Kumagai,[97] and Inagaki[98] were all there. In the evening, Mr. Harada Goichi[99] came over to visit.

11.16. Monday. Fine.
Our Ambassador, Minister of the Right Iwakura [Tomomi], along with Mr. Kido [Takayoshi] and Mr. Ōkubo [Toshimichi] came today from England.[100] They arrived at a hotel on the Rue de Présbourg.[101]

---

[97] Kumagai Naotaka 熊谷直孝 (1850–1942) was the nephew of Kurimoto Joun and a student of French at the Yokohama French academy. Ryūhoku would thus likely have met him while serving as a cavalry instructor at the school in the mid-1860s. After finishing his studies in Yokohama, Kumagai went on to teach in the Numazu military academy, and then at the Yokosuka foundry. In the early summer of 1872, he left Japan with Kawazu Sukeyuki to study shipbuilding in France. He returned to Japan in 1874 for a career as an instructor of shipbuilding.

[98] Inagaki Kitazō 稲垣喜多造 (b. 1848) began studying French in Yokohama and went on to teach the language at the Yokosuka foundry in 1869. He also worked in the foundry's accounting department and in 1871, he went to further his studies in France. He returned to Japan in 1874, where he contributed to the establishment of modern accounting practices.

[99] Harada Goichi 原田吾一 (1830–1910), also known as Harada Kazumichi or Ichidō 原田一道, had accompanied the bakufu's 1863–64 Ikeda mission to France as a military student. Upon returning to Japan he continued his military career, and in early Meiji, he accompanied Yamada Akiyoshi on the Iwakura Mission. It should be noted that Harada Goichi and Harada Ichidō appear as two separate individuals in Tomita Hitoshi's extremely useful dictionary of early Japanese who traveled abroad, but comparing Ryūhoku's diary with those of his contemporaries such as Shimaji Mokurai shows that Goichi and Ichidō in fact are the same person.

[100] The Iwakura Mission was a tremendous undertaking by which many of the Japanese government's top officials traveled to Europe and the United States to meet Western dignitaries and to study Western social, political, legal, and cultural institutions between 1871 and 1873. Those whom Ryūhoku mentions here were three of the most prominent men among the forty-plus officials traveling on the mission: Ambassador Iwakura Tomomi 岩倉具視 (1825–1883) and Vice-Ambassadors Kido Takayoshi 木戸孝允 (1833–1877) and Ōkubo Toshimichi 大久保利通 (1830–1878). For an excellent introduction to the Mission, see Marlene Mayo's article. A complete English translation of the five-volume report compiled by the Mission's chief secretary, Kume

Utsunomiya Saburō[102], Kawaji Kandō[103], and Tomita Tōzan[104] checked into my hotel. I went for a stroll with Mr. Utsunomiya at night.

11.17. Tuesday. Fine.
I went to see the zoological gardens today with Mr. Utsunomiya and Mr. Honma Kōsō. By the time we were making our way back, the sky had grown dark. When we passed in front of the gates to the royal palace, we used a telescope to look at Venus. It was shaped like a semicircular moon, and was a reddish purple color. In the evening, Mr. Tanabe

---

Kunitake, was published in 2002.

[101] Although Ryūhoku uses the term *ryokan* 旅館 or "inn," the Iwakura Mission was actually not staying in a public hotel. As Kume Kunitake noted in his report, "This mansion had originally been leased to the Turkish Legation, but because of the arrival of our Embassy the French government had given us use of the building as our diplomatic residence for the duration of our stay, and had selected a steward to attend to all our needs. The house looks out upon the north-west {south-east} side of the Arc de Triomphe, although the front entrance is at {No. 10} Rue de Presbourg" (Andrew Cobbing's translation, III: 29); see also Kume, III: 40–41 and Tomita, *Iwakura*, 21–23.

[102] Utsunomiya Saburō 宇都宮三郎 (1834–1902) was a student of Dutch whom Ryūhoku befriended in the mid-1860s while he was in domiciliary confinement. In his early career, Utsunomiya pursued military studies, focusing principally on chemistry, which he studied in France in 1867. Upon his return to Japan, he taught at the Kaisei Academy, and then went to work for the government as an engineer in 1872. Later that year, he traveled to England and the United States to arrange the purchase of equipment. He went on to establish the Japanese cement industry (Imaizumi, 256).

[103] Kawaji Kandō 川路寛堂 (1844–1927), also known as Tarō 太郎, had pursued Chinese studies under Asaka Gonsai (1791–1860) and Dutch studies under Mitsukuri Genpo (1799–1863) as a young man. He also studied French under Mermet de Cachon and trained in the infantry. In 1866, he headed a group of students bound for England, but was prevented from entering the University of London because of his age, leading him to study navigation with a private tutor. The collapse of the shogunate brought him back to Japan, but he soon returned to Europe as a translator for the Iwakura Mission. He later tried his hand in business before settling into a career in education.

[104] Tomita Tōzan 富田冬三, also known as Tatsuzō 達三 or Noriyasu 命保, was a former shogunal official who had traveled on the Shibata mission to France and England in 1865 with Fukuchi Gen'ichirō; see the latter's *Kaiō jidan*, 304; and Tomita, *Yokohama Furansu*, 33. When Ryūhoku met him, it seems Tomita was part of the Iwakura Mission.

Taichi[105] came over for a chat, as did Matsumoto Tamenosuke. He is the son of Judayū and told me about how he had been in the United States for some time.[106]

11.18. Wednesday. Overcast; rainy in the afternoon.
Mr. Chanoine[107] came over for a visit today, and we reminisced about old times. He left after several hours. During the reign of the shogunate, he had been ordered by Napoleon III to come to our country as an army instructor. He and I were on very familiar terms with one another then, and today we found ourselves reunited here of all places. How marvelous the workings of fate are! In the afternoon, I went to the Embassy's lodgings and met with the officials there. I invited Mr. Tanabe out, and went to see the Panorama again. He was also quite impressed with it.

---

[105] Tanabe Taichi 田邊太一 (1831–1915), whose name is also read Yasukazu, served on several of the shogunate's early missions to France. When Ryūhoku encountered him in Paris, he was traveling as a secretary for the Iwakura Mission. Under the sobriquet Renshū 蓮舟, Tanabe was also an accomplished Chinese poet, teaching Shimazaki Tōson *kanshi* and Chinese vernacular fiction. He contributed a preface to *Ryūhoku zenshū* and perhaps also to the second volume of *New Chronicles of Yanagibashi*.
[106] Matsumoto Judayū 松本壽太夫 was a shogunal official who had been part of Japan's first mission to the United States in 1860. He went on to become the principal of the Kaisei Academy in 1866 and was chosen to accompany Ono Tomogorō and Fukuzawa Yukichi to the United States to acquire a ship in 1867 (Fukuzawa, *Autobiography*, 166; Tanabe, *Bakumatsu Gaikōdan* I: 248; Fujii, 101–122 includes a photograph of the group). Judayū apparently fled to the United States in the wake of the Meiji Restoration, and in 1871, Iwakura Tomomi encountered his son (Tamenosuke) in San Francisco; the son had apparently "already forgotten Japanese" and Iwakura took him under his wing (Fujii, 137).
[107] In 1866, Charles Sulpice Jules Chanoine (1835–1915) was invited by the shogunate to establish a training program in Yokohama for a modernized infantry, cavalry, and artillery. Soon after Chanoine and his officers arrived in 1867, Ryūhoku began training under them and also learned the French language. Ryūhoku would thus have spent a full year with Chanoine, who returned to France a few months after the collapse of the shogunate in 1868. In 1872, Chanoine was chosen by the French government to welcome the Iwakura Mission members and escort them to several sites.

11.19. Thursday. Rainy.

Utsunomiya and I braved the rain to visit Osada and go for a walk downtown. In the evening, Masuda Katsunori came over to talk, and I went with him to watch the dancing at the Valentino.

11.20. Friday. Overcast.

I visited Kurimoto, and then Masuda. Today I obtained several old German coins. At night, Shioda Saburō,[108] Komatsu Seiji,[109] and Hayashi Tadasu[110] came over to chat.

11.21. Saturday. Fine.

I spent the whole day in the hotel, writing letters home and attending to various matters. I gave the proprietor of the inn several kinds of Japanese items that I had brought with me in my suitcase. His expression of joy was nearly palpable. Mr. Kawaji Kandō came over from the Embassy's lodgings and informed me that our country has

---

[108] Former shogunal retainer Shioda Saburō 鹽田三郎 (1843–1889) had gotten an early start studying French under Mermet de Cachon while in Hokkaido, where he also befriended Kurimoto Joun. He served on several shogunal missions to Europe before taking up a post in the Yokohama French academy during Ryūhoku's tenure as cavalry head. After the Restoration, he served as a secretary for Japan's Paris legation and was also called into service en route by the Iwakura Mission.

[109] Komatsu Seiji 小松濟治 (1847–1893) became Japan's first student to enroll in a German university when he began studying law at Heidelberg in 1868. At the time Ryūhoku met him, he was serving as a secretary for the Iwakura Mission while also assisting with Japan's participation in the Viennese exhibition (Araki, esp. 28–30). Upon his return to Japan, he served in the Foreign Ministry briefly before going on to a career in the Ministry of Justice.

[110] Hayashi Tadasu 林董 (1850–1913) had studied English under Japanese castaway Joseph Heco and American missionary James Hepburn before getting a chance to study at the University College School in England in 1866. As in the case of Shioda and Komatsu, Hayashi's extensive overseas experience led the Iwakura Mission to employ him as a secretary. He went on to a career in diplomacy with posts in Russia, Scandinavia, and England.

reformed its calendrical system. This means that today is December 21 in the fifth year of Meiji.[111]

December 22 by the new calendar. Sunday. Fine.
Kurimoto came over and we went to find suitable new lodgings for us. After looking at several places, we finally decided on an inn at Number 5 Rue Corneille.[112] While we were out, we stopped by Irie Fumio's lodgings,[113] and also by Kurimoto's house. We then went together for a quick drink at the Kai. This evening, there was a fire next door to our hotel. Ishikawa and Matsumoto said they raced to the scene to help.[114] At night, I met Minister Itō.[115] Tanabe, Fukuchi,[116] Komatsu, Andō, and I stayed up chatting leisurely until the wee hours.

---

[111] The Meiji government's proclamation adopting the solar calendar was announced on 11.08, but the official statement did not reach the Iwakura Mission until February 3 of 1873. The Mission nevertheless learned of the reform two months prior to this date because Terashima Munenori of the Japanese legation in London forwarded the telegram he had received to the Japanese legation in Paris, which in turn conveyed the information to Mission members. Kido Takayoshi notes the change on 11.21, and Kume Kunitake notes it on 11.22 (III: 62; see also his extensive note in III: 365–366). Reactions varied to the news of calendrical reform; Kume was upset and bewildered by what he saw as an unnecessary change, and similarly Matsumoto Hakka noted his "mounting unease" in his diary. Many Japanese diarists began using the solar calendar to date their journal entries immediately after learning of the reform, but others such as Shimaji Mokurai elected to continue using the lunar calendar (see his entry for 12.03).

[112] The 1874 Baedeker's *Paris* places the Hôtel Corneille at the head of a list of "*Hôtels Garnis* in the Quartier Latin, suitable for the traveller of moderate requirements" (8).

[113] Irie Fumio 入江文郎 (1834–1878), also read Bunrō, was one of the earliest Japanese students of French, which he first learned from a diplomat at the French legation in Yokohama. He went on to teach at the shogunate's French academy, and after the Restoration, the Ministry of Education sent him to study in Paris, where he also supervised the Japanese students resident in France.

[114] Hakka's diary entry for this day records how he went out to observe the fire that had engulfed the house next door only to find himself the object of attention when he fell down.

[115] Future prime minister Itō Hirobumi 伊藤博文 (1841–1909) had come to Europe as a vice ambassador with the Iwakura Mission. He was also serving as Minister of Public Works, hence Ryūhoku's reference to him as Minister Itō.

[116] Fukuchi Gen'ichirō 福地源一郎 (1841–1906), who used the sobriquet Ōchi 櫻痴,

December 23. Monday. Fine.
Tanabe, Andō, and I went for a bath. We then wandered around the Bois de Boulogne, had a drink and returned. Tonight as well, several friends came over to visit.

December 24. Tuesday. Fine.
I got up early, gathered together my things and took them over to the inn on the Rue Corneille with the other members of our group. The inn faces the Luxembourg Gardens. At night, I went for a walk and visited Bouché's house. This evening I caught a cold.

December 25. Wednesday. Fine.
Today is "Christmas." Several members of our group went out today to have a look at several churches, and they said that they were packed with people. I was taking care of my cold and so I lay in bed all day.

December 26. Thursday. Overcast.
Beginning today, a female teacher named Legrand will be coming over to give English lessons to several people. I will also study with her.[117]

December 27. Friday. Overcast.
The teacher came. In the afternoon, I went to a bathhouse nearby. The price was just fifty *centimes*; it is quite an inexpensive place. Recently I

---

was a seasoned diplomat who had been on multiple shogunal missions. He was employed by the Treasury at the time and was traveling with the Iwakura Mission as a high-ranking secretary. Fukuchi went on to a career as an important dramatist and journalist (for a biography, see Huffman). In the second decade of Meiji, Fukuchi staked out a "gradualist" approach to the implementation of popular sovereignty, constitutional government, and other political reforms; Ryūhoku frequently criticized such a stance as unnecessarily dilatory.

[117] The name "Legrand" is a conjecture; the identity of this English teacher, who visited Ryūhoku's lodgings over fifty times during his stay in Paris, is unknown.

have not been taking walks because of my cold, and every night I go to bed early.

December 28. Saturday. Fine.
The teacher came. Today I visited Hayashi and Komatsu, and met Mr. Harada Goichi. A letter arrived from Osada, informing me that he agreed to go out with me tomorrow.

December 29. Sunday. Fine.
I visited Osada, and together we went to the Hotel de Capucin to invite Sugiyama Shūtarō[118] and Tomita Tatsuzō out. We boarded the 1:50 train, and arrived in Saint Germain after forty-five minutes. I hear that when railroad tracks were first laid in France, it was between these two cities. This place is like Yokohama in my own country.[119] On top of a tall hill is a palace that was built by King François I.[120] It is just seven miles from Paris. We visited a museum inside the palace. It would be impossible to recount all of the items on display, from ancient vessels of metal, stone, and pottery, to old coins, human and animal bones (some of which are from beasts very rarely seen) to swords, bows, crossbows, hair ornaments and earrings from Roman times. Outside

---

[118] Sugiyama Shūtarō 杉山秀太郎 (1843–1880), or Kazunari 一成, was a former shogunal retainer who was traveling as an attendant on the Iwakura Mission. He went on to become a commissioner for Japan's participation in the 1876 International Exhibition in Philadelphia, and later worked as a secretary in the Home Ministry.
[119] Japan's first railroad was established between Tokyo's Shinbashi and Yokohama, and service commenced on 09.12 (October 14) of 1872, the very day that Ryūhoku departed from Tokyo to Yokohama, whence he embarked on his trip to Europe. It is clear from the partial copy of Ryūhoku's original diary made by Matsumoto Hakka that Ryūhoku made this journey by carriage rather than rail, but the inauguration of rail service to Yokohama would nevertheless have been fresh in his mind.
[120] The Château in St-Germain-en-Laye was built by François I; it houses the Musée des Antiquités Nationales.

the palace there was a restaurant overlooking the steep cliff.[121] We went there for a cup of tea and feasted our eyes on the lovely view.

半似鴻臺半鳥邱　風光想起故山秋　登臨今日旗亭酒　一洗胸襟萬斛愁
A cross between the Wild Goose Platform and the Flying Bird Hill,[122]
The view here calls to mind autumn in the mountains of home.
Surveying the scene from on high today, I take a drink from the tavern;
Washing away the surfeit of melancholy that lingered in my breast.

Gazing from our mounted position here, the Seine River looks like a single strand of silk thread, and I can see the fortress at Mont Valérien as well. The Prussian soldiers were unable to capture this fortress, which is the largest base outside of Paris. We gave the waiter our order of drinks and food and then took a few moments to go stroll about in the woods. As dusk drew near, we went up to the restaurant again, where the wine was delicious and the meat fresh. We enjoyed ourselves to our heart's content and then at five o'clock returned on the train.

December 30. Monday (12.01 by the old calendar). Rainy.[123]
The teacher came today as usual. I went to the Boulevard de Capucines to have my hair cut. Today I was able to buy two different kinds of old Egyptian relics.

---

[121] In his recent annotated edition of *Kōsei nichijō*, Ida Shin'ya notes that Ryūhoku is describing the restaurant at the Pavillon Henri IV, still open for business, which commands panoramic views of the Seine (197). Ryūhoku visited the restaurant a second time on April 20.
[122] The first Japanese location mentioned is Kōnodai 国府台, in Ichikawa city, Chiba prefecture (Terakado, *Edo hanjōki*, 175, n. 26); the second is Asukayama 飛鳥山, a famous site for cherry blossom viewing in northern Tokyo.
[123] I have followed a minor correction to the text proposed by editors of *Meijihen* here and in the January 2 entry.

December 31. Tuesday. Fine.
The teacher came today. At night, I had a drink with Ishikawa. We stayed up quite late talking about how it felt to be celebrating the end of the year overseas. Today I posted several letters home.

January 1, Meiji 6 [1873]. Wednesday (12.03 by the old calendar). Pleasant and fine.
This morning I got up, put on my new clothes, and headed for the legation to offer my New Year's greetings. I met with the Secretary. The legation staff had some champagne, which they served in place of the spiced *toso* wine of New Year's Day. I went by the Hôtel de Lord Byron to visit my friends there, but they were all gone. I visited Kōno, Tsuruta, Komuro,[124] Kawaji, and Sugiyama, and on the way back I stopped in for a quick drink at the Capucin tavern.[125] Today, I climbed the Arc de Triomphe. It is thousands of stone steps high, and from the top one can look down on the whole city of Paris: quite a splendid feeling. There is little else particularly worth seeing here on New Year's Day, just crowds of men and women wandering around the city, and a vast array of various goods displayed on sale. I composed two poems.

草廬猶在墨江濆 何事閑身去若雲 萬里清音河上舍 無端逢着舊東君
My grass cottage still lies at the Sumida's edge;
What on earth has sent my idle soul adrift like a floating cloud?

---

[124] In the 1860s, Komuro Shinobu 小室信夫 (1839–1898) had been a fiery nativist who was involved in the decapitation of statuary at Tōjiin, the Kyoto temple dedicated to the Ashikaga shoguns. After the Restoration, however, he served in the Sain (Chamber of the Left), which sent him and four others to Europe in 1872 to investigate its legal institutions. Leaving aboard the same ship was the lord of Tokushima, Hachisuka Mochiaki 蜂須賀茂韶 (1846–1918), whom Komuro had befriended years earlier in his activist days.

[125] Perhaps Ryūhoku's destination was the Hotel des Capucines at 37 Boulevard des Capucines.

Ten thousand miles away, at an inn on the Seine,
I chance to encounter the old god who brings us spring.

客裏新正趣更奇　蠻奴相對不相知　一瓶傾盡三鞭酒　唱出東京舊竹枝
Ringing in the New Year abroad is really rather odd;
Face to face with the barbarian, and yet we remain strangers.
I drank a whole bottle of champagne, down to the last drop,
And sang out an old "bamboo branch" ballad of Tokyo.[126]

January 2. Thursday. Rainy.
The teacher came as usual. I went to Beiran's house with Ishikawa.[127] After we returned to the hotel, Reverend Mokurai came over to chat.

---

[126] "Bamboo branch" (Ch. *zhuzhi*; J. *chikushi*) ballads are a genre of poems that treat local customs or popular manners, often of a romantic nature. The term translated here as "barbarian" is *bando*, a term Ryūhoku used earlier to refer to the service staff aboard his ship (09.17 poem) and the natives peddling goods in Singapore (10.01 poem).

[127] The identity of the person whom Ryūhoku and Ishikawa visit is uncertain. Ryūhoku uses the characters 米蘭, suggesting something like *beiran* or *mairan*, characters he uses elsewhere to represent the city "Milan." In an earlier article, I suggested the possibility that this name might refer to Charles Buland (1837–1871), who served as an assistant to Mermet de Cachon at the French Language School in the last days of the shogunate. In his 1866 diary, Ryūhoku wrote of being led around Yokohama by a Frenchman named 比蘭 (Ōshima, 62), a person whom Maeda Ai identified as Charles Buland (*Narushima Ryūhoku*, 151). Buland continued to teach French in Osaka until the tenth month of 1870, when he returned to France escorting several Japanese students. However, Buland died in April 1871, just a few months after his return to France (Meiji Ōsaka, *Nichi-Futsu*, esp. 90–106). It is possible that Ryūhoku's visit was to the Buland family, though since they lived in Bourg-la-reine at the time such an interpretation is rather unlikely. For these reasons I have come to think that the most likely interpretation is that Ryūhoku and Ishikawa visited a brothel on this day. Some of the otherwise obscure names that occur elsewhere in Ryūhoku's diary have been convincingly shown to refer to prostitutes (Emma on March 4, Rochelle on March 15, Alba on March 30, Teresa on April 1, and Ida on April 5). The name "Beiran" may thus represent "Maureen" or "Brienne," or perhaps simply a prostitute from Milan. In a quatrain Ryūhoku composed upon his return to Yokohama (see Afterword), he used the term in the following couplet: "Famous Milanese courtesans and Parisian wine / Whom shall I call to regale with these grand adventures of yesterday?" 米蘭名妓巴黎酒　豪興呼誰話昨游.

January 3. Friday. Fine.
The teacher came. In the afternoon, I visited Kurimoto and Osada, and then headed to Ambassador Iwakura's hotel to offer my New Year's greetings. I celebrated together with Itō, Yamaguchi,[128] Tanabe, and Andō, and since the hour was quite late, I stayed there for the night.

January 4. Saturday. Fine.
I returned at dawn. The teacher came. Today, Nitta came and told me that he would be leaving here tomorrow morning. At night, we went for a stroll in the Luxembourg Gardens.

January 5. Sunday. Fine.
I went to the Rue des Ecoles to visit Mr. Shimaji and Mr. Umegami, and with the two of them went to view the Cluny Museum. Long ago, the building was the site of the palace where Emperor Julian, the nephew of Emperor Constantine, lived.[129] Apparently, some of the Roman Popes also lived here. Inside the building are some walls that have been preserved just as they were back then. There were also a great many old vessels, coins, and other relics including crowns from the Roman period. In the garden, there were carved stone figures of humans and animals lined up, all of which were marvelous to see. In front of the gate to the building, there was an antique shop called Bōban, and here as well, there were many old items on display. When I went to see Mr. Chanoine today, he was not in. I visited Mr. Komeda

---

[128] Saga native Yamaguchi Naoyoshi 山口尚芳 (1839–1894), whose given name is also read Masuka, was a Vice Ambassador on the Iwakura Mission. Some authorities state that he was born in 1842.
[129] The Musée de Cluny is located in the Place des Ecoles; the building housing it was once known as the "Palais de Julien," after Julian (331–363; Roman Emperor, 361–363), the nephew of Constantine the Great.

Keiji,¹³⁰ and he was not in either. Harada Goichi came over to talk. At a stall set up on the bank of the Seine, I bought old copper coins from several different countries. They were quite inexpensive.

January 6. Monday. Fine.
The teacher came. I visited Mr. Chanoine again, but he wasn't in. When evening came, Komeda visited me, and we went to the Théâtre de l'Odéon together. I was struck by how gorgeous the theater was. The play they were performing was about a woman who dies with a grudge and becomes a vengeful spirit. It was apparently based on an old tale, but since I was unable to understand the language very well, it is difficult for me to give a clear account of it.¹³¹

---

130 Komeda Keiji 米田桂次 (1843–1917), or Keijirō 桂次郎, was another name for Tateishi Onojirō 立石斧次郎, who became a celebrity when he traveled to the United States as part of the 1860 Man'en Embassy. The adopted son of interpreter Tateishi Tokujūrō 立石得十郎, this precocious and affable young man had been christened "Tommy" by the American ship captain (based on his name Tamehachi) before the ambassadors even reached San Francisco. As the Japanese ambassadors proceeded from city to city, "Tommy" was the focus of overwhelming media attention and much fanciful speculation (Kanai Madoka, esp. 69–116; Miyanaga, *Man'en*, esp. 126–135, 160–167, 222). After his return to Japan, Tateishi served as an interpreter for American envoy Townsend Harris while at the same time teaching in an English academy (Masuda Takashi, 36; 59–60; Imai Ichiryō, 25–28). In 1871, Tateishi was chosen to accompany the Iwakura Mission as a "secretary of the second rank" under the name Nagano Keijirō 長野桂二郎 (Tanaka Akira, 10), but Ryūhoku's use of the older name suggests that they knew each other, perhaps from Tateishi's tenure at the Kaiseijo or in Yokohama. Tateishi went on to hold posts in the development office of Hokkaido and in the immigration office in Hawaii.
131 Ryūhoku saw the premiere of *Les Érinnyes* by Leconte de Lisle (1818–1894) with a score by Jules Massenet (1842–1912). The work was a two-act distillation of the *Oresteia* of Aeschylus, concerning the murder of Agamemnon by his wife Clytemnestra, and the revenge that their son, Orestes, takes by slaying his mother. The "vengeful spirit" Ryūhoku mentions presumably refers to Clytemnestra's ghost, who sends the female goddesses of the play's title to pursue Orestes for his matricide.

January 7. Tuesday. Fine.

I visited Beiran, who was not in. At night, Mr. Kurimoto and his wife came over, bringing the younger brother of Lord Hachisuka with them.[132] Today, we made the decision to send Seki Shinzō to go study in London.

January 8. Wednesday. Fine.

Today, Seki Shinzō left for England. The teacher came as usual. I visited Mr. Irie and Mr. Harada. I went to visit Mr. Rosny,[133] but he was not in. I went to see the Cluny Museum again.

January 9. Thursday. Fine.

I went to the Comptoir d'Escompte Bank with Kurimoto to meet with Mr. Coullet about a money order to cover our travel expenses.[134] I

---

[132] Lord Hachisuka presumably refers to Hachisuka Mochiaki, who traveled with Komuro Shinobu to England in 1872, studying there until 1879. According to the diaries of Shimaji Mokurai and Kido Takayoshi, he was traveling with his wife Ayako 斐子. Hachisuka went on to become a resident minister in France. While Hachisuka seems to have been an only child, perhaps the "younger brother" Ryūhoku mentions was Hachisuka Makijirō 蜂須賀萬亀次郎 (1864–1901), with whom the elder Hachisuka had departed Japan (*Meijihen*, 291).

[133] Léon de Rosny (1837–1914) was an early Orientalist scholar and extraordinary Japanophile who interacted with many Japanese visitors to Paris in the 1860s and 1870s. Ryūhoku had likely heard of him from Fukuzawa Yukichi, Mitsukuri Shūhei or Fukuchi Gen'ichirō, all of whom had spent a good deal of time with Rosny in 1862 while they served on the Bunkyū mission to Europe. He may also have learned about Rosny from the diaries of other participants on such late-Tokugawa diplomatic missions. Ryūhoku was not, however, the first in his group to make Rosny's acquaintance, for Shimaji Mokurai had escorted Hakka and several others to visit Rosny's home at 15 Rue Lacépède on December 30.

[134] The Comptoir d'Escompte was established in 1848 and located at 14 Rue Bergère. Its director was named Paul Jacques Coullet (b. 1830), but the person mentioned here may be A.M. Coullet, who had longstanding financial dealings with the Japanese government. In 1865, the latter Coullet was deputy manager of the Messageries Impériales, and had been sent to Japan as a representative of a large bank that sought to coordinate trading ventures with Japan (Medzini, 114).

went to the Hôtel de Lord Byron, and then with Komeda Keiji, Nishimura Katsurō,[135] and a certain Mr. Noguchi,[136] paid a visit to the tomb of Napoleon I. The gravestone itself was made from precious stone of a purplish cast like lustrous amber, and the lower platform was of green marble. The floor of the whole crypt was tiled with stones of various colors. The structure's iridescent splendor struck me with its solemn grandeur. There was a chapel to either side holding the sarcophagi of the Emperor's parents and his younger brother. Truly there can be few graves in the entire world to rival this one.

哂彼驪山錮九泉　祖龍血肉霎時烟　英雄身後無遺憾　玉碣巍然億萬年

I scoff at Mt. Li, its crypt made to stanch the underworld's nine streams;
Still the Qin Emperor's flesh and blood became but fleeting mist.
A true hero, Napoleon died leaving no regrets behind,
His jeweled tombstone will tower mightily for eternity.[137]

---

[135] Nishimura Katsurō 西村勝郎 (1846–1879) was the younger brother of Nishimura Katsuzō 西村勝三; he went to Europe in 1872 to study shoe and leather production and to negotiate the purchase of necessary machinery and samples (Nishimura-ō Denki Hensankai, 67, 198–199; Kakuyūkai, 79).

[136] Kokumai Shigeyuki identifies the individual Ryūhoku meets here as Noguchi Tomizō 野口富蔵 (1841–1883), a young man from Aizu who began learning English in Hakodate (78). In 1865, Noguchi became the assistant, secretary, and occasional bodyguard of British diplomat Ernest Satow. In his diary, Satow reminisced, "Noguchi eventually went with me in 1869 to England, where I paid for his schooling during a couple of years. After my return to Japan he stayed on awhile in London at the expense of the Japanese government and eventually came back to Tôkiô, where he obtained a minor appointment in a public office … He was honest and faithful to the end" (174–175). While studying in London, Noguchi was called into service by the Iwakura Mission as a translator and guide; and upon his return he worked in Kobe (Miyazaki Tomihachi, 257–288). According to his diary, Takasaki Masakaze encountered Noguchi and Shibusawa Kisaku in New York and San Francisco as they made their way back to Japan in August of 1873.

[137] Ryūhoku refers here to the despotic first Qin Emperor, whose quest for immortality and excessiveness in mobilizing thousands of men to build a massive and lavish tomb for him were decried by later historians.

Although it may seem a little unusual to use the phrase "jeweled tombstone," the Emperor's headstone is in fact made of jewels and not stone. Do not let conventional assumptions lead you into dismissing the term as baseless.

Behind Napoleon's tomb, there is a center for veterans.[138] When we went inside to have a look, we saw that several hundred flags and banners that Napoleon captured in battles with various countries over the course of his life are on display. When we had a look inside the kitchen, we saw a huge pot three feet in diameter for brewing coffee. The cauldron for boiling vegetables was over six feet in diameter, and they say that one batch can feed six hundred veterans. Outside the veteran's center were arrayed several cannons plundered from various foreign countries. Many of the cannons had Arabic writing inscribed on them. I imagine that those with Chinese characters are probably the spoils of Napoleon III's recent attack on that country.[139] Among the cannons, I spotted one that was cast with the crest of the Mōri house, and I suspect this may have been captured during the Shimonoseki campaign.[140] We left the veterans' center and went to see the Entrepôt (warehouse), which is located along the bank of the Seine.[141] It houses a large quantity of wine, and the facility's stone cellars with bowed

---

[138] Ryūhoku is describing the Hôtel des Invalides, a home for retired and disabled soldiers. The vestibule of the Salle du Conseil on the first floor contains the captured flags Ryūhoku mentions (Baedeker's *Paris*, 221).
[139] Ryūhoku refers to the 1856–1860 Anglo-French hostilities against China that are sometimes called the "Second Opium War."
[140] In 1864, the combined forces of England, France, Holland, and the United States struck Shimonoseki in retaliation for the Chōshū domain's firing on European ships the previous year.
[141] Ryūhoku may have visited one of the many warehouses close to the Hôtel des Invalides along the Seine, or he may be referring specifically to the Entrepôt at the Halle aux Vins, the "wine-depôt of Paris" located further upstream; "Some half million casks here lie in bond, the duty being paid on their removal" (Baedeker's *Paris*, 37).

roofs bear a striking resemblance to earthen caverns. The proprietor gave me some fine wine to drink, which had a delightful flavor. We left the Entrepôt and went to have a look at a reservoir.[142] It seems that all of the drinking water used daily by the people of the entire city of Paris is drawn from here. They have constructed the reservoir by digging down into the earth to lay water pipes underneath. We first entered into one of the caverns to a depth of 140 paces. We took lanterns with us and descended, coming into another cavern that was several thousand *kyū* wide. The water is stored at two levels and the iron pipes that run between them are so big that a man could not wrap his arms all the way around them. With the pipes running horizontally and vertically, the sound of water is deafening. This large reservoir constructed underground with its interconnected waterways is almost like something out of this world. I found it truly impressive that the wonders of human ingenuity have reached such heights. Just a few yards away from the reservoir was a large park.[143] On a steep cliff, they have built a precarious bridgeway. There were caves and caverns. On top of the mountain, they have built a pavilion, and sitting down here gives you the chance to gaze out over all of Paris. It is like a miniature realm of the immortals. As we were going back, we saw them manipulating the water gates of the canal in such a way as to transport a boat upstream.[144] I was surprised at how cleverly designed it was. Today, Napoleon III died while sick in England. It was truly tragic.

---

[142] Ryūhoku probably visited the Réservoir de Ménilmontant, which was the largest operating in Paris at the time.
[143] Immediately adjacent to the reservoir is the Parc de Belleville, one of the highest parks in the city, but Ryūhoku's description strongly suggests that he visited the Parc des Buttes Chaumont, which is located slightly further north and had opened in 1867. In addition to many grottoes and a restaurant overlooking the city, Buttes Chaumont is known for two famous bridges (a suspension bridge and another made of brick and ominously called "Pont des suicides").
[144] Ryūhoku presumably refers here to the nearby Canal Saint-Martin, which runs to

January 10. Friday. Fine.

The teacher came. In the afternoon, Komeda came to visit, and the two of us went together to tour the Luxembourg Minerals Building.[145] I cannot even guess how many millions of precious jewels, unusual stones, and other minerals they had on display. Komeda is knowledgeable about mineralogy, and so I was quite fortunate to be able to view the exhibition with him. The American Kassei came over to talk in the evening.[146]

January 11. Saturday. Fine.

The teacher came. I went with Shuntai to several bookstores and purchased dozens of volumes. We went to the Rue de Louvre to visit Mr. Cachon,[147] but he was not in. We visited several of our friends at the Hôtel de Lord Byron, and it was late at night before we returned to the hotel.

January 12. Sunday. Rainy.

I visited Harada. Tonight, I wrote several letters home so that I could entrust them to Komeda for delivery.

---

the Bassin de la Villette.

[145] Ryūhoku seems to be describing the Musée de Minéralogie, de Géologie, et de Paléontologie at the Ecole Supérieure des Mines in the Luxembourg Gardens.

[146] The identity of "Kassei" is unknown.

[147] Ryūhoku writes "Kashon" here, which I have conjectured refers to Mermet de Cachon (1828–1889). During his tenure as a cavalry officer in Yokohama, Ryūhoku received private lessons from Cachon, who had come to Japan in 1855 to learn Japanese and work as a missionary. The date of Cachon's demise was long thought to be 1871 (Tomita Hitoshi, *Merume*, 166; Miyanaga Takashi, *Keiō*, 43; even Nishino and Polak, 151), but historian of Franco-Japanese relations Christian Polak has acquired a copy of Cachon's death certificate, which confirms that he died in 1889 (personal communication with the author; see also Nishino and Polak, 50, 58).

January 13. Monday. Fine.
The teacher came. I visited Tanabe and Andō. Komeda is going to leave here on the fifteenth and return to Japan. I therefore asked him to deliver some letters for me and we parted. I went by the legation and met Kanematsu.[148]

January 14. Tuesday. Fine.
The teacher came. I visited Mr. Kurimoto, but he was not in. I visited Tanabe, Andō, Osada, and Komatsu. Mr. Hayashi Tadasu says that he will be leaving here for London tomorrow evening. As I returned home late tonight, I composed one poem while overlooking the Seine.

鐵欄橋畔夜無風　夾岸萬燈波亦紅　金像當頭烟忽散　月輪輾上古王宮
  Along the iron railings at the bridge-side, there is no wind tonight;
  Myriad lights line the river's banks, shading its waves red too.
  Mist suddenly disperses from the statue before my eyes,
  Revealing the moon as it arcs up over the old palace.[149]

January 15. Wednesday. Overcast and cold.
The teacher came. I spent the whole day reading my books.

January 16. Thursday. Fine.
The teacher came. In the afternoon, I went out for an excursion. On the way, I met the naval officer Mr. Bazin. We went together to the Naval Cartography Office, and there met with General Manier.[150] We

---

[148] Kanematsu Naoshige 兼松直稠 (d. 1886) was a former shogunal retainer who served as a secretary at the Japanese legation in Paris. After returning to Japan, he held posts in the Foreign and Home Ministries (Sameshima, 506).
[149] Ida Shin'ya suggests that the "statue" mentioned in the poem is the bronze equestrian statue of Henri IV on the Pont Neuf (204).
[150] The men's names are conjectures; Ryūhoku records them as "Fuzon" and "Banaru."

agreed to meet again, and I left. I also went to the Louvre, and met with Mr. Sasaki Takayuki[151] and a certain Mr. Higashikuze.[152] In the evening, I stopped by the legation and went for a walk together with Osada and Ono Yaichi. We went for a drink at a place on the Boulevard des Italiens. The drinks and food were well prepared and delicious. I then invited Utsunomiya to come with us to see the Gaîté Theatre.[153] The show was about three poor men who obtained golden chicken's eggs and tossed them to become kings.[154] The staging was wonderful, especially the chorus of girls who performed the mayfly dance. It was quite similar to the butterfly dance of Japan, and startled me with its beautiful allure.

January 17. Friday. Overcast.

The teacher came. I visited Mr. Irie Fumio today and asked him about Sanskrit. On the way back, I went by a mineral shop on the banks of the Seine. At night, Reverend Mokurai came over to chat.

---

[151] Tosa native Sasaki Takayuki 佐々木高行 (1830–1910) was Senior Assistant to the Minister of Justice at the time, and was accompanying the Iwakura Mission as a Councilor. A conservative, he later served in a variety of high posts in the Meiji government including vice chairman of the Genrōin and adviser to the Privy Council.

[152] Kyoto-born Higashikuze Michitomi 東久世通禧 (1834–1912) was a member of the nobility who had been active in loyalist causes in the 1860s. Like Sasaki, he was accompanying the Iwakura Mission as a Councilor, and he went on to serve as vice chairman of the Genrōin and vice chairman of the Privy Council.

[153] The Théâtre de la Gaîté, which Ryūhoku visited three times, seated 1800 and had been re-opened in 1862 in the Square des Arts et Métiers; it was, according to Baedeker's, "for melodramatic pieces and fairy scenes" (*Paris*, 48).

[154] Ryūhoku saw *La Poule aux œufs d'or* (The Hen with the Golden Eggs) by Adolphe d'Ennery and Louis-François Clairville. In the play, a person has only to break open one of the golden eggs that a magical hen lays in order to have his every wish fulfilled. The "butterfly dance" that Ryūhoku goes on to mention is part of the repertoire of *gagaku* court music.

January 18. Saturday. Fine.
The teacher came. Today, it was extremely cold. This evening at the invitation of Sakata and the others, I again went to the Gaîté Theatre. We stopped in at a place near the Palais-Royal for a drink. At night, it rained.

January 19. Sunday. Rainy.
The teacher came as usual. I stopped by the hotel of Commissioner Takasaki,[155] but he was not in. I visited my old acquaintance Mr. Chanoine to thank him for his friendliness years ago. I met his wife for the first time. He had the Japanese sword and the copy of *Edo meisho zue* [Illustrated guide to the famous sites of Edo] that I had given him on display in his study. Moreover, he had placed photographs of me and my wife in his photograph album.[156] I was genuinely moved to see that he had not forgotten our old feelings for each other. When we Japanese people meet old acquaintances, many of us treat them like mere streetside passersby; how could I not feel ashamed? After that, I visited Osada, and then went to the Ambassador's hotel for a dinner banquet. I met Mr. Hida Hamagorō.[157] This evening, there was a thunderstorm and a shower of hail; the air was quite warm.

---

[155] Satsuma native Takasaki Masakaze 高崎正風 (1836–1912) had been active in pro-imperial causes in the 1860s. After the Restoration, he became an official in the Sain, and in 1872 he lead a group of five who were investigating European legal institutions. An accomplished *waka* poet, Takasaki instructed the Meiji Emperor in Japanese verse.

[156] *Edo meisho zue* is the gazetteer completed by Saitō Gesshin in 1836 that Ryūhoku quotes at the outset of *New Chronicles of Yanagibashi*. The photographs of Ryūhoku and his wife Ochō that Chanoine preserved in his photograph album have been reprinted in Suzuki Akira, *Tsuiseki*, 151. See Figure 11 for the photograph of Ryūhoku.

[157] Hida Hamagorō 肥田濱五郎 (1830–1889) began studying Dutch, navigation, and shipbuilding in the 1850s, and traveled abroad twice during the 1860s (Fujii Tetsuhiro, 53–56, 94–95). When Ryūhoku met him, Hida was in Paris as an attendant on the Iwakura Mission, and after his return to Japan, he served in several naval posts.

Figure 11. Photograph of Narushima Ryūhoku taken in Japan, circa 1867. This is presumably the actual photograph that Ryūhoku presented to Chanoine in Japan, prior to the latter's return to France. Historian of Franco-Japanese relations Christian Polak was entrusted with the photograph by one of Chanoine's descendants. The verso, at right, is inscribed "Narushima Kinetarō," the name by which Ryūhoku was known to Chanoine. Courtesy of the Christian Polak Collection.

January 20. Monday. Overcast.

By noon, the weather had cleared. I went with Shuntai to visit the naval officer Mr. Manier at his house in Rue du Cherche-Midi. I heard that his neighbor, Duval, is fond of Japanese containers, so I went over to pay him a visit. He had many different kinds of Japanese items, including lacquer-ware, pottery, and bronzes, all of them objects to be carefully treasured. After arranging to meet again, I left. On the way back, I went to see the Church of St. Sulpice. I was impressed with its solemnity. The parishioners all thronged together to listen to the priest's sermon, just like the places of worship back home in Japan.

January 21. Tuesday. Rainy and cold.

The teacher came. I accompanied Reverend Gennyo to both the legation and the Embassy's lodgings. At night, Kawazu and Inagaki came over to chat. At the churches all around the country today, there were services in honor of the spirit of Louis XVI.[158] As I was returning home, I obtained a posthumous photograph of Napoleon III, which put me in a dolorous mood.

January 22. Wednesday. Rainy.
I woke up at dawn, and went again with Reverend Gennyo to the Embassy's lodgings. We accompanied Iwakura, Kido, and Ōkubo to the Luxembourg Observatory.[159] We observed the various instruments and machines, none of which was lacking in precise and expert craftsmanship. The roof of the observatory is made of stone, and on the highest level, there is a circular room. It is made from iron, and can be moved to facilitate observation of the stars. The observatory had so many holes in it from artillery shells that it looked like a beehive. When we asked about it, they said that the damage was suffered during the recent uprising of a rebellious faction.[160] There are five large telescopes, and the largest of them is more than ten feet in length and can be rotated at will. In the garden there were several other separate buildings, some of which measure light from the sun, and some of which are

---

[158] January 21 was the day that Louis XVI was beheaded in 1793.
[159] Ryūhoku is describing the Observatoire within the Palais du Luxembourg, established in 1672. Kume Kunitake's narrative of the Mission's subsequent visits on this day to the Cour d'Assizes in the Palais de Justice, the Sainte-Chapelle church, and the jail at La Santé can be found in *The Iwakura Embassy*, III.131–135.
[160] The uprising refers to the Paris Commune, which had erupted in March 1871.

built for detecting new stars. They said that even the most basic model of the instrument they use to detect new stars costs four thousand francs. When we finished our tour, we went to the courthouse. We went to see the court chambers, and it turned out that they were in the middle of hearing a case. The judges sat in the middle and to the right and left. One of the people seated at the side was wearing a crimson robe, but all of the others were dressed in everyday clothing. The criminal was a woman, and she stood before the judges. I gathered that she had been brought before them on suspicion of killing her husband. There were two witnesses present, a man and a woman. Each came forward to testify to the circumstances of the crime. There were scores of people observing the proceedings, all of whom listened in silence. Among the officials, there was one who wore black robes similar to the priest's robes of our country. He had a white cloth hanging under his throat and would frequently pace back and forth. This was the "lawyer," or representative of the accused. To the side of the courthouse, there was a large church, quite splendid.[161] Its walls were covered with images depicting people being punished; these included some very strange punishments. It is said that these were probably forms of punishment from the barbarous times of antiquity. We left the church and then went to the prison for a tour.

The prison was located in an area not very far from the observatory.[162] A sturdy earthen fence encircles the perimeter, its height a little over twenty feet. It is constructed so that even an agile and fleet-footed man could not easily scale it to escape. The inside of the prison is extremely

---

[161] The church Ryūhoku mentions is likely Sainte Chapelle, adjacent to the Palais de Justice. Its stained glass windows feature representations of Christ's crucifixion and various biblical episodes of martyrdom.

[162] The Iwakura Mission report clarifies that the group visited the Prison de la Santé, which had just been constructed in 1867.

clean; it simply cannot be mentioned in the same breath as the prisons of our land. Moreover, they only have one inmate in each cell. There are some large rooms that accommodate several prisoners, but the individual cells where the inmates sleep are without fail occupied by only one person. Inside each cell, there is a pillow, bedclothes, a bed, and a chair. The prison is hexagonal and has a surveillance station in the center from which the guards can command a view of all six wings. There is also a bathing room, which was quite clean. The prisoners are allowed to bathe once every month, and there is also a place for them to wash up and rinse their mouths out every morning. There is also a free exercise ground, and an additional ground for group marching. The inmates all pursue their own individual industrial projects. Some of them weave textiles, and others make "matches." Half of the money they earn goes to the government, and the other half they get to keep for themselves. They can use it to buy things, and apparently most of the inmates use their money to buy alcohol. There are facilities inside the prison for religious services in both the old Catholic and the new Protestant faiths. It seemed to me that the seating area in the Protestant chapel was cramped, whereas the Catholic chapel was more spacious. There was also a place for an instructor to lecture on texts. As for meal service, bread and water are provided every day, and soup is also provided twice daily. Twice a week, the prisoners are allowed to eat meat. At the present time, the prison population numbers over one thousand men. They have their own infirmary, where sick prisoners stay, and it was also extremely spacious. There is a pharmacy located next door, and there is also a surgical room, which contains a large examination table. The prisoners' clothing and the personal effects they may have brought with them are all stored in another room. It seems that these items are deposited when the inmates first enter the prison; each item is recorded in a ledger-book, and the inmate is made to sign his name. There is also a room in which the inmates can meet relatives who have come to visit. Everything has been organized and planned to the last detail; *it is the pinnacle of strictness where strictness is called for and the height of mercy when mercy is in order.* Truly one cannot help but marvel at it. Today at the prison, I saw a device that allows the guards on the lower and upper levels to talk to each other. It is shaped like a bugle, and one removes its cap to blow into it, producing a sound like a whistle.[163] After this, one puts his mouth to the device and speaks into it. In no time, the whistle rings out again to indicate that a reply has come from the party on the other side. One then presses his ear up against the pipe and listens. This can certainly be called a useful device. Today the various churches in the city were conducting services for Napoleon III.

January 23. Thursday. Fine.
The teacher came. In the afternoon, I visited Utsunomiya. I also paid a visit with Ono to the house of Mr. Coteau, the watchmaker. Today I paid our lodging expenses for January to the proprietor of the hotel.

January 24. Friday. Rainy, then fine.
The teacher came. I visited Bouché and then went to the Oriental Bookstore to purchase some books.[164] I went to see Mr. Kurimoto and we had a drink together at a bar downtown.

---

[163] The device Ryūhoku describes here is a "speaking tube," a mid-nineteenth century precursor to the intercom.
[164] The "Oriental Bookstore" 東洋書林 that Ryūhoku visits here is likely Maisonneuve & Cie, a bookstore and publishing house that specialized in Oriental materials and printed several books by Léon de Rosny. Ryūhoku's traveling companion Matsumoto Hakka had visited the bookstore a month earlier, and wrote in his diary: "With Seki and Ishikawa I visited a bookstore to the south of the Seine, at 15 Quai Voltaire, where I bought the *Lotus Sutra*, the *Koran*, a dictionary, a Japanese French conversation book, and a list of Indian books. Ishikawa bought the *Koran*, a history of

January 25. Saturday. Fine.
The teacher came. I spent the whole day reading.

January 26. Sunday. Fine.
The new cold weather is extremely severe. I visited Coteau again. Today, I gathered together some items to send back home. At night, Mr. Irie Fumio came over to chat.

January 27. Monday. Fine, cold.
The teacher came. In the evening, I went to the Embassy's lodgings, where I talked to Tanabe, Ikeda, and Andō. We all went over to Komatsu's hotel, where we stayed the night. It was a stroke of luck, since Yokoyama Magoichirō[165] had come from Switzerland and he told us about conditions there.

January 28. Tuesday. Fine.
The cold was fierce today. I saw that we have had our first ice. I returned to the hotel early in the morning. The teacher came. I entrusted a parcel and some letters home to Shioda today.

January 29. Wednesday. Fine.
The teacher came. I went to the legation, where I met with Osada and Kurimoto. On the way back, I went to the Lord Byron to have a drink with Tanabe, Komatsu, and Yokoyama. Mr. Nishimura Katsurō was

---

India, Renan's *Life of Jesus*, and a German dictionary."
[165] Yokoyama Magoichirō 横山孫一郎 (1848–1911) was a businessman born in Ibaraki. He began studying English in Yokohama, where he got a job as a translator for the British legation. When Ryūhoku met him in Europe, Yokoyama had been hired by the Ono financial conglomerate to supervise the studies of Ono Zenjirō in Switzerland. While abroad, he met Ōkura Kihachirō, with whom he later collaborated in numerous international business ventures in textiles, lumber, and tea trading. He was also involved in introducing electrical illumination to Tokyo's city streets.

also there. I spent the night there again. Today was the first day of the New Year according to the old calendar.

January 30. Thursday. Overcast.
At noon, there was a downpour of snow mixed with rain. I spent the whole day at the Lord Byron. At night, I returned. The scenery was extremely beautiful.

January 31. Friday. Overcast, cold.
Today, the American Kassei came over to talk. We agreed to go see the catacombs tomorrow. I will record the poems I have recently had occasion to compose here.

哭那破侖第三世　　*Lament for Napoleon III*
勝敗何論鼠嚙猫　英雄末路奈蕭條　判他獨逸新天子　高枕而眠從此宵
No point rehashing the battle's outcome; a cornered rat will bite a cat;
Such a bleak demise awaited the hero at the road's end.
We can be sure that over in Germany, the new Emperor
Sleeps easily tonight with his pillow propped high.

雪中口占　　*An extemporaneous poem composed in the snow*
樓臺幾處捲羅帷　點綴六花觀更奇　身似邯鄲枕中客　黃粱一夢未醒時
Everywhere the tall buildings have rolled up their thin silk curtains;
Snowflakes scattered like blossoms make the sight even more fine.
I feel like the traveler in Handan, resting on a pillow,
Not yet roused from his dream while the millet cooks.[166]

---

[166] The Tang classical tale "The World in a Pillow" 枕中記 by Shen Jiji (c. 741–805) tells of an encounter at a Handan inn between a dejected young man named Lu Sheng and a Daoist priest. While the two wait for the innkeeper to serve them millet, the priest attempts to cheer Lu Sheng by offering him a pillow. Placing his head upon it, Lu Sheng finds himself transported inside, where he experiences a full life of success and

四邊鶯鏡皎無塵　身是水晶宮裏人　不識門前三尺雪　金爐銀燭滿堂春
Elegant mirrors all around the room shine without a trace of dust;
I feel like one inside a crystalline palace.
Oblivious to the three feet of snow piled up outside,
The golden furnace and silver lamps fill the whole room with spring.

February 1. Saturday. Looks like snow.
The teacher came today as usual. At one o'clock in the afternoon, I went to see the catacombs (that is, the old underground cemetery) with the American Mr. Kassei and three others from my hotel. The entrance to the underground caverns is beside the observatory. One after another, visitors of both sexes bought candles mounted on small boards (which resemble the hand lanterns we use in Japan), set them alight, and went inside. After going down several hundred steps, we came to a four-way crossroads that looked for all the world like a city street. Several hundred paces past this, we entered another cavern, and from that point on, everywhere we looked right or left there were human skeletons. Arms and legs were stacked up just like firewood and on top of these were piled skulls. I can't even guess how many thousands or even millions there might have been. I felt rather like I had entered the underworld. During ancient times in France, the dead had been borne down and buried in this underground city, a practice that was apparently discovered around 1800. The bodies were gathered together and people were allowed to come see the ruins once every year. [167] I am not sure how many miles this underground city

---

fame, only to wake up and discover that it was all a dream and the millet is still not cooked. For a translation see Minford and Lau, I: 1021–1024.

[167] The catacombs had been used as limestone quarries since Roman times, but in the eighteenth and nineteenth centuries, bones from several cemeteries were relocated there. Baedeker's notes that "these somber caverns used to form one of the usual sights of Paris, but visitors are now admitted two or three times a year only" (*Paris*, 229–230).

encompasses. At those points where the path becomes half buried in earth and stone making entry dangerous, there were signs posted reading, "Passage forbidden." Moreover there were patrol guards standing at these places to prohibit people from entering recklessly. After winding our way along, we came to another passage that led to the surface. When we exited through this passage, we found ourselves quite far away from the place where we had originally entered. The foreign tourists all said that there was nothing to rival this strange place even in other lands. At night, I visited Ono. We had a drink together and went to the Valentino dance theater.

February 2. Sunday. Fine.

I went to a photographer's studio and had my picture taken.[168] I then went over to have a look at the "Musée Louvre" (a museum). I found myself struck by the objects on display, from the Egyptian and Roman statuary and other relics to the oil paintings, with their superb technical execution. Today, Kurimoto came over for a chat.

February 3. Monday. Rainy.

The teacher came. I went to the legation, where I met with Consul Sameshima. I returned after I asked him to prepare a letter on my behalf asking permission to tour the Mint.[169] Today, I met Ōkura Kihachirō,[170] and received a letter from home. We went to the legation

---

[168] In addition to this entry, Ryūhoku also mentions having photographs taken on Feburary 7. The image in Figure 12 was taken by the photographer Langerock of Paris. Ryūhoku presented this photograph to numerous individuals he met in Europe. It is contained in Mori Arinori's album of *cartes de visite* (Inuzuka and Ishiguro, 81).

[169] The workrooms of the Hôtel des Monnaies were open by special permission only (Baedeker's *Paris*, 211).

[170] Ōkura Kihachirō 大倉喜八郎 (1837–1928) was a leading Meiji businessman active in munitions, engineering, mining and a variety of other concerns. When Ryūhoku met him, he was making a tour of European industrial institutions.

together and then went to see the Panorama. Afterward I went by the Lord Byron and invited Mr. Fukui[171] to come for a stroll with me in the city. When I got back to my hotel, Mr. Utsunomiya and Mr. Inagaki had come over to inform me that they would be leaving for the Netherlands tomorrow.

February 4. Tuesday. Fine.
The teacher came. Today I was invited to a drinking engagement at Mr. Chanoine's residence. I went with Shioda, Harada, and Osada. Because Mr. Chanoine was most intimate with me during his stay in Japan and moreover since my rank at the time had been higher than the other three, he made me the guest of honor. His uncle and family all joined us, and we had quite a wonderful time. The food they served was abundant and delicious.

February 5. Wednesday. Rainy.
The teacher came. I went with Ono to visit Ōkura, but he was not in. I went to see Mr. Tsuruta, Mr. Namura, and Mr. Iwashita,[172] and together we went to a sleight-of-hand theater on the Boulevard des Italiens.[173] While some of the tricks they did were similar to those performed in Japan, there were also some that were quite mysterious and captivating. The magician first threw some beans into an empty

---

[171] Presumably this refers to Fukui Junzō 福井順三, also known as Jundō 順道, a physician traveling with Kido Takayoshi (Ōkubo, 170; Izumi, II: 42).

[172] Satsuma native Iwashita Chōjūrō 岩下長十郎 (1853–1880) had been one of the early Japanese students sent to study in France in 1866; after the Restoration, he continued to study military subjects in France, where he was called upon to assist the Iwakura Mission. The Japanese government later relied upon Iwashita's knowledge of French as it modernized its military legal codes, but his career was cut short when he drowned in a swimming accident (see the brief chapter on Iwashita in Kasumi Nobuhiko, *Nori o koete*).

[173] A conjurer named Clevermann performed shows featuring sleight-of-hand and automata at the Théatre Robert Houdin, located at 8 Boulevard des Italiens.

Figure 12. Photograph of Narushima Ryūhoku taken at Langerock of Paris, circa 1873. It is signed on the verso (shown here at right), and inscribed "Souvenir d'amitié à Madame Chanoine." This photograph is also one of the items presented to Christian Polak by Chanoine's descendant. Courtesy of the Christian Polak Collection. Perhaps it was one of the photographs Ryūhoku had taken on February 2; he may have presented it to Mme. Chanoine when they met on February 4.

pot, covered it with a lid, and then fired a pistol at it. When he took off the lid, the beans inside the pot had turned into coffee, which he then had members of the audience drink. I myself had a sip of it. There were also tricks such as one in which he manipulated a silver coin and then concealed it in his hand. He then brought out an orange, and when he cut it in half with a knife, the blade struck the silver coin, knocking it from inside the orange. Today I wore my new shoes, but my left foot started to hurt, making it impossible for me to walk. I went into a shoe repair shop to get it fixed, and the cobbler said to me, "For some reason there are many Japanese whose left foot is bigger than their right. Are you that way too?" After I had pondered the matter a while, it seemed to me that because samurai from our land carry two swords from the time they are young, they put more force into their left foot, and naturally this causes it to become larger than the right foot. When I asked my friends what they thought about this idea, they all agreed with me.

February 6. Thursday. Snowy.
I went with Ono to a machinery exhibition hall, which was located right in front of the Théâtre de la Gaîté.[174] They had things like water wheels, ploughs and looms, telescopes, microscopes, chronometers, cameras, miniature models of boats and carriages, and scale replicas of palaces (the ancient Indian temple hall, for example, looked very much like the architecture of Japan). There was hardly anything that had not been put on display. On the way back, we went by the church of Notre Dame, a large church that is one of the most famous in Paris. I was struck by how solemn it appeared. The church faces the Seine. On the church grounds was a building into which the bodies of those who have drowned in the river are apparently put in expectation that the deceased's relatives will come inquiring. The room that holds the corpses is enclosed in glass walls, and at the time of our visit there was in fact an old woman's corpse inside. It is said that she died of drowning several days ago. I was impressed again at the depth of charitable feeling among the religious faithful.[175]

---

[174] Located near the Théâtre de la Gaîté, the Conservatoire des Arts et Métiers contained "the most extensive industrial and scientific collections in Europe," including both working devices and replicas (Baedeker's *Paris*, 147).
[175] Ryūhoku is describing the Morgue, located behind the church at the southeast end of the Ile de la Cité. Baedeker's describes it as "a building where corpses of unknown

February 7. Friday. Wind, snow.

The teacher came. Ōkura came over to visit. He told me that he will leave Paris for London tomorrow. I went with the other members of my traveling group to have our picture taken at a photographer's studio. At night, Kawazu and Ono came over to chat.

February 8. Saturday. Snowy again.

The teacher came. Umegami, Shimaji, Sakata, and Ono came over to chat. We shared a meal together at Duval, and then went to the Calvaire Circus to watch the show.[176] Graceful petite women rode astride fine horses and made them gallop like rolling thunder. At the same time, they also performed various feats. It was yet another marvelous sight to behold. The most spectacular thing was a horse that danced in time to music. I composed a poem:

鐵蹄翔處翠裙披　狂蝶穿簾鶯遶枝　千古誰追項王感　烏騅背上舞虞姬

The hem of her emerald skirt rises as the horse's iron-clad hoofs fly,
A butterfly darting through a blind, a warbler flitting in the branches.
Who calls to mind those bygone days when King Xiang grieved,
For astride this dappled steed dances the consort Yu.[177]

---

persons who have perished in the river or otherwise are exposed to view for three days. The bodies are placed on marble slabs, kept cool by a constant flow of water, and their clothing is hung above them. The corpses thus exposed number about 290 annually, 50 of them being those of women. The painful scene attracts many spectators daily, chiefly persons of the lower orders" (*Paris*, 178).

[176] Duval was the name of an inexpensive restaurant chain with locations throughout the city; Ida Shin'ya suggests that the "low-class" cafeteria Ryūhoku visited with Kurimoto Teijirō on 11.03 may have been a branch of this chain (189). The Cirque de Napoleon (Cirque d'Hiver) was located on the Boulevard des Filles du Calvaire (Baedeker's *Paris*, 49).

[177] The allusion is to a famous scene narrated in Sima Qian's *Records of the Grand Historian*. In 203 BCE, when Chu general Xiang Yu 項羽 was surrounded by the Han army and knew his defeat was imminent, he consoled himself with drink: "With him were the beautiful Lady Yu, who enjoyed his favour and followed wherever he went,

February 9. Sunday. Snowy again.
I set out with Ono to visit Osada, but we ran into each other along the way. Together, we went to the Palais-Royal. In the evening, we had a drink at a bar near the Théâtre de l'Odéon. We also enjoyed a round of billiards at a café on the Boulevard Saint-Michel. Today Ono transferred his lodgings to our hotel.

February 10. Monday. Snowy again.
The teacher came. I went to the Ambassador's hotel to meet Shioda and give him some letters to take home. In the middle of the night at one o'clock, I braved the blizzard and returned to the hotel. It was so cold.

February 11. Tuesday. The skies cleared.
The teacher came. Shimaji and Umegami came over for a chat. Kawazu also came over to talk in the evening, and the two of us had a cup of tea nearby. Starting today, I began to read some French texts in the spare time between my English studies.

February 12. Wednesday. Overcast.
The teacher came in the evening. I went to the Ambassador's hotel to say goodbye to Shioda.

February 13. Thursday. Rainy.
The teacher came. In the afternoon, Ono, Ishikawa, and I endured the cold to go to the Bois de Vincennes, a wooded park with supremely

---

and his famous steed Dapple, which he always rode. Xiang Yu, filled with passionate sorrow, began to sing sadly, composing this song: 'My strength plucked up the hills, My might shadowed the word; But the times were against me, And Dapple runs no more, When Dapple runs no more, What then can I do? Ah, Yu, my Yu, What will your fate be?'" (Watson, *Records*, Han I: 45).

pleasant scenery located on the outskirts of Paris. Rivers and lakes wound around the perimeter, and dense vegetation grew lushly. The teahouse and the bridge had a distinctly quiet and secluded feeling about them. There were many cottages belonging to aristocrats and wealthy people. We went to a café in a wooded area to have a drink. Inside the café was a young girl reading a book. Just ten years old, she was as beautiful as a fine piece of jade. I can easily imagine what a lovely woman she will become in the future. As evening approached, we took the old road back. It was fiercely cold today, and it felt as though my whole body was going to be frozen solid.

February 14. Friday. Fine.
The teacher came as usual. In the afternoon, I took my letter from the legation and went to the Mint for a tour with my traveling companions. The machines for producing currency are quite grand yet crafted with precision. They are able to make silver coins (worth five francs) at the rate of one every second. The effortlessness of the process is enough to make one stare wide-eyed with amazement. I am told that the face value of the money they produce in one day would correspond to roughly forty thousand yen in our currency. The production of commemorative coins and medals also takes place in the same facility. They have gold, silver, and copper coins from ancient times, as well as the currencies of various countries on display at the Mint. There must have been more than a hundred million items there. In the evening, I went to the Ambassador's lodgings and met with Mr. Itō. Osada also came and so we met too.

February 15. Saturday. Overcast.
The teacher came. Osada and Gotō both came over and invited me to accompany them and Umegami, Shimaji, and Sakata to go see a school

for the blind.[178] The blind students read books together and produce texts. Their teachers are blind as well. When the students were asked about the materials they had studied, their answers came flowing back immediately. The letters in the books that they read are encoded with small convex protrusions on the paper, which they can read by touching them with their hands. It is quite a miraculous method. In addition to their studies, the blind students engage in various crafts, such as making wooden vessels and weaving wicker, playing the organ, and setting type. There was a wide range of skill levels. The school next door is for blind women, and there are two courses of study: one in music and the other in sewing. The students sell the items they produce in order to offset their living expenses. Before we left, I bought a wooden cup that was made by a blind person. At night, I went to the Ambassador's lodgings, and met with Mr. Iwakura and Mr. Kido. Somewhere along the way today I lost my umbrella.

February 16. Sunday. Fine.
I went to an antique shop in front of the Mint, where I bought two old gold coins. One of them was a request from Mr. Kido.[179] On the way back, I went by the Ambassador's lodgings, and spoke with Mr. Kido for several hours. Tanabe and Andō also told me that the date of their departure was growing near. When I went back to my hotel, there were some letters from home that had been delivered by Osada. Several months have passed since I left Japan, and today was the first time I had received letters from home. My joy was incomparable. The senders of the letters were my brothers Mori and Kusu[yama], my wife, my son

---

[178] Students in the Institution des jeunes Aveugles on the Boulevard des Invalides were mainly nine to thirteen years old; the school held concerts and gave tours of its printing office and work rooms (Baedeker's *Paris*, 227).
[179] Kido Takayoshi's diary notes "With Narushima's help I obtained several varieties of old Roman coins of gold, silver, and copper" (II: 287).

Ken[kichi], Funabashi Gyokukei, Kunii Tadao, and Takeuchi Zaiji[rō].[180]

February 17. Monday. Fine.

The teacher came. Today Ambassador Iwakura and the rest of the mission are going to leave France for Belgium. I went to their lodgings to say goodbye with my other traveling companions. We all went together to the train station at Rue de Dunkerque where we saw them off. On the way back, I went to relax and have some tea in the Buttes-Chaumont Park. This park was quite clean and secluded. There was a waterfall, providing another splendid view. Today, the weather was fine, and I could feel hints of spring in Paris for the first time. When evening came, our group and Ono invited Umegami and Shimaji to a place on the Boulevard Saint-Michel for a drink. We wanted to say goodbye to Umegami, who is leaving for England.

February 18. Tuesday. Fine.
The teacher came. I spent the whole day reading books.

February 19. Wednesday. Overcast.
The teacher came. I visited Mr. Bouché's house with Ono and Osada. Our host brought us to the place next door to eat.

---

[180] In addition to his wife, Ryūhoku received letters from his biological brothers, Kusuyama Kōichirō 楠山孝一郎 and Mori Shōgo 森省吾, and his adopted son Kenkichi, with whom he would reunite shortly in Paris; on the brothers, see Maeda, *Narushima*, 34. The other letters came from former students of Ryūhoku's who were employed by the Higashi Honganji academy in Asakusa: Funabashi Shin 舟橋振 (b. 1846), who used the literary name Gyokukei 玉卿, Kunii Tadao 國井忠雄 (b. 1848), and Takeuchi Zaijirō 竹内財次郎 (b. 1833). These three individuals would go on to join the staff of the temple's Translation Office; for further details on the Office, see the articles by Kataoka. It seems that this was not actually the first time during his trip that Ryūhoku had received a letter from home (see the February 3 entry).

February 20. Thursday. Overcast.

Misty fog casts a gloomy darkness on the city, and it is extremely chilly. The teacher came. Harada came and invited me to visit Mr. Rosny. Mr. Rosny's house is outside the city gate at Porte de Courcelles.[181] Mr. Rosny took out scores of books from his library and showed them to me. Harada and I enrolled in Mr. Rosny's ethnography society and will receive its new publications.[182] Tonight I went to see a performance at the Gymnase Theatre. The production was about Camellia, the famous courtesan of recent years. From the time Camellia and her lover chance to meet, their feelings for each other grow more and more intimate by the day until they are reprimanded by his father. When Camellia learns that her lover is living in seclusion on the outskirts of the city, she goes to the house in search of him. She is lectured by his father, and has no choice but to resign herself to deceiving her lover and breaking off relations with him. From that time, she becomes the object of his scorn and is thoroughly humiliated in a café. Finally, she falls ill and becomes bedridden. On January 1, her condition has become perilous, and her lover receives his father's permission to go and visit Camellia at her home. Overcome with joy to see him, the ailing Camellia dies. The play has apparently enjoyed an extremely favorable response from audiences recently.[183]

---

[181] Léon Rosny's address is recorded as 15 Rue Lacépède in the diaries of other Japanese who met him, but this was an address used for academic correspondence and not the location of his residence.

[182] Rosny founded the Société d'ethnographie in 1858, and Ryūhoku's name appears alongside Harada's and Shimaji Mokurai's in its 1875 member list: "Harada Kadumiti (le colonel), à Yédo; Simadi Mokurai, prêtre bouddhiste, à Tokuzi; Narusima, à Yédo" (Société d'Ethnographie, 52). It is possible that at this point, Ryūhoku and Harada had only indicated their intent to join, or perhaps merely subscribed to the Society's publications. Ryūhoku's formal entry into the Society may not have come until March 11, when he paid a fee and received a certificate.

[183] The play Ryūhoku saw at the Théâtre du Gymnase was of course Alexandre Dumas fils' *La Dame aux camélias*. In a letter sent from Paris to his biological brother Kusuyama

February 21. Friday. Overcast. Cold.
The teacher came. Mr. Imamura Warō[184] came over for a chat. Starting tonight, I began to translate a book about Sanskrit.[185]

February 22. Saturday. Overcast.
The teacher came. I put my luggage in order and cleaned and swept the room.

February 23. Sunday. Overcast. Rainy.
Sakata was returning to Lyon today, and I saw him off. I visited Mr. Fukuchi Gen'ichirō at the Grand Hôtel and talked to him late into the night. He is planning to go to Turkey in the near future.

February 24. Monday. Overcast. Wind and rain in the afternoon.
The teacher came as usual. At night, I went for a stroll with Ono around the Palais-Royal. We shared a quick drink and came back.

February 25. Fine. Tuesday.
Today is Carnaval in the Christian faith, and so all of the shops are closed, just like Sunday. I visited Osada with Ono, and together we

---

in Tokyo, Ryūhoku recounted the plot of the play, praised it, and noted that human feelings were the same East and West. The letter was published in the *Yūbin hōchi shinbun* 54 (May 1873), one of Tokyo's major newspapers, where Ryūhoku's friend Kurimoto Joun was editor; see Ōshima 118–120, as well as the Afterword to this volume.

[184] Tosa native Imamura Warō 今村和郎 (1846–1891) had begun learning French in 1869 and was an assistant to the Iwakura Mission. He began to work as an instructor of the Japanese language under Rosny at the Ecole des langues orientales vivantes in 1873. Upon returning to Japan, he continued to work as a civil servant.

[185] The translation that Ryūhoku began to work on that evening was most likely the one that his grandson Ōshima Ryūichi later came into possession of, entitled "Seisokuritsu bunten" (A grammar of Sanskrit); see Ōshima, 125–126. The source text seems to have been H. H. Wilson's 1841 *An Introduction to the Grammar of the Sanskrit Language: for the Use of Early Students*.

went to the Grand Hôtel in order to accompany Fukuchi and Shimaji to the railway station and see them off on their journey.[186] The strong winds we had today blew the door to my room shut and the door locked on its own. Since the key for the lock was inside the room, I was very much at a loss for what to do. The hotel bellboy called a workman on my behalf. He opened the door and at last I was able to get back inside my room. I had quite a laugh at this mishap.

February 26. Wednesday. Rainy, then the skies cleared and it became quite pleasant.
The teacher came. With Ono, I visited the lodgings of a certain American dentist, whom I asked to manufacture some false teeth for me. On the way back, we went and had a look inside a hall with an exhibition about the reparations from the Franco-Prussian War.[187] In order to convey to French citizens the amount of reparations the country was forced to pay to Prussia after its defeat in the war, the sum was converted into gold bullion and put on display. Instead of actual gold, they fashioned rectangular blocks of wood and covered their

---

[186] Shimaji Mokurai's diary traces his very busy trip with Fukuchi through Italy, Greece, Turkey, Egypt, and India on their way back to Japan. Fukuchi had apparently grown tired of attending on the Iwakura delegates, and so when the opportunity arose to go investigate legal systems in Turkey and Egypt, he seized the chance to escape (Yanagida, 149).

[187] France was made to pay reparations of five billion francs to Prussia after the Franco-Prussian War. From the account left by another visitor to Paris in February 1873, it seems that the exhibition was not officially sponsored: *"Ce que c'est que cinq milliards en or monnaye!* ... We were accosted in front of No. — Boulevard St. Denis by the above question. At the same time a polite French boy hands us a handbill, which told us that *un bloc d'or*, eight metres long, five metres high, and three and two-third metres deep, could be seen for fifty centimes ... This cube of one hundred and fifty metres contained one hundred thousand *rouleaux* of fifty thousand francs each; each one of the rolls—*rouleaux*—contained two thousand five hundred pieces of twenty francs, and the whole two hundred and fifty million (250,000,000) pieces" ("A Block of Gold," 855). This account goes on to quote a French report that the entire amount in one-franc pieces "would encircle the globe twice and seven-eighths."

surface with gold foil. The blocks are stacked here several dozen feet high. According to the man at the hall, if you stretched all of this gold into a single thread, it would be able to circle the globe twice. I said that in my own country, it would be a very peculiar thing indeed for the defeated country to try to show its people the vast extent of reparations extracted by the enemy. On the other hand, I wonder if this might not be a method for boosting the citizenry's morale.

February 27. Thursday. Overcast.
The teacher came. I wandered leisurely around the Palais-Royal with Ono again. It snowed tonight.

February 28. Friday. Rainy, and then fine.
The teacher came. Today, I went to the post office to send a letter home. It cost thirty francs.

March 1. Saturday. Steady snowfall.
The teacher came. In the afternoon, I visited the home of the dentist. Namura came over for a chat this evening.

March 2. Sunday. Fine.
This morning, there was a fire in the bookstore next door on the Rue Racine, but it was put out immediately. I visited Mr. Harada's hotel. There was a brief shower this afternoon, but the skies soon cleared. I went to see the Luxembourg Museum with my traveling companions. They have a great number of oil paintings and sculptures carved of stone. I was told that the works of living artists are put on display in this museum and that when the artists die, the works are moved to the

Louvre and exhibited there.[188] We left the museum and went to stroll around the Garden of Acclimatization.[189] There was a cockfighting arena inside the park. The park also houses a wide variety of exotic birds and strange beasts; there were scores of animals, ranging from zebras and kangaroos to members of the monkey family. They also had a pool filled with seawater into which fish and shellfish had been released. The pool was enclosed by glass walls, enabling one to closely observe the fish swimming through the water. They let children who visit the park enjoy a ride on an elephant, camel, or ostrich. They also cultivate many unusual kinds of plant life in the park. Tropical plants and grasses are all raised inside a glass building. Camellias, azaleas, and other such flowers were all in full bloom, producing a riot of color. This place is yet another miniature realm of the immortals.

March 3. Monday. Fine, then rainy.
The teacher came. Kawaji Toshiyoshi came over for a visit with Iwashita. In the afternoon, I visited Irie Fumio, and then visited Osada, but he wasn't in. Today, I received my second letter from home.

March 4. Tuesday. Rainy.
The teacher came. I visited Osada with Ono, and also went by the Lord Byron to meet with Ikeda. At night, I went out to the Folies Bergère.[190]

---

[188] Baedeker's notes that "works of living artists" are exhibited in the Musée de Luxembourg, and that those by "the most distinguished masters are generally transferred to the Louvre about ten years after their death" (*Paris*, 187).

[189] The original purpose of the Jardin d'Acclimatation was to acclimatize foreign plants and animals to the French climate, but it also served the recreational demands of the city (and it did in fact offer an ostrich ride for children). Ryūhoku's reference to a cockfighting arena may have been to the Poulerie (Baedeker's *Paris*, 131–132).

[190] Baedeker's describes the Folies Bergère as "a theatre of very humble pretension to which the public are admitted gratis ... the profits being derived from the refreshments sold" (*Paris*, 48). *Yose* is a form of popular entertainment akin to vaudeville.

The theater was a small one, something like a *yose* in Japan. The audience members can drink alcohol as they wish and smoking is also permitted. It does not have the stiff and dignified air of a theater. The price of the seats was just two francs. The music they performed and the dancing was not different from the theater. Two men stood on the right and left of the stage and threw a young boy back and forth almost as though he was a ball. The little boy flew lightly through the air like a butterfly. At times he would soar through the air, and other times he would be suspended upside down from a rope. His nimble agility was astonishing. There was also a performer who mounted a bicycle and wove his way through an array of several hundred glass bottles without touching a single one. His wife was also a good rider, and at the end of their routine, the performer hoisted her onto his shoulders and rode his bicycle around the theater. Even in this, he was leisurely and relaxed. In the next act, a clown entered a wine cellar to steal some wine, but the wine bottles all transformed into beautiful women who started to dance. Next, they put on a shadow play, which was quite magnificent. It was not like the minuscule scale of similar productions back in Japan. On the way home, I visited Emma at Number 13 Rue Fontaine.

March 5. Wednesday. Rainy.
The teacher came. I boarded a horse-drawn carriage with my traveling companions and went to visit the Sèvres Ceramics factory, which is located on the lower reaches of the Seine. We traveled alongside the river for about two miles and then came to the factory. The great magnificence of the edifice astonished me. The kilns were all constructed of brick. There were several hundred workers involved in production, all of them divided into separate sections where they carried out their work. There was also a separate exhibition hall: a vast space where the ceramics of various countries had been collected.

However, the attractiveness and precise craftsmanship of the design, as well as the beauty of the source material, make it evident that this factory's products are the most impressive. Moreover, there was a flower vase that was priced at six thousand yen, which gives one some idea of the West's wealth. On the way back, we had a late-night drink at the Palais-Royal. My traveling companions wanted to go to the Folies Bergère, and so I went to see the show again.

March 6. Thursday. Fine. Cold.
The teacher came. I visited Bouché's house and also stopped in at the Grand Hôtel, where I met Mr. Shibusawa Seiichi[191] and Mr. Nakajima Saikichi.[192] They had both come from Italy and they had brought me a letter from Reverend Mokurai.

March 7. Friday. Rainy.
The teacher came. Tsuruta and Namura came over for a chat. Today, I spent the day at the hotel getting my luggage in proper order, for it has been decided that we will soon be leaving here. I will append here two parting poems that I composed while a traveler myself.

---

[191] Shibusawa Seiichi 澁澤誠一 (1838–1912), or Kisaku 喜作, was the cousin of pioneering Meiji businessman Shibusawa Eiichi (1840–1931). Though he had been jailed after fighting alongside Enomoto Takeake and other pro-Tokugawa forces, Kisaku received amnesty after the Restoration and attained a Treasury post. He was deployed to Italy in the winter of 1872 to investigate the silk industry, but quit his post after returning to Japan in September 1873, becoming a businessman. In his diary, Shimaji Mokurai mentions meeting him in Milan on February 28 and traveling on the same train with him to Venice on March 4 (60).

[192] Nakajima Saikichi 中島才吉 (1846–1925) was in the first cohort of students at the Yokohama French academy and was chosen to serve as a translator for Chanoine. He taught French in the Yokosuka Arsenal after the Restoration, and then took up a post in the customs office at the Treasury; he went on to become a diplomat in Italy.

送鹽田三郎歸本邦 *Seeing off Shioda Saburō on his return to Japan*
故園曾唱送君詞　猶記淒風吹客衣　誰料離鄉五千里　又操舊調送君歸

Back in our native land, I once saw you off with a farewell poem,
I still recall the fierce winds that blew on your traveler's clothes that day.
Who could predict that now I would be five thousand miles from home,
Calling up the old verses as I send you on your return journey?[193]

別島地默雷　　*On parting from Shimaji Mokurai*
客身同値海西春　來燕去鴻情更親　何事夢間添一夢　他鄉翻送故鄉人

Two travelers, together we welcomed spring overseas;
Arriving swallows and departing geese brought our feelings even closer.
How strange it is—a dream within a dream,
To say goodbye to you, my countryman, in this foreign land.

March 8. Saturday. Fine.

The teacher came. I visited Bouché with Ono, and went by the house of the clock shop proprietor Coteau. I also went to the Lord Byron, where I met with Shibusawa, Nakajima, as well as Matsumura Toshisaburō from the Mitsui Group and Shimizu Kihei from the Shimada Group.[194] On the way back, I went with Nakajima to the Valentino.

---

[193] In the winter of 1870, Ryūhoku wrote a poem entitled *Sending off Shioda Saburō, who has received an Imperial order to go to Europe* 送鹽田三郎奉　敕之歐羅巴, which reads, "I bid you farewell, and my sidelocks grow frosty white in just one evening; / Stirred by the past, moved by the present, my feelings grow ever deeper. / How can I celebrate your accompanying this mission to foreign lands? / Your old friend's mind is like Li Ling's when he parted from Su Wu on the bridge." 送君一夜鬢將霜　感舊感今情轉長　爭賀節旄臨異域　故人心似上河梁 (*Ryūhoku shishō*, III: 1). The allusion in the last line is to a paradigmatic poem of parting included in the *Wen xuan*; it suggests that the poet is uncertain he will meet his friend again.

[194] Along with the Ono, the Mitsui and Shimada Groups were the three largest financial conglomerates in the first years of the Meiji period, and all sent family scions or other representatives abroad to study Western business and banking practices and

March 9. Sunday. Beautiful and clear.

I went to relax with my traveling companions in the Bois de Boulogne, where we took in the view of the whole place. At night, we went to the Théâtre de l'Odéon. They performed a play about a harridan who is plotting to poison her stepdaughter, only to have the plan discovered by her own biological daughter, who then steals the poison and dies after drinking it in her stepsister's place.[195] It made me feel miserable.

March 10. Monday. Fine.

The teacher came. I went to the Comptoir d'Escompte and saw Mr. Coullet to withdraw ten thousand francs of the money we had deposited there. Receiving the money, I returned. I also visited Mr. Kawazu. Utsunomiya and Inagaki have returned from Germany. The venerable American Mr. Hepburn has recently come to Paris.[196] Today,

---

explore overseas markets. Shimizu Kihei 清水喜兵衛 was dispatched to Europe by the Shimada-gumi just a few years before the conglomerate collapsed in 1874 (Miyamoto Mataji, IV: 588). Matsumura Toshisaburō 松村利三郎, representing the Mitsui-gumi, was affiliated with a Kyoto commercial organization and left Japan for France in the winter of 1872, traveling on to New York in May 1873 (Mitsui Hachirōemon, 99). Matsumura was sent to France at the same time as Sakura Tsuneshichi 佐倉常七 (1835–1899), who played an important role in modernizing the Nishijin weavers of Kyoto by introducing mechanized Jacquard looms (Kyōto Furitsu, 53). Takasaki Masakaze had met Matsumura and Shimizu a week before Ryūhoku, describing them in his diary as "clerks" of the Mitsui and Shimada respectively (321).

[195] Ryūhoku saw *L'Aïeule* by Adolphe D'Ennery and Charles Edmond, which had premiered in 1863, and was being reprised in 1873. The play concerns an elderly woman (Ryūhoku's "harridan") whose daughter, married to a duke, has died after giving birth to a daughter, Jeanne (whom Ryūhoku mis-identifies as the elderly woman's "daughter" instead of granddaughter). The duke remarries and has a daughter named Blanche (Ryūhoku's "stepdaughter"). The elderly woman perceives Blanche as a threat to Jeanne and plots to poison her, but Jeanne discovers her grandmother's plot and drinks the poison in her half-sister's place (*Meijihen*, 311).

[196] The Presbyterian minister and physician James Curtis Hepburn (1815–1911) first went to Japan in 1859, where he operated a clinic in Yokohama, began translating the Bible, and edited the first Japanese–English dictionary. In October 1872, he traveled home to the United States with his wife Clara, returning to Japan in November 1873 (Mochizuki, 242).

he paid a visit and very cordially agreed to meet again before he took his leave. In the evening, I went with Ishikawa and Matsumoto to visit Mr. Rangardo at the Grand Hôtel, but he was not in. We ran into him on the way back, and together we went to drink at the Dîner Européen (a tavern). This evening, I wrote a couplet: "The singing bird dances with a flower in its mouth / the surging stream flows with a stone in its embrace."[197] Today there was a light snowfall, but by night it had turned to rain.

March 11. Tuesday. Shifting weather: first overcast, then fine.
The teacher came. I visited Mr. Rosny with Ono and Ishikawa, and we enrolled in his Society. I paid the fee and received a certificate. In the office, I met a Polish man named Robaroa who hopes to travel to Japan. Mr. Rosny was an exceedingly generous host. I asked him several questions I had concerning Indian script. We also had a tour of his Society's typesetting facilities and then returned. At night, it rained. We went to the Valentino, where we met Ono Zensuke and a certain Mr. Kamizawaya.[198] Today a student became drunk and disorderly in our

---

[197] The identity of Mr. Rangardo is unclear, but Ryūhoku and his traveling companions were in a particularly celebratory mood that evening it seems, for the Dîner Européen was a well regarded restaurant on the Boulevard des Italiens (Baedeker's *Paris*, 12). Moreover, in a fascinating article, Maeda Ai deciphered Ryūhoku's cryptic couplet using Matsumoto Hakka's diary, which notes that the group went to a brothel on the Rue d'Amboise after their drink. In Hakka's diary, the couplet appears as 啼鳥啣華舞　奔川抱石流 with interlinear notes reading 芹菜 after the first, and 馬利亜 after the second lines. As Maeda discovered, the characters 華 and 石 mean not "flower" and "stone" but are rather coded references to the names of Ryūhoku's traveling companions, Hakka and Ishikawa. The interlinear names, Maeda deduced, are those of the prostitutes that the men engaged that evening, Celina and Maria (*Kōsei*, 81).

[198] Along with the Shimada-gumi and Mitsui-gumi, the Ono-gumi was a major financial conglomerate that ran an exchange company, brokered rice, silk, and other commodities, and provided financing for the Meiji government before the Group collapsed in 1874. Given the Ono family's complex practice of name usage and inheritance (i.e., a single individual using multiple names and multiple individuals using the same name) it is difficult to be certain, but it seems that Ryūhoku met Ono Zensuke 小野善助

hotel's dining room, and broke a glass door. In the several months that have passed since I came to Europe, this is the first time I have seen someone become violent from drink. The fineness of Western manners deserves admiration.

March 12. Wednesday. Overcast and cold.
The teacher came. Today was the final day of our classes since my traveling companions and I will soon leave for Italy. I presented the teacher with several different Japanese products as gifts. Ono and I went to the Grand Hôtel to meet with the Italian Mr. Dell'Oro,[199] and then went for a drink with him and Asano Kōbē[200] at the Dîner Européen. Tonight Bouché invited my traveling companions and me to come see a performance at the Opera.[201] The opera is the finest theater in all the land (one seat costs eighty francs). The place is large enough to accommodate twenty-five hundred people. In the front are box seats for the Emperor and Empress. It is customary for members of the

---

(1831–1887) in Paris, and his son Zenjirō in London (Miyamoto Mataji, IV: 585–589). Kamizawaya was the name of a shop exporting silkworm seeds that was run in Yokohama by Shibusawa Sōgorō 澁澤宗五郎, the cousin of Shibusawa Eiichi (Yamamoto, 75–76). Shimaji Mokurai's diary notes that a person named "Kamizawaya" and employed in Japan's customs office was traveling between Milan and Venice with Asano Kōbē and Shibusawa Kisaku (60).

[199] Joseph Dell'Oro and his elder brother Isidoro (d. 1900) were importers of raw silk. Isidoro had founded a trading company in Yokohama in 1868 and published an Italian translation of the 1803 Japanese sericultural text *Yōsan hiroku* (Tomita, *Merume*, 90–96). Matsumoto Hakka's diary for 03.19 confirms that it was Joseph whom Ryūhoku and the others met in Paris and then Milan: "There is a man named Dell'Oro in Milan. He was in Yokohama for two years and understands Japanese. His elder brother is now in Yokohama. Narushima and Ono are old acquaintances of his."

[200] Asano Kōbē 浅野幸兵衛 helped run the Ono group's Tokyo businesses, and seems to have been in Europe to explore the exportation of silk eggs (Miyamoto, 584).

[201] Ryūhoku's visit to the Opéra (Salle de la rue Le Peletier) came just a few months prior to the house's destruction in a fire, and just over a year before the present Opera House was complete. Nakamura Kōsuke has identified the opera performed that evening as *La coupe du Roi de Thulé*, a work by Louis Gallet and Édouard Blau based upon *Faust* (93–95).

audience to dress in formalwear. The opera is performed in archaic language and seems to have a flavor quite similar to Sangaku in our country.[202] As far as the actresses' dancing is concerned, however, there is little difference between the opera and other theaters; the opera is just more lavishly beautiful. There was an undersea scene during the performance. They had secretly strung up silver wires on which were suspended green water plants and bluish floating weeds. It was truly a dazzling sight to behold. We returned after enjoying ourselves to the fullest. It rained tonight.

March 13. Thursday. Overcast and then clear.

My traveling companions and I boarded a steam train, and departed for Versailles to see the palace of Louis XIV and XVI. The gardens and ponds were magnificently gorgeous and vast, surpassing even the royal palace in Paris. We also went to a museum, where the larger oil paintings seemed to even better than those in the Louvre. We also had another tour of Trianon Palace, and returned on the six o'clock train. Today I saw Marshal Mac-Mahon on the street.[203] With his white hair and venerable expression, he is a formidable and dignified man.

March 14. Friday. Fine.

I went to the legation and the Lord Byron, stopping in to see Mr. Ikeda, Mr. Osada, Mr. Matsuda, Mr. Tsuruta, and Mr. Namura, and to tell

---

[202] Sangaku was the name of a variety of acrobatic and mimetic popular entertainment traditions with roots on the continent that took shape in Japan during the Heian period. The medieval period saw the emergence of more dramatic forms, known as *sarugaku*, that were ultimately the source of the Noh theatrical tradition. It is this latter form, consolidated in the fourteenth century and evolving to become more stately over subsequent centuries, that Ryūhoku has in mind here.

[203] Maréchal Patrice de Mac-Mahon (1808–1893) was known for leading troops to put down the Paris Commune; just two months after Ryūhoku saw him at Versailles he became president.

them that I was leaving for Italy. Today, I went to a building housing ancient currency and met with its attendant. He didn't understand anything and so I soon bid him farewell and left.

March 15. Saturday. Rainy, clear in the afternoon.
I assembled my traveling clothes with the rest of the group since we will be leaving here tomorrow. I entrusted three boxes of books and clothes to Bouché, and then headed for Lyon Station where I made a reservation for the train tomorrow and returned. At night, I went for a walk with Ono and visited Rochelle at Montmarte.

March 16. Sunday. Fine.
I got up at dawn and visited Irie Fumio, leaving a box of books with him at his hotel and then returning. At 3:05 in the afternoon, we boarded a steam locomotive at Lyon Station and departed on our journey to Italy. Our traveling group all sat together. Ono was our guide. We passed through Melun and at 4:40 we stopped to rest in Fontainebleau. This place is the source of the clay used to make Sèvres ceramics. At 7:20, we reached Laroche, and at 8:20, we had dinner in Tonnerre. We reached Mâcon at 3:40, where we changed trains. I drank some of the famous Mâcon wine and it was delicious. At five o'clock, we left there and rode all through the night.

March 17. Monday. Rainy.
At dawn we reached Pont d'Ain, and at seven o'clock we reached Ambérieu, where we stopped for forty minutes.

客身遠逐汽烟飛　千里風光一望奇　來路未収紅旭影　前山已濺雨霏々
    I fly on this journey, chasing after the locomotive's steam,
      Taking in a thousand miles of scenery in a single spectacular glimpse.

The crimson light of sunrise yet unfaded from the path we've come,
While the mountains ahead are already sprinkled with light rains.

From this point onward, I could see to my right the stern crags of mountain ridges with waterfalls cascading down. Small lakes would from time to time appear and then vanish; it was quite lovely scenery. The area is called Rossillon. At 9:28, we reached Culoz, where we changed trains. We passed by the side of a large lake and also through several tunnels. A little after three o'clock, the train ran through a charming place where a small bridge spanned a stream flowing through the valley. At 4:10, we reached Modane, which is the border between France and Italy. We entered the customs office, where our luggage was examined in the most cursory way. After we had a meal, we changed trains and departed, passing through two tunnels before we came to the famous Mont Cenis Tunnel, which is three *ri* and nine *chō* long.[204] It took us twenty-three minutes just to pass through it. This tunnel was built by digging into the sides of these great layered mountains, and the project took thirteen years to complete. Apparently the first train passed through it in 1871. Along the passageway through the tunnel, they have installed lamps, over twenty of them in all. It is the biggest tunnel in the world. As soon as we emerged from the darkness of the tunnel, we were in Bardonecchia, where snow flurries had covered the ground to a depth of one foot.[205] Everyone in our group was astonished.

---

[204] Mont Cenis Tunnel was built between 1861 and 1870, and is just over eight miles long. Ryūhoku slightly understates its length.

[205] Ida Shin'ya points out that the orthography Ryūhoku uses for Bardonecchia, "Sebarudoneshiya," suggests that French was the medium through which he interacted with his fellow train passengers. Presumably Ryūhoku asked the name of the region they were passing through and was told "C'est Bardonèche," misunderstanding the sentence as the toponym (269).

斜陽影裏破雲行　地道冥々三里程　走出洞門天未晩　滿山積雪照人明

 Our train races ahead, breaking through the setting sun-lit clouds,
 Then a passage through the earth, with darkness for three *ri*.
 Emerging from the cavern's gate, I find the sky has not yet darkened;
 The snow covering the whole mountain range shines brightly on us.

At nine o'clock, we reached Turin, where we checked into the Hôtel d'Europe. The building is another grand one, quite a pleasant sight. We ate noodles made from dried buckwheat, which tasted very delicious. Many houses in Italy are constructed with bow-shaped roofs, and these are covered in reddish tiles, quite similar to houses in Japan. However, the difference is that whereas tiles in Japan face downward, those in Italy face up. Since this country is rich in minerals, there are a great many places that use marble, and since they are skilled at painting, there are many buildings here and there that have paintings decorating the walls. On the street, the large horse-drawn carriages used for transporting passengers and also for hauling goods are more beautiful than those in France. One is struck by their brilliance, radiant with gold and vermilion. Tonight, I heard a clanging sound that resembled a stringed instrument. It must have been the bells of a church.

March 18. Tuesday. Rainy.
After breakfast, we left Turin and boarded a steam locomotive. We could see the surging rapids of a river, which I imagine comes from the melting of snow on the Mont Cenis range. The fields visible on either side of the train were full of yellow rape blossoms in full bloom, reminding me very much of the scenery back in Japan. At 5:40, we reached Milan, where we checked into the Hôtel de Milan. Today there were national flags hoisted up in front of the houses to honor soldiers

who were killed in past battles; the streets were bustling with activity.[206] After dinner, I went out with Ono. There are many brothels in this area, and it is said that the rates are very inexpensive in comparison to those in France. Today I wrote one quatrain:

想見富饒冠各州 滿城士女自優游 鉦聲斷續天將暮 細雨春寒古石樓
   I imagine its wealth and riches must crown all the provinces;
   Throughout the city, gentlemen and ladies live in unfettered contentment.
   Church bells ring out and fall silent as the sky begins to darken;
   A slight rain, chilly this spring, falls on the old stone buildings.

As one of the most prosperous cities in all of Italy, there are several things about Milan that bring France's Paris to mind. There are many giant cathedrals throughout the city and one can hear their bells ringing by day and by night. Moreover, the city has an unrushed manner and is quite charming.

March 19. Wednesday. Overcast, rainy.
After breakfast, I visited Mr. Dell'Oro at his house at Number 18 Via Cusani. The head of the shop acted as our guide, taking us for a tour of the great cathedral of Milan.[207] The church and its towers were made entirely of marble, jutting up high above us like swords. Inside, they had used various colors of glass to decorate the structure, and the iridescence struck my eyes. We also went to see the Galleria arcade, which was extremely beautiful.[208] In the afternoon, Mr. Dell'Oro

---

[206] March 18 was the anniversary of the 1848 Insurrection of Milan.
[207] The Duomo di Milano is the largest gothic cathedral in Europe, noted for its stained glass depictions of biblical scenes.
[208] The Galleria Vittorio Emanuele II, an arcade covered by a glass and iron ceiling, connects the Piazza della Duomo with the Piazza della Scala. When it opened in 1867,

himself came and invited us to go to the station where we made a reservation and paid the train fare for a tour around Italy. The fare was 180 francs for each person. The fare will be very inexpensive if we see the country this way. If on the other hand we purchased our tickets at each individual station, then the fare would apparently be nearly twice as much. We went to see a museum. In front of the museum building was a bronze statue of Napoleon I, which was quite magnificent.[209] Inside the museum, there were many ancient stone statues and oil paintings on display. It seems that other countries cannot match Italy in this regard, for I understand that there is no end to the stream of artists who come here from England, France, and elsewhere to copy the ancient paintings. Even now, there are forty or fifty individuals who have come to the museum to imitate the paintings. We then boarded a carriage for the Arc de Triomphe, that is, the "Pavilion to celebrate triumph," which we scaled and looked out from.[210] There were statues of a goddess and fast horses atop the structure. They were made from bronze and were several times the size of a real human and horses. The tower itself was made from stone, all of it marble. Compared to the French Arc de Triomphe, this one is a little smaller, but when it comes to beauty, it is far superior. In the evening, Mr. Dell'Oro became our guide again, taking us to see a show at the Santa Radegonda Theater.[211]

---

it was one of the largest and most elaborately decorated arcades in Europe.

[209] In the court of the Palazzo di Brera stands Canova's bronze statue of Napoleon as a Roman emperor. The Palazzo contains the Accademia di Belle Arti and the Pinacotéca di Brera gallery (Baedeker's *Northern Italy*, 126).

[210] The Arco della Pace at the Piazza Sempione was a triumphal white marble arch built between 1804 and 1838 (Baedeker's *Northern Italy*, 139). It is crowned with a figure of the goddess of peace leading a chariot of horses.

[211] The Teatro di Santa Radegonda, near the Duomo di Milano, staged a variety of operettas and operas before it was demolished and turned into a power plant in 1883. Publisher Edoardo Sonzogno, whom Ryūhoku met the following day, was a major patron of this theater, enabling it to install gas lamps in 1875 (Manzella and Pozzi, 71–75).

The piece they performed was about two men who went swimming in the ocean, encountered gods and female immortals, and also fell into a cave of demons. The scenery and stage effects, including gusting winds, surging waves, and a volcano that spewed fire, were truly spectacular.

March 20. Thursday. Fine, then rainy.
This morning, I went for a stroll downtown, had a cup of tea, and returned to the hotel. Mr. Dell'Oro came over and took us to the Cova, the finest restaurant in Milan, where we had a splendid meal.[212] After that, we visited the home of Mr. Sonzogno, who lives at Number 14 Via Pasquirolo.[213] He is a newspaper publisher, and his business is very prosperous. Up until two years ago, his press machinery could print three thousand sheets in an hour, but now he says that his machines can produce eight thousand sheets in an hour. We also saw how they print images in color, and these were quite similar to our *nishikie*. The precision of the artistry was very impressive. We also went to the Church of San Carlo, which is tiled in precious stones.[214] Its beauty was striking. On the way back, we stopped by a park that quite resembled the scenery of Japan. The park was very spacious, and there was a large building housing a hospital behind it. Inside the park was a museum, with many different varieties of birds and beasts, bugs and fish.[215] There were all sorts of human bones and dried corpses on

---

[212] The Cova was a café "with a garden" located at "Via S. Giuseppe, near the Scala" and offering "concerts in the evening" (Baedeker's *Northern Italy*, 119–120).
[213] Edoardo Sonzogno (1836–1920) was the publisher of *Il Secolo*, a daily Milan newspaper that had one of the largest circulations in Italy. He was also a patron of musical theater and a publisher of inexpensive musical editions.
[214] The Chiesa di San Carlo al Corso was located on Corso Vittorio Emanuele II.
[215] The Nuovo Giardino Pubblico had been newly expanded in 1860; the Museo Civico (di storia naturale) opened in 1838 (Baedeker's *Northern Italy*, 138). Two large hospitals, the Fate-bene-fratelli and Fate-bene-sorelle, were located on Porta Nuova, near the garden.

display, as well as dried snakes, fossils, and curious shells. I went with Mr. Dell'Oro to the train station and bought the tickets. Today, we changed our gold currency into paper currency, gaining 13 percent in the process. The discrepancy between France's wealth and Italy's poverty is an obvious one. Today, I bought some old jewels, old vessels and paintings. I went to have a bath and found that the bathing tub was made of a reddish marble. In Italy, it is very common to use items made of stone. Tonight, I invited Mr. Dell'Oro to our hotel to be our guest for a meal and thank him for generously facilitating so many things for us. I gave him a photograph of our group and some gold and silver coins from Japan.

March 21. Friday. Fine.
At ten o'clock, we left Milan. Mr. Dell'Oro saw us off at the station, where he presented us with two bottles of Milan wine as a parting gift. It was similar to champagne, and quite delicious. From the train, we could see the great lake of Desenzano to our left. The scenery was gorgeous. At five o'clock, we reached the famous old city of Venice, which is on the sea and has lovely scenery. Its islands apparently number forty-eight. Canals run this way and that throughout the whole city, and Venice is certainly unrivaled anywhere in its great number of bridges. As soon as we got off the train, we immediately boarded a boat, which is the mode of transportation used here. Horse-drawn carriages are extremely few in number. The boats have a long and narrow shape and are painted black. We left the station, poling off into a small canal. After a while we reached the coastline, where we got off and went to check in at the Hotel la Luna (that means the "Inn of the Moon"), a first-rate hotel in this city.[216] My old friend Nakayama

---

[216] The Hôtel Luna was located very close to the Piazza of St. Mark (Baedeker's *Northern Italy*, 231).

Umonta[217] lives in this city, and he had one of his staff members, Tanaka Kenzaburō, come to meet our group.[218] The buildings in this city are all old, and the bridge spans are all made from stone or brick. Though one may say that Venice falls far short of Milan in prosperity, it nevertheless greatly surpasses Milan in elegant charm. After a meal, we went for a stroll on the Piazza di San Marco, which brought the Palais-Royal in Paris to mind. The tiles are all made of a white marble with a reddish cast. We relaxed for a bit in a coffee shop, where many of the tables and chairs were constructed from stone.[219] There are many shops in the city center that sell coral, and the price is also quite reasonable. I imagine that for all kinds of things, from watches to everyday goods and knickknacks, the prices are often less expensive in Italy than in France. Mosquitoes come out at night, and so I slept with a cloth screen hanging over the bed. This is the first time in my trip of Europe that I have heard the sound of mosquitoes, which are said to thrive here because of the city's numerous canals.

March 22. Saturday. Fine.
We hired a boat and went for a tour around the bay that lies in front of the hotel. It is called the Laguna. Right on the water is the political headquarters of the Republican government. From 418 until 1797, it was the place where the business of government was transacted.[220]

---

[217] Former shogunal retainer Nakayama Umonta 中山右門太, or Jōji 譲治 (1839–1911), had trained under Chanoine in Yokohama. He became Japan's Minister to Italy in 1872, and later worked on Japanese immigration to Hawaii.
[218] Hiroshima native Tanaka Kenzaburō 田中健三郎 (1845–1908) joined the Foreign Ministry soon after the Restoration and held appointments as a consular official in Venice and Rome. After returning to Japan, he served in the Imperial Household Agency and also wrote a brief history of modern Italy called *Itari kenkoku kiryaku* in 1886.
[219] Ida Shin'ya concludes that Ryūhoku visited Caffé Florian, which was established in 1720 and is still in operation (221).
[220] The Palazzo Ducale, or Palace of the Doges, was the center of Venetian

The Republican Senate's Council Chamber is extremely vast, and the architectural craftsmanship is quite fine. On its walls were murals depicting the people of this ancient city victoriously battling the Austrians. There were also images of the presidents from ancient times. Inside the hall were housed 150,000 volumes of old books, most of which were manuscripts. The seats of the 310 "Senators" were still there, preserved in the same arrangement as in former times. The paintings on the four walls were done in vivid colors. There were places where some paintings had been removed, and according to our guide, these were the remains of when Napoleon I came here and plundered the famous paintings that suited his tastes. We also saw the prison cells attached to the Senate house.[221] They were enclosed in stone with steel bars, quite sturdy and imposing. There was a well-sweep apparatus that was used for torturing prisoners. These sights all allow one to visualize conditions in ancient times. We left the prison, and after a very short walk came to the Cathedral of San Marco, which has 544 rounded pillars encircling it. The building was constructed entirely out of marble, gold, silver, and copper. It is quite an astonishing sight to behold. In front of the gate, there is a tall tower built to commemorate the founding of the Republic.[222] The ancient palace soars up adjacent to it.

---

government until Napoleon took possession of the city in 1797. The initial date that Ryūhoku gives is perhaps a mistake for 1418 (the year Matsumoto Hakka recorded in his diary), which roughly corresponds to the time when the construction of the present building was nearing completion. Alternatively, many guidebooks date the original founding of the Palazzo on this site to 814; perhaps Ryūhoku transposed the numbers of this year to 418. Ryūhoku goes on to describe the Sala del Maggior Consiglio, which is adorned by Tintoretto's seventy-six portraits of the Doges (whom Ryūhoku calls "presidents").

[221] There were interrogation and torture rooms in the Palazzo itself, but across the so-called Ponte dei Sospiri (Bridge of Sighs) was the Palazzo delle Prigioni. While the dark, dank cells in this prison were called "pozzi" (wells), by "well-sweep apparatus" Ryūhoku is describing some sort of leverage-based torture device.

[222] The Campanile di San Marco was originally built in 888, but had been rebuilt (Baedeker's *Northern Italy*, 244).

This is the liveliest part of the city. Moreover, since there was a festival today for the anniversary of the Republic, men and women were out in droves. They filled the streets with their skirts fragrant and hair ornaments radiant, the sounds of celebratory music delighting the ears. In this city, there are many young girls selling flowers.

漕渠百道入江流　畫舫雕梁鏡裏浮　女伴賣花郎弄笛　春風搖曳小瀛洲
    A hundred canals cross the city, flowing into the Lagoon;
    Painted boats and carved bridges float on the water's mirror.
    Women sell flowers while men play flutes,
    As a spring wind sweeps leisurely over this little paradise.

We also went to have a tour of a glass manufacturing plant. The manager, Fureru Rubi, was a gracious host. The men work at a furious pace, and yet their work is extremely precise and fine. Our host said that they are all renowned glass craftsmen hailing from various provinces. We also went to the church of Santa Maria dei Gesuiti, which had drapes and curtains that had been carved from marble—quite an unusual sight.[223] We then went to see the church of Santa Maria dei Frari, which had a triangular tower.[224] Finally, we went to the church of Santa Maria del Carmine, which was decorated with jewels of five colors.[225] It was the most beautiful of all. On the roof, there remained the marks from where cannon fire had struck the building. Apparently, this damage was done long ago during the battle with the Austrians. From there, we left our boat and went ashore to rest

---

[223] The interior of the Santa Maria dei Gesuiti, built in 1715–30, was lined entirely with marble (Baedeker's *Northern Italy*, 268).
[224] The Santa Maria Gloriosa dei Frari was a Gothic church built in the thirteenth or fourteenth century (Baedeker's *Northern Italy*, 276–277).
[225] The Santa Maria del Carmine was a Gothic church and Carmelite convent built in 1290–1348 (Baedeker's *Northern Italy*, 279).

in a botanical garden. Here, too, there was a musical concert to commemorate the military festival. When evening drew close, we returned to the hotel.

March 23. Sunday. Fine.
We hired a guide to take us by boat to see the Murano glassworks, which are located on islands in the middle of the lagoon. The place we saw yesterday cannot even compare to its magnificent size. The factory's artisans produce glass cups, forming them as freely and easily as they might shape candy. Since many of the bridges in the area are made of wood, there were several places that resembled the scenery back in Japan. The people from the lower classes have dark, sallow complexions, reminding me of Asian people's faces. Children were flying paper kites in the air that were not unlike the design of our kites back home. From there, we went to see the Anjihikagaa glass shop, and we also saw a museum devoted solely to glass pieces.[226] Though it was quite a grand facility, I was not particularly impressed. We then went ashore on an island where there was a large church called San Michele.[227] There was a cemetery on the church grounds and we asked the priest to let us have a look around. Patches of green grass grew luxuriantly here and there. There was little to distinguish this place from Japan. Most of the graves were for coffins that would accommodate a body lying prone; these were buried in the earth and covered by a stone tablet, on which the deceased's name and date of death were recorded, appearing above ground. There were also some similar to those in Japan, in which a stone tablet had been placed vertically above the grave.

---

[226] The museum is the Museo Vetrario; perhaps the glass shop is that of Pietro Bigaglia (1786–1876).
[227] Hakka's diary notes the presence of Catholic, Protestant, and Greek Orthodox cemeteries on the Isola di San Michele.

Furthermore, there were some graves marked only by a crucifix, made from either iron or stone. There were also some newer headstones into which a recess had been carved to accommodate a photograph of the deceased; the photographs were covered with plates of glass to permanently protect them from damage. People who had come to pay their respects at the graves of their relatives and friends placed a standard wreath of vines or flowers before the graves. There were also some who left behind the leaves of a tree that resembled a Japanese star anise, though it was slightly different. All of the priests in the church seemed to wear their hair in the style of the *gobu-sakayaki* of our country.[228] My traveling companions and I exchanged looks and had a laugh at this halfway hairstyle, a tonsure somewhere between priest and layman. After that, we headed to the Palais-Royal.[229] Nakayama Jōji and Miwa Hoichi had arrived from Trieste, and they are both staying in our hotel.[230] At night, I went out for a stroll again in the city. There are many poor people in this place. They pluck their harps and blow their whistles, begging for change in the street. It is quite a nuisance. Tonight, I received word that my son Ken[kichi] had arrived without incident in Trieste. My joy as his father can be imagined.[231]

---

[228] The *sakayaki* was a popular hairstyle during the Edo period in which a man shaved the top of his head while leaving the sidelocks intact. A *gobu-sakayaki* was a *sakayaki* hairstyle that had grown out a bit (lit. "five *bu*" or about half an inch). It was the name of a men's wig used in the kabuki theater and was used for the roles of rōnin and the infirm.

[229] The Palazzo Reale was the southern palace of the Piazza di San Marco. The group's guides were likely using French, and thus Ryūhoku's use of French names such as "Palais-Royal" and "Arc de Triomphe" for Italian sites.

[230] Miwa Hoichi 三輪甫一 was a diplomat whom the Meiji state had sent to Hawaii in 1869 to assist Ueno Kagenori in negotiating on behalf of Japanese agricultural laborers for better working conditions (Yamashita, 11).

[231] Narushima Kenkichi 成島謙吉 (d. 1910) was born into the Osada family, but was adopted as a spouse for Ryūhoku's daughter Hata in 1868 (Ōshima, 410). He had studied French in Yokohama and was later employed by Japan's Agricultural Office. He published translations of several French works including basic primers and texts on

March 24. Monday. Fine.

After getting up early for breakfast, we boarded a boat and headed for the train station. On the boat, they had raised the national flag of Japan, a good indication of the hospitality and respect they show guests. At 5:40, the train departed. As we raced along, I gazed out at the ocean to our left. The blossoms on the peach and apricot trees along the way were in full bloom like a sheet of brocade. The grass of farm pastures added an intermittent touch of green. At twelve o'clock, we arrived at Bologna, another large city. We had a meal and were on our way again. After that, we passed through a valley with a river running along it, the train twisting its way around as we advanced. Looking back in the direction whence we had come, I could see a bridge over the river rapids. The scenery was refreshing and vivid. These mountains are called the Appennino range. On the way from Bologna to Florence, we passed through forty-two tunnels, three of which were particularly large.

石洞吞車又吐車　蜿蜒鐵路入雲斜　深山亦有韶華在　瞥見紅桃一樹花
 The stone cavern swallows up our train, only to spit it out again;
 Iron rails writhe in curves as we ascend the slope into the clouds.
 Here deep in the mountains, the loveliness of spring lingers:
 I catch a glimpse of a red peach tree blossoming in full flower.

At 5:40 in the afternoon, we arrived in Florence, the capital of the old king of Tuscany, who was in recent years deposed by the Italian king.[232] Its population numbers 114,000, and the houses and streets downtown

---

forestry, agriculture, and animal husbandry.
[232] Leopold II (d. 1870) had been banished in the revolution of 1859, just before Tuscany was annexed by Sardinia in 1860. The "Italian king" mentioned here is Vittorio Emanuele II (1820–1878), King of Sardinia, who went on to become the first king of the unified Kigdom of Italy in 1861.

are all constructed from giant stones. It is a genuinely splendid and impressive sight. Florence truly has the feeling of a regal city. We checked into the Hotel di Milano. There are very few people here who speak French, which makes things rather inconvenient. At night, I went for a stroll in the city streets. I found a coffee shop but it was rather rough and not at all appealing. It is interesting how each city has its own strengths and weaknesses.

赴弗稜蘭途中作　*Composed along the way to Florence*
客程南入弗稜蘭　恍覺風光肖故山　曖々烟霞春十里　桃紅點綴菜黃閒

My traveler's route brings me southward into Florence;

Entranced by the scenery that so resembles the mountains back home.

A vague and hazy mist covers the spring for ten miles;

The peach trees' crimson hue is dappled with yellow rape blossoms.

March 25. Tuesday. Fine, a little hot.
We hired a guide and went to tour the Duomo church. We climbed up inside of its tower, high enough to bring us soaring into the clouds. There were 417 stone steps, although some say there are 418.[233] As I looked out over the entire city, the pedestrians on the streets below all looked like swarming ants. We also went to see the stone and bronze statuary around the Palazzo Vecchio, all of which were carved by famous craftsman of antiquity. After that, we went to see the Palazzo Pitti, that is, the old castle of the King of Tuscany. The wall in front was constructed entirely from immense stones. When we went inside, we found the interior all inlaid with precious stones. Known as "mosaic," it is the most renowned craft of Italy, and its beauty is a wonderful

---

[233] The Duomo, or Cattedrale di Santa Maria del Fiore, had a 276-foot campanile constructed in the fourteenth century; contemporary guidebooks put the number of steps at 414.

delight for the eyes. After a leisurely look around the palace, we went out into the garden. There was a place where green trees came together from right and left to meet and form a passage rather like a long, cavernous corridor. A fountain burbled steadily, and the fragrant grasses grew luxuriantly. There were stone statues and stone sculptures arranged here and there. The castle is uninhabited at present and is used only occasionally when the Italian king comes to entertain guests. However, the people of this province still yearn for their former sovereign the Tuscan king and have not surrendered their feelings to the Italian king. Apparently when the Italian king comes here to visit, it is very rare for the people of this province to take off their hats as a sign of respect. When I toured the garden of this castle, I felt as though I were strolling around Gusu and I could almost see the old palace of the King of Wu.[234] I composed one quatrain:

知有遺民記大家　當年一曲後庭花　石人不語春如夢　滿苑藨蕪夕日斜
    I know adherents of the old regime still recall its great house;
    In those days, there would be music, and flowers in the rear courtyard.
    But now the stone statues do not speak, and that spring is but a dream;
    In the gardens grow only vines, as the evening sun sets.

---

[234] Located in modern Suzhou, Gusu 姑蘇 was the capital of Wu, a Chinese state during the Spring and Autumn Period. More specifically, Gusu refers to the terrace where King Fuchai of Wu consorted with the beautiful Xi Shi before meeting his demise at the hands of the rival state of Yue (whence Xi Shi hailed). Gusu figured in the ominous warning that one of the King's advisors, Wu Zixu, gave him: deer would play in its ruins if the King underestimated the rival state. As Wu Zixu predicted, King Goujian of Yue did in fact later defeat Fuchai, who commited suicide at Gusu. The site was a famous topic for poems of remembrance; see, for example, the pair by Li Bo translated by Hinton (33–34). The phrase about flowers in the rear courtyard presumably refers to Xi Shi and other palace ladies.

We left the inner garden and wandered around the outer garden. The view was absolutely splendid. We also went to see the church of Santa Maria Novella, which was again quite grand. Crossing the iron bridge over the Arno River, we returned to the hotel. At 8:50, we got on a train and left this place. We passed through several tunnels during the night, but since I fell asleep onboard, I do not know anything beyond that.

March 26. Wednesday. Fine.
In the morning, I could see pastures for grazing cows. The green grasslands spread out as far as the eye could see, extending for I don't know how many dozens of miles. At 6:50, we reached Rome, where we checked into the Hotel di Milano.[235] I went to a public bath on Via del Corso. The bathing basins were all made out of marble. Corso is the city's largest street. After lunch, we first went to see the famous Basilica di San Pietro. Of all the churches in Europe, none is more grand or beautiful than this one. In the front of the church was a great Egyptian obelisk, about forty meters tall. To the side was a fountain that sent water shooting up to a height of several dozen feet. To the right and left were tiered passageways supported by round columns, upon which stone figures were arrayed. This church is adjacent to the pope's palace. Since there are so many places to see here, we arranged to come again another day and went back. We also went to see the prison in which Jesus' disciples Peter and Paul were incarcerated. The upper level was where Paul was kept, and the lower level was Peter's cell. Inside was a spring, and we were informed that this is the place where Peter converted the prison guards and administered the rite of baptism to

---

[235] The Hotel di Milano was located on Piazza di Monte Citorio near the Piazza Colonna, had a restaurant, and was, according to Baedeker's *Central Italy*, "patronized ... by Italian deputies" (116).

them.[236] We also stopped by the Triumphal Arch of Constantine.[237] Tonight, I was tired and went to bed early.

March 27. Thursday. Clear.

We hired a guide and went by horse-drawn carriage to tour a series of scenic spots.

• The Pantheon: This was an ancient crematorium, and the mouth of the chimney was visible in the center of the roof.[238] The entire building was constructed out of marble. In front was an Egyptian obelisk.

• The Piazza Colonna: This was built by Emperor Antony of Rome, and on top of it was a statue of St. Peter.[239]

• Popolo Church: There was another stone Egyptian obelisk, with a crucifix affixed to its top. This obelisk was plundered from Egypt by Emperor Heliopolis.[240] In front of the obelisk were two churches, one on each side of the Via del Corso. The first was called San Montesanto and the other was called San Miracoli.[241]

---

[236] The jail mentioned here is the Carcer Mamertinus, which lies under the Church of San Giuseppe dei Falegnami. Formerly a well, the jail had two subterranean chambers lying one on top of the other, and was held to be the site of Peter and Paul's captivity and martyrdom. The lower chamber "contains a spring, which, according to the legend, St. Peter, who was imprisoned here under Nero, miraculously caused to flow in order to baptise his jailors" (Baedeker's *Central Italy*, 228).

[237] The arch, celebrating Constantine I's victory over Maxentius in 312, was dedicated three years later.

[238] Ryūhoku seems to have misunderstood the function of the oculus at the center of the Pantheon's dome.

[239] The Piazza Colonna takes its name from the Column of Marcus Aurelius (Antoninus), whom Ryūhoku may have had in mind when he wrote "Emperor Antony of Rome." Incidentally, the statue atop the column is actually St. Paul.

[240] The obelisk in the Piazza del Popolo was thought to have been brought by Augustus from the Egyptian city of Heliopolis, hence Ryūhoku's confusion; it came to its present location in the sixteenth century (Baedeker's *Central Italy*, 133).

[241] The two churches are the Santa Maria dei Miracoli (on the west) and the Santa Maria in Montesanto (on the east).

- Barcaccia: This fountain contains a massive stone sculpture in the shape of a boat.[242] The patina seemed very ancient.
- Immacolata Column: At its top was a standing figure of Mary.
- The Column of Emperor Trajan was 132 feet in height and at its top was a statue of Saint Peter. Beneath this column, there were several smaller columns, but they were all partially crumbled or broken, some to such an extent that the foundations had barely survived. I was told that they were probably destroyed in ancient wars. Behind the tower was a lookout tower made of brick. In ancient times, the nefarious Emperor Nero decided to set fire to the city and climbed up in this tower to watch as it burned. The details are in Roman history.[243]
- The Academy of St. Luke: There were a great variety of oil paintings.[244]
- The Triumphal Arch of Septimius Severus was constructed out of Greek stones. I understand that it was built to commemorate the accomplishments of Emperor Septimius and his two sons.[245] Below the arch was the ancient city center of Rome, which even now preserves some of its original appearance. To the side were three pillars that remain standing from the Temple of Emperor Vespasian. Eight pillars remain standing from the Temple of Saturn, while the Column

---

[242] Near the steps of the Piazza di Spagna is the *La Barcaccia*, a fountain in the shape of a warship (its name means "barque") by Lorenzo Bernini (1598–1680). In the same square stands the Column of the Immacolata.

[243] Though several sites are associated with the story, Ryūhoku is presumably referring to the Torre delle Milizie, "erected about 1200 by the sons of Petrus Alexius, also called *Torre di Nerone*, because Nero is popularly believed to have witnessed the conflagration of Rome from the top" (Baedeker's *Central Italy*, 149).

[244] The Accadémia di San Luca was founded in 1577.

[245] This marble arch was erected on the tenth anniversary of Severus's accession in 203 CE to honor him and his sons Caracalla and Geta for their victories over the Parthians, Arabs, and Adiabenians (Baedeker's *Central Italy*, 218).

of Phocas consists of just one column. Phocas was the Eastern Roman Emperor and reigned around 608 CE.[246]

- To the side of the Column of Phocas were the remains of an ancient hall. This is where Caesar held audiences with ambassadors from the east. The stone tiled flooring of the hall is still intact.[247]
- The Capitol has now become the houses of parliament.[248] In front was a bronze sculpture of Marcus Aurelius astride a horse. Beneath that was a balustrade and several stone statues along the steps. All of them were wise and great men from antiquity. To the side, there was a cage with a wolf inside. This is because the first Emperor of Rome was raised by wolves. Inside the Capitol, there was a tremendous statue called the Marforio, with water gushing out from beneath. There were also many ancient relics inside: old coffins, grave lanterns, lachrymatories and other such things; it would be impossible to list them all.[249] In addition, there were busts of the emperors, kings, and scholars of the ages, so numerous that I cannot even guess how many there were.

---

[246] The inscription on the Column of Phocas itself notes that it was dedicated "in 608 in honour of the tyrant *Phocas* of the Eastern Empire, by the exarch Smaragdus" (Baedeker's *Central Italy*, 219).

[247] Ida Shin'ya concludes that Ryūhoku is describing the Rostra, a large orator's platform (227–228). Another possibility is the Basilica Giulia, a site used for tribunals and other public business.

[248] The Piazza del Campidoglio was the site of the Palazzo del Senatore and housed the civic administration of Rome. The bronze statue of Marcus Aurelius that Ryūhoku mentions was situated on a pedestal designed by Michelangelo, who also designed the steps leading to the Palazzo del Senatore. Along the approach to the Piazza was the cage with the "she-wolf," and in the court of the Capitol itself a fountain with the "colossal river-god" Marforio (Baedeker's *Central Italy*, 206–207). The numerous relics that Ryūhoku mentions were gathered in the Museo Capitolino.

[249] A lachrymatory was a glass "tear bottle" buried along with the deceased. In his 1877 essay "Doyōboshi no ki" (A record of summer airing), Ryūhoku explains the custom and how he acquired one of the antique objects while in Rome (*Ryūhoku zenshū*, 16–17).

- The Pavilion created by Emperor Antoninus and Empress Faustina had a crucifix attached to the top, and a tower to Romulus to the side.[250]
- The Church of Constantine now lies in dilapidation, only its ruins remaining. I gather that this church was constructed to celebrate the ending of hostilities after the battle with Maxentius.[251]
- The Temple of Caesar is the ancient site most worth visiting in this city.[252] It lies in a location originally chosen by the patriarch Romulus and one at which Caesar himself later came to live. The tomb is situated on a large hill, and was built on an immense scale. When we scaled the stone steps and went inside, we found a fountain and pool, as well as a bathing room. The entrance to the corridor was multi-tiered, rather like the mouth of a cave. Apparently whenever the Roman Emperors would triumph in battle, they would proceed through this corridor. When we looked in one room, we could see a statue of Caesar at its center, with statues of Napoleon I and the present king of Italy to the left and right, for these are the three men who have ruled Rome over the centuries. Ah, how splendid it is that the deeds of a heroic man never fade away, but are instead passed down in perpetuity! We proceeded through the tiered passageway, and everyone in our group picked up one of the stray tiles. There was also a large circular great bath. We went out into the rear garden, where the flowers and trees were numerous. One of the trees had blossoms that were the same as those of a Japanese plum, and the fragrance was identical as well. When

---

[250] The Temple of Faustina was "dedicated by Antoninus in A.D. 141 to his wife, the elder Faustina, and re-dedicated to that emperor also after his death" (Baedeker's *Central Italy*, 221). The round building nearby is the Templum Divi Romuli.

[251] The Basilica of Constantine was "erected by Maxentius, but afterward altered by his conqueror Constantine, whose name it bears" (Baedeker's *Central Italy*, 222).

[252] Ryūhoku narrates a sequence here through the Roman Forum, describing the Temple of Julius Caesar, the Via Sacra, the Balnea, and then the Palatine Hill.

I inquired as to its name, I was told that the tree was called an "amando."²⁵³ I am quite certain it was a plum. They are very seldom seen in Europe. From within the garden, we gazed out over the city stretching far into the distance. We could see a large building below us, and the guide explained that this was where Pompilius was murdered.²⁵⁴ The walls of the Senate and the other buildings all had miniature paintings in color drawn on top of their tiles. The pipes used for heating the rooms were still intact. There were also the remains of a circular horse-racing track, a school, and a hall used for victory banquets. Moreover, the ruins of structures like the room used for conducting heat by fire were all extant. The palace's area was so vast that it would be impossible to make an exhaustive tour. I composed one quatrain:

捄築當年鑿斷崖 殘墻今見暮雲埋 深園春綠離々草 兒女時來拾墜釵
  Back then, they built this place by chiseling it out of a sheer cliff;
  Now I see the remains of those walls, buried by the evening clouds.
  The greens of spring have come to the deep garden, grasses grow lush;
  A young girl happens by, picking up a fallen hair ornament.

I was also moved to thinking about the affair with Brutus, and I composed one poem (the word *jun* in the poem does not refer to one's lord).²⁵⁵

---

²⁵³ Perhaps the guide identified the tree as an almond tree, using the French *amande*.
²⁵⁴ Perhaps this refers to the Regia, a residence said to have been constructed by Numa Pompilius, the second King of Rome. Numa Pompilius was not murdered, however, but died of old age.
²⁵⁵ The 君 (Ch. *jun*; J. *kun*) in the first line of the poem might easily be thought to mean "lord," so Ryūhoku clarifies that it is the second person pronoun "you," and thus that the poem is an apostrophic address to Julius Caesar. In *Ryūhoku shishō*, the poem appears with a note: "Some would say that Brutus's stabbing of Caesar in the Senate was a righteous act; others would call it villainy. It is a tragedy for all time" (III: 38).

莫問殺君忠不忠 霜鋩一閃百圖空 千秋遺恨誰能雪 敗瓦殘磚弔古宮

I shall not ask if killing you was loyal or disloyal;
With a single flash of the sparkling blade, all your plans came to naught.
A thousand springs of lingering resentment, and who can wash it away?
Gazing at the broken tiles and leftover stones, I lament the old castle.

- The arena for the dueling of beasts (Amphitheatre) is a strikingly magnificent structure composed of immense stones. Even today, half of the circular structure remains.[256]
- The Arch of Titus was built at the time of the victory in the attack against Jerusalem.[257] In the same area was the Triumphal Arch of Emperor Constantine. To the side of it, there was an old well that Emperor Nero cursed.
- Although the palace of Emperor Nero was quite grand, it was pitch black inside.[258] Our guide used a torch to illuminate the interior and show it to us. The walls were covered with the multicolored tiles of a mosaic, giving us a glimpse of the past.
- In front of the Church of St. Jion, there was an Egyptian obelisk with a crucifix at the top.[259]
- At the Church of Scala Santa, there was a stairwell with one hundred steps. At this point, our guide hired a carriage and took us through some old city gates and away. The gates were also part of an ancient structure.

---

[256] This is of course the Colosseum, also known as the Flavian Amphitheatre.
[257] The Arch of Titus was erected in 81 to commemorate the sacking of Jerusalem a decade earlier in the Judaean War.
[258] This may be the remains of Nero's "Golden House" upon which Vespasian founded the Colosseum.
[259] In the piazza of the Church of San Giovanni in Laterano is the oldest obelisk in the city and the tallest in existence.

• At the Church of San Pietro in Vincoli, there was a great statue of Moses made out of white stone. He had horns growing from his head, reminding me of our god of agriculture.[260]
• Mars Ultor formed something like the walls of the city, and its ancient elegance was so obvious that one could tell from a single glance that it was thousands of years old.[261]
• The fountain of Trevi is also one of the ancient sites, and here we met the Crown Prince of Italy and his wife, the Princess. We all took off our hats and bowed, to which the Crown Prince kindly bowed in return.
• The Palazzo del Quirinale is the palace of the present king, where tours of the public hall, the tower, and the garden and pool are permitted. It was extremely beautiful.
• The Monte Pincio (Park) is situated on top of a mountain and the view is splendid. We arrived just when workmen were in the middle of constructing a cave in the park out of stones and tiles. Some soldiers had come and were playing music in the park. Throngs of men and women from the aristocracy had come to enjoy themselves.
• The French Academy was a magnificent structure.[262] I saw irises in full bloom here, making me feel quite homesick. On the way back, we went to a restaurant and ordered Roman cuisine for our meal (the hotels and other such places prepare French cuisine).[263] All of the dishes had a slight smell. One was a stew with something resembling *dango* dumplings floating in it, and it tasted dreadful too. We were all

---

[260] Shennong 神農, the Chinese god of agriculture, is often represented with two horns on his head.
[261] The Temple of Mars Ultor was dedicated in 2 BCE (Baedeker's *Central Italy*, 229).
[262] The Villa Medici, built in the sixteenth century, had been the site of the French Academy of Art since 1801.
[263] Ida Shin'ya conjectures that Ryūhoku visited La Casina Valadier, a restaurant that has operated atop Monte Pincio for two hundred years (231).

thoroughly disappointed. We returned to the hotel, and then later in the evening we went out again to a grand theatre. It was quite fine, only one notch below the French opera. They were performing the story of William Tell, who is ordered by the king to place an apple on top of his son's head and then shoot it off with an arrow. The actresses' dancing was superb, and I was also surprised at the deftness with which they closed the curtain from the sides.

March 28. Friday. Clear.
We hired a guide again to take us around to see the various sites.
• The Palazzo Borghese had an exhibition gallery with many oil paintings hanging on display. We also saw a large decorative plate made of precious stones which was truly an astonishing sight to behold.
• There are "catacombs" in the Church of the Cappuccini. They have made lanterns out of old dried bones and also arranged them on the walls to form various patterns. In addition, there were several dried corpses.[264]
• Palazzo Pamphili Doria [265] had many oil paintings and stone sculptures.
• The old Theater of Marcellus is still preserved in the city center. The lower level is occupied by merchants. It is recorded in Roman history that in ancient times Caesar built theaters, and it is said that this theater was constructed by Caesar too.[266]

---

[264] The Church of the Cappuccini, founded in 1624, also known as the Santa Maria della Concezione, has catacombs that are home to the bones and skeletons of over four thousand Capuchins (Baedeker's *Central Italy*, 139).
[265] The Galleria Doria-Pamphili in the Palazzo Doria had a large collection of paintings (Baedeker's *Central Italy*, 170).
[266] The theater was planned by Julius Caesar and dedicated in 13 BCE by Augustus to Marcellus, who was his nephew and son-in-law. The next site Ryūhoku mentions seems to be the Portico d'Octavia, built by Augustus in honor of his sister; enclosing two temples, it functioned as a gallery exhibition space (Baedeker's *Central Italy*, 196).

- The ruins of the Portico Theatre are also a kind of theatre, this one built by Octavia.
- The Israelite Church is a temple for "Jews," and on the front was a placard written in "Hebrew letters."
- The Palazzo Farnese houses old paintings. Some of the paintings on its ceiling could almost be classified as *shunga*. It is said that the famous artist Zangaru once spent time here.[267]
- Santa Maria in Trastevere Church has ornamentation above the gates in front of the church that is made entirely of mosaic. The human figures and other subjects portrayed have been executed with marvelous craftsmanship and were quite a striking sight.

We then returned to the Cathedral of Saint Peter and went to see the Vatican of the Pope, which is located behind it. It is the palace in which the pope lives. The interior of the palace is extremely spacious, and half of it has been made into a museum. Its unusual exhibits, from ancient stone carvings of humans and animal figures to stone and copper vessels, pottery and other objects, were marvelous to see. The large stone bowl of Emperor Titus was made of purple marble. I saw two other large coffins made of purple stone, both of which were finely carved. Our guide explained that they were the coffins of

---

[267] The Palazzo Farnese had been designed by Antonio da Sangallo the Younger (1485–1546), who seems to be the individual Ryūhoku had in mind in referring to the "famous artist Zangaru." Given that Sangallo's distinction was prinicipally as an architect, however, there is good reason to think that Ida Shin'ya is correct in concluding that "Zangaru" refers instead to the French neo-classical painter Jean Auguste Dominique Ingres, who drew inspiration from the frescoes in the Palazzo Farnese (232–233). As for the particular ceiling frescoes that reminded Ryūhoku of Japanese erotic prints, Ida suggests the spandrels by Raphael depicting Cupid and Psyche, but the frescoes executed by Annibale Carracci (1560–1609) and his brother, which were entitled "The Loves of the Gods," are equally likely candidates (Baedeker's *Central Italy*, 193). A few days later, Ryūhoku described erotic images excavated from Pompeii as *shunga* too.

Emperor Constantine and his Empress.[268] Truly the gorgeous grandeur of these pieces is unparalleled. Among the exhibits were a Chinese bell carved during the Qianlong period [1736–1795] and numerous Chinese Buddhist statues. This is without question one of the very finest museums in all of Europe. When we ventured out into the palace garden, we saw that there was an old iron boat (in miniature) floating in the middle of the pond. It was quite a lovely scene, with dozens of willow trees that looked to be the West Lake type. We left the palace and went to see the Vesta Tower built by Emperor Titus, after which we passed by the Monte Aventino.[269] I imagine that this small hill would be an excellent place to get a good view of the city, but since we were in a hurry, we did not climb it. From there, we went to the outskirts of the city to see the pyramid of Caius Cestius (it was built as a replica of the ancient Egyptian ruins).[270] We also went to the Church of San Paolo, an immense church that is the largest in Rome next to the Cathedral of St. Peter.[271] I am told that it can in fact boast of having inside it the largest and most numerous stone pillars of any church in the world. Just as we were passing by the Triumphal Arch of Trajan, we happened to encounter the King of Italy's carriage in the street. We all removed our hats and bowed, and the King also removed his cap to return our bow. There was nothing about him to suggest imperiousness. Today, I have caught a cold, and so I went to bed early. Ono departed by himself for Pisa. Today, I composed one poem during our tour.

---

[268] The Museo Vaticano houses the sarcophagi of Constantine the Great's daughter and mother, Constantia and St. Helena (Baedeker's *Central Italy*, 297).
[269] Ryūhoku is presumably referring to the Temple of Vesta, site of the sacred fire.
[270] The Pyramid of Cestius is the tomb of Caius Cestius, a magistrate who died in 12 BCE (Baedeker's *Central Italy*, 244–245).
[271] The church of San Paolo fuori le Mura was founded in 386, and "prior to the great fire of 1823, which destroyed almost the entire building except the choir, this was the finest and most interesting church in Rome" (Baedeker's *Central Italy*, 350).

風意吹春舊帝都　獨憐臺閣委烟蕪　干戈畢竟爲何用　石柱空留百戰圖

A breeze blows spring into the old Emperor's capital;
A shame that the pavilion has long yielded to mists and curling vines.
In the end, what use are spears and halberds?
The stone pillars vainly preserve images from a hundred battles.

March 29. Saturday. Fine and pleasant.

My sickness is a bit improved. In the afternoon, I went for a stroll downtown. I bought several ancient articles and returned.

March 30. Sunday. Fine again.

In one of the streetside shops, I bought several decorative objects made out of "lava." Lava is the substance formed when the molten matter that has erupted from a volcano returns to a solid state again. In the evening, I visited the home of a Tuscan named Alba with my traveling companions. Tonight, Ono returned.

March 31. Monday. Overcast.

I went for a stroll with Ono on the Corso. We went for a tour of the Esupangiyo building.[272] We encountered a brief shower in the afternoon, and at two o'clock we left Rome. On board the train, we saw what looked like the remains of the old city walls stretching out endlessly to our right. We could see the remains of the old market shops and the ruins of old buildings scattered here and there among the fields. At 9:30, we reached Naples, where we checked into the Hôtel de Genève.[273] Because the hotel's rooms were all occupied, three of

---

[272] Ono and Ryūhoku presumably toured the Palazzo di Spagna in the Piazza di Spagna.
[273] Baedeker's *Southern Italy* notes that the Hôtel de Genève on the Strada St. Giuseppe and the Hôtel Central on the Strada Medina were "second-class" hotels located near the harbor and appealing to a "commercial" clientele (21).

273

the members of our group checked into the Hotel Central. Naples is one of Italy's particularly beautiful cities.

都城如錦港如弧　多少樓臺負海嵎　好是佳人迎客笑　玻璃窓底賣珊瑚
The city a beautiful brocade, its port a sweeping arc;
Many buildings lie with the edge of the sea behind them.
What a joy it is to have charming women greet this traveler with a smile;
Beneath glass windows, they sell their coral.

April 1. Tuesday. Fine.
We hired a guide and toured the city's museum. Most of the items on display there had been excavated from the famous site of Pompeii. Stone and bronze statues and the like were numerous. But the difference between the statues we have seen elsewhere and these is that the penises and scrotums and so forth are all still intact on their bodies. We saw ancient armor and something that looked quite like a Japanese *naginata*. Also, there were stones shaped liked gingko nuts that were used in catapults during ancient battles. A great many Egyptian objects were also on display, with old bronzes and pottery heaped nearly on top of one other. The variety of the exhibited pieces was quite impressive. There was one place in the museum that women were not allowed to tour. We went in to have a look and it turned out the objects on display were fixtures from an old brothel that had been excavated at Pompeii. The lamp stands and everything else as well were phallic in shape. Ancient erotic paintings, all of them quite elegant, adorned the walls. In both the ancient coin room and the ancient documents room, many of the items on display had been unearthed from Pompeii. I was surprised to see that the paints, raw silk, bread, grains and other such things that had been buried in the earth for over one thousand years still retained their original form. However, things like the silk and the bread had

been singed pitch black, and I imagine that if you so much as touched them with your hands they would immediately crumble into pieces. As for the paints, colors like blue, yellow, red, and white were still sharp and unchanged, which is surely something curious. We left the museum, and headed to the Vomero Hill. On the side of the hill is a giant stone fortress. We reached the Church of Carthusia.[274] The Church overlooks the ocean, and the view is absolutely splendid. To the left you can see the volcano: Vesuvius. The mountain now has two pointed peaks, one of which was pouring forth fire quite vigorously. I understand that in ancient times there were three peaks, but that one of the peaks erupted and broke apart, burying the whole city of Pompeii underground. All of the houses in the city lay before us, stretching along the shore of the bay. With islands rising up here and there, and ships crisscrossing the water, it is a very bustling place. Since it is in the southernmost part of Italy, the climate is warm and quite similar to our own country's. We surveyed the various items in the church, among which was the golden palanquin of the old King of Naples. It was a dazzlingly beautiful sight.

Many of the people of Naples keep donkeys, which they will rent out to tourists to ride. In addition, we saw donkeys and horses harnessed up and pulling the same carriage: quite an unusual sight. The outside of the palace of the old King of Naples faces the sea and is very beautiful. The coastal scenery is especially splendid, and the houses are all also clean and well tended. There is no reason not to call this place the most beautiful city in all of Italy, and on top of that the climate is also temperate and agreeable. Off to the right from the coastline, there was

---

[274] The fourteenth-century monastery La Certosa di San Martino (St. Martin's Charterhouse) stands atop the Vomero hill, next to the Castel Sant'Elmo fortress (Baedeker's *Southern Italy*, 90).

a small tunnel entering the mountainside. Just for fun we took the carriage in, and it took us just five minutes to pass through. Along the way there were several burning lights. This is apparently an old tunnel that was dug in ancient times.[275] We went for a stroll in a park. The park was bounded on one side by the sea, and was extremely spacious. There were many flowers and trees, and not a few stone sculptures. There was even a place for training horses. The park was thronged with men and women. Even Paris would perhaps not quite measure up to this scenery. There were purple wisteria blossoms almost in full bloom: quite a lovely scene. We left and went to look at a coral shop. There was an astonishing array of coral gathered together there, from deepest scarlet to light pink. We returned to the hotel and had dinner. At night, I went with the others to the house of Teresa. She is from Lyon in France.

April 2. Wednesday. Clear.
At nine o'clock we hired a horse-drawn carriage to take us around the ancient ruins of Pompeii. Along the way, we saw a series of wholesale companies that gather coral from the seaside and sell it all over the world. I couldn't begin to guess how many thousands of coral items are stocked in their warehouses. If Shi Chong were to see these riches, he would no doubt pass out from the shock.[276] When we asked about their prices, we were told that one kilogram of the finer items was worth four hundred francs, and the same weight of the lower grade

---

[275] Ida Shin'ya suggests that Ryūhoku and his traveling companions passed through the Galleria della Vittoria, which is 800 meters long (236).
[276] As mentioned earlier, Shi Chong was a wealthy man from the Jin Dynasty; Ryūhoku's reference to him here is especially appropriate, for a story recorded in Shi Chong's biography in the *Jin shu* as well as in the *Shi shuo xin yu* tells of how he once destroyed a man's fine specimen of coral only to flaunt his wealth by making reparations with several coral objects that were superior to the original item; for a translation see Minford and Lau, I: 477–478, 671–672.

items was worth two hundred francs. The sand on this beach is like ash, and since the wind was blowing fiercely, traveling along it was quite a challenge. Looking at the volcano nearby, I saw that it was pouring forth "lava" like oil. Two and a half hours outside of Naples, we reached Pompeii. There was a gate. We all got out of the carriage and went inside. This was quite a thriving city in ancient times, but in 79 CE, the volcano erupted, burying the whole city in molten rock. Then in 1755, residents of the surrounding area were digging a well and for the first time discovered houses buried in the earth. Gradually the site was excavated, and eventually the whole city saw the light of day again. Thus a steady stream of tourists from all over the world comes here to see the curious sight. What a marvelous stroke of good luck that I have chanced to come here too! One can easily imagine how prosperous the city must have been in antiquity. The city streets were all paved with cobblestones, just like European cities of today. There were graves that still stood somberly, and such structures as the barrier gates and military garrisons have also survived intact. In a breadmaker's shop, there was still a stone pestle in place, and in an oil shop there were giant jugs like sake barrels lined up. The public bathhouses were round in shape and made out of stone. The remains of taverns, theaters, and arenas for dueling beasts were all apparent. In the churches, courthouses, and prisons, one could see what life must have been like in those days. Among the most unusual sights was a brothel. By the gateway stood a stone pillar, atop which was a carved penis. Entering the gate, there were miniature paintings of fish and vegetables on the wall. In the bedrooms, there were erotic paintings on all of the walls. From this, one could imagine the customs of the time. When the city was buried, all of its residents fled to other locations, but the physical forms of those who unfortunately died are still preserved through plaster casts of their whole bodies. Some, soldiers apparently, had died while still clutching their swords or staffs. There were others that looked like pregnant women. Deep within one room there was a body that had become dried bones, half buried in the earth. Perhaps this was the body of someone who was gravely ill at the time. There were also the dried corpses of dogs, horses, and other birds and beasts. I cannot record each and every one of the strange sights there. Since they are still in the process of excavating the place today, I cannot even venture a guess as to just how expansive the perimeter of the city must have been originally. I composed one poem:

天勝人耶人勝天 殘楹再映舊峯烟 酒壚詩壁依然在 借問當年有八仙
  Does Heaven overcome man? Or does man overcome Heaven?
  The pillars re-emerge, standing out against the smoking old peak.
  Taverns with poems inscribed on the wall are still intact today;
  I wonder if this city once had eight immortals too.[277]

We took a rest in a coffee shop, and drank some wine, which was nine francs for a bottle. In this city, we saw some pumpkins that were several times the size of a watermelon. We took the same road back to the hotel. Tonight we left Naples at 10:05.

April 3. Thursday. Fine.
At 6:40 we reached Rome, where we had a meal, and then departed at nine o'clock on a different train. The scenery we saw from the train was spectacular: tall hills, flowing water, a riot of cherry blossoms in full splendor. We had lunch in Foligno, and then we traveled across a river

---

[277] The final line refers to the "eight immortals of the winecup," a group of Tang era scholars (including Li Bo) whose fondness for drink was celebrated in a poem by Du Fu. The question posed at the outset recalls Wu Zixu's statement as recorded in Sima Qian's *Records of the Grand Historian*: "I have heard that when people are numerous, they can overcome Heaven; but Heaven can certainly also break people."

flowing through a mountain valley, passing through several tunnels. At 6:47 in the evening, we reached Florence, where we checked into the Hotel di Milano again.

April 4. Friday. Fine.
At dawn, I got up and went to a bathhouse in the city. It was immaculate. Inside the bathing rooms there was a toilet, which is something I had not seen in other places. The bathing tubs were all constructed out of marble. I then had my hair cut in one of the city shops. It cost one and a half francs. Tonight at seven o'clock we left by train, and at 1:15 we reached Modena. At 3:30 we reached Piacenza, where we changed trains, and since we were hungry had a meal.

April 5. Saturday. Fine.
The fields were quite enchanting: a lovely late spring scene, with peach and apricot blossoms fluttering down to the ground. At 8:40, we reached Alessandria, which is a large city. We changed trains again, and at eleven o'clock reached Turin, where we checked into a hotel called the Trombetta.[278] I went for a stroll around a flower garden. There was one street that very much resembled the Palais-Royal in Paris. There was a strikingly beautiful young woman in a small bookshop; I have not seen one so beautiful in my journey through Europe thus far. At night, my companions and I visited the home of Ida, a Greek.

April 6. Sunday. Fine.
At nine o'clock, we left Turin. Gazing out at Mont Cenis, we could still see snow on its peaks. At 12:12, we entered the great tunnel, and thirty-three minutes later, we came out through the other side, where

---

[278] Located near the Piazza Castello, the Hôtel Trombetta was, according to Baedeker's *Northern Italy*, a "first class" establishment (66).

snow was falling steadily in the wind. This is just how different the climates of France and Italy are from one another. At 12:20, we passed through Modane, where the French officials checked our luggage. They were quite perfunctory about it. I adjusted my watch here. I believe the difference between Italy and France is about forty minutes. When we left Modane, the rain was pouring down, the mountains were covered by clouds and mist, and everywhere I looked, it was dark and hard to see. At just after four o'clock, I could make out a great lake to our left. Seeing the scenery in the rain has its own charm. We had a meal in Culoz.

April 7. Monday. Overcast.

At 6:50, we arrived in Paris, and checked in at the old hotel again. It was as though we had come back home. After a meal, we went to the legation and met with Osada. Hearing that my son Ken had arrived and was on the Rue de Saint-Sulpice, I went there immediately, but he was not in. In the afternoon, Ken came together with Ono. Naturally I was delighted, for this was the first time since I left Japan that I had the opportunity to hear news about my family. However, I heard that my youngest daughter had become ill and passed away. How could I, her father, restrain my tears upon receiving such unexpected news? At night, I visited Irie, and went with Ken to have a drink at Duval.[279]

April 8. Tuesday. Fine.

In the morning, I visited Inagaki's hotel and went to Bouché's house. In the afternoon, I went to the Grand Hôtel, and met with Ōkubo Toshimichi. He will leave here tomorrow.[280] I returned to the hotel and

---

[279] Ida Shin'ya reasons that Ryūhoku, freshly returned from an expensive tour of Italy, may have chosen to economize by taking his son-in-law to the cafeteria Duval (237).
[280] Ōkubo Toshimichi, one of the Vice Ambassadors traveling on the Iwakura Mission,

wrote a letter home. I went again to the Grand Hôtel, where I met with Ikeda Kanji and entrusted the letter to him.

April 9. Wednesday. Overcast.

Irie Fumio, Takabatake Bizan[281] and Kanbe Yoshikata[282] came over to visit. In the afternoon, I went for a stroll in the floral gardens in front of our hotel. I also went to have a look at the Cluny Museum.

April 10. Thursday. Overcast.

My son Ken came over. We visited Fukazawa Katsuoki at the Grand Hôtel.[283] We discussed our group's plans for studying abroad and together we had dinner at the Dîner Européen.

April 11. Friday. Fine.

Today is the day that Christ was executed, and pious parishioners crowded churches throughout the city. Namura and Fukazawa came over. At night, I visited Osada and discussed my son Ken's plans for studying abroad.

---

had been summoned back to Japan early in order to attend to a variety of policy divisions that had arisen in the Meiji government.

[281] Tokushima-born Takabatake Gorō 高畠五郎 (1825–1884), who used the sobriquet Bizan 眉山, pursued Chinese studies and Dutch studies, becoming an instructor and translator at the shogunate's Institute for the Study of Barbarian Books in 1856. He continued his work as a translator in the War Ministry and Navy after the Restoration. When Ryūhoku met him, he was part of the Japanese delegation attending the International Exhibition in Vienna.

[282] Kanbe Yoshikata 神戸義方 (1840–1882) was from Shōnai (Yamagata) and had accompanied the sons of his daimyo, Sakai Tadazumi (1853–1915) and Tadamachi (1856–1921), to Germany in 1872. Kanbe stayed in Germany for eight years, attending on the Sakai brothers and studying law himself.

[283] Nagasaki-born Fukazawa Katsuoki 深澤勝興 (d. 1883), also read Shōkō, served in the Finance Ministry and had been dispatched to Europe to assist the Japanese delegation to the Vienna Exhibition in its financial dealings (Tanaka and Hirayama, appendix, 10); as Ryūhoku's references to him suggest, he also consulted with other Japanese in Europe on such matters. He went on to become a banker.

April 12. Saturday. Overcast.
The members of my traveling group and I visited Fukazawa. We have decided to go our separate ways: Matsumoto will go to Germany, and Ishikawa and I will go to England. Ono came over to chat.

April 13. Sunday. Fine.
I visited Takabatake at the Hôtel de Gibraltar. Together we went to the Louvre Museum, where we looked at the old paintings and antiquities. After that, we went for a stroll in the park. Today was warm and pleasant, just like the weather in Japan around April. There were cherry blossoms in full bloom, all of their blossoms white.

April 14. Monday. Fine.
I went to the bank with Ono to discuss withdrawing the money we had deposited. At night, I went with Takabatake to watch the show at the Gaîté Theatre. They were still performing the same play that I saw last time about the golden eggs.

April 15. Tuesday. Fine.
I went to the bank again to meet with Mr. Coullet, and brought our transactions to a close. I then had lunch at a place on the Boulevard des Italiens, where the shrimp was quite delicious. At night, I visited Osada.

April 16. Wednesday. Fine.
I went to visit Mr. Chanoine at his home on the Rue Saint-Marc with Ken, but he was not in. I visited Tsuruta, Namura, and the others. It was a little hot today, and a gentle wind blew through the branches of the green trees to create a very lovely early summer scene.

April 17. Thursday. Rainy.
I went to Coteau's place to buy a watch. I went with Ono again to the Palais-Royal to have a stroll and bought some "labradorite" (a precious stone produced in Russia). At night, I went with Osada, Kanematsu, and my son Ken to Mr. Chanoine's home for a banquet. We came back after a wonderful time.

April 18. Friday. Rainy.
Today Shuntai transferred to the Lord Byron. I went with Takabatake to the Center for Naval Maps, after which we wandered around the Buttes-Chaumont Park. The scenery was crisp and fresh. We had dinner in the Dîner Européen.

April 19. Saturday. Fine.
I visited Osada, Takabatake, Ishikawa, and Ono. I also visited Mr. Nakai Hiroshi at the Hôtel de Bâle.[284]

April 20. Sunday. Overcast.
I took Osada, Ono, Ishikawa, and my son Ken to Saint Germain. The railway passes through Rueil, where the tomb of Napoleon's former wife Josephine lies. Just as I had done last time I came, I went for a stroll around the woods atop the hill, but this time the grasses were in

---

[284] Born in Satsuma, Nakai Hiroshi 中井弘 (1838–1894), who used the sobriquet Ōshū 櫻洲, was a samurai active in loyalist causes in his youth. He first traveled to the West in 1866, an experience he recorded and published as *Seiyō kikō kōkai shinsetsu* (A new account of navigation: Western travelogue, 1870). He traveled abroad again in the early Meiji period, leaving just a few months before Ryūhoku; he stayed in Europe for several years, and composed a second travel piece, *Man'yū kitei* (Record of a leisurely journey), which was published in 1877 after his return to Japan. Ryūhoku provided some of the editorial commentaries printed alongside Nakai's poems in this edition. Ida Shin'ya suggests that Ryūhoku's cryptic "Baaree" in his transcription of the name of Nakai's hotel refers not to "Bâle," but to the Hotel de la place du "Palais" Royal (237).

lush growth and the flowers in radiant bloom, making it particularly charming. At the inn in the woods, we had a drink and also ate some carp, which was quite delicious.

April 21. Monday. Rainy, then fine.
I visited Takabatake. Watanabe Yoshinori[285] from Kaga came over to chat.

April 22. Tuesday. Overcast, cold.
I went with my son Ken to visit Rosny, but he was not in. We met with a Polish man named De Zélinski, who was extremely kind and hospitable to me.[286] Whenever Poles attend on foreigners they are always so friendly and gracious. It certainly is impressive. My traveling companions and I went for a drink at a tavern on Saint-Michel this evening; the time had come for us to exchange our parting cups.

April 23. Wednesday. Fine.
Today, I transferred to the Hôtel de Lord Byron. Since I have been staying in the Hôtel Corneille for such a long time, when I said goodbye to the proprietor and his wife, it was almost as though I was leaving my family behind. In the afternoon, we went to have a tour of a cigarette factory.[287] They use one type of machine at the factory to cut

---

[285] The identity of Watanabe Yoshinori 渡邊賀治 is obscure; Hakka's diary entry for April 19 suggests that he was seeking to return home with Ryūhoku and Ishikawa via the United States.
[286] Louis de Zélinski, a professor based in Nijni-Novogorod, was a member of Rosny's Ethnographic Society and translated Rosny's Japanese primer *Dialogues japonais* from French into Polish in 1874.
[287] The Manufacture des Tabacs occupied "the whole block between the Rue Nicot, the Rue de l'Université, and the Rue de la Boucherie des Invalides ... 1800–1900 hands are employed, of whom 1400 are women, and 60–70 children; the women earn 2½ fr. per diem on an average" (Baedeker's *Paris*, 226).

the tobacco plants and another type to transport the leaves along. The machines move with a surprisingly nimble agility. Next, we saw the machine that breaks apart the clusters of tobacco: it was a large iron rod that revolved around in a giant mortar. There were many young girls weighing the tobacco out on scales. We also saw girls rolling the tobacco up in paper, a task they performed with astonishing swiftness. They also produce tobacco that is about the length of a piece of string. We were told that this product is chewed by members of the lower social classes. In addition, there was a kind of tobacco that is sniffed. There were mountains of the stuff piled up—I can't imagine how many millions of pounds it all weighs. The aroma was intoxicating and it was quite fragrant to sniff. Since it is prohibited for followers of certain sects to smoke tobacco, they apparently put it up to their nostrils and sniff it. I imagine that the tobacco is grown in France (the Calais region is said to produce a lot of it). The tobacco coming from America resembles that grown in Japan, but the leaves are a little longer. German tobacco is the same variety as Japanese tobacco. Tobacco produced in Mexico is speckled with a star pattern. Tobacco grown in Turkey has small leaves, is yellowish in color, and is considered to be of the highest quality. The factory girls also roll "cigars" with great dexterity. It is said that they can each produce four hundred cigars in a single day. The factory girls' wages are two francs and twenty-five centimes per day. Men receive five francs. Women from the city have banded together with the Turks to found a group that has rented a space inside the factory and used it for a separate production unit. The machines in the factory are all very large and powered by steam. Even without asking how much they produce, it is clear that the amount is quite large. This evening, I visited Osada, and we went to visit Ōkura Kihachirō and Yokoyama Magoichirō.

April 24. Thursday. Fine.

Inagaki came over to visit. I took Ōkura and my son Ken to see the collection of cannons at the museum. There were scores of cannons that had been plundered from various countries. There were also a great many suits of ancient armor and horse armor on display, including the armor of Emperor François, Louis XIV, and Joan of Arc. We saw ancient swords, halberds, and also a device for hurling stones (it resembled a catapult). Today, Ōkura went to London. This evening, the Minister to the United States, Mr. Mori Kinnojō, came and stayed in our hotel.[288] We met and talked for several hours. Mr. Sameshima, Mr. Takasaki, and Mr. Osada all came over to meet him. These past few days, I have written two poems, which I will record here.

海西二月漸韶華　此際征人最憶家　縱使東君催剪綵　風香不似故山花

    The second month visits splendor on these western shores;
    In this season, the traveler longs most for home.
    Even if the god of spring should fashion lovely silken blossoms,
    The scent wafting on the breeze is not that of the flowers back there.

石獅蹯處賽旗斜　日暖街頭賣百花　生怕薔薇香萬斛　春風吹送美人車

    Festive flags flutter where the stone lions stride;
    The sun warms the street, where hundreds of flowers are sold.
    An overpowering fragrance of roses leaves me anxious and unsettled,
    As a spring breeze sends off a beautiful woman in her carriage.[289]

---

[288] Satsuma native Mori Kinnojō, better known as Mori Arinori 森有禮 (1847–1889), had studied in Europe and the United States in the 1860s, and would go on to become a leading advocate of Japan's Westernization, founding the Meirokusha society immediately upon his return to Japan in 1873 and serving as Minister of Education. He was assassinated by a nationalist in 1889.

[289] Ida Shin'ya suggests that the pair of white stone lions at the Luxembourg Gardens inspired Ryūhoku to write this quatrain (238).

April 25. Friday. Overcast. Occasional snow.
It is extremely cold. I visited the lodgings of Reverend Gennyo, followed by those of Mr. Irie, Mr. Takabatake, Mr. Tsuruta, and Mr. Namura, and then dropped by the houses of Mr. Chanoine and the female teacher Legrand to say my goodbyes. In the market downtown, I bought some flower and plant seeds. In the evening, I went with Ishikawa and Ono to Véfour (a famous restaurant) for a drink. Tonight at eleven o'clock, Reverend Gennyo is going with Matsumoto and Ono to Germany. I went to the station to see them off and I found it hard to leave them.

April 26. Saturday. Snowy and then rainy.
Tsuruta, Takasaki, and Kawaji came over and I said goodbye to them. In the afternoon, I went to the legation and informed Minister Sameshima of my plans to depart. At night, I attended a going-away party at a tavern on the Boulevard des Italiens with Osada, Takabatake, Inagaki, Ishikawa, and my son Ken.

April 27. Sunday. Rainy and then clear.
I left early in the morning, and at 7:35, I boarded a train at the Gare du Nord. My son Ken and Inagaki came and saw me off. As I looked back over these roughly four months I have spent in Paris, I felt as though I could not bear to leave it behind. We passed through some mountains and fields, and then at 1:20 reached Calais and had lunch. When we boarded the small steamship there, the winds were blowing fiercely, and there were snow flurries. The waves came crashing onto the deck, and of the fifty-odd passengers on board, there were just two who did not become nauseated. After two hours, we reached Dover in England. The fortresses here were quite sturdy and imposing. We took a carriage to customs, where our luggage was examined upon arrival. Once I slipped

the inspector two "shillings," the inspection was very cursory. We boarded a steam locomotive and entered London. We reached Victoria Station at 6:50. We checked into a hotel called the Golden Cross.[290] It was located in Charing Cross. By evening, I was exhausted and went to bed early.

April 28. Monday. Fine.
I visited the inn where Ōkura and Tejima are staying, and made plans to switch our accommodations.[291] I went to the legation, where I met with Mr. Okada Yoshiki.[292] I visited Mr. Takeda Masatsugu at Kensington, and we spoke of old times.[293] Today after dinner, I moved

---

[290] The Golden Cross Hotel was located at 452 Strand, opposite Charing Cross Station (Baedeker's *London*, 8).
[291] Ryūhoku refers only to "Tejima," making the man's identity uncertain. The editors of *Meijihen* identify him as Tejima Seiichi 手島精一 (1849–1918), a central figure in the establishment of industrial education in Japan who was in England at this time. In 1870, Tejima had begun to study architecture at Lafayette College in Philadelphia, and in 1872, just as his funds were running short, he accepted a position as interpreter for the Treasury officials then in Washington with the Iwakura Mission (Ōkubo, 127). He accompanied these officials to England, where he continued to serve as interpreter before returning to Japan in 1874 (Tejima, 17–22). Nevertheless, given the fact that the Tejima Ryūhoku meets is staying with pioneering enterpreneur Ōkura Kihachirō, it seems quite likely that "Tejima" refers not to Tejima Seiichi, but to Ōkura's assistant, Tejima Eijirō 手嶋鍈次郎 (d. 1897), who was hired to serve as an interpreter during Ōkura's observational tour of the West. Tejima Eijirō worked for Ōkura his entire life, eventually reaching the rank of vice president in one of Ōkura's companies (Kakuyūkai, 58; Sunagawa, 33, 103).
[292] Okada Yoshiki 岡田好樹 (1848–1926) was an early student and teacher of English in Nagasaki who went on to produce the first French–Japanese dictionary printed with movable type, the *Nouveau dictionnaire français-japonais*, in 1871. Soon after joining the Foreign Ministry, he was sent to London with Terajima Munenori in the summer of 1872, and went on to work in the Home Ministry upon his return to Japan; for further details, see Nakai Eriko's detailed article.
[293] Takeda Masatsugu 武田昌次 had gone to London in January 1873 in preparation for the International Exposition in Vienna. He was a prolific translator of materials concerning agriculture and manufacturing methods, and continued his work in the Agricultural Promotion Office upon returning to Japan; his most notable accomplishments in this capacity were his efforts to introduce new apiary techniques to Japan and his 1878 attempt to cultivate Javanese coffee in the Ogasawara Islands (Itō

to a new hotel at Number 146 Buckingham Palace Road. The maids and service staff at this hotel are all sincere and friendly, and the furnishings are elegant and clean. It is a most suitable hotel. It costs just over three pounds a week, and meals are provided. At night, I met Masuda Katsunori nearby.

April 29. Tuesday. Rainy and then clear.

This city is unlike Paris in that there is perpetually a thick fog covering the city in hazy darkness. The weather is thoroughly unpleasant. In the afternoon, Takeda came over for a chat. In the evening, I went out with Masuda and Tejima to Charing Cross. There was a giant column with four lions at its base that had at its top a statue of Mr. Nelson.[294] We also saw the Houses of Parliament. Their magnificent grandeur was impressive. We saw the Waterloo Bridge over the River Thames, which is truly one of the most splendid views on earth. We went to the station downtown and took an underground train. In just ten minutes, we had returned to our hotel. Today, I saw someone walking with a drunken man leaning on his shoulder, something one almost never sees in Europe.

April 30. Wednesday. Clear.

I went to see Westminster Bridge. In the afternoon, I visited Kikuchi Dairoku.[295] Tonight, Seki Shinzō and Horikawa Gorō came over to chat.[296]

Hiroshi, 213–215; Funakoshi, esp. 21–30; Tanaka and Hirayama, 49–53).

[294] A 145-foot granite monument to Admiral Nelson stands in Trafalgar Square; Nelson died in the Battle of Trafalgar, but in destroying the French fleet he averted Napoleon's planned invasion of England (Baedeker's *London*, 128).

[295] Kikuchi Dairoku 菊池大麓 (1855–1917) was the son of Mitsukuri Shūhei, the man Ryūhoku claims was the sole person in whom he confided his plans to go abroad before departing. Kikuchi was just eleven when he was first sent to study in England, and on this, his second period of study, he was at University College School. Kikuchi's

May 1. Thursday. Clear.

Akamatsu came over to visit.[297] I went to London's "City" with Ōkura and Tejima, where we saw a variety of shops, including money changers and the like. The size of the Royal Exchange was truly astounding. We also walked down Queen [Anne] Street, Oxford Street, and Redienbirugu Street, and saw a great statue in Hyde Park. The statue was cast out of cannons and guns that had been captured in the Battle of Waterloo.[298] I stopped by the Alexandra Hotel to visit Ōtori, but he was not in.[299] I went to have a look at the Exhibition in Kensington.[300] Although they were only exhibiting some new oil paintings, as well as tobacco, grains, food products, silk and fabrics, and ceramics, I was

---

prodigious academic success abroad was reported in Tokyo newspapers in 1872–1873; he went on to become a major mathematician and later president of the University of Tokyo; see Koyama's *Hatenkō*, esp. chapters 1–3.

[296] Horikawa Gorō 堀川五郎, also known as Kyōa 教阿, was a Kyoto priest who had traveled with Umegami Takuyū and Shimaji Mokurai's Nishi Honganji group to Europe in early 1872. Mokurai's diary notes that Horikawa left Paris with Akamatsu Renjō to begin studying in London on 03.24 (May 1) of that year (30).

[297] Akamatsu Renjō 赤松連城 (1841–1919) was the second of Nishi Honganji's students dispatched to study in London. He returned to Japan in 1874 and served in several important positions in temple administration.

[298] The Statue of Achilles was erected in 1822 to honor Arthur, Duke of Wellington; its metal came from French cannons captured in France, Spain, and at Waterloo (Baedeker's *London*, 236). Perhaps "Redienbirugu" is a corruption of "Regent" Street.

[299] A former bakufu retainer and early student of Dutch and military subjects, Ōtori Keisuke 大鳥圭介 (1833–1911) made Ryūhoku's acquaintance while the two were posted in the shogunate's Western-style military units in Yokohama in the 1860s. Unlike Ryūhoku, however, Ōtori did not resign his post when the Restoration came, choosing instead to fight for the shogunate in the northeast. He was imprisoned for this by the Meiji administration but received clemency in 1872, and began working for the new government's Treasury Department. Late that year, he accompanied Yoshida Kiyonari (1845–1891) to the United States. After returning to Japan he served in a variety of posts before becoming a Minister to China and Korea. The Alexandra Hotel, at 16–21 St. George's Place, was close to both Hyde Park and the Exhibition at Kensington.

[300] The International Exhibition was held at nearby Hyde Park in 1851, and many of the items exhibited there were acquired by the South Kensington Museum when it was founded shortly thereafter. The Music Hall that Ryūhoku mentions is surely the Royal Albert Hall, built in 1867–1871.

surprised at the number of objects on display. Inside, there was a coffee shop, and a girl was selling things there. The Music Hall was an immense round structure, and outside there was a garden with a pond, and beautiful flowers and trees. Various types of carriages had been lined up and put on display. One of them was the carriage of the queen. There were also several machines that seemed to be powered by steam. At night, I went to the legation with Masuda and Ōkura.

May 2. Friday. Clear.
I saw London Bridge and Blackfriars Bridge, and the second of these was a most beautiful and grand structure. I took Regent Street, and from there went to Charing Cross to have a look at the shops that sell old coins and currencies. At night, Takeda and I went again to Regent Street, where we saw the "Royal Polytechnic." There were a hundred different machines lined up on display, and various items were for sale. I saw a large diving bell. I also saw a shadow-show.[301] The show takes place on a screen, upon which the images appear, kaleidoscopically transforming themselves into scenes depicting the customs and features of various countries. The most impressive was when they showed a boat sailing on the ocean. There was also a play performed, in which a queen, a princess, a gallant youth, and a monster all made an appearance; it too was a delight to see.

May 3. Saturday. Clear.
I visited Yoshida Jirō at the Alexandra Hotel.[302] We went to see the

---

[301] This presumably refers to a "magic lantern" show.
[302] Kumagaya (Saitama) native Yoshida Jirō 吉田二郎 (1842–1905) had first been abroad when he traveled ahead of merchant Shimizu Usaburō to Paris in 1866, accompanying the items that the shogunate had sent to the International Exhibition in Paris scheduled for the following year (Sawa, 498). After the Restoration, he joined the Ministry of Finance and was dispatched twice to the United States to investigate its

statue of the famous general Wellington that is in front of Hyde Park.[303] In the afternoon, Akamatsu came over and invited me out. The two of us went to see Buckingham Palace, and then St. James's Park. It was quite a lovely park with elegant and serene fountains and gardens. We also went to see the India Museum.[304] From jewels and treasures on down, there is nothing Indian that the museum lacks. On the contrary, they say that there are things here that can no longer be found in India. Next we saw the library of Indian books. There were mountains of books, and the library was stocked with all of the classics—it is fair to say that Indian literary and material culture have all been gathered together here. After that, we went to Westminster and saw the upper and lower houses of Parliament. The grand scale and solemn orderliness of the building were awe-inspiring. We also went to Westminster Abbey, where the gravestones of Henry VII and other kings are reposed. The old grave markers all have the reclining figures of the kings preserved above the stones. There was a stone carving of a skeleton trying to stab a scoundrel in the Abbey.[305] It is apparently famous. There was a wooden bench in one part of the Abbey. This old

---

banking system: in 1871 with Fukuchi Gen'ichirō and Iwakura Tomomi, and then again in 1872 (Yanagida Izumi, 137). On this latter journey, he was traveling with five young men from the Mitsui group, who were on their way to New Brunswick to study English and learn about banking practices (Mitsui Ginkō, 62–63; Miyamoto Mataji IV: 585–586). He later served as Consul General of New York and London.

[303] The thirty-foot-high "equestrian statue of Wellington" by Wyatt stands at Hyde Park Corner (Baedeker's *London*, 236).

[304] When Ryūhoku visited, the India Museum and the Library were housed next to one another within the India Office on Downing Street.

[305] Presumably this refers to the tomb of Sir Joseph and Lady Elizabeth Nightingale by Louis-François Roubiliac, which depicts Joseph attempting to shield his wife from Death's attack. Elizabeth's death came in premature labor that had been precipitated by a frightening lightning storm, but Ryūhoku may have misunderstood the tomb sculpture as representing the death of an adulterous couple. The term translated "scoundrel" (姦夫; J. *kanpu*) usually means a man who has sexual relations with another man's wife.

and quite plain bench was apparently the one used in the coronation ceremony of King Henry (six hundred years ago).³⁰⁶ After sunset, we went to the Alhambra Theatre. The fiery battle scene was grippingly realistic, and there were also many humorous scenes. The dancing girl named D'Anka was extremely beautiful and sang very well.³⁰⁷

May 4. Sunday. Rainy and then clear.
Mr. Kikuchi Dairoku came over to visit, and Takeda also dropped by to invite me out. We boarded a train and went to have a look at some botanical and agricultural exhibition grounds. I was astonished at the fineness of the lumber and the beauty of the flowers and plants. There was a "Palm Stove" there, which was as large as an enormous house.³⁰⁸ In this space surrounded by glass, they grow betel palm, coconut palm, bamboo, and other tropical plants. They run hot water through iron pipes in the room, insuring warmth throughout the day and night. Today, we crossed the upper reaches of the River Thames and along the way the pastoral scenery was exquisite. The peach and apricot blossoms were just coming into full bloom. When we got back to the hotel, Okkotsu came over to chat.³⁰⁹ I will record here a composition that I made the other day in Calais.

---

³⁰⁶ It seems quite likely that Ryūhoku is describing the "old coronation chair" used in the coronation ceremony of every English monarch since Edward I in 1297 (Baedeker's *London*, 193–194). "Henry" is likely a mistake for "Edward I."
³⁰⁷ Located in Leicester Square, the Royal Alhambra Theatre was then known for its "operettas, ballets, and spectacular plays" (Baedeker's *London*, 35–36). Singer and actress Cornélie D'Anka (c. 1852–1927), also known as Mrs. J. E. Ingham, had made her debut in 1871 and was then a popular prima donna in the London theater world. It seems that the performance Ryūhoku saw this evening was *The Black Crook*, a work that had been tremendously successful when it opened in New York and is sometimes called the "first American musical" (Knapp, 21–29). The fairy-opera version that opened in London late in December 1872 featured music by Georges Jacobi and Frederic Clay.
³⁰⁸ The "Palm-Stove" or the "Great Palm House" was a glass-enclosed structure in the Kew Gardens where tropical climes could be simulated.
³⁰⁹ Okkotsu Kenzō 乙骨兼三 (1852–1923) was the third son of shogunal official and

渡英佛海海峡　*Crossing the Strait Between England and France*
風濤之險世無雙　判得天公界二邦　君見佛郎王若虎　一生不渡此長江

Wind and waves so wild, without equal in the world;
Plain to see, Heaven has forged a border between the two countries.
Behold the King of France, fierce tiger though he was,
Never once in his life crossed this great channel.

May 5. Monday. Windy and rainy, but clear in the afternoon.
I went to a bathhouse in the city, and the price was six pence. The basin was ceramic. Akamatsu came over for a visit. This evening, I had a cold, and so I went to bed early.

May 6. Tuesday. Fine.
Takeda came over and together we went to visit Mr. Beal at George Yard. Mr. Beal is able to read Chinese, and edits an eastern newspaper.[310] We went to the British Museum and toured the

---

scholar Okkotsu Taiken 乙骨耐軒 (1806–1859), and was studying English in London when Ryūhoku met him. Kenzō's elder brother Wataru 亙 (1844–1888) was the father of Ueda Bin (1874–1916), the Meiji poet and scholar of English literature (Nagai Kikue, 220–233).

[310] Samuel Beal (1825–1889) was a Wesleyan minister and scholar of Buddhism who became a Professor of Chinese at University College, London, in 1877. In this entry, however, Ryūhoku seems to have confused Beal with another man, Beal's friend James Summers, who was publishing several newspapers about East Asia at the time. Summers had begun studying classical Chinese and the Cantonese dialect in Hong Kong in 1848, taking up a teaching post at Kings College upon his return to England in 1852. He edited the *Chinese and Japanese Repository*, published between July 1863 and December 1865, and *The Phoenix*, published between July 1870 and June 1873. In addition, Summers published a Japanese newspaper called the *Tai Sei Shinbun* 大西新聞 (Ebihara, 43–52). According to its masthead, the *Tai Sei Shinbun* was at "3 George Yard, Lombard Street, London." Presumably Ryūhoku refers either to this paper or *The Phoenix* when he writes of the "eastern newspaper" 東方新聞 at "George Yard." Ryūhoku met Summers just when the latter had been invited by members of the Iwakura Mission to teach in Japan. Arriving later that year, Summers taught logic and English literature for three years at the Kaisei Gakkō, then went on to teach English at a variety of schools throughout Japan; see Koyama Noboru's informative essay.

numismatic exhibits. Among the old Chinese coins were some circular silver pieces that I had never seen before. I also saw some old gold coins from Venice that were enormous. I found myself staring in awe of the towering stacks of old gold, silver, and copper coins from all over the world.

May 7. Wednesday. Clear, then overcast.

I dropped by the Victoria Hotel and visited Kawamura, the Vice Assistant to the Minister of the Navy.[311] I also went to stroll around Regent's Park. This park had lions, tigers, and leopards (and a black panther too), a host of wild cats that were as large as great mastiffs, white bears, giant snakes, sea cows, "hippopotami," and some very peculiar members of the monkey family—so many varieties of exotic birds and curious beasts that I couldn't possibly count them all. After we returned to the inn, Masuda and Mr. Tomita Atsuhisa came over to chat.[312]

May 8. Thursday. Fine.

We went to see University College on Gower Street. We were shown around by Mr. Horton, who is a second-rank teacher at this school, and

---

[311] Satsuma native Kawamura Sumiyoshi 川村純義 (1836–1904) had been involved in loyalist causes in the 1860s and joined the new Military Affairs Ministry after the Restoration. He had been sent to Europe as part of the Japanese delegation to the International Exhibition in Vienna in late 1872 and returned to Japan the following year. He led the imperial troops that put down the Satsuma Rebellion in 1877, and served several years as the Minister of the Navy.

[312] Tomita Atsuhisa 富田淳久 had been dispatched in January 1873 to London with Takeda Masatsugu to observe and report on the products exhibited at the London Exhibition grounds. A retrospective piece by Tomita (under his later surname Nishiyama 西山) is included in Tanaka and Hirayama (49–53). Elsewhere in the same report by Tanaka are annotated lists of the copious documents produced by the Japanese observers of the Exhibition, including many translations by Tomita on such topics as road construction, the silk trade, and the history of the London Exhibition.

Kikuchi Dairoku.[313] We toured the Latin studies, Greek studies, French studies, arithmetic, mathematics, and penmanship classrooms. There were also recreational grounds for walking and a ball-throwing area (an arena where one throws a ball at a stone wall). At the school, we saw a pair of young twin boys who were handsome in their appearance and gifted in their abilities: truly charming children. We also went to Baker Street to have a look at the waxworks.[314] Carved statues of ancient heroes, along with Washington, Napoleon, Napoleon III, the present English sovereign, the French President Thiers, the present King of Italy, and many other famous people, were lined up on display; each and every one of them seemed almost alive. There was also a beautiful woman lying asleep, and when I peered at her chest, I saw that her heart moved as though she were alive. This sleeping beauty is named Madame Tussaud, a famous Swiss woman who lived in Paris. The exhibits here are truly like living dolls, their exquisite craftsmanship on a par with the Paris Panorama. On display as well here are the carriage of Napoleon I, which was taken at Waterloo, as well as the shroud and other items used at his funeral. I cannot possibly remember all of them. On the way back, I visited Yasukawa Shigenari, but he was not in.[315] Osada Tōichi, a man from Koga, has come to stay in our hotel.[316]

---

[313] Koyama Noboru notes that Ryūhoku was likely led around by Elias Robert Horton (1835–1884), a classics scholar who was then Vice Master of University College School (*Hatenkō*, 39–40). Perhaps "Vice Master" is what Ryūhoku had in mind by writing that his guide was a "second-rank" instructor.

[314] The waxworks were those of Madame Tussaud's Waxwork Exhibition, on Marylebone Road near Baker Street.

[315] Yasukawa Shigenari 安川繁成 (1839–1906) was part of a group of five Meiji officials (the others were Takazaki Masakaze, Komuro Shinobu, Nishioka Yumei, and Suzuki Kan'ichi) dispatched by the Sain in 1872 to investigate Western legal systems. They are sometimes considered a second cohort of the Iwakura Mission. Yasukawa went on to serve in various government agencies upon his return, including the Ministry of Works and the Printing Office.

[316] The identity of Osada Tōichi 長田藤一 is unknown.

May 9. Friday. A light rain in the afternoon.
I went shopping and bought scores of books. I also went to the White Star Company and made the arrangements for our trip to America. I agreed to make a single payment to this company that would also include the domestic railway fares in America and the Pacific Ocean return trip. I took the subway with Mr. Tejima and Mr. Nagasawa and went to a certain trading company, one that trades in Yokohama.[317] At Charing Cross, I bought forty different varieties of minerals. At night, Seki Shinzō and I went to visit Mr. Hamilton on Stanley Street, where we had the Indian fruit known as "coconut."[318] It was very delicious.

May 10. Saturday. Fine.
Takeda and Akamatsu came over to chat. I went with Akamatsu to the "Tower of London." It is the city's old castle, and they have mountains of ancient weaponry there. The armor, swords, and spears of famous kings of the ages are also on display. Old cannons and old swords are piled up on top of each other, as though to form a wall. Some were arranged in flower patterns, which was quite an unusual sight. Mr. Wellington's clothing was on prominent display, along with many regal crowns and golden vessels. There were also Japanese and Indian armor, swords, and halberds among the exhibits. The walls of the castle were several feet thick, which was in order to protect it from enemy troops in the old days. Apparently it has never once been captured. In ancient times, there was a decapitation area inside the castle. Today, we took a

---

[317] Ryūhoku writes only "Nagasawa," making this individual's identity unclear, but the editors of *Meijihen* propose Nagasawa Korekazu 長沢惟和 (1843–1893), a Shōnai (Yamagata) man who had accompanied Kanbe Yoshikata to Europe in 1872; the following year, Nagasawa returned to Japan after becoming ill (348).
[318] The editors of *Meijihen* suggest the possibility that Ryūhoku and Seki met Lord George Francis Hamilton (1845–1927), a politician who soon went on to serve as Under-Secretary of State for India.

boat back and forth across the River Thames. The grandeur of the bridge beams was truly striking. Tonight, Yasukawa Shigenari came over to chat.

May 11. Sunday. Fine.
I visited Ōtori Keisuke at Gower Street, and together we went for a stroll in the Cremorne Gardens.[319] At night, the street lamps lit up the place as though it were midday. It is a lively area, thronged with men and women hustling and bustling about. Today, Seki left and went back to his lodgings.

May 12. Monday. Fine.
With Ishikawa, I went to visit the British Museum again. Indian, Egyptian, and Roman relics and minerals, the feathers, bones, and skins of unusual birds and exotic beasts, and a great many other things—there was nothing that they did not have. It truly is the greatest museum in all of Europe. At night, Takeda came over to visit, and we went to Cremorne Gardens again.

May 13. Tuesday. Fine.
Mr. Scott, an employee of the White Star Corporation, came over to discuss our travel plans, and we settled on a price. I visited Yasukawa at his hotel, and together we went to see the City Prison (jail).[320] It was even cleaner than the French prison, but it was also a little smaller. Inside the prison, there was a garden. The inmates braid rope, weave mats, make bricks, and cultivate vegetables. The women wash clothing

---

[319] According to Baedeker's *London*, the Cremorne Gardens, located west of Battersea Bridge on the northern side of the Thames, were formerly "a very popular place of amusement" but were closed in 1877 (38).

[320] The City Prison in Holloway was erected in 1852.

and linens. Unlike the French system, the beds in the prisoners' cells are put away in the morning and then brought out again in the evening. There was a chapel in which a minister could deliver sermons, and a darkened room as well. Prisoners who are sentenced to death are held in this darkened room for three days prior to being executed. Tonight Masuda came over to chat.

May 14. Wednesday. Overcast.
Takabatake Bizan and Inagaki Kitazō came from Paris, and are staying in the same hotel as we are. I went again to the White Star Corporation. Tonight, Takeda and Akamatsu came over to talk.

May 15. Thursday. Overcast and cold.
Inagaki is headed back to Paris. Kawamura, the Assistant to the Minister of the Navy, is also departing on the same vessel. I took leave of them at Victoria Station. I went to see the Crystal Palace with Takabatake Bizan and Okkotsu Kenzō.[321] The palace is covered by a great roof made out of glass, so it is fair to say the whole palace is inside a glass encasing. A great number of different varieties of live fish were on display inside. It must require a considerable amount of labor to transport seawater all this way. Oil paintings and human mannequins, along with products from all over the world were on exhibition inside the Crystal Palace. The gardens and ponds were also very lovely, and the fountains and green foliage made for a truly splendid scene. Inside the garden was an archery range. The bows and arrows resembled those used in Japan. I imagine that archery is an ancient art here. At night,

---

[321] The Crystal Palace, a massive building of iron and glass, had been constructed at Hyde Park for the Great Exhibition of 1851. It was moved a few years later to Sydenham Hill, where it continued to be an exhibition space until the building was destroyed by fire in 1936.

when we returned Takeda presented us with two barrels of Japanese sake. Taking a sip of it was like meeting an old friend.

May 16. Friday. Fine.
I went to explore Windsor Castle with Takabatake, Takeda, Ishikawa, Akamatsu, Okkotsu, and someone named Masuno from Yamaguchi.[322] It was twenty-two English miles outside of London, and the fare for the train was six shillings. We went inside the Queen's castle, where we toured the royal stables and saw the royal carriage. There was a chapel inside the castle, very beautiful and grand. Inside the castle grounds, there was a high tower built up from stones stacked on top of each other. It is said to rise 220 feet above the level of water in the River Thames. We scaled to the top of this, and beheld the spectacular view.[323] Outside the castle, there was a large garden park area. They keep cattle there, from which they obtain milk, and also raise horses and animals that resembled deer. Outside of this enclosure and facing the castle was a broad and level road, at the end of which was a stone sculpture of George III. The road is three miles long.[324] If you continue along a separate road, you come to another garden where there is a lake. It is a man-made lake, kept artificially full of water, and with its own fishing platform. There is also a small battleship complete with a cannon, but this is surely provided for amusement's sake only.

---

[322] Perhaps Mr. Masuno was Masuno Sukezō 増野助三 (1848–1908), who was from Yamaguchi and was in Germany from 1871 to 1874 doing military research; he went on to a career in the Army.
[323] Ryūhoku is describing the "Round Tower, or *Keep*, used as a prison down to 1660" (Baedeker's *London*, 304).
[324] Ryūhoku is describing the 1800-acre Great Park, lying south of Windsor and "stocked with several thousand fallow deer." The elm-lined, three-mile-long Long Walk with its statue of George III connected with another road, at the end of which lay "Virginia Water, an artificial lake, formed in 1746 … in order to drain the surrounding moorland. A model of a man-of-war is so placed on the lake as to appear almost like a real ship" (Baedeker's *London*, 306–307).

The apricot and wisteria blossoms were in full bloom, and there was a waterfall as well. Very close nearby is the Crown Prince's detached summer palace. All in all, not only was the scenery in the garden splendid, its setting was also remarkably serene. What's more, it is really quite admirable that they grant even us visitors from abroad the privilege of strolling around it as we wish.

四野無人訴凍饑　君王拱默在深闈　請看靈囿能偕樂　麋鹿爲群白鳥飛
  In all four directions, none complain of cold or hunger;
  The King folds his arms in silence, deep within the castle gates.
  Behold the Ling You Garden, the King and his people sharing pleasure;
  Antelopes and deer roam together where swans take flight.[325]

When I return to Japan and try to express to people what I thought and how I felt when I came here, there will be things I won't be able to convey. *Ah! How good the British system is!* We boarded the steam locomotive again, and at 7:55 returned to our hotel in London.

May 17. Saturday. Fine.
Okkotsu came over. I visited a bookstore and bought several volumes. I paid the White Star Corporation the full fare for our sea and land passage at their offices. It was ninety-eight pounds and eleven shillings for transport from Liverpool to Yokohama. I went by the Doctor Ken Museum.[326] They had fetuses, pregnant women, a variety of organs,

---

[325] The allusion is to the Lingyou, translated variously as "Magic Park" or "Divine Menagerie," constructed by the sagely King Wen in remote Zhou antiquity. The park became idealized from Mencius's praise of Wen for sharing his amusements with his people; see Waley, *The Book of Songs*, 259–260; and Lau, *Mencius*, 61–62.
[326] Ryūhoku seems to be describing the museum of the Royal College of Surgeons, opened in 1835, which exhibited an extensive anatomical collection of normally formed and pathological organs (Baedeker's *London*, 159–160).

and genitalia all lined up on display. There were dried specimens and also specimens that had been preserved in alcohol. There were also wax models. Today Ono Zenjirō and Yokoyama Magoichirō came to stay in our hotel.[327]

May 18. Sunday. Slight rain.
I visited Kikuchi Dairoku to ask him about a variety of matters. In the afternoon, Seki and Tejima came over. Today, I visited Minister Mori but he was not in.

May 19. Monday. Fine.
We are just about ready to leave London. This morning, I went with Mr. Takabatake to the Consulate, and met with Minister Terajima.[328] In the afternoon, Ishikawa and I went to have a tour of the exhibition grounds (a small exhibition was then being put on). They only had things like iron vessels, textiles, oil paintings, foods, fish, and shellfish on display. There were weaving machines, and they were also making small candies like *confeito* for sale to the exhibition-goers. It was quite a grand hall. I dropped by the Alexandra Hotel to visit Yoshida Jirō, but he was not in. Takeda and Tejima came over and said goodbye. I will record the poor poems I composed during my time in London here.

---

[327] Ono Zenjirō 小野善次郎 (b. 1854) was the scion of the Ono financial conglomerate who had been sent to study abroad in 1872 and whose father, Ono Zensuke, Ryūhoku had met in Paris two months earlier. Yokoyama Magoichirō was hired by the Ono-gumi to act as the young man's translator and help him get established in his studies, which was apparently easier said than done (Miyamoto Mataji IV: 586–587).

[328] Terajima Munenori 寺島宗則 (1832–1893) took up his post as the Japanese Minister to England in 1872. As a young man, he was known as Matsuki Kōan 松木弘安, and had traveled with Fukuzawa Yukichi on the first shogunal mission to Europe in 1862, during which time he, Fukuzawa, and Mitsukuri Shūhei became close friends with Léon de Rosny. He also led a group of students to England in 1865. After the Restoration, he became a diplomat, with posts in England and the United States.

倫敦市上作　　*Composed in the city of London*
汽車烟接汽船烟　四望冥冥不見天　忽地長風來一掃　倫敦橋上夕陽妍
　Smoke from the trains blends with that of the ships;
　Everywhere I look, the same haze, and no sign of sky.
　Just then a great wind comes to sweep it all away,
　Revealing the splendid sunset atop London Bridge.

頂上晴雷脚底烟　一車入地一車天　中間吾亦車中座　驀過東西陌與阡
　Thunder rolls through clear skies overhead, smoke billows underfoot;
　One train enters the earth, the other races through the heavens.
　And here I sit on another car, running in their midst;
　Charging headlong through city streets, east and west, north and south.

謁維靈敦之像　　^(ウエルリングトン)　*Seeing the statue of Wellington*
莫怪遺容凜有神　將軍功績足千春　輸嬴一決窪多路　擒得驕龍是此人
　No wonder his semblance still stands so awesome and spirited:
　This general whose valor will live on for a thousand springs.
　Victor and vanquished fixed in a moment at Waterloo;
　He who took the proud dragon Napoleon alive was this man.

禽獸園　　*The Zoo*
鐵檻劃園豹虎橫　蹈青士女趁晚晴　誰圖釵影裙香裡　聽箇空山嘯月聲
　An iron cage marks off the park where wild dogs and tigers prowl;
　Strolling along the green grass, men and women savor the clear evening.
　Amid the shine of hair ornaments and the fragrance of dresses,
　Who would expect to hear howls on the bare moonlit hill?

May 20. Tuesday. Fine.
Yoshida, Yokoyama, and Ono came over to say their goodbyes. Seki and Horikawa saw me off at Euston Station. At 2:45 in the afternoon,

Ishikawa and I departed London. Once we had gotten underway, I could see a long canal to our right. This is a waterway that goes all the way to London. We passed the station at Crewe, and then went through a tunnel that is said to be one and a half English miles long. At ten minutes of eight o'clock, we reached the port of Liverpool, where we checked into the Angel Hotel.[329] We are two hundred English miles from London. This hotel is large and there are many guests staying here. Breakfast is served from seven o'clock until ten o'clock, and dinner is served from one o'clock until nine o'clock; the guests may take their meals as they wish at any point in between those times.

May 21. Wednesday. Overcast.
I visited the ship dispatch office at Number 10 Water Street. Afterward, I went for a walk and looked at the scenery around the harbor. I then boarded a carriage and rode for about two miles to Prince's Park, where the refreshingly secluded garden and pool were quite lovely. Today I went to a currency exchange shop and obtained two one-*bu* notes from Japan. I bathed at the public bath on Cornwallis Street, where the bathing area was quite large.[330]

May 22. Thursday. Fine.
I went to stroll around the city. At four o'clock in the afternoon, we boarded a small steamship that took us out to where the steamship *Celtic* was anchored. The ship is 3,888 tons. The Liverpool harbor is long and also deep. It is said to lie 3,200 nautical miles from New York in America. I gazed at the lighthouse to my left as the ship headed

---

[329] The Angel Hotel was located at 22 Dale Street, near the docks and the Exchange Buildings (Baedeker's *Great Britain*, 324).
[330] The Corporation Baths on Cornwallis Street were located southeast of Ryūhoku's hotel.

north. We proceeded out into the open seas and headed west, and all I could see were some distant mountains to the south.

May 23. Friday. Fine.
I heard the second bell ring at 8:30, and we all went to have breakfast. This morning, I could see mountains to our right. The ship continued to head south, and at eleven o'clock, we entered the port of Queenstown in Ireland where some more passengers boarded before we set off again. All of these passengers were traveling in the lowest class of transport. The mouth of this port is very narrow, and is suited to defense. We are 236 nautical miles from Liverpool. At one o'clock, at the sound of the second bell, we had lunch. At six o'clock we ate dinner.

May 24. Saturday. Fine. Windy.
The ship rocked slightly. At dusk, it started to rain. Today, the ship traveled 317 nautical miles.

May 25. Sunday. Overcast.
Great winds arose and made the boat pitch and dance wildly. The passengers all lay down in their beds and did not leave their cabins. At night, the skies cleared, and the winds calmed a little bit. When I went out onto the deck, I found the Irish and German passengers in steerage so amusing that they made me double over in laughter. Whether East or West, low-class people have the same sensibilities. Today the ship traveled 306 nautical miles.

May 26. Monday. Pouring rain.
In the morning, the winds were calm, but great winds and waves rose up as evening approached. It is really quite exhausting. I never want to

travel across this ocean again. Today the ship traveled 294 nautical miles.

May 27. Tuesday. Intermittently clear and rainy.
The wind and waves are extremely large. The "purser" is the "commissionaire" on board a ship. He took the passengers' "tickets" and asked us our ages. At one o'clock in the afternoon, I saw a ship to our left. Today the ship traveled 215 nautical miles. We are at a latitude of 49° and a longitude of 37°.

May 28. Wednesday. Overcast.
It was stormy today. At around noon, the weather cleared and the winds ceased. At last the ship was freed from the misery of leaning from side to side. All of the passengers then went to the cafeteria to eat dinner; and our joy was considerable. Today we traveled 230 nautical miles.

May 29. Thursday. Rainy.
There is a tremendously thick fog and I can't see a foot in front of me. The ship's crew sounded the foghorn incessantly in order to prevent us from colliding with something. Today there was no wind, and the waves were placid. We came to the fishing waters of Newfoundland. The sea is remarkably shallow. For the past two or three days, it has been intensely chilly on board, and this is because the winds have been blowing down from the northern Arctic Sea. I spent the entire day chatting amiably with the Englishman Morton. Today the ship traveled 231 nautical miles. Several dozen of the Western passengers were betting on the number of nautical miles we would travel. I was in the losing camp, and lost five shillings.

May 30. Friday. Overcast.
Just as yesterday, we were surrounded by a thick fog today. The wind and waves were calm. All day long, I whiled away the boredom by talking to the English passengers. The ship traveled 336 nautical miles today.

May 31. Saturday. Pleasant and fine.
The passengers were overjoyed. Today, I bought a copper medal and fastened it to my suitcase. In the afternoon, I went to take a close look at the ship's steam machinery. We traveled 351 nautical miles.

June 1. Sunday. Fine.
At four o'clock, I could see a long island to our right, and thus I could tell that we were close to New York. The passengers were all excited. At ten o'clock this evening, we reached New York. Today, the ship traveled 335 nautical miles. I composed only three quatrains during our passage across the Atlantic Ocean.

經過東球三大洲　直將餘勇向西球　閣龍針路吾能認　山大風濤葉大舟
 I have trekked across three great continents of the Eastern Hemisphere,
 And now with my remaining courage, I head straight for the Western.
 I know that we trace the course of Columbus's compass,
 Among mountainous wind-blown waves weaves our little leaf of a ship.

長天積水碧茫々　獨倚鐵欄潮氣凉　萬丈風濤一輪月　客舟夜度大西洋
 Across the horizon, emerald water as far as the eye can see;
 Alone, I lean against the iron railing, enjoying the cool sea breeze.
 Stormy waves ten thousand feet high, and the single moon above,
 Our passenger ship crosses at night through the Atlantic Ocean.

老鯨出沒碧瀾間　五月朔風吹裂顏　自發英倫二千里　行舟未見一螺山

　　Great whales surface and dive amid the emerald waves;
　　The raging north winds of May lash my face.
　　Two thousand leagues since we left England;
　　And our ship still hasn't seen a sliver of shore.

Afterword

Glossary

Works Cited

Index

Afterword

Ryūhoku began serializing *Diary of a Journey to the West* in his literary magazine *Kagetsu shinshi* in November of 1881, almost a decade after his journey. The travelogue appeared in nearly successive installments until August 8, 1884, when Ryūhoku had become too ill to continue his duties as the magazine's editor. The issue that appeared on this date carries the travelogue through the June 1, 1873, diary entry, in which Ryūhoku records his arrival in New York Harbor, and no further installments would be published in the magazine. In the course of his travels a decade earlier, Ryūhoku had surely kept a complete record of the remaining five weeks of his world tour, during which time he took a rail trip across the United States and then traveled across the Pacific Ocean to Japan in July 1873. Yet this final portion of the travelogue never saw the light of day, for publishing the successive installments of it in *Kagetsu shinshi* was not simply a mechanical matter of taking the next section of the diary and setting it in movable type. As he serialized the travelogue, Ryūhoku had been transforming his original *kanbun* (literary Chinese) diary into a *kanbun kundoku* (Sino-Japanese) prose style, and had also been making some minor changes in the diction of the poems and in the content and order of narrated events. Clearly this was not a task that could be simply delegated to others. With Ryūhoku absent from the journal's helm, *Kagetsu shinshi* suspended its publication after just two more issues, and a month later Ryūhoku himself died. Unfortunately the original *kanbun* diary that Ryūhoku was using as the basis of his published travelogue is no longer extant. The last mention of it seems to have been in 1935, when Ryūhoku's grandson Ōshima Ryūichi lent a listing of his grandfather's diary titles to the scholar Ōno Mitsutsugi, who was then preparing an article on Ryūhoku's career after his return to Japan. According to Ōno, among the diary volume titles once in Ōshima's possession was one inscribed "Diary of a Journal to the West No. 2; From April 8 to My Return to Tokyo on July 8" (33). This volume of Ryūhoku's diary seems to have already been missing at the time that Nagai Kafū spent seven months copying out nearly thirty diary volumes that he received from Ōshima in 1926. In any case, fires from American incendiary strikes on Tokyo in 1945 destroyed most of these original diary volumes as well as the copy that Kafū had made.[1]

In the preface to the serialized *Diary of a Journey to the West*, Ryūhoku notes that he has unearthed "three volumes" from his trunk and that they contain the outline of his journey and the poems he composed along the way. Given the inscription on the volume that Ōno

---

[1] On the copy that Kafū made of the diary, see his "Nisshi." Indeed, that any portion of Ryūhoku's original diary survives is something of a miracle. After Kafū returned the originals, Ōshima left them in the care of his aunt Nobu. In 1974, however, seven volumes of these original diaries mysteriously surfaced at a used book sale in Tokyo, where literary scholar Maeda Ai had the good fortune to acquire them. It seems that Ryūhoku's son Toshirō, a somewhat lackluster playboy who was down on his luck and taking up residence in the homes of various relatives in the late 1920s, came across the diaries while staying at his sister Nobu's house. Figuring no one would notice their absence, Toshirō apparently sold a few of them for drinking money. Though his readiness to part with his father's diaries might seem unfilial, we must be thankful that Toshirō had inherited Ryūhoku's fondness for Tokyo nightlife, or else the diaries would surely have been completely destroyed in the air raid fifteen years later (Maeda, *Narushima*, 21–26). The extant diaries are held today by the Maeda Bunko of Cornell University Library.

notes, it seems reasonable to conclude that the first of the three volumes contained the narrative of Ryūhoku's overseas travelogue from his departure in the summer of 1872 to April 7 of the following year, the second contained the remainder of the prose narrative from April 8 to July 8, and the third perhaps contained his poems. Whether Ryūhoku composed his poems in a separate volume or not, what is clear is that these poems did survive long enough to be accessible to Mori Shuntō when he compiled *Tōkyō saijin zekku*, a two-volume anthology of quatrains published in 1875, as well as to the editors who compiled *Ryūhoku shishō*, the anthology of Ryūhoku's *kanshi* that appeared posthumously in 1894. While we have no direct narrative account of Ryūhoku's return to Japan, it is nevertheless possible to weave these poems together and thereby trace the outline of the final five weeks of Ryūhoku's Western journey.

Before beginning to look at these poems that Ryūhoku composed after arriving in New York, it is important to note one other poem that appears in the posthumous anthology but not in the published travelogue. This poem stands out as the sole instance where we can be almost certain that Ryūhoku chose to exclude from the serialized work a poem that he had written in the course of his European travels and that had been included in the base text of overseas poems that later anthologizers used.

題伯德^{ペートル}寺寺則羅馬法王所居
On Saint Peter's Basilica. This church is where the Pope of Rome resides.
西教誨民將□民　祠堂宏壯壓宮闌　法王冠履皆金玉　不賑門前凍饑人
　　Western religion teaches people, making them ＿＿＿＿＿＿
　　Its churches in their grandeur exceed even palaces.²

---

² A square □ appears as the penultimate character for the first line in the *Ryūhoku shishō* edition, presumably a printer's error or perhaps an indication that the original

313

> The Pope's crown and sandals are all made with gold and jewels,
> Yet charity does not extend to the cold and hungry at the church gates.

In the *Ryūhoku shishō* anthology, this poem appears immediately after a poem composed on the ruins at Pompeii (which appears in the published travelogue in the entry for April 2), and immediately before a poem on Ryūhoku's return to Paris (which is the next poem in the published travelogue, appearing in the entry for April 24). Given the topic and the exact match of sequence, we can be confident in concluding that Ryūhoku wrote this poem in Rome in April 1873 and that it originally appeared alongside the other overseas poems.

When he was serializing this portion of the travelogue a decade after the events it narrated had occurred and after the poems they inspired had been written, why did Ryūhoku choose to remove only this poem from the published installments?[3] The obscurity of the wording in the poem's first line raises the possibility that Ryūhoku had abandoned it or rejected it on technical grounds, but it seems more likely that the poem was sacrificed because its tone was at odds with the travelogue's overall positive evaluation of Western legal and political systems, technological and social structures, and cultural and religious institutions. By the time he was anthologizing the travelogue in the 1880s, Ryūhoku had established himself as a staunch supporter of the

---

character could not be deciphered. Given the occasional typographical oddities in the *Ryūhoku shishō* edition, it is not completely inconceivable that the character is actually 口 (J. *kō*; Ch. *kou*), meaning mouth. This would indeed be grammatically peculiar, but we might nevertheless attempt a provisional reading of what appears on the page: "Western religion teaches its people, but pays only lip-service to treating them as people." In any case, the thrust of the poem is unambiguous from the second couplet.

[3] We know from the partial copy of Ryūhoku's original diary made by Matsumoto Hakka that Ryūhoku had composed several other poems while abroad that were not included in the posthumous anthology *Ryūhoku shishō*. The poem on St. Peter's Basilica is, however, the only poem that is included in this posthumous anthology but clearly excluded from the published version of the travelogue.

implementation of many of the institutions and practices that he had observed personally in the West. To be sure, Ryūhoku was by no means in favor of a wholesale abandonment of traditional Japanese cultural forms. As many of the episodes in the second volume of *New Chronicles of Yanagibashi* portended, Ryūhoku would remain a fierce critic of the superficial modes of Westernization that some of his contemporaries mistook for genuine modernization. Far from calling for the remaking of Japanese life in a Western guise, Ryūhoku used his position as a celebrated essayist and satirist to articulate nuanced responses to the question of how best to achieve Japan's modernization.

The journalist Ryūhoku's involvement in such debates from the mid-1870s onward undoubtedly had some effect on the final form that his 1872–1873 travelogue took when it was published in *Kagetsu shinshi* in the 1880s. To take just one example, in 1876 Ryūhoku had spent four months in prison as punishment for his relentless criticisms of the Meiji government's restrictive press laws. This experience presumably shaped the way in which he recounted his earlier observations of Western penal institutions when he made the travelogue public. Ryūhoku states in the January 22 entry of his travelogue that Japanese prisons "cannot be discussed in the same breath" as the prisons of Paris, and goes on to exclaim, using marks of emphasis in the original, that the French penal system is *"is the pinnacle of strictness where strictness is called for and the height of mercy when mercy is in order."* Such emphatics are extremely rare in the travelogue, and the intensity with which Ryūhoku writes about the Paris prison surely reflects the personal experience he had being incarcerated three years after his return to Japan.

While some of what we see in the travelogue in this way seems to have been informed by Ryūhoku's later experiences and sensibilities, it is also the case that from the very beginning of his career as a journalist, Ryūhoku cultivated a cosmopolitan persona, drawing extensively on his knowledge and experience of Western culture to advocate an eclectic form of modernization. We can see this persona emerging not only in Ryūhoku's own early journalistic writings, but from the way in which his works were regarded by his contemporaries shortly after his return to Japan. When Mori Shuntō published the *Tōkyō saijin zekku* anthology in 1875, he included a diverse sampling of works from a staggering array of active Japanese *kanshi* poets. Shuntō chose to include ten poems by Ryūhoku, a comparatively large number that fewer than a dozen of the 160 poets represented in the anthology achieved. Yet what is particularly striking is that all ten of the poems were taken from Ryūhoku's overseas compositions. A handful of poems composed overseas by other Japanese poets are contained in the anthology, but by far the highest number of *kanshi* composed in Western settings are those by Ryūhoku.

On the whole, the sites Ryūhoku visited in France, England, and Italy were impressive to him, a point he makes unambiguously in the travelogue. Even the occasional unpleasant experience could be readily transformed into further praise of European institutions and manners simply by an assertion of its exceptionality, as in the following entry from March 11:

> Today a student became drunk and disorderly in our hotel's dining room, and broke a glass door. In the several months that have passed since I came to Europe, this is the first time I have seen someone become violent from drink. The fineness of Western manners deserves admiration.

The contrast to his representation of China and Southeast Asia could not be more plain.

Diary of a Journey to the West is almost uniform in its depiction of a gregarious Ryūhoku amiably socializing with a variety of

Westerners, but there are nevertheless a few exceptions. On New Year's Day of 1873, Ryūhoku went to the Japanese Legation to celebrate the holiday. Spending the important holiday abroad was undoubtedly an alienating experience, perhaps further complicated by the fact that while he was abroad, the Meiji government had suddenly abandoned the traditional Japanese lunar calendar in favor of the Western solar calendar.[4] As Ryūhoku used champagne in place of the spiced *tōso* wine customarily imbibed in Japan on the first of the year, he seems to have felt a bit homesick, as the following quatrain suggests:

客裏新正趣更奇　蠻奴相對不相知　一瓶傾盡三鞭酒　唱出東京舊竹枝
  Ringing in the New Year abroad is really rather odd;
  Face to face with the barbarian, and yet we remain strangers.
  I drank a whole bottle of champagne, down to the last drop,
  And sang out an old "bamboo branch" ballad of Tokyo.

The reference to "barbarians," the emphasis on the cultural rift between the author's persona and the Westerners who surround him, and the yearning for Japan expressed in this quatrain, are part of a rhetoric that

---

[4] New Year's was clearly an important holiday for Ryūhoku; in a later essay, he wrote that in his entire life, he had only been away from home on New Year's twice—on this occasion in France, and in 1884 when he was in Atami; see "Atami no ganjitsu" (New Year's at Atami) in the 6 January 1884 edition of the *Chōya shinbun*. Yet Ryūhoku gives no sense in his Western travelogue that he is at all troubled about adopting the new calendrical system; his dates suddenly switch on 1 December 1872 with little fanfare. By contrast, Kume Kunitake, Shimaji Mokurai, and other Japanese in Paris at the time either refused to adopt the new custom or grumbled about it in their diaries. In this connection, it is worth noting that Masao Miyoshi has argued that by continuing to reckon the days according to the Japanese calendar even as they were traveling in the United States, 1860 mission members to the United States were allowed a "capsule of time, a protective bubble … as though they were carrying a bit of Japan along, a sacred time-space precluding their being plunked directly into the middle of the American reality" (111). At least so far as we can judge from his self-presentation in *Diary of a Journey to the West*, Ryūhoku felt no need.

is decidedly muted in *Diary of a Journey to the West*. Aside from this one exception, the consistent emphasis in the text is on Ryūhoku's sociability, his effortless familiarity with Westerners, and his utter lack of discomfort at living within a new cultural setting.

About 130 personal names are scattered throughout the travelogue, impressing the reader with the breadth of Ryūhoku's social sphere. In addition to detailing his regular contacts with the sizable Japanese community of students and envoys then resident in Europe, Ryūhoku highlights his meetings with various Westerners, including old friends like Chanoine, businessmen like Bouché, Western scholars such as Léon de Rosny and James Summers, as well as a variety of others who cannot be positively identified. Coupled with the text's frequent references to events from European history, as well as the incorporation of historical incidents and persons into its *kanshi*, the cumulative effect is to suggest the author's assured and intimate familiarity with the people and culture of Europe. *Diary of a Journey to the West* also makes frequent reference to holidays and other events of which Europeans would take note, thereby narrowing any distance that might exist between Ryūhoku as he appears in the text and the Europeans around him.

Ryūhoku's figuration of his authorial persona in *Diary of a Journey to the West* as a man possessed of linguistic and social facility, cultural familiarity, and sophisticated discernment as a connoisseur thus distinguishes the work from many other travelogues written by Japanese who ventured abroad in the late Tokugawa and early Meiji period. Likewise, while lyrical expressions of homesickness formed a characteristic feature of these early travelogues, such sentiment surfaces only rarely in Ryūhoku's diary. From the posthumous poetry anthology, however, we see a slightly different story, with the following three poems on the topic of "Thinking of home:"

憶郷三首 *Three poems on thinking of home*

一白雲踪出故山 飛鴻幾度報平安 爲儂枕上多郷夢 絜得縞衾夜々寒
　Like a drifting white cloud, I departed the old mountains of home;
　Wild geese in flight have repeatedly brought reports that all is well.
　But these only make my dreams of home grow more numerous;
　I draw together my silken nightclothes, cold night after night.

想汝遊嬉在舊盧 誦詩習字近何如 阿爺囊橐無餘物 爲汝賒來數卷書
　I imagine you frolicking gleefully around our old cottage;
　Reciting poems and practicing characters, how have you been recently?
　Alas your old man has no more left in his purse,
　But he has scraped together enough to buy you a few books.

絃歌久不夢潯陽 萬里青衫客恨長 何當喚取江樓酒 笑看凉月照紅裳
　String music and songs: long have I had no dreams of Xunyang;
　A blue-coated young man a thousand miles away, my woes linger on.
　Oh whenever shall I be able to call for wine in that riverside tavern,
　And gaze with a smile at moonlight shining on crimson skirts?[5]

These three poems appear in *Ryūhoku shishō* in the section preceding his trans-Atlantic passage from London to New York. In other words, since Ryūhoku was still well enough to prepare the serialized installments through the diary's narration of his arrival in New York, the absence of these poems (assuming the order in the posthumous anthology is indeed the order in which they were composed) means that in addition to the poem on Saint Peter's Basilica, Ryūhoku

---

[5] Ryūhoku alludes here to Bo Juyi's "Song of the Lute," in which the poet writes of chancing to hear the exotic sound of a lute while in exile in Xunyang. He discovers that a Chang'an singing girl is the source of the music, and her affecting tale causes the poet to identify with her situation and to "wet his blue coat" with tears; for a translation, see Minford and Lau, I: 890–893.

probably made the decision to exclude these poems on the theme of homesickness from the published travelogue as well.[6]

About two dozen additional poems that were originally written after Ryūhoku's arrival in New York appear in *Ryūhoku shishō*, and they allow us to trace the remainder of his journey back to Japan. According to the May 9 entry of the travelogue, Ryūhoku had made arrangements for both the North American transcontinental rail tickets and the trans-Pacific ship booking while still in London. At the time, the Pacific Mail Steamship Company offered service to Yokohama from San Francisco on the first and sixteenth of every month, and Ryūhoku and Ishikawa had apparently decided to depart for Japan on the June 16 ship. The need to get across the country in two weeks necessarily limited the extent of their touring in the United States, but they did have the leisure to enjoy a visit to New York's Central Park:

遊紐育中央園 (ニウヨルクセントラルパアク)　*A trip to Central Park in New York*
輪蹄鎮入洞門來　鳥自和鳴花自開　好是仙郷新引客　劉郎不問老天台
Horse-drawn carriages enter through the cavernous gates;
Birds naturally sing in harmony, flowers open on their own.
How lovely this immortal realm that beckons the traveler anew;
Liulang need not call on old Mount Tiantai for his dalliances.[7]

---

[6] Unlike the poem on St. Peter's, it is difficult to be certain in this case, however, since there are several slight shifts in order between the poem sequence in *Diary of a Journey to the West* and the posthumous poetry anthology; in addition there are occasional discrepancies of a few days between the placement of poems in *Diary of a Journey to the West* and the copy of Ryūhoku's original diary made by Matsumoto Hakka. Because this sequence came so near the end of the published portion of the diary, it is possible that the poems would have been included had Ryūhoku been able to continue editing.

[7] Ryūhoku also alludes to this Tang era supernatural story in the second volume of *New Chronicles of Yanagibashi*.

The process of building Central Park had been underway since the late 1850s, but construction was officially completed in 1873, the same year that Ryūhoku made his visit. While his enthusiastic comparison of the Park to the mysterious dreamlike realm of delight that Liulang discovered on Mount Tiantai might seem hyperbolic, it is worth remembering that the Park was not only rather new at the time, but had been conceived on a scale unmatched by most of the public parks in the other major European urban centers that Ryūhoku had just visited. Indeed, Ryūhoku's exaltation is perhaps exceeded only by the author of the following piece from the *New York Times*; it appeared on June 2, 1873, which might well have been the very day that Ryūhoku visited the Park, for he had arrived in New York at 10 PM the night before:

> How joyous, how refreshing, and delightful to all our senses is the first ramble of the season in Central Park, so soon as nature has decked herself in all the glories of her new Summer garb … Never did the Park look more beautiful than it does now … No metropolitan city in the world boasts of so lovely a public resort as New York. London has its innumerable parks, very nice and very valuable to her population. Poor Paris had her Bois de Boulogne; Berlin has her Unter den Linden; Naples has her Giardini Reale; but dear as are all these to the memory of our naturalized citizens, they all fail before the natural beauties of the Central Park.

In addition to enjoying this bit of well-planned "nature" within the urban setting, Ryūhoku was equally stirred by less artificial natural scenes nearby. After departing New York City, he traveled with Ishikawa to Niagara Falls, a spectacular sensory experience that figures as either the focus or a key image in the following four poems. At no other point in his travels was Ryūhoku so moved to compose this many poems on a single site.

那耶哥羅觀瀑詩二首 *Two poems on viewing the waterfalls at Niagara*
危巖迎瀑碎爲烟　烟迸兩飛斜照天　最是山靈逞奇幻　橫溪幾道彩虹懸

> Steep crags welcome the plunging water, shattering it into mist;
> The mist surges up again, hovering as it illuminates the sky.
> This is a marvelous wonder the mountain gods present to us;
> Over numerous forks in the river stretch iridescent rainbows.

匡盧猶覺小涓々　蔽日涵雲漲半天　絕勝誰能運仙筆　人間無復李青蓮

> The great Mount Lu seems but a meager trickle;
> Blocking the sun and soaking the clouds, it fills half the sky.
> Who could wield his immortal brush before this peerless sight?
> For in our mortal realm, there has never been another Li Bo.[8]

客夢警醒枕上雷　起攀老樹陟崔嵬　夜深一望乾坤白　萬丈珠簾捲月來

> The dreams of this traveler are disturbed by thunder at his pillow;
> I rise and cling to old trees as I scale the steep crags.
> Late in the night, yet all is white as far as the eye can see,
> A pearly curtain a thousand feet high embraces the light of the moon.

過蘇格都古戰場　*On passing the old battleground of Scott*
立馬林皋望古營　當年陳迹認分明　歸雲陣々來爭岫　飛瀑猶爲巨礟聲

> Halting my horse on the wooded hill, I survey the old battleground;
> The ancient traces left back then are still clearly visible.
> Returning clouds, one after another enter the mountain cavern;
> In the plummeting cascade, one still hears the sound of giant cannons.

---

[8] Li Bo was so well known for his compositions on gazing at Mount Lu that visual representations of him viewing the waterfall there are common in East Asian painting; for translations of two of his famous poems on the falls see Hinton, 6–7.

Composed in the mode of "reflecting on the past," this final poem is followed by a note explaining the relevant history of the setting: "Scott was a famous American general. He fought a great battle with the British, and defeated them. The location is near Niagara." During the War of 1812, Winfield Scott (1786–1866) fought against the British, winning the Battle of Chippawa and becoming wounded in the Battle of Lundy's Lane. Both battles were fought in July 1814 along the Niagara River, as the United States attempted to invade Canadian territory.

　　Given this poem on the Niagara battlefield and the earlier composition in which the poet's sleep is disturbed by the sound of the waterfall, it seems likely that Ryūhoku and Ishikawa crossed to the Canadian side of the Niagara River and spent the night there. They could then have taken the Great Western Railway through Ontario to Detroit, where they presumably switched to the Michigan Central Railway for Chicago, and then switched to yet another railway line that carried them across Illinois and Iowa to Omaha. From the lack of poems preserved in the posthumous anthology, we may surmise that the trip through the Midwest was rather rushed, but not long after they had boarded a Union Pacific train to continue their westward journey across the Great Plains, the two men found themselves caught up in an unexpected catastrophe:

渡亞兒栩甫浪河〔アルクホルン〕 橋架摧裂 車陷急流有死傷者 余幸而免 爲賦此詩
　　Upon crossing the Elkhorn River, the bridge supports buckled and collapsed, and the carriage fell into the rapids. There were injuries and some people died. I was fortunate to escape, and for this reason I wrote the following poem.

323

霹靂推人迫急湍 倏然萬膽一時寒 棧摧車覆儂無恙 笑唱青蓮蜀道難

A crash of thunder sends me hurtling toward the rapids;
In a flash my vitals are momentarily frozen.
The pillars broken, the train overturned, but I emerge unscathed,
With a smile I sing out Li Bo's "The Road to Shu Is Steep."[9]

The accident that Ryūhoku refers to here took place on June 8, as his train crossed the Elkhorn River in Nebraska. As an article appearing in the local *West Point Republican* newspaper on June 12 reports, the derailing of the train had even more unexpected consequences for the Elkhorn River ecosystem, introducing several non-native fish species:

> On Sunday as a western bound passenger train on the Union Pacific railroad was crossing a trestle work near Elkhorn Station, the timbers suddenly gave way, precipitating the engine and two cars into the water. The trestle work was about four hundred feet long and twelve feet high, and was built over a slough on the east side of the Elkhorn river. The train was running at the rate of about three miles an hour, which fact is all that prevented a serious loss of lives. Roadmaster M. Carey was riding upon the engine at the time of the accident, and has not been seen since. It is supposed his body is fast in the wreck, which is still partially submerged, and must remain so until the waters subside, which are now about ten feet in depth. The engineer and fireman had a very narrow escape. Mr. Wood, the engineer, dove through the window of the cab and swam some distance from the wreck and arose to the surface uninjured. Fireman Hays was taken from the water insensible, but recovered in a short time. One human life, $30,000 worth of fish, and injury to the railroad stock, is, in brief the summing up of the results of the accident. The fish of which there were an

---

[9] A translation of the Li Bo poem alluded to here, which memorializes the treacherous road to Shu (modern Sichuan), can be found in Cooper, 129–132.

immense number consisted of various species of trout, pike, eels, lobster, bass, &c. These fish were being removed from the piscicultural breeding farm of Seth Green, on the Connecticut river, in Massachusetts, to California, for propagating purposes on the Pacific coast. This, although a great loss to some private parties, is a valuable acquisition to the Elkhorn, as they were confined in open tanks, and escaped unharmed into the river. Mr. Carey leaves a wife and four small children to mourn his sudden and terrible death. Trains now go by the way of Fremont and Blair, so that travel is not checked on this great thoroughfare. A large force is now at work repairing damages, and trains will doubtlessly be running in a few days over the old route.[10]

According to another report published in the *Lincoln Journal*, the unusual cargo that the train was transporting produced a rather bizarre scene in the aftermath of the tragedy: "A car load of little fishes collected in the east at a cost of $30,000, was precipitated into the Elkhorn river, by the Sunday accident. The oysters were fished out and roasted by the wrecked passengers."[11] Whether Ryūhoku and Ishikawa partook of the roasted oysters is unclear, but they were soon on their way again, continuing the steady climb in altitude from Omaha to Sherman, the highest point of the Union Pacific Railway.

過 綠 魋 山　　*On crossing the Rocky Mountains*
　　　ロッキイモンテイン

崎嶇路在老巖間　落月斷雲相對閑　怪獸有聲人不語　火輪輾上綠魋山

　A precipitous road winds through the ancient mountain crags;
　In the evening stillness, the falling moon sets off the scattered clouds.
　A mysterious beast cries out, but no human voices are heard.
　The steam engine rolls up into the Rocky Mountains.

---

[10] Entitled "Railroad accident," this article appeared in the 12 June 1873 edition of the *West Point Republican* (p. 5, col. 3).
[11] Reprinted in the 19 June 1873 edition of the *West Point Republican*, p. 5, col. 3.

午炎烘地夜亦蒸　警鐸敲醒夢一肱　向曉空山人患渇　停車爭嚙澗頭氷

Midday heat scorches the earth, and at night it is still sultry;
An alarm bell is struck, waking me from my dreams, elbow for a pillow.
As dawn approaches these empty mountains, all are desperately thirsty;
When the carriage stops, everyone races to eat the ice in the river.

Perhaps Ryūhoku was having a bit of fun with his choice of Chinese characters to represent the toponym "Rocky Mountains." He assigned the characters 綠 ("green"; Ch. *lü*; J. *roku*) and 魁 ("ghoulish"; Ch. *qi*; J. *ki*) principally for their phonetic value, of course, but the semantic content of the characters also suggested both the verdure of the mountains and the forbidding "mysterious beasts" he encountered there. A note accompanying the first of these two poems explains the identity of these unfamiliar creatures: "The Rocky Mountains have strange beasts that resemble bulls but are larger. I saw them in person. They are called 'buffalo.'" In the next poem, he used the character "green" again, but for its semantic value, assigning it to the Green River in Utah:

グリンリバー
綠　河　　*Green River*

濃綠涵雲是綠河　爲誰新樣染輕羅　縱然日夜東流去　難洗吾儂客思多

The deep green suffusing the clouds is the Green River;
For whom does it present this fresh visage, like delicate dyed silk?
Even if its waters poured day and night, flowing off to the East
They could not wash away this traveler's thoughts of home.

ソールトレイキ
鹽　湖　二首　　*Two poems on the Salt Lake*

綠河太駛綠山危　看到鹽湖意轉怡　風月一灣晴更好　烟波萬頃兩還奇

The Green River charges on, the green Rocky Mountains craggy;
When I saw Salt Lake at last, my mind was at ease.

The scenery in this inlet is even better on a clear day;
Mist and waves stretch for a thousand acres, and both are lovely.

隔岸翠螺收夕陽　晴瀾涵月鏡光涼　他年若憶鹽湖景　應是黃粱夢一場
On the far bank, emerald butterflies soak up the evening sun;
Clear waves bathe the moon: cool light on a mirror.
If in some future year I recall the scenery at the Salt Lake,
It will surely be in a dream, like the Handan traveler awaiting his millet.

Perhaps it was the strikingly unfamiliar scenery that led Ryūhoku to compare his present surroundings to a dreamscape, alluding as he had in his January 31 entry in Paris to the story of Lu Sheng and the magical pillow he borrowed in a Handan inn.

Having entered the Salt Lake Valley, Ryūhoku had only one more mountain range to cross before reaching the Pacific Coast:

過寧婆陀山　*Crossing the Sierra Nevada*
虯車奔壑勢如抛　征客坐捫栖鶻巢　夾路松杉皆百尺　瀜輪軋過最高梢
The dragon carriage races through the valley with unleashed force
While the traveler sits and plucks the nests of resting hawks.
On either side of the path, pines and cedars grow a hundred feet tall;
The steam engine rattles along through the tallest of peaks.

The sheer cliffs and gorges around the Donner Pass presumably provided the inspiration for this poem, in which Ryūhoku evokes the disorienting feeling of traveling above the high treetops that lined the valley floor. In its juxtaposition of the stationary calm of the traveler and the dynamic force of the moving locomotive, the poem resonates the poem he composed on his first encounter with train travel, speeding from Marseille to Paris (see the 10.30 entry).

The terminus of Ryūhoku's transcontinental journey on the Union Pacific would have been Sacramento, from which point he would have switched trains again for the short trip to San Francisco.

達桑港書喜二首<ruby>サンフランシスコ</ruby>
Two poems composed to record my joy at reaching the port of San Francisco
滊機雖疾客程長　毒熱酸寒子細甞　鐵路三千三百里　今朝始望太平洋

    Though the steam engines are fast, the traveler's route is long;
    Poisonous heat and bitter cold, I have tasted it all.
    On iron rails for three thousand three hundred miles,
    This morning, I have my first glance at the Pacific Ocean.

西來桑港似歸家　忘卻家山萬里遐　蒼靄薰風好天氣　園々開遍杜鵑花

    Westward, I have come to San Francisco, and it is like returning home;
    I forget that my hometown lies a thousand miles away.
    Azure mists, fragrant winds: such lovely weather;
    In each garden, azalea flowers in full bloom.

Whether it was the sight of the familiar Pacific Ocean or the agreeable climate, Ryūhoku was clearly pleased to have reached San Francisco, though the fact that he does not record any poems about the city itself suggests that he did not stay long. While the precise date of his arrival is unclear, if we consider that he was involved in the Nebraska train accident on June 8, we can estimate that the earliest he would have reached San Francisco would have been around June 12.

    Ryūhoku's departure for Yokohama came on June 16 when he boarded the Pacific Mail's *Great Republic*.[12] That Ryūhoku was aboard this ship is strongly suggested by his chance encounter with a

---

[12] The June 17 edition of the *Daily Alta California* records that the *Great Republic* left San Francisco under Capt. Howard's command on June 16.

British businessman named David Carr Binnie, who was at the time making his way around the world. Binnie's diary and album are now held by Cambridge University, and as Noboru Koyama of the University Library has discussed, the album contains a photograph of Ryūhoku seated beside Binnie (see Figure 13).

Figure 13. Photograph by Shimooka Renjō of Narushima Ryūhoku and David Carr Binnie, from the latter's photograph album. Beneath Ryūhoku's seated figure, "Narushima" is inscribed on the mounting paper. Reproduced by kind permission of the Syndics of Cambridge University Library.

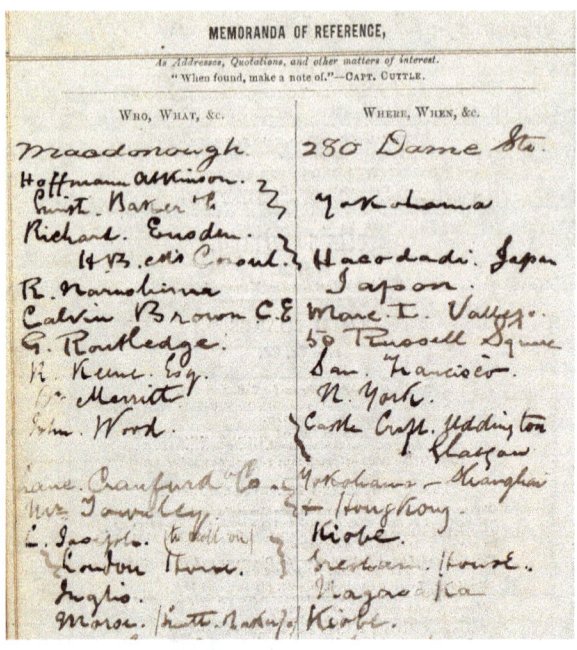

Figure 14. List of names in David Carr Binnie's travel diary. "R. Narushima … Japan" appears on the sixth line. Reproduced by kind permission of the Syndics of Cambridge University Library.

The name "Narushima" appears written on the photograph in pencil, and the inscription on the photograph's verso details how it was taken by pioneering Japanese photographer Shimooka Renjō in Yokohama. It is unclear how Ryūhoku and Binnie became acquainted—whether it was during Ryūhoku's stay in London, the tour of the United States, or the voyage back to Japan—yet it is clear that they did attain some degree of familiarity, for Ryūhoku's name also appears in a list of names in Binnie's travel diary: "R. Narushima Japan"[13] (Figure 14). Though the entries in Binnie's travel diary are sporadic, they do help

---

[13] I am grateful to Noboru Koyama for generously providing me with copies of the text of his presentation ("Opening") and of the relevant section of Binnie's diary.

shed some light on Ryūhoku's return to Japan. Binnie notes on June 14, 1873: "We are very hurried on this trip as we must catch Japan steamer on Monday." June 14 fell on a Saturday in 1873, which makes it almost certain that Binnie and Ryūhoku returned on the June 16 ship.

In the course of his journey across the Pacific Ocean, Ryūhoku wrote the following four poems. All are tinged with a sense of weariness with travel and an eager anticipation of reunion with family and friends. The first one, for example, evokes the song of the nightingale, whose call is thought to sound like the phrase "better go home" (*burugui*) in Chinese:

太平洋舟中之作四首
Four poems composed during a ship's journey across the Pacific
啼禽催我不如歸　夢繞家山情更痴　海舶日馳三百里　客心猶覺太遲々

    The cries of the nightingale urge me "Better go home";
    My dreams linger on the hills of home, feelings all the more maudlin.
    On our seaborne vessel, each day we race ahead three hundred miles;
    But to the heart of a traveler, this is just too slow.

征人西去復西還　帆影長飛雲水間　誰信滄溟如許濶　二旬不見五洲山

    Having departed west, the traveler returns now, still headed west;
    Our sail has long flown between the sea and sky.
    Who would believe the dark blue depths could be so vast?
    Two-times-ten days with none of the five great continents in sight.

水滑天沈雨氣冥　孤帆無力度蒼溟　封姨驀地吹雲裂　滿目晴瀾月亦青

    The waters smooth, the sky low and gloomy in the rain;
    Our lone ship weakly crosses the dark blue depths.
    But then the wind god gusts at full force, breaking apart the clouds;
    Filling the scene with clear waves bathed in limpid moonlight.

鎖海濃雲黯不開　濕霖時節我歸來　想他澨上舊茅宇　幾顆金丸摽有梅

Thick clouds seal off the sea, the darkness does not lift;
It is the monsoon season, and I am returning home.
I think of my old thatched hut along the Sumida River;
Where the golden fruit will have withered and plums appeared.

While Ryūhoku wrote of being simply impressed by the speed of the *Mei Kong* on the outbound journey, the same speed of the *Great Republic* on the return journey now seemed insufficient and the journey across the Pacific protracted. But to use these terms of "outbound" and "return" is somewhat misleading, for as Ryūhoku points out in the second poem in the series, his trip did not neatly conform topologically to the familiar routes that travelers had been describing in their travelogues for centuries. It consisted neither of an outbound leg followed by a return along the same path nor of some more circular path that involved a change of direction midway, for Ryūhoku had basically continued west for the course of his circumnavigation. In a note he appended to the poem, he made the following droll observation:

余發橫濱針路西向而達歐洲再西馳而到米國又西面而走二十三日達橫濱地球如橙之説可以證也

I left Yokohama, navigating a course to the west and reaching Europe. I then traveled west again to America. I then again continued going to the west. After twenty-three days, I arrived in Yokohama. The theory that the Earth is round like an orange can thus be substantiated.

The specific date of Ryūhoku's return is not noted in the poems surviving in the posthumous anthology, but judging from the "twenty-three days" of the journey mentioned in this note, we can conlude that he arrived in Yokohama on July 8, twenty-three days after his departure from San Francisco.¹⁴

歸家口號二首　　*Two poems chanted on returning home*
無爵無田且莫憂　天公縱我自由遊　人間快樂汝知否　雙脚踏來全地球
   I have no rank, no rice paddies, but also no worries;
   Heaven has granted me leave to travel freely.
   I wonder if you know what pleasures there are in this world of ours;
   To walk with one's own two legs over the entire globe.

休送新霜上鬢頭　風蒿瑟々故園秋　米蘭名妓巴黎酒　豪興呼誰話昨游
   Don't add another layer of frost to the hair at my temples;
   Wind soughs softly through the mugwort in my old autumn garden.
   Famous Milanese courtesans and Parisian wine—
   Whom shall I call to regale with these grand adventures of yesterday?

到橫濱二首追綠　　*Two poems appended on reaching Yokohama*
渺々鯨濤來路長　忽看蓮嶽立蒼洋　三峯迎我粲然笑　萬里歸人喜欲狂
   Over vast leviathan waves, the journey has been long;
   Suddenly I glimpse the Lotus Peak rising up from azure seas.
   Its three crests welcome me with a brilliant smile;
   After ten thousand miles, my joy upon returning approaches ecstasy.¹⁵

---

¹⁴ Many commentators have interpreted 二十三日 to be a date, the 23ʳᵈ (of June), rather than "twenty-three days;" such a reading is grammatically possible, but is not the sense here. The July 8 return date is corroborated by Naramoto and Momose, and also Ōno (33).
¹⁵ Ryūhoku seems to be combining a specific term for Japan's Mt. Fuji ("the Lotus Peak") in the first couplet with the "three crests" of China's Mt. Hua near Chang'an along the Wei River in the second couplet. This latter reference to the "three crests," as well as the references to the passage of time in the previous poem, recall the final lines of Bo Juyi's "On returning to my old home on the Wei River" 重到渭上舊居, in which the poet observes the impermanence of things and concludes: "My ruddy complexion fades unremittingly / On my head, countless strands of white hair / There

去時江月照人清 今夕歸來復月明 相送相迎意何厚 金蟾是亦可憐生

When I left, the moon over the river shined its clear light on me;
As I return this evening, the moon again is bright.
Sending me off and welcoming me home, how thoughtful it is!
The golden toad must also have a sensitive soul.

In this final poem Ryūhoku makes use of a common synecdoche for the moon based on a Chinese legend of a moon-dwelling golden toad, a manifestation of the lunar goddess Chang'e. He also harks back to the first poem in the travelogue, which commemorated the group's departure under the "night of the later moon" in Yokohama Harbor nine months earlier. Though Ryūhoku's travelogue was never published in its entirety, the appearance of this poem at the end of the sequence thus marks an appropriate close for the travelogue, bringing his journey full circle.

  Immediately after his return to Japan in July 1873, Ryūhoku helped to found the Higashi Honganji Temple's Translation Office in Kyoto. Drawing upon the knowledge he had gained during his journey abroad, Ryūhoku served as the director of this office, which oversaw the translation and publication of several Western texts concerning the world's religions, including some of the first modern treatments of Sanskrit published in Japan. Before long, however, budgetary problems and tensions with the temple administration arose, and Ryūhoku grew frustrated in his position. When an invitation came in the summer of 1874 to join a new newspaper publishing venture in Tokyo, he leapt at the opportunity. Clearly this marked a major transition point in Ryūhoku's life, but it was not altogether unexpected. Ryūhoku's interest in newspapers was longstanding, as his production of a handwritten

---

is just one thing: outside the gate / the three crests still look the same" 朱顔銷不歇、白髮生無數、唯有山門外、三峰色如故.

"newspaper" called *Tōkyō chinbun* (Strange news from Tokyo) in the immediate aftermath of the Meiji Restoration, and his comparison of *New Chronicles of Yanagibashi* to a "newspaper," both illustrate. In fact, Ryūhoku had begun to contribute to Japan's fledgling newspapers even while he was still abroad. Among the items in the May 1873 edition of the *Yūbin hōchi shinbun* was an excerpt from a letter Ryūhoku sent to his biological brother, Kusuyama Takasaburō. In the letter, Ryūhoku gives a brief outline of his various nocturnal adventures in Paris, including a recent trip to the theater, where he saw a theatrical version of Alexandre Dumas fils' *La Dame aux Camélias*. It was Ryūhoku's response to this production that formed the bulk of the excerpt published in the *Yūbin hōchi shinbun*:

> The night before last, I went to see a play at a theatre called the Gymnase. The play they performed, if one were to put it in Japanese terms, was about a geisha who falls in love with a playboy, but who is forced to break up with him when the man's parents disapprove of her; after this, she remains tormented by her love and ends up falling ill and dying; the man meanwhile goes mad. This is based upon actual events, and the courtesan's name is Camellia. Her grave is within the city of Paris, and the playboy is apparently an old man now, but still alive. It had closed after a smashing success the other day, but the night before last, it was performed just one night more in accordance with the man's request. Since it had been very highly regarded, I also went to see it. The play truly had me in tears. People's feelings are exactly the same no matter where you go; the West is absolutely no different.[16]

The 1869 experiments with the *Tōkyō chinbun* notwithstanding, this dispatch from Paris was Ryūhoku's first newspaper publication. It is

---

[16] Reprinted in the *Hon'yaku bungei hen* volume of *Meiji bunka zenshū* (Tokyo: Nihon Hyōronsha, 1927; 14: 586).

335

difficult to know if Ryūhoku intended the letter to be published, but it resonates thematically and structurally with many of the essays he would write first as an occasional correspondent for the *Yūbin hōchi shinbun* and then as the head of the *Chōya shinbun*.[17]

Until his death ten years later, Ryūhoku occupied a leading role in the founding of modern journalism in Japan, serving in a variety of key positions at the *Chōya shinbun*, including editor and president. Ryūhoku established the *Chōya* as one of the outspoken voices of criticism against various Meiji policies. This oppositional stance could sometimes be a boost to sales, but it could also cost the paper severely in an era when increasingly restrictive press laws were used against newspapers the Meiji regime found troublesome. On numerous occasions, the *Chōya* was ordered to suspend publication, resulting in a devastating loss of revenue and readership; its reporters and editors were regularly fined, and not infrequently incarcerated. Over time, Ryūhoku's journalistic activities expanded beyond the publication of the daily *Chōya shinbun*. In 1877, Ryūhoku founded *Kagetsu shinshi* (New journal of the moon and blossoms), one of Japan's very first literary magazines. The journal, which was printed by the *Chōya shinbun* and ran continuously until Ryūhoku's death in 1884, featured Chinese and Japanese poetry and prose works composed by Ryūhoku and his poetic confreres but also provided a forum for newly emerging talents. Several travelogues, including Ryūhoku's own *Diary of a Journey to the West* appeared in its pages.

---

[17] For a discussion of Ryūhoku's emergence as a journalist with a focus on his *zatsuroku* or miscellaneous essays, see Fraleigh, "The Fire Guard."

Glossary

chawanmori — A dish made from seafood, chicken, or vegetables that are boiled and served in a bowl with a lid.

chikushi(shi) — Literally meaning "bamboo branch" (ballads), this refers to a genre of *yuefu* ("music bureau") poetry focused on local customs that was developed by Tang poet Liu Yuxi (772–842). It became an especially popular genre in Japanese *kanshi* composition in the late Edo period, where the local customs of the pleasure quarter became a particular focus of interest.

chin — The "Japanese chin" is a breed of small dog of originally Chinese ancestry that was first produced in the Edo period.

choki — Also written with the characters "boar's tusk boat" 猪牙舟, a *chokibune* was a long and thin unroofed boat used in the Edo period for fishing and for ferrying passengers speedily along the river, especially to Yoshiwara. Ryūhoku also uses the characters 飛舸, suggesting a "flying lighter boat."

confeito — A confection of flour and sugar that had originally entered Japan from Portugal and become relatively widespread by the seventeenth century.

daimyō — A daimyo is a feudal lord. During the Tokugawa period there were about two hundred hereditary lords whose holdings qualified them for the title.

dango	Round dumplings made from a steamed or boiled dough (typically made by mixing rice flour and water).
dodoitsu	A form of ditty that was popular at the end of the Tokugawa period; using colloquial language, and typically focused on romantic themes, the lyrics fell into a syllable pattern of 7-7-7-5.
funayado	The term refers to boathouses that arranged river trips for their patrons, summoned geisha for their entertainment, and doubled as houses of assignation.
furoshiki	A sheet of cloth that is used to wrap and carry objects.
fūryū	A term originally deriving from the Chinese *fengliu*, the term can refer to grace and panache, stylish elegance, or sophisticated sense in amorous or artistic matters.
geisha	Female professional entertainers who are engaged to dance, sing, play shamisen and perform other traditional arts. The characters from which the word is composed literally mean something like "arts person."
geta	Traditional Japanese clog-like footwear that are made out of a wooden base supported by two teeth. Like sandals, they are open on top.
gikun	"Playful glosses" that are typically written in Japanese to the left side of Chinese characters and offer a variety of expressive possibilities beyond simple explanations of meaning or guides to pronunciation.
go	A game played with black and white markers on a grid, *go* entered Japan from China and was the

	inspiration for the contemporary board game Othello.
gōkan	A genre of extended illustrated fiction that became popular in the early nineteenth century and consisted of smaller books that had been bound together. It was especially popular with female readers.
hakama	A form of trousers loose-fitting in the legs that are worn by men on formal occasions.
hako(ya)	The agency who dispatched a porter to carry the shamisen of a geisha, or the porter himself.
hakomawashi	The porter who was responsible for carrying the shamisen of a geisha.
haori	A short, coat-like garment that is worn over kimono.
hara-awase	An obi sash that is made with different kinds of fabric.
hatamoto	Often translated as "bannerman," the term refers to those retainers who were especially close to the daimyo or shogun whom they served.
hidarizuma	Literally "left skirt," the term refers to geisha, whose practice it is to gather up the skirts of their kimono to the left.
hikitejaya	A teahouse that served as an intermediary between a customer and courtesan.
hikyaku(ya)	Literally "flying legs," the term refers to messengers or porters who conveyed letters, money, and goods.
hitoe	An unlined, single-layered kimono.
hitoyado	In addition to its primary meaning of "inn," the term refers to any kind of intermediary agency. Ryūhoku uses it in reference to the agencies that provided porters to accompany geisha to their engagements.

hōkan	The *hōkan* or *taiko-mochi* was responsible for providing verbal and musical entertainment at banquets. The term is sometimes translated as "male geisha." Sexual services were not typically part of the picture.
jorō	A prostitute. Throughout *New Chronicles of Yanagibashi*, Ryūhoku draws a distinction between the female entertainer or courtesan 妓 (J. *gi*; Ch. *ji*), which he often glosses *geisha*, and the prostitute 娼 (J. *shō*; Ch. *chang*), which he sometimes glosses *jorō*. Occasionally, he uses the conventional characters 女郎 for *jorō*. The term was also pronounced *jōro*. See also *shōgi*.
jusha	A term that refers broadly to Confucian scholars, either those who supported themselves by teaching privately, or who were in the employ of daimyo or the shogun. Ryūhoku himself was the eighth in a line of *okujusha* or "*jusha* of the interior," men assigned to oversee the shogun's education.
kanbun gesaku	Literally, "playful writings" in literary Chinese, *New Chronicles of Yanagibashi* is an exemplary modern work of the genre.
kawabiraki	The annual opening of the Sumida River for summer, the event was typically celebrated on the twenty-eighth day of the fifth month with a fireworks festival from Ryōgoku Bridge.
ken	A parlor game popular in the Edo and Meiji periods in which several people competed by making hand gestures representing concrete objects or people. One simple form is "paper, scissors, rock" but various versions with more elaborate rules were developed.

kenban	Originally meaning a "lookout," the term also referred to an agency that dispatched geisha to banquets or parties in Yoshiwara.
Kiyomoto	A style of song accompanied by shamisen that was developed by Kiyomoto Enjudayū (1777–1825) and became popular in the Edo period. It was particularly common as the music for kabuki dance.
kōgai	A bodkin-like hair ornament made from a simple metal bar.
kōshaku	A type of oral entertainment popular from the Edo to the Meiji period in which the performer who recite texts, especially battle epics.
koshiobi	A sash that is worn beneath the decorative outer sash to preserve the form of a kimono.
kōzo	A species of tree known as the "paper mulberry," its fiber is used to make Japanese paper.
kusazōshi	A large category of popular illustrated fiction that circulated widely in the Edo period, the term embraces more specific genres such as *kibyōshi* and *gōkan*. Ryūhoku uses the term as a gloss on the Chinese 稗史 (Ch. *baishi*; J. *haishi*), a term for anecdotes, fictionalized accounts, and other forms of "unofficial history."
kyōgen	A form of light comic theater that grew out of the Noh tradition in the Muromachi period.
maru	A suffix that is commonly attached to the names of boats and ships in Japan.
mochi	Pounded rice cakes that are hard when uncooked and soft and glutinous when boiled or baked.
nagajuban	Undergarments that are worn beneath kimono.

nagauta	Literally "long songs," the term refers to a genre of music that become popular in the Edo period and was performed along with kabuki and dance. Typically several singers would be accompanied by shamisen, but the arrangements might also include drums and other instruments.
naginata	Sometimes translated as "Japanese halberd" or "partisan," the *naginata* was a weapon with a long handle with a curved blade.
najimi	A regular customer of a certain courtesan. In the Yoshiwara, it was customary for a customer who had engaged a courtesan three or more times to be considered one of her steady clients.
nishikie	Literally, "brocade pictures," this refers to woodblock prints printed using color. The technique was developed by *ukiyoe* artist Suzuki Harunobu in the mid-eighteenth century.
nitari	A form of small freight-bearing boat that was used in the Edo period, it is typically written with the characters 荷足, meaning "load legs."
obi	A decorative sash worn like a belt with Japanese kimono.
okyūji	Literally "servers," the term was used in reference to junior *machi-geisha*, women who, like their senior counterparts the *shakujin* or *shakutori*, fulfilled the roles of geisha outside of the licensed districts of Fukagawa and Yoshiwara.
oshaku	Literally "drink pourers," the term designated young women who poured drinks, danced, and provided other entertainment to customers. This was one term

	by which "little" or "junior" apprentice geisha were known.
rakugo	A form of verbal entertainment that became popular in the Edo period. Told by a single performer, *rakugo* typically involved a rather simple story that was made complex by much comic digression, and culminated in a joke or punchline.
sarugaku	Emerging from *sangaku* 散楽, a form of farce and acrobatic entertainment that had continental roots, *sarugaku* entered Japan in the Heian period. Originally referring to comic impersonation acts and other light diversions that were performed in association with sumō wrestling matches and other events at Shinto shrines, the genre became more dramatic in the Kamakura period and eventually developed into the two classic theatrical forms of Noh and kyōgen.
shakujin	The term is a Sino-Japanese equivalent of *shaku-tori*, or "drink pourer." While the *machi-geisha* (those geisha based outside of the officially licensed districts of Yoshiwara and Fukagawa) in fact were commonly referred to as "geisha," they were technically not allowed to use this name, and thus *shaku-tori* served as a substitute term.
shirabyōshi	A form of dance performed by courtesans from the Heian to the Kamakura period. The term later became used in reference to courtesans.
shirukoboshi	Ryūhoku writes this term with characters meaning "spilling liquid" (汁翻), it refers to a slightly smaller version of the *yakata* river boat that was propelled by four or five rowers.

shōgi 将棋	A form of chess that entered Japan from China in the Heian period.
shōgi 娼妓	Generally translated "courtesans," Ryūhoku uses the term to refer to female entertainers, geisha, and prostitutes, as a collective.
shōji	Sliding paper doors typically made from translucent paper attached to a bamboo frame.
shunga	Literally "pictures of spring," this refers to erotic prints, a genre that was especially popular in Japan's early modern period.
soba	Buckwheat noodles.
sumi	Black ink used for calligraphy and painting.
taikomochi	Also known as a *hōkan*, the term literally means "drum holder" and refers to a "male geisha," who was responsible for providing diverting verbal and musical entertainment at banquets, rather in the manner of a jester.
tatami	Straw mats of fixed size used as flooring in Japanese-style architecture.
Tokiwazu	A form of *jōruri*, or popular narrative songs played on the shamisen, made popular by Tokiwazu Mojidayū (1708–1781).
Tomimoto	A form of *jōruri*, or popular narrative songs played on the shamisen, pioneered by Tomimoto Buzennojō (1716–1764).
yakata(bune)	A term for a large-scale pleasure boat outfitted with a roof. To restrict excessive expenditure and unseemly ostentation, the shogunate imposed sumptuary edicts that subjected these boats to regulation.

yanebune	A roofed pleasure boat, smaller than a *yakatabune*, that was popular for river excursions during the Edo period. Typically the term is written 屋根船 ("roofed boat"), but Ryūhoku sometimes uses the characters 遊舫, "pleasure excursion boat."
yashiki	Written with characters meaning "estate boat" 邸船, the term refers to large pleasure boats that samurai were allowed to keep at riverside boathouses.
yose	Sometimes compared to "vaudeville," the term refers to a hall in which various forms of oral and musical entertainments popular in the Edo and Meiji period were performed.
yotsude(kago)	Literally "four-hand palanquin," this refers to a simple kind of platform that was suspended from a long pole that was carried by two porters, one in front of the passenger and the other in back.
yukata	Literally "bathing robe," the term refers to a light kimono worn after bathing or in summer.

Works Cited

Versions of *Kōsei nichijō* and *Ryūkyō shinshi*
For both translations, I have used the first published version of the work as the base text. I list these below, along with additional anthologized editions that I have consulted. I should note that I have benefited tremendously from the detailed and illuminating annotations of *Ryūkyō shinshi* provided by Maeda Ai and Hino Tatsuo. Many of the notes I have provided to my translation of this work are indebted to their meticulous scholarship. The first annotated editions of *Kōsei nichijō* were published in Japan within a few months of each other in the summer and autumn of 2009, after my translation had been completed and the manuscript had already been copy-edited. I was, however, able to incorporate some additional information from the thorough notes in these editions, which I have indicated in the translation itself.

Narushima Ryūhoku 成島柳北. *Kōsei nichijō* 航西日乗. Serialized in 34 installments in *Kagetsu shinshi* from issue no. 118 (November 30, 1881) to issue no. 153 (August 8, 1884). The installments begin on p. 420 of vol. VI and end on p. 277 of vol. VIII in the photoreproduction: *Kagetsu shinshi* 花月新誌, 8 vols. Tokyo: Yumani Shobō ゆまに書房, 1984. {Base text.}

———. *Kōsei nichijō*. In Shioda Ryōhei 塩田良平, ed., *Narushima Ryūhoku Hattori Bushō Kurimoto Joun* 成島柳北・服部撫松・栗本鋤雲, *Meiji bungaku zenshū* 明治文学全集 vol. 4, 117–144. Tokyo: Chikuma Shobō, 1969.

———. *Kōsei nichijō*. In *Gaikoku bunka hen* 外国文化篇, *Meiji bunka zenshū* 明治文化全集, vol. 17, 403–441. Tokyo: Nihon Hyōronsha 日本評論社, 1992.

———. *Kōsei nichijō*. In Horikawa Takashi 堀川貴司, Sugishita Motoaki 杉下元明, Suzuki Ken'ichi 鈴木健一, and Hihara Tsutae 日原傳, eds., *Kaigai kenbunshū* 海外見聞集, *Shin Nihon koten bungaku taikei: Meiji hen* 新日本古典文学大系：明治編, vol. 5, 249–357. Tokyo: Iwanami Shoten 岩波書店, 2009.

———. *Kōsei nichijō*. In Ida Shin'ya 井田進也, ed., *Bakumatsu ishin Pari kenbunki: Narushima Ryūhoku 'Kōsei nichijō' Kurimoto Joun 'Gyōsō tsuiroku'* 幕末維新パリ見聞記：成島柳北「航西日乗」・栗本鋤雲「暁窓追録」, 7–136. Tokyo: Iwanami Shoten, 2009.

———. *Ryūkyō shinshi* 柳橋新誌, 2 vols. Tokyo: Yamashiroya Masakichi 山城屋政吉, 1874. {Base text.}

———. *Ryūkyō shinshi*. In Itō Sei 伊藤整, ed., *Meiji shoki bungakushū* 明治初期文學集, *Nihon gendai bungaku zenshū* 日本現代文學全集, vol. 1. Tokyo: Kōdansha 講談社, 1969.

———. *Ryūkyō shinshi*. In Maeda Ai 前田愛, ed., *Meiji kaikaki bungakushū* 明治開花期文学集, *Nihon kindai bungaku taikei* 日本近代文学大系, vol. 1. Tokyo: Kadokawa Shoten 角川書店, 1970.

———. *Ryūkyō shinshi*. In Hino Tatsuo 日野龍夫, ed., *Edo hanjōki, Ryūkyō shinshi* 江戸繁昌記・柳橋新誌. *Shin Nihon koten bungaku taikei*, vol. 100. Tokyo: Iwanami Shoten, 1989.

Biographical Reference Materials

In identifying the individuals whom Ryūhoku met during his journey abroad, I have made use of the following reference materials. When not otherwise indicated, the biographical notes I have provided are a composite of information drawn from these works. In particular, Tomita Hitoshi's *Umi o koeta Nihon jinmei jiten* has been an invaluable source.

Dictionnaire de Biographie Française. J. Balteau, M. Barroux, M. Prevost, et al, eds. Paris: Letouzey et Ané, 1933–.

Ishitsuki Minoru 石附実. *Kindai Nihon no kaigai ryūgakushi* 近代日本の海外留学史. Tokyo: Chūō Kōronsha 中央公論社, 1992.

Kasumi Kaikan Shoka Shiryō Chōsa Iinkai 霞会館諸家資料調査委員会, ed. *Kazokukei taisei* 華族系大成, 2 vols. Tokyo: Yoshikawa Kōbunkan 吉川弘文館, 1982–1984.

Miyazaki Tomihachi 宮崎十三八 and Yasuoka Akio 安岡昭男. *Bakumatsu ishin jinmei jiten* 幕末維新人名事典. Tokyo: Shinjinbutsu Ōraisha 新人物往来社, 1994.

Meiji jinmei jiten 明治人名辞典, 3 vols. (Vol. 1 is a reprint of *Gendai jinmei jiten* 現代人名辭典, originally published 1912; vol. 2 is a reprint of *Nihon genkon jinmei jiten* 日本現今人名辞典, originally published 1900; vol. 3 is a reprint of *Dai Nihon Jinbutsushi* 大日本人物誌, originally published 1913.) Tokyo: Nihon Tosho Sentā 日本図書センター, 1987–1994.

Ōue Shirō 大植四郎. *Meiji kakochō: bukko jinmei jiten* 明治過去帳：物故人名辞典. Tokyo: Tōkyō Bijutsu 東京美術, 1971. [Originally published 1935.]

Tamai Gensaku 玉井源作. *Hiroshima jinmei jiten: Geibi sentetsu den* 広島人名事典・藝備先哲傳. Tokyo: Rekishi Toshosha 歴史図書社, 1976.

Teraoka Juichi 寺岡寿一. *Meiji shoki no kan'inroku, shokuinroku* 明治初期の官員録・職員録, 6 vols. Section 1 of *Meiji shoki rekishi bunken shiryōshū* 明治初期歴史文献資料集. Tokyo: Teraoka Shodō 寺岡書洞, 1977–1981.

Tezuka Akira 手塚晃. *Bakumatsu Meiji kaigai tokōsha sōran* 幕末明治海外渡航者総覧, 3 vols. Tokyo: Kashiwa Shobō 柏書房, 1992.

Tomita Hitoshi 富田仁. *Umi o koeta Nihon jinmei jiten* 海を越えた日本人名事典, new corr. ed. Tokyo: Nichigai Asoshiētsu 日外アソシエーツ, 2005.

Other Works Cited

Allison, Anne. "American Geishas and Oriental/ist Fantasies." In Purnima Mankekar and Louisa Schein, eds., *Media, Transnationalism, and Asian Erotics*. Durham, NC: Duke University Press, forthcoming.

Araki Yasuhiko 荒木康彦. *Kindai Nichi-Doku kōshōshi kenkyū josetsu: saisho no Doitsu daigaku Nihonjin gakusei Mashima Seiji to Kāru Rēman* 近代日独交渉史研究序説：最初のドイツ大学日本人学生馬島済治とカール・レーマン. Tokyo: Yūshōdō Shuppan 雄松堂出版, 2003.

Ariga, Chieko M. "Dephallicizing Women in Ryūkyō Shinshi: A Critique of Gender Ideology in Japanese Literature." *The Journal of Asian Studies* 51.3 (1992): 565–586.

———. "The Playful Gloss: Rubi in Japanese Literature." *Monumenta Nipponica* 44.3 (1989): 309–335.

———. *Reading Ryūkyō Shinshi: An Investigation in Literary Hermeneutics*. Ph.D. dissertation, University of Chicago, 1986.

Baedeker, Karl. *Central Italy and Rome. Italy: Handbook for Travellers*, part 2, 11th rev. ed. Leipzig: Karl Baedeker, 1893.

———. *Great Britain: Handbook for Travellers*, 2nd ed., rev. and augmented. Leipzig: Karl Baedeker, 1890.

———. *London and Its Environs: Handbook for Travellers, Including Excursions to Brighton, the Isle of Wight, etc.* Leipzig: Karl Baedeker, 1878.

———. *Northern Italy Including Leghorn, Florence, Ravenna, the Island of Corsica and Routes Through France, Switzerland and Austria*, 7th remodeled ed. Leipzig: Karl Baedeker, 1886.

———. *Paris and its Environs, with Routes From London to Paris, and From Paris to the Rhine and Switzerland: Handbook for Travellers*, 4th ed. Remodeled and augmented. Leipzig: Karl Baedeker, 1874.

———. *Southern Italy and Sicily*, 9th rev. ed. Leipzig: Karl Baedeker, 1887.

Barnstone, Tony and Chou Ping. *The Anchor Book of Chinese Poetry*. New York: Anchor Books, 2004.

Bell, William Morrison. *Other Countries*, 2 vols. London: Chapman and Hall, 1872.

Bible. O.T. *Jiu yue quan shu* 舊約全書, 7 vols. Hong Kong: Yinghua Shuyuan 英華書院, 1864–1865.

Bin Chun 斌椿. "Cheng cha bi ji" 乘槎笔记. In Zhong Shuhe 钟叔河 and Gu Jishe 谷及世, eds., *Cheng cha bi ji wai yi zhong* 乘

槎笔记：外一种. Changsha: Hunan Renmin Chubanshe 湖南人民出版社, 1981.

———. *Jōsa hikki* 乘槎筆記, punctuated and annotated Japanese edition. Eds. Shigeno Yasutsugu (Seisai) 重野安繹 (成齋) and Ōtsuki Seishi (Tōyō) 大槻誠之 (東陽). Tokyo: Fukuroya Kamejirō 袋屋龜次郎, 1872.

Birrell, Anne. *New Songs From a Jade Terrace*. Harmondsworth: Penguin Books, 1986.

"A Block of Gold." *Catholic World* 18 (1874): 855–856.

Bolitho, Harold. "The Tempō Crisis." In Marius B. Jansen, ed., *The Cambridge History of Japan Volume 5: The Nineteenth Century*, 116–167. New York: Cambridge University Press, 1989.

Burton, Richard F., trans. *Plantains in the Rain: Selected Chinese Poems of Du Mu*. London: Wellsweep Press, 1990.

Campbell, Robert ロバート　キャンベル. "Tenpōki zengo no shogakai" 天保期前後の書画会. *Kinsei bungei* 近世文芸 47 (November 1987): 47–72.

———. "Yomikaki no fūkei" 読み書きの風景. In *Koten Nihongo no sekai: kanji ga tsukuru Nihon* 古典日本語の世界：漢字がつくる日本, 217–240. Tokyo: Tōkyō Daigaku Shuppankai 東京大学出版会, 2007.

Chan, Wing-Tsit. *A Sourcebook in Chinese Philosophy*. Princeton: Princeton University Press, 1963.

Chinpunkan Shujin 陳奮館主人, pseudonym of Kita Sōichirō 喜多壯一郎. *Edo no geisha* 江戸の芸者. Tokyo: Chūō Kōronsha, 1989. [Originally published 1948.]

Collcutt, Martin. "Buddhism: The Threat of Eradication." In Marius B. Jansen and Gilbert Rozman, eds., *Japan in Transition: From Tokugawa to Meiji*, 143–167. Princeton: Princeton University Press, 1986.

Cooper, Arthur. *Li Po and Tu Fu*. Harmondsworth: Penguin Books, 1973.

Dalby, Liza. *Geisha*. Berkeley: University of California Press, 1983, 1998.

DeBecker, J. E. *The Nightless City: or the History of the Yoshiwara Yūkwaku*, 5th ed., rev. Rutland, VT: Charles E. Tuttle, 1971. [Originally published 1899, rev. 1905.]

Downer, Lesley. *Madame Sadayakko: The Geisha Who Bewitched the West*. New York: Gotham Books, 2003.

———. *Women of the Pleasure Quarters: The Secret History of the Geisha*. New York: Broadway Books, 2001.

Ebihara Hachirō 蛯原八郎. *Kaigai hōji shinbun zasshishi* 海外邦字新聞雑誌史. Reprinted with *Kaigai hōjin gaiji shinbun zasshishi* 海外邦人外字新聞雑誌史. Tokyo: Meicho Fukyūkai 名著普及会, 1980. [Originally published 1936.]

Endō Shizuo 遠藤鎮雄. *Kanbun bunkaron* 漢文文化論. Tokyo: San'ichi Shobō 三一書房, 1973.

Fessler, Susanna. *Musashino in Tuscany: Japanese Overseas Travel Literature, 1860–1912*. Ann Arbor: Center for Japanese Studies, University of Michigan, 2004.

Fogel, Joshua. *The Cultural Dimension of Sino-Japanese Relations: Essays on the Nineteenth and Twentieth Centuries*. Armonk, NY: M. E. Sharpe, 1994.

Foreman, Kelly M. "Bad Girls Confined: Okuni, Geisha, and the Negotiation of Female Performance Space." In Laura Miller and Jan Bardsley, eds., *Bad Girls of Japan*, 33–47. New York: Palgrave Macmillan, 2005.

———. *The Gei of Geisha: Music, Identity and Meaning*. Burlington, VT: Ashgate, 2008.

Fraleigh, Matthew マシュー・フレーリ. "Kōsei no Tōdō Shujin: Narushima Ryūhoku *Kōsei nichijō* to sore izen no kaigai kikōbun" 航西の東道主人―成島柳北「航西日乗」とそれ以前の海外紀行文. *Kyōto Daigaku kokubungaku ronsō* 京都大学国文学論叢 8 (2002): 64–92.

———. "Narushima Ryūhoku no yōkō: *Kōsei nichijō* no shokontekusuto" 成島柳北の洋行―「航西日乗」の諸コンテクスト. *Kokugo kokubun* 國語國文 71.11 (2002): 1–55.

———. "Ryūhoku (Narushima Ryūhoku)." In Jay Rubin, ed., *Modern Japanese Writers*, 313–330. New York: Scribners, 2001.

———. "The Fire Guard and the Hired Bard: Narushima Ryūhoku's parodic journalism." In Joshua Mostow and Sharalyn Orbaugh, eds., *Parody (PAJLS* 10): 17–31. West Lafayette, IN: Association for Japanese Literary Studies, 2009.

Fuchibe Tokuzō 淵邊德蔵. "Ōkō nikki" 歐行日記. In Nihon Shiseki Kyōkai 日本史籍協会, ed., *Kengai shisetsu nikki sanshū III* 遣外使節日記纂輯三, *Nihon shiseki kyōkai sōsho* 日本史籍協会叢書, vol. 98. Tokyo: Tōkyō Daigaku Shuppankai, 1987. [Originally published 1930.]

Fujii Tetsuhiro 藤井哲博. *Kanrinmaru kōkaichō Ono Tomogorō no shōgai: bakumatsu Meiji no tekunokurāto* 咸臨丸航海長小野友五郎

の生涯:幕末明治のテクノクラート. Tokyo: Chūō Kōronsha, 1985.

Fukuchi Gen'ichirō (Ōchi) 福地源一郎 (櫻痴). *Kaiō jidan* 懐往時談. In Yanagida Izumi 柳田泉, ed., *Fukuchi Ōchi shū* 福地櫻痴集, *Meiji bungaku zenshū* 明治文学全集, vol. 11, 264–324. Tokyo: Chikuma shobō, 1966.

Fukui Tatsuhiko 福井辰彦. "Aru jusha no bakumatsu: Kikuchi Sankei den shōkō" ある儒者の幕末:菊池三渓伝小攷. *Ronkyū Nihon bungaku* 論究日本文學 89 (December 2008): 1–13.

Fukuzawa Yukichi. *The Autobiography of Yukichi Fukuzawa*. Trans. Kiyooka Eiichi. New York: Columbia University Press, 1966.

Funakoshi Masaki 船越真樹. "Ogasawara shotō ni okeru ginnemu hayashi no seiritsu: inyū to bunpu no kakudai o meguru oboegaki, sono 4" 小笠原諸島におけるギンネム林の成立−移入と分布の拡大をめぐる覚え書−その 4. *Ogasawara Kenkyū nenpō* 小笠原研究年報 14 (1991): 21–51.

Guth, Christine. *Longfellow's Tattoos: Tourism, Collecting, and Japan*. Seattle: University of Washington Press, 2004.

Haeckel, Ernst. *A Visit to Ceylon*. Trans. Clara Bell, 2nd American ed. Boston: S. E. Cassino, 1883.

Haga Tōru 芳賀徹. *Taikun no shisetsu: bakumatsu Nihonjin no seiō taiken* 大君の使節:幕末日本人の西欧体験. Tokyo: Chūō Kōronsha, 1968.

Hawkes, David, trans. *The Songs of the South: An Ancient Chinese Anthology of Poems*. New York: Penguin, 1985.

Hikawa Naoya 飛川直也. *Shinjuku Nichōme urisen bōizu* 新宿二丁目ウリセン・ボーイズ. Tokyo: Kawade Shobō Shinsha 河出書房新社, 2006.

———. *Shinjuku Nichōme Urisen monogatari* 新宿二丁目ウリセン物語. Tokyo: Kawade Shobō Shinsha 河出書房新社, 2004.

Hinton, David, trans. *The selected poems of Li Po*. New York: New Directions, 1996.

Huffman, James L. *Politics of the Meiji Press: the Life of Fukuchi Gen'ichirō*. Honolulu: University of Hawai'i Press, 1980.

Imai Ichiryō 今井一良. "Sano Kanae no Eigaku to Tommy Tateishi Onojirō no koto" 佐野鼎の英学と Tommy・立石斧次郎のこと. *Eigakushi kenkyū* 英学史研究 15 (1982): 15–32.

Imaizumi Mine 今泉みね. *Nagori no yume: Ran'i Katsuragawa-ke ni umarete* 名ごりの夢：蘭医桂川家に生れて. Tokyo: Heibonsha 平凡社, 1963.

Imamura Eitarō 今村栄太郎. "Narushima Ryūhoku shōkō" 成島柳北小攷. Serialized in six parts in *Nihon kosho tsūshin* 日本古書通信, 42.9 (1977)–43.2 (1978).

Inoue Kowashi 井上毅. "To-Ō nikki" 渡歐日記. In Inoue Kowashi Denki Hensan Iinkai 井上毅傳記編纂委員會, ed., *Inoue Kowashi den* 井上毅傳, vol. 5, 333–342. Tokyo: Kokugakuin Daigaku Toshokan 國學院大學圖書館, 1966.

Inui Teruo 乾照夫. *Narushima Ryūhoku kenkyū* 成島柳北研究. Tokyo: Perikansha ぺりかん社, 2003.

Inuzuka Takaaki 犬塚孝明 and Ishiguro Keishō 石黒敬章. *Meiji no wakaki gunzō: Mori Arinori kyūzō arubamu* 明治の若き群像：森有礼旧蔵アルバム. Tokyo: Heibonsha, 2006.

Itō Hiroshi 伊藤博. *Kōhii hakubutsushi* コーヒー博物誌, new ed. Tokyo: Yasaka Shobō 八坂書房, 2001.

Iwasaki Mineko [岩崎峰子] with Rande Brown. *Geisha, a Life*. New York: Atria Books, 2002.

Iwashita Tetsunori 岩下哲典. *Edo no Naporeon densetsu: seiyō eiyū wa dō yomaretaka* 江戸のナポレオン伝説：西洋英雄伝はどう読まれたか. Tokyo: Chūō Kōronsha, 1999.

Izumi Saburō 泉三郎. *Beiō Kairan hyakunijūnen no tabi: Iwakura Shisetsudan no ashiato o otte* 「米欧回覧」百二十年の旅：岩倉使節団の足跡を追って, 2 vols. Tokyo: Tosho Shuppansha 図書出版社, 1993.

Jiromaru Kenzō 治郎丸憲三. *Mitsukuri Shūhei to sono shūhen*. 箕作秋坪とその周辺. Kume, Okayama: Mitsukuri Shūhei Denki Kankōkai 箕作秋坪伝記刊行会, 1970.

Kakuyūkai 鶴友会, ed. *Ōkura Kakugen'ō* 大倉鶴彦翁. Reprinted in *Kindai Nihon kigyōka den sōsho* 近代日本企業家伝叢書, vol. 8. Tokyo: Ōzorasha 大空社, 1998. [Originally published 1924.]

Kamei Hideo 亀井秀雄. *Kansei no henkaku* 感性の変革. Tokyo: Kōdansha, 1983.

———. *Transformations of Sensibility: The Phenomenology of Meiji Literature*. Trans. by Michael Bourdaghs et al. Ann Arbor: Center for Japanese Studies, 2002.

Kanai Madoka 金井圓. *Tomii to iu na no Nihonjin: Nichi-bei Shūkō shiwa* トミーという名の日本人：日米修好史話. Tokyo: Bun'ichi Sōgō Shuppan 文一総合出版, 1979.

Kanda Kiichirō 神田喜一郎, ed. *Meiji kanshibunshū* 明治漢詩文集. Vol. 62 of *Meiji bungaku zenshū* 明治文学全集. Tokyo: Chikuma Shobō, 1983.

Kano Hisatsune 鹿野久恒, ed. *Kessō Ishikawa Shuntai Genkōroku* 傑僧石川舜台言行録. Kanazawa: Bukkyō Bunka Kyōkai 佛教文化教會, 1951.

Kasumi Nobuhiko 霞信彦. *Nori o koete: Meiji hōseishi danshō* 矩を踰えて：明治法制史断章. Tokyo: Keiō Gijuku Daigaku Shuppankai 慶應義塾大学出版会, 2007.

Kataoka Takaaki 潟岡孝昭. "Meiji shonen ni okeru Higashi Honganji Hon'yakukyoku" 明治初年に於ける東本願寺翻訳局. *Shiritsu Daigaku Toshokan Kyōkai Kaihō* 私立大学図書館協会会報 36 (1962): 11–26.

———. "Narushima Ryūhoku no hon'yakukyoku jidai: shiryō honkoku *Hon'yakukyoku zakki*" 成島柳北の翻訳局時代：資料翻刻「翻訳局雑記」. *Obihiro Ōtani Tanki Daigaku kiyō* 帯広大谷短期大学紀要 2 (March 1963): 103–115.

Kawaguchi Hisao 川口久雄, ed. *Bakumatsu Meiji kaigai taiken shishū: Kaishū Keiu yori Ōgai Sōseki ni itaru* 幕末明治海外体験詩集：海舟・敬宇より鴎外・漱石にいたる. Tokyo: Daitō Bunka Daigaku Tōyō Kenkyūsho 大東文化大学東洋研究所, 1984.

Keene, Donald. "The First Japanese Tourist in Italy." In Adriana Boscaro and Maurizio Bossi, eds., *Firenze, il Giappone e l'Asia orientale: Atti del convegno internazionale di studi, Firenze, 25–27 marzo 1999*, 219–230. Firenze: Leo S. Olschki, 2001.

Ketelaar, James Edward. *Of Heretics and Martyrs in Meiji Japan: Buddhism and Its Persecution*. Princeton: Princeton University Press, 1990.

Kido Takayoshi. *The Diary of Kido Takayoshi*, 3 vols. Trans. Sidney Devere Brown and Akiko Hirota. Tokyo: University of Tokyo Press, 1983–1986.

Kitagawa Morisada 喜田川守貞. In Usami Hideki 宇佐美英機, ed., *Kinsei fūzokushi: Morisada mankō* 近世風俗志：守貞謾稿, 5 vols. Tokyo: Iwanami Shoten, 1996–2002.

Knapp, Raymond. *The American Musical and the Formation of National Identity*. Princeton: Princeton University Press, 2004.

Kojima Noriyuki 小島憲之. *Kotoba no omomi: Ōgai no nazo o toku kango* ことばの重み―鷗外の謎を解く漢語. Tokyo: Shinchōsha 新潮社, 1984.

Kokumai Shigeyuki. 國米重行. *Ānesuto Satō to Noguchi Tomizō* アーネスト・サトウと野口富蔵. Itami: Kokumai Shigeyuki, 2000.

Kornicki, Peter. *The Book in Japan: A Cultural History from the Beginnings to the Nineteenth Century*. Honolulu: University of Hawai'i Press, 2001.

Koyama Noboru 小山騰. *Hatenkō: Meiji ryūgakusei retsuden Daiei Teikoku ni mananda hitobito* 破天荒〈明治留学生列伝〉大英帝国に学んだ人々. Tokyo: Kōdansha, 1999.

———. "James Summers, 1828–91: Early Sinologist and Pioneer of Japanese Newspapers in London and English Literature in Japan." In J. E. Hoare, ed., *Britain & Japan: Biographical Portraits*, vol. 3, 25–37. Richmond, Surrey: Japan Library, 1999.

———. "The Opening of Japan and Tours around the World: An English Travel Diary (1873) and Photographs." Presentation given at EAJRS Conference, Prague, 2000.

Kume Kunitake 久米邦武. *The Iwakura Embassy, 1871–73: A True Account of the Ambassador Extraordinary & Plenipotentiary's Journey of Observation Through the United States of America and Europe*, 5 vols. Ed. Graham Healey, Chushichi Tsuzuki, et al. Matsudo: The Japan Documents, 2002.

———. *Tokumei zenken taishi Bei-ō kairan jikki* 特命全権大使米欧回覧実記, 5 vols. Ed. Tanaka Akira 田中彰. Tokyo: Iwanami Shoten, 1977–1982.

Kuniyoshi Sakae 国吉栄. *Seki Shinzō to kindai Nihon no reimei: Nihon yōchien shi josetsu* 関信三と近代日本の黎明：日本幼稚園史序説. Tokyo: Shin Dokushosha 新読書社, 2005.

Kyōto Furitsu Sōgō Shiryōkan 京都府立総合資料館, ed. *Shōkō-hen* 商工編, vol. 2 of *Kyōto-fu hyakunen no nenpyō* 京都府百年の年表. Kyoto: Kyoto-fu, 1970.

Laidlaw, Christine Wallace, ed. *Charles Appleton Longfellow: Twenty Months in Japan, 1871–1873*. Cambridge, MA: Friends of the Longfellow House, 1998.

Lanfant, Jean. *Historique de la flotte des Messageries maritimes, 1851–1975*. Cholet: Hérault, 1997.

Lau, D. C., trans. *The Analects*. Harmondsworth: Penguin, 1979.

———. *Mencius*. Harmondsworth: Penguin, 1970.

Legge, James, trans. *The Chinese Classics*, 5 vols. Hong Kong: Hong Kong University Press, 1960.

Levy, Howard S., trans. *A Feast of Mist and Flowers: The Gay Quarters of Nanking at the End of the Ming*. Yokohama: Howard S. Levy, 1966.

Lloyd's Register of British and Foreign Shipping from 1ˢᵗ July, 1875, to the 30ᵗʰ June, 1876. London: Wyman and Sons, 1875. [Reprinted edition published in London: Gregg Press Limited, 1964.]

Lynn, Richard John. *The Classic of Changes: A New Translation of the I Ching as Interpreted by Wang Bi*. New York: Columbia University Press, 1994.

———. "Huang Zunxian (1848–1905) and His Association with Meiji Era Japanese Literati (Bunjin 文人)." *Japan Review* 15 (2003): 101–125.

Maeda Ai 前田愛. *Bakumatsu, ishinki no bungaku* 幕末・維新期の文学. Tokyo: Hōsei Daigaku Shuppankyoku 法政大学出版局, 1972.

———. *Narushima Ryūhoku* 成島柳北. Tokyo: Asahi Shinbunsha 朝日新聞社, 1976.

———. "Narushima Ryūhoku no nikki" 成島柳北の日記. *Bungaku* 文学. Part One: 43.2 (Feb. 1975): 109–120; Part Two: 43.3 (Mar. 1975): 53–63.

———. "Ryūhoku *Kōsei nichijō* no genkei" 柳北「航西日乗」の原型. In *Kindai Nihon no bungaku kūkan: rekishi, kotoba, jōkyō* 近代日本の文学空間：歴史・ことば・状況, 69–87. Tokyo: Shin'yōsha 新曜社, 1983.

———. *Text and the City: Essays on Japanese Modernity*. Ed. James Fujii. Durham, NC: Duke University Press, 2004.

Mair, Victor, ed. *The Columbia Anthology of Traditional Chinese Literature.* New York: Columbia University Press, 1994.

Mair, Victor, trans. *Wandering on the Way: Early Taoist Tales and Parables of Chuang Tzu.* Honolulu: University of Hawai'i Press, 1998.

Manzella, Domenico and Emilio Pozzi. *I Teatri di Milano.* Milano: Mursia, 1971.

Markus, Andrew. "*Shogakai*: Celebrity Banquets of the Late Edo Period." *Harvard Journal of Asiatic Studies* 53.1 (June 1993): 135–168.

Masuda Sayo 増田小夜. *Autobiography of a Geisha.* Trans. G. G. Rowley. New York: Columbia University Press, 2003.

———. *Geisha: kutō no hanshōgai* 芸者苦闘の半生涯. Tokyo: Heibonsha, 1973.

Masuda Takashi 益田孝. *Jijo Masuda Takashi ō den* 自叙益田孝翁伝. Ed. Nagai Minoru 長井実. Tokyo: Chūō Kōronsha, 1989. [Originally published 1939.]

Mather, Richard, trans. *Shih-shuo hsin-yü: A New Account of Tales of the World*, 2nd ed. Ann Arbor: Center for Chinese Studies, University of Michigan, 2002.

Matsumoto Hakka 松本白華. "Matsumoto Hakka Kōkairoku" 松本白華航海録. In Kashiwara Yūsen 柏原祐泉, ed., *Ishinki no shinshū* 維新期の真宗, *Shinshū shiryō shūsei* 真宗資料集成, vol. 11, 371–416. Kyoto: Dōhōsha Shuppan 同朋舎出版, 1983.

———. "Matsumoto Hakka Kōkairoku" 松本白華航海録, transcribed by Tokushige Asakichi 徳重淺吉. Kyoto: Tōrin Shobō 東林書房, 1932.

Mayo, Marlene. "The Western Education of Kume Kunitake: 1871–6." *Monumenta Nipponica* 28.1 (Spring 1973): 3–67.

McCullough, Helen Craig, Trans. *The Tale of the Heike*. Stanford: Stanford University Press, 1988.

Medzini, Meron. *French Policy in Japan During the Closing Years of the Tokugawa Regime*. Cambridge, MA: Harvard East Asian Monographs, 1971.

Meiji Ōsaka Heigakuryō Futsukoku Ryūgakuseishi Kenkyūkai 明治大坂兵学寮仏国留学生史研究会, ed. *Nichu-Futsu kōryū reimeiki no kaimei: Ōsaka heigakuryō daiikki ryūgakusei to Furansugo kyōshi Sharuru Byuran no sokuseki to kōseki* 日仏交流黎明期の解明：大坂兵学寮第一期留学生とフランス語教師シャルル・ビュランの足跡と行績. [Tokyo]: Meiji Ōsaka Heigakuryō Futsukoku Ryūgakusei Kenkyūkai 明治大坂兵学寮仏国留学生史研究会, 2006.

Mertz, John Pierre. *Novel Japan: Spaces of Nationhood in Early Meiji Narrative, 1870–88*. Ann Arbor: Center for Japanese Studies, 2003.

Minford, John and Joseph S. M. Lau. *Classical Chinese Literature: An Anthology of Translations*. New York: Columbia University Press, 2000.

Mitsui Ginkō Hachijūnenshi Hensan Iinkai 三井銀行八十年史編纂委員会. *Mitsui Ginkō hachijūnenshi* 三井銀行八十年史. Tokyo: Mitsui Ginkō 三井銀行, 1957.

Mitsui Hachirōemon Takamune Den Hensan Iinkai 三井八郎右衛門高棟伝編纂委員会, ed. *Mitsui Hachirōemon Takamune den* 三

井八郎右衛門高棟伝. Tokyo: Mitsui Bunko 三井文庫, 1988.

Miyachi Masato 宮地正人 and Matsudo-shi Kyōiku Iinkai 松戸市教育委員会, eds. *Tokugawa Akitake bakumatsu taiō nikki* 徳川昭武幕末滞欧日記. Tokyo: Yamakawa Shuppan 山川出版社, 1999.

Miyamoto Mataji 宮元又次. *Onogumi no kenkyū* 小野組の研究, 4 vols. Tokyo: Shinseisha 新生社, 1970–1977.

Miyanaga Takashi 宮永孝. *Keiō ninen bakufu Igirisu ryūgakusei* 慶応二年幕府イギリス留学生. Tokyo: Shinjinbutsu Ōraisha, 1994.

———. *Man'en gannen no Amerika hōkoku* 万延元年のアメリカ報告. Tokyo: Shinchōsha, 1990.

Miyazaki Tomihachi 宮崎十三八. *Aizujin no kaku Boshin sensō* 会津人の書く戊辰戦争. Tokyo: Kōbunsha 恒文社, 1993.

Miyoshi, Masao. *As We Saw Them: The First Japanese Embassy to the United States (1860)*. Berkeley: University of California Press, 1979.

Mochizuki Yōko 望月洋子. *Hebon no shōgai to Nihongo* ヘボンの生涯と日本語. Tokyo: Shinchōsha, 1987.

Mori Ōgai 森鷗外. *Ōgai zenshū* 鷗外全集, 38 vols. Tokyo: Iwanami Shoten, 1971–1975.

Mori Shuntō 森春涛, ed. *Tōkyō saijin zekku* 東京才人絶句, 2 vols. Tokyo: Nukada Shōzaburō 額田正三郎, 1875.

Murata Fumio 村田文夫. *Seiyō bunkenroku* 西洋聞見録. In Asakura Haruhiko 朝倉治彦, ed., *Meiji Ōbei kenbunroku shūsei* 明治欧米見聞録集成, vol. 1. Tokyo: Yumani shobō, 1987. [Originally published 1869.]

———. *Seiyō bunkenroku* 西洋聞見録. In *Gaikoku bunka hen* 外國文化篇, *Meiji bunka zenshū* 明治文化全集, rev. ed., vol. 7, 189–276. Tokyo: Nihon Hyōron Shinsha, 1955. [Originally published 1869, and in this edition 1928.]

Murray, John. *A Handbook for Visitors to Paris; Containing a Description of the Most Remarkable Objects, with General Advice and Information for English Travellers in That Metropolis, and on the Way to It*, 6th ed., rev. London: John Murray, 1874.

Nagai Hiroo 永井啓夫. *Terakado Seiken* 寺門静軒. Tokyo: Risōsha 理想社, 1966.

Nagai Kafū 永井荷風. "Narushima Ryūhoku no nisshi" 成嶋柳北の日誌. *Kafū zenshū* 荷風全集, vol. 16, 267–281. Tokyo: Iwanami Shoten, 1964. [Originally published 1927.]

———. "Ryūkyō shinshi ni tsukite" 柳橋新誌につきて. *Kafū zenshū*, vol. 16, 283–292. [Originally published 1927.]

———. *Shitaya sōwa* 下谷叢話. Tokyo: Iwanami Shoten, 2000. [Originally published 1924–1926.]

Nagai Kikue 永井菊枝. *Shōden Okkotsu-ke no rekishi: Edo kara Meiji e* 小伝乙骨家の歴史：江戸から明治へ. Musashino: Firia フィリア, 2006.

Nakai Eriko 中井えり子. "*Kankyo Futsuwa jiten* to Okada Yoshiki o megutte." 『官許佛和辭典』と岡田好樹をめぐって. *Nagoya Daigaku Fuzoku Toshokan kenkyū nenpō* 名古屋大学附属図書館研究年報 6 (2007): 47–62.

Nakai Hiroshi (Ōshū) 中井弘（櫻洲）. *Man'yū kitei* 漫遊記程. In *Gaikoku bunka hen* 外國文化篇, *Meiji bunka zenshū* 明治文化全集, rev. ed., vol. 7, 299–346. Tokyo: Nihon Hyōron

Shinsha 日本評論新社, 1955. [Originally published 1877, and in this edition 1928.]

Nakamura Kōsuke 中村洪介. "Ishinki Nihonjin no yōgaku taiken: Kume Kunitake hen *Tokumei zenken taishi Beiō kairan jikki* to Narushima Ryūhoku *Kōsei nichijō* o chūshin ni" 維新期日本人の洋楽体験：久米邦武編『特命全権大使米欧回覧実記』と成島柳北『航西日乗』を中心に. *Hikaku bunka* 比較文化 4 (Summer 1987): 69–110.

Nakamura Shikaku 中村芝鶴. *Yūkaku no sekai: Shin Yoshiwara no omoide* 遊廓の世界：新吉原の想い出. Tokyo: Hyōronsha 評論社, 1976.

Nakao Tatsurō 中尾達郎. *Edo Sumidagawa kaiwai* 江戸隅田川界隈. Tokyo: Miyai Shoten 三弥井書店, 1996.

Naramoto Tatsuya 奈良本辰也 and Momose Meiji 百瀬明治. *Meiji ishin no Higashi Honganji* 明治維新の東本願寺. Tokyo: Kawade shobō 河出書房, 1987.

Narushima Ryūhoku 成島柳北. *Kenhoku nichiroku: Narushima Ryūhoku nikki* 硯北日録：成島柳北日記. Ed. Maeda Ai 前田愛. Tokyo: Taihei shooku 太平書屋, 1997.

———. "Meiji gonen Ryūō yōkō kaikeiroku" 明治五年柳翁洋行會計録. In *Gaikoku bunka hen* 外国文化篇, *Meiji bunka zenshū* 明治文化全集, vol. 17, 443–451. Tokyo: Nihon hyōronsha 日本評論社, 1992.

———. *Ryūhoku shishō* 柳北詩鈔. Ed. Ōhashi Shintarō 大橋新太郎. Tokyo: Hakubunkan 博文館, 1894.

———. *Ryūhoku zenshū* 柳北全集. Tokyo: Hakubunkan, 1897.

Niina Noriko 新稲法子. *Hanjōkimono no kenkyū* 繁昌記ものの研究. Ph.D. dissertation, Osaka University, 1998.

Nishimura-ō Denki Hensankai 西村翁伝記編纂会, ed. *Nishimura Katsuzō'ō den* 西村勝三翁伝傳. Reprinted in vol. 6 of *Kindai Nihon kigyōka den sōsho* 近代日本企業家伝叢書. Tokyo: Ōzorasha 大空社, 1998.

Nishino Yoshiaki 西野嘉章 and Christian Polak クリスティアン・ポラック. *Ishin to Furansu: Nichi-Futsu gakujutsu kōryū no reimei* 維新とフランス：日仏学術交流の黎明. Tokyo: Tokyo Daigaku Sōgō Kenkyū Hakubutsukan 東京大学総合研究博物館, 2009.

Nozaki Sabun 野崎左文. *Watakushi no mita Meiji bundan* 私の見た明治文壇. In Hiraoka Toshio 平岡敏夫, et al., eds., *Meiji Taishō bungakushi shūsei furoku 1* 明治大正文学史集成付録１. Tokyo: Nihon Tosho Sentā 日本図書センター, 1982. [Originally published 1927.]

O'Brien, Suzanne G. "Splitting Hairs: History and the Politics of Daily Life in Nineteenth-Century Japan." *Journal of Asian Studies* 67.4 (November 2008): 1309–1339.

Oda Kenshin 織田顕信. "Wagakuni yōchien kyōiku no senkakusha: Ankyūji Yūryū (besshō Andō Ryūtarō Seki Shinzō) denkō" 我国幼稚園教育の先覚者 安休寺猶龍 (別称 安藤劉太郎 関信三)伝攷. *Dōhō Daigaku ronsō* 同朋大学論叢 37 (December 1972): 55–84.

Ōkubo Toshiaki 大久保利謙. *Iwakura shisetsu no kenkyū* 岩倉使節の研究. Tokyo: Munetaka Shobō 宗高書房, 1976.

Ōno Mitsutsugi 大野光次. "Gaiyūgo no Narushima Ryūhoku" 外遊後の成島柳北. *Kokugo to kokubungaku* 国語と国文学 12.5 (May 1935).

Ōshima Ryūichi 大島隆一. *Ryūhoku dansō* 柳北談叢. Tokyo: Shōwa Kankōkai 昭和刊行会, 1943.

Owen, Stephen. *An Anthology of Chinese Literature: Beginnings to 1911.* New York: Norton, 1996.

———. *The End of the Chinese Middle Ages: Essays in Mid-Tang Literary Culture.* Stanford, CA: Stanford University Press, 1996.

Pastreich, Emanuel. "The Pleasure Quarters of Edo and Nanjing as Metaphor: The Records of Yu Huai and Narushima Ryūhoku." *Monumenta Nipponica* 55.2 (2000): 199–224.

———. *The Reception of Chinese Vernacular Narrative in Korea and Japan.* Ph.D. dissertation, Harvard University, 1997.

Pflugfelder, Gregory M. *Cartographies of Desire: Male-Male Sexuality in Japanese Discourse, 1600-1950.* Berkeley: University of California Press, 1999.

Pyle, Kenneth. *The New Generation in Meiji Japan: Problems of Cultural Identity, 1885–1895.* Stanford: Stanford University Press, 1969.

Rimer, J. Thomas, ed. *Not a Song Like Any Other: An Anthology of Writings by Mori Ōgai.* Honolulu: University of Hawai'i Press, 2004.

Rosny, Léon de. *Cours Pratique de Langue Japonaise.* Paris: Ernest Leroux, 1903.

Rouzer, Paul F. *Articulated Ladies: Gender and the Male Community in Early Chinese Texts.* Cambridge, MA: Harvard University Asia Center, 2001.

Saitō Mareshi 齋藤希史. *Kanbunmyaku no kindai: Shinmatsu Meiji no bungakuken* 漢文脈の近代－清末＝明治の文学圏. Nagoya: Nagoya Daigaku Shuppankai 名古屋大学出版会, 2005.

———. *Kanbunmyaku to kindai Nihon: mō hitotsu no kotoba no sekai* 漢文脈と近代日本：もう一つのことばの世界. Tokyo: NHK Books, 2007.

Saitō Shōzō 斎藤昌三. *Gendai hikka bunken dainenpyō* 現代筆禍文献大年表. 1932. Reprinted as vol. 2 of *Saitō Shōzō chosakushū* 斎藤昌三著作集. Tokyo: Yashio Shoten 八潮書店, 1980.

Sameshima Monjo Kenkyūkai 鮫島文書研究会. *Sameshima Naonobu zaiō gaikō shokanroku* 鮫島尚信在欧外交書簡録. Kyoto: Shibunkaku Shuppan 思文閣出版, 2002.

Sanetō Keishū 実藤恵秀. *Ōkōchi bunsho: Meiji Nitchū bunkajin no kōyū* 大河内文書：明治日中文化人の交遊. Tokyo: Heibonsha, 1964.

Satow, Ernest. *A Diplomat in Japan: the Inner History of the Critical Years in the Evolution of Japan When the Ports Were Opened and the Monarchy Restored, Recorded by a Diplomatist Who Took an Active Part in the Events of the Time, with an Account of His Personal Experiences During That Period*. Berkeley: Stone Bridge Press, 2006.

Sawa Mamoru 澤護. *Oyatoi Furansujin no kenkyū* お雇いフランス人の研究. Chiba: Keiai Daigaku Keizai Bunka Kenkyūjo 敬愛大学経済文化研究所, 1991.

Screech, Timon. "Going to the Courtesans: Transit to the Pleasure District of Edo Japan." In Martha Feldman and Bonnie

Gordon, eds., *The Courtesan's Arts: Cross-Cultural Perspectives*, 255–279. Oxford: Oxford University Press, 2006.

Seigle, Cecilia Segawa. *Yoshiwara: The Glittering World of the Japanese Courtesan.* Honolulu: University of Hawai'i Press, 1993.

Seigle, Cecilia Segawa, et al. *A Courtesan's Day: Hour By Hour.* Amsterdam: Hotei Publishing, 2004.

Seki Sekkō 関雪江. *Sekkō sensei harimaze* 雪江先生貼雑, 2 vols. Ed. Robert Campbell. Tokyo: Kokuritsu Kōbunshokan Naikaku Bunko 国立公文書館内閣文庫, 1997.

Shibusawa Eiichi 渋沢栄一 (Seien Gyoho 青淵漁夫) and Sugiura Yuzuru 杉浦譲 (Aisan Shōsha 靄山樵者). *Kōsei nikki* 航西日記, 6 vols. Tokyo: Taikan Dōsha 耐寒同社, 1871.

Shimaji Mokurai 島地黙雷. *Kōsei nissaku* 航西日策. In Futaba Kenkō 二葉憲香 and Fukushima Kanryū 福嶋寛隆, eds., *Shimaji Mokurai zenshū* 島地黙雷全集, vol. 5, 19–114. Kyoto: Honganji Shuppanbu 本願寺出版部, 1978.

Shimamura Teru 島村輝. "Pari o mita Nihonjin/Nihonjin o mita Pari: Narushima Ryūhoku to Kurimoto Joun" パリを見た日本人／日本人の見たパリ―成島柳北と栗本鋤雲. *Joshi Bijutsu Daigaku kiyō* 女子美術大学紀要 27 (1997): 107–117.

Shioda Ryōhei 塩田良平. "Kaidai" 解題. In Narushima Ryūhoku 成島柳北, *Ryūkyō shinshi* 柳橋新誌, 93–101. Tokyo: Iwanami Shoten, 1940.

———. "Ryūkyō shinshi zenpen no genkei ni tsuite" 柳橋新誌前編の原形に就いて. *Bungaku* 9.8 (1941): 57–66.

Shirane, Haruo. *Early Modern Japanese Literature: An Anthology, 1600–1900.* New York: Columbia University Press, 2002.

———. "Lyricism and Intertextuality: An Approach to Shunzei's Poetics." *Harvard Journal of Asiatic Studies* 50.1 (1990): 71–85.

Société d'Ethnographie. *Annuaire de la Société d'Ethnographie.* Paris: La Société, 1875.

Strassberg, Richard E. *Inscribed Landscapes: Travel Writing from Imperial China.* Berkeley: University of California Press, 1994.

Sugi Magoshichirō (Chōka) 杉孫七郎 (重華). *Kankai shishi* 環海詩誌. [Tokyo]: Sugi Chōka, 1904.

Sunagawa Yukio 砂川幸雄. *Ōkura Kihachirō no gōkai naru shōgai* 大倉喜八郎の豪快なる生涯. Tokyo: Sōshisha 草思社, 1996.

Suzuki Akira 鈴木明. *Tsuiseki: ichimai no bakumatsu shashin* 追跡：一枚の幕末写真. Tokyo: Shūeisha, 1984.

Swinton, Elizabeth da Sabato. *The Women of the Pleasure Quarter: Japanese Paintings of the Floating World.* New York: Hudson Hills, 1995.

Takahata Takamichi 高畑崇導. "Ishikawa Shuntai: 1842–1931 Tenpō 13–Shōwa 6: sono sonzai shōmei no toki" 石川舜台<1842〜1931 天保 13〜昭和 6>その存在証明の時. *Hokuriku shūkyō bunka* 北陸宗教文化 12 (2000): 23–37.

Takasaki Masakaze 高崎正風. "Zaigai nikki" 在外日記. In Kitasato Takeshi 北里闌, ed., *Takasaki Masakaze sensei denki* 高崎正風先生伝記, 261–362. Kobe: Keibunsha Insatsu Kōgyō 啓文社印刷工業, 1959.

Tanabe Taichi 田辺太一. *Bakumatsu gaikōdan* 幕末外交談. Ed. Sakata Seiichi 坂田精一. Tokyo: Heibonsha, 1966. 2 vols. [Originally published 1898.]

Tanaka Akira 田中彰. *Iwakura Shisetsudan "Beiō Kairan Jikki"* 岩倉使節団『米欧回覧実記』. Tokyo: Iwanami Shoten, 1994. [Originally published 1977.]

Tanaka Kenzaburō 田中健三郎, ed. *Itari kenkoku kiryaku* 伊太利建国紀略. Tokyo: Hakubunsha 博文社, 1886.

Tanaka Ryūji 田中隆二. *Bakumatsu Meijiki no Nichifutsu kōryū* 幕末・明治期の日仏交流. Hiroshima: Keisuisha 渓水社, 1999.

Tanaka Yoshio 田中芳男 and Hirayama Narinobu 平山成信. *Ōkoku hakurankai sandō kiyō* 澳國博覧会参同記要. Reprinted in Fujiwara Masato 藤原正人, ed., *Meiji shoki sangyō hattatsushi shiryō* 明治初期産業発達史資料 8:2. Tokyo: Meiji Bunken Shiryō Kankōkai 明治文献資料刊行会, 1964. [Originally published 1897.]

Tanaka Yūko 田中優子. *Geisha to asobi: Nihonteki saron bunka no seisui* 芸者と遊び：日本的サロン文化の盛衰. Tokyo: Gakushū Kenkyūsha 学習研究社, 2007.

Taniguchi Iwao 谷口巖. "Mori Ōgai *Kōsei nikki* ni miru bungei ishiki: Fukuzawa Yukichi *Seikōki* to taihi shitsutsu Narushima Ryūhoku *Kōsei nichijō* to no ruijisei ni tokioyobu" 森鷗外「航西日記」にみる文芸意識―福沢諭吉『西航記』と対比しつつ成島柳北『航西日乗』との類似性に説き及ぶ. *Aichi Kyōiku Daigaku kenkyū hōkoku dai ichibu: jinbun shakai kagaku hen* 愛知教育大学研究報告第一部人文社会科学編 25 (1976): 190–175.

Taya Raishun 多屋頼俊. "Ishikawa Shuntai to Higashi Honganji" 石川舜台と東本願寺. In *Rekishi hen* 歴史編, vol. 2 of *Kōza:*

Kindai Bukkyō 講座：近代仏教. Kyoto: Hōzōkan 法蔵館, 1961.

Tejima Kōgyō Kyōiku Shikindan 手島工業教育資金團, ed. *Tejima Seiichi sensei den* 手島精一先生傳. Tokyo: Tejima Kōgyō Kyōiku Shikindan 手島工業教育資金團, 1929.

Terakado Seiken 寺門静軒. *Account of the Prosperity of Edo*. Alternative title: *Asakusa Kannon, Ryōgoku Bridge: Two Segments from Edo Hanjōki (1832–36)*. Trans. Andrew Markus. No. 1 of *An Episodic Festschrift for Howard Hibbett*. Hollywood: Highmoonoon, 2000.

———. "Blossoms Along the Sumida." Trans. Andrew Markus. *Sino-Japanese Studies* 3.2 (April 1991): 9–29.

———. *Edo hanjōki* 江戸繁昌記. In Hino Tatsuo 日野龍夫, ed., *Edo hanjōki, Ryūkyō shinshi* 江戸繁昌記・柳橋新誌, vol. 100 of *Shin Nihon koten bungaku taikei*. Tokyo: Iwanami Shoten, 1989.

Thelle, Notto R. *Buddhism and Christianity in Japan: From Conflict to Dialogue, 1854–1899*. Honolulu: University of Hawai'i Press, 1987.

Tomita Hitoshi 富田仁. *Furansu ni miserareta hitobito: Nakae Chōmin to sono jidai* フランスに魅せられた人びと：中江兆民とその時代. Tokyo: Karuchā Shuppansha カルチャー出版社, 1976.

———. *Iwakura Shisetsudan no Pari: Yamada Akiyoshi to Kido Takayoshi sono ten to sen no kiseki* 岩倉使節団のパリ：山田顕義と木戸孝允その点と線の軌跡. Tokyo: Kanrin Shobō 翰林書房, 1997.

———. *Merume Kashon: bakumatsu Furansu kaisōden* メルメ・カション：幕末フランス怪僧伝. Yokohama: Yūrindō 有隣堂, 1980.

———. *Yokohama Furansu Monogatari* 横浜フランス物語. Tokyo: Hakusuisha 博水社, 1991.

Tsuruta Tōru 鶴田徹. *Genrōin gikan Tsuruta Akira: Nihon kindai hōten hensan no kiseki* 元老院議官鶴田皓：日本近代法典編纂の軌跡, rev. and corr. ed. Tokyo: Kakumeisha 鶴鳴社, 1999.

Ueda, Atsuko. *Concealment of Politics, Politics of Concealment: The Production of "Literature" in Meiji Japan.* Stanford: Stanford University Press, 2007.

Ueda Masayuki 上田正行. "*Kōsei nikki* no seikaku"「航西日記」の性格. *Kanazawa Daigaku Bungakubu ronshū: Bungakkahen* 金沢大学文学部論集：文学科篇 9 (1989): 15–90.

———. *Matsumoto Hakka Kōkairoku* 松本白華航海録. *Kanazawa Daigaku Fuzoku Toshokan hō Kodama* 金沢大学附属図書館報こだま. Part One: No. 93 (January 1, 1989): 6–7; Part Two: No. 94 (April 1, 1989): 5–7.

Umezawa Hideo 梅沢秀夫. "Shushi gakusha Ōtsuki Bankei no seiyōkan" 朱子学者大槻磐渓の西洋観. *Seisen Joshi Daigaku kiyō* 清泉女子大学紀要 34 (1986): 21–39.

Waley, Arthur, trans. *The Analects of Confucius.* New York: Vintage, 1989.

———. *The Book of Songs.* New York: Grove, 1987.

Wang Ping. *Aching for Beauty: Footbinding in China.* Minneapolis: University of Minnesota Press, 2000.

Watson, Burton, trans. *Records of the Grand Historian,* 3rd ed., 3 vols. New York: Columbia University Press, 1993.

---. *Selected Poems of Su Tung-po*. Port Townsend, WA: Copper Canyon Press, 1994.

---. *The Tso Chuan: Selections From China's Oldest Narrative History*. New York: Columbia University Press, 1989.

Wixted, John Timothy. "Kanbun, Histories of Japanese Literature, and Japanologists." *Sino-Japanese Studies* 10.2 (April 1998): 23–31.

Yamada Kumiko 山田久美子, trans. *Rongufero Nihon taizaiki: Meiji shonen Amerika seinen no mita Nippon* ロングフェロー日本滞在記：明治初年、アメリカ青年の見たニッポン. Tokyo: Heibonsha, 2004.

Yamamoto Shichihei 山本七平. *Shibusawa Eiichi: kindai no sōzō* 渋沢栄一近代の創造. Tokyo: Shōdensha 祥伝社, 2009.

Yamashita Sōen 山下草園. *Nihon Hawai Kōryūshi* 日本布哇交流史. No. 8 of *Tōa bunka sōsho* 東亜文化叢書. Tokyo: Daitō Shuppansha 大東出版社, 1943.

Yanagida Izumi 柳田泉. *Fukuchi Ōchi* 福地櫻痴. Tokyo: Yoshikawa Kōbunkan, 1965.

Yoshida Asako 吉田朝子. "Kyōsai o meguru gaka." 暁斎をめぐる画家. *Kyōsai* 暁斎 10.96 (December 2007): 18–22.

Yoshimi Kaneko 吉見周子. *Baishō no shakaishi* 売娼の社会史, rev. and enlarged ed. Tokyo: Yūzankaku 雄山閣, 1992.

Yu Huai 余怀. *Banqiao zaji (wai yi zhong)* 板桥杂记（外一种）. Ed. Li Jintang 李金堂. Shanghai: Shanghai Guji Chubanshe 上海古籍出版社, 2000.

Index

Abe Hisomu, 191, 192
abortion, 101
Aceh, 168
Aden, 172, 174–75, 175, 176, 179
Africa, 176, 177
Aioi. *See* Ayasegawa Sanzaemon
Akamatsu Renjō, 290, 292, 294, 297, 299, 300
Andō Tadatsune. *See* Andō Tarō
Andō Tarō, 193, 194, 195, 197, 202, 203, 208, 215, 223, 233
Anegakōji Kimitomo, 150
Arabia, 173, 174, 176, 177
Ariga, Chieko, xxxv, lix
Asakusa, 140
Asano Kōbē, 245
Ayasegawa Sanzaemon, 98
Bab-el-Mandeb, 178
Ballagh, J. H., xliii
bamboo branch ballads, 75, 207, 317
Beal, Samuel, 294

Beiran, 207, 210
biblical references, 160, 176, 178, 262, 269, 281
Bin Chun, 167
Binnie, David Carr, 328–29
Bo Juyi, 64, 68, 75, 86, 88, 116, 125, 129, 319, 333
boathouses. *See funayado*
Boshin War, 78, 96, 111
Bouché, 192, 193, 197, 203, 222, 234, 241, 242, 245, 247, 280, 318
Buland, Charles, 207
bunmei kaika, xiii, 87
Cachon, Mermet de, 191, 199, 201, 207, 214
Caesar, Julius, 268
calendar, 90, 147, 149, 161, 163, 189, 202, 205, 206, 224, 317
Canada
  Niagara Falls, 321–22
Candia, 183
Cape of Good Hope, 180
Celtic, 304
Ceylon. *See* Sri Lanka

Chanoine, Charles, xlii, 191, 200, 208, 209, 217, 227, 241, 254, 282, 283, 287, 318
China, 155, 158, 178, 189, 212
  Brother Islands, 154
  Qinhuai River, 75, 130
  Xiamen, 154
  Yangzhou, 75
choki, 8, 13, 14, 68, 337
Chōya shinbun, ix, 317, 336
Chu Lianxiang, 65
Columbus, Christopher, 307
Confucian classics, 36, 44, 119
  misappropriation, xxxii, 9, 11, 17, 19, 24, 28, 31, 38, 45, 67, 91, 97, 115, 124
Confucian scholars, 35, 37, 133, 135, 340
Confucianism, 6–7, 64, 67, 127
Confucius, 35, 97, 120, 133
Coullet, A. M., 210, 243, 282
Coullet, Paul Jacques, 210
Crete. *See* Candia
currency, 83, 93–94, 113, 155, 164, 165, 173, 174, 175, 178, 188, 193, 197, 201, 204, 208, 209, 232, 233, 247, 253, 274, 291, 295
D'Anka, Cornélie, 293
de Zélinski, Louis, 284
Dell'Oro, Isidoro, 245
Dell'Oro, Joseph, 245, 250, 251, 252, 253
dodoitsu, 112, 118, 338
Du Fu, 278
Du Mu, 70, 75, 129
Edo geisha. *See machi-geisha*
Edo meisho zue, 7, 217
Egypt, 176, 178, 181, 237, 263
  Ismaïlia, 180
  Port Said, 181, 182
  Suez, 176, 177, 179, 180
England
  Dover, 287
  Liverpool, 304–5, 305
    Prince's Park, 304
  London, lvi, 150, 288–304, 320
    Alhambra Theatre, 293
    Blackfriars Bridge, 291
    British Museum, 294, 298
    Buckingham Palace, 292
    City Prison, 298
    Cremorne Gardens, 298

Crystal Palace, 299
Houses of Parliament, 289, 292
Hyde Park, 290, 292, 299
Kew Gardens, 293
London Bridge, 291, 303
Madame Tussaud's, 296
Regent's Park, 295
Royal Albert Hall, 290
Royal Exchange, 290
Royal Polytechnic, 291
South Kensington Museum, 290
St. James's Park, 292
Tower of London, 297
Trafalgar Square, 289
University College, 295
Victoria Station, 288, 299
Waterloo Bridge, 289
Westminster Abbey, 292
Westminster Bridge, 289
zoo, 303
Windsor Castle, 300
English language, 92
France
    Calais, 285, 287, 293
    Corsica, 184
    Culoz, 280
    Lyon, 188, 236, 276
    Mâcon, 247
    Marseille, 182, 183, 185–88, 189
        Château Borély, 187
        Grand Hôtel, 185, 186
        Musée des Antiques, 187
        Musée des Beaux-Arts, 187
    Modane, 280
    Paris, lvi, 147, 150, 167, 187, 188–247, 250, 276, 279, 280–87, 289
        Arc de Triomphe, 191, 199, 206, 251, 258
        Bois de Boulogne, 193, 197, 203, 243
        Bois de Vincennes, 231
        Buttes-Chaumont, 213, 234, 283
        Café Anglais, 194
        Catacombs, 224, 225, 270
        Church of St. Sulpice, 218
        Cirque de Napoleon, 230
        Cluny Museum, 208, 210,

281
Comptoir d'Escompte, 210, 243, 282
Conservatoire des Arts et Métiers, 229
Dîner Européen, 244, 245, 281, 283
Folies Bergère, 239, 241
Grand Hôtel, 188, 236, 237, 241, 244, 245, 280, 281
Hôtel Corneille, 202, 284
Hôtel de Lord Byron, 191, 206, 211, 214, 223, 224, 227, 239, 242, 246, 283, 284
Hôtel des Invalides, 212
Institution des jeunes Aveugles, 233
Jardin d'Acclimatation, 193, 239
Louvre Museum, 216, 226, 239, 246, 282
Luxembourg Gardens, 203, 208, 286
Luxembourg Museum, 239
Luxembourg Observatory, 219
Mint, 226, 232
Morgue, 229
Notre Dame, 229
Palais de l'Élysée, 194, 199, 246
Palais-Royal, 194, 217, 231, 236, 238, 241, 254, 258, 279, 283
Panorama, 194, 200, 227, 296
Pavillon Henri IV, 205, 284
Prison de la Santé, 220
Réservoir de Ménilmontant, 213
Théâtre de l'Odéon, 209, 231, 243
Théâtre de la Gaîté, 216, 217, 229, 282
Théâtre du Gymnase, 235
Valentino, 195, 201, 226, 242, 244
Véfour, 287
Sèvres, 240, 247
St-Germain-en-Laye, 204,

283

Toulon, 185
Versailles, 196, 197, 246
Fukagawa, xvi, xviii, xx, 5, 6, 10, 16, 25
Fukazawa Katsuoki, 281, 282
Fukuchi Gen'ichirō, 188, 199, 202, 210, 236, 237
Fukui Junzō, 227
Fukuzawa Yukichi, 104, 149, 188, 200, 210, 302
Funabashi Gyokukei, 234
funayado, 12–13, 83, 338
    boat types, 13–14, 118–19
    customers, 16
    proprietors, 14–15
fūryū, 30, 63, 65, 79, 85, 115, 129, 132, 140, 338
gagaku, 216
Gao Linglong, 65
Ge Ruifang, 66
geisha, xvi–xxvi, 10, 16–26, 25, 34–35, 338
    "rolling", 25–28, 29, 31, 32, 42, 57, 85
    arts, 34, 37, 54, 56
    association with cats, 121–22
    children of, 101–2
    clothing, 33, 52–54
    customers, 28–31, 39, 85, 28–31
    expenses, 52
    fees, 33, 38, 93
    haori geisha, 51
    houses, 39–41
    idle time, 49–50
    male. *See hōkan*
    mothers, 41–44, 93
    muguri geisha, 51–52
    redemption, 43–46, 101, 105, 115
    religious practices, 38–39
    seniority, 32–34, 54, 57
Gennyo, xlii, 148, 149, 197, 219, 287
gesaku, xxxiv
gikun, xxxiii, xxxv, xxxvi, lviii, 338
Godavéry, 149, 150, 156, 159, 193
gōkan, 339, 341
Golden, Arthur
    Memoirs of a Geisha, xxiii,

379

Gonchan. *See* Ichikawa Danjūrō IX
Gotō Tsune, 189, 190, 195, 206, 232
gozumezu, 49
Great Republic, 328, 332
Greece, 183
Gu Mei, 66
Hachisuka Makijirō, 210
Hachisuka Mochiaki, 206, 210
Haeckel, Ernst, 178
haibutsu kishaku, xliii
haiku, 27
hairstyles, 95, 99–101, 114, 123, 258
hakoya, 46–50, 93, 339
Han Yu, 131, 135, 159
hanjōkimono, xxxii, lix
Harada Goichi, 198, 204, 209, 210, 214, 227, 235, 238
Harada Kazumichi. *See* Harada Goichi
Harris, Townsend, 209
hauta, 34
Hayashi Jussai, xxxi
Hayashi Tadasu, 201, 204, 215

Hayashi Teiu, xxxii
Hekiun Sanjin, 78
Henry VII, 292
Hepburn, James, xliii, 160, 201, 243
Hida Hamagorō, 217
hidarizuma, 33, 339
Higashi Honganji, xlii, xliii, 334
Higashikuze Michitomi, 216
hikitejaya, 16, 339
Hindu, 174
Hino Tatsuo, lviii
Hirose Kyokusō, xlii
hōkan, 86, 340
Hon'ami Kōetsu, 106
Hong Kong, 155–59
  Shing Ping Theatre, 158
  Taiping Shan Water and Moon Temple, 157
  Victoria Peak, 155
  Ying Wa College, 158, 160
Hongfu, 65, 116, 142, 144
Honma Kōsō, 151, 191, 193, 199
Horikawa Gorō, 289, 303
Horton, Elias Robert, 295
Hou Fangyu, 141

Hu Quan, 143
Ichijō Jūjirō. *See* Gotō Tsune
Ichikawa Danjūrō IX, 97
Igawa Totsurō, 157
Ijichi Suekata, 157
Ikeda Kanji, 191, 192, 194, 195, 223, 239, 246, 281
Ikeda Masayoshi. *See* Ikeda Kanji
Imamura Warō, 236
Inagaki Kitazō, 198, 219, 227, 243, 280, 286, 287, 299
Inoue Kowashi, 150, 151, 181
Ireland
    Queenstown, 305
Irie Fumio, lx, 202, 210, 216, 223, 239, 247, 280, 281, 287
Ishikawa Shuntai, xlii, 148, 149, 163, 165, 195, 202, 206, 207, 214, 218, 222, 231, 244, 282, 283, 284, 287, 298, 300, 302, 304, 320
Islam, 165
Italy
    Alessandria, 279
    Bologna, 259
    Elba, 184
    Florence, 259–62, 279
        Duomo, 260
        Palazzo Pitti, 260
        Palazzo Vecchio, 260
        Santa Maria Novella, 262
    Foligno, 278
    Messina, 183
    Milan, 249–53, 254
        Arco della Pace, 251
        Chiesa di San Carlo al Corso, 252
        Duomo, 250
        Galleria arcade, 250
        Teatro di Santa Radegonda, 251
    Modena, 279
    Murano, 257
    Naples, 184, 273–78
        Castel Sant'Elmo, 275
        Church of Carthusia, 275
    Piacenza, 279
    Pompeii, 274, 276–78, 314
    Rome, 262–73, 278, 314
        Academy of St. Luke, 264
        Arch of Constantine, 263
        Arch of Septimius Severus, 264

Arch of Titus, 268
Barcaccia, 264
Basilica di San Pietro, 262, 271, 313
Basilica of Constantine, 266
Church of San Giovanni in Laterano, 268
Church of San Pietro in Vincoli, 269
Church of Scala Santa, 268
Church of the Cappuccini, 270
Colosseum, 268
Column of Emperor Trajan, 264
Column of Phocas, 265
Forum, 266
French Academy of Art, 269
Galleria Doria-Pamphili, 270
Immacolata Column, 264
Monte Pincio, 269
Palazzo Borghese, 270
Palazzo del Quirinale, 269
Palazzo Farnese, 271
Pantheon, 263
Piazza Colonna, 263
Piazza del Campidoglio, 265
Popolo Church, 263
Portico Theatre, 271
Pyramid of Cestius, 272
San Paolo fuori le Mura, 272
Santa Maria dei Miracoli, 263
Santa Maria in Montesanto, 263
Santa Maria in Trastevere, 271
synagogue, 271
Temple of Faustina, 266
Temple of Julius Caesar, 266
Temple of Mars Ultor, 269
Temple of Vesta, 272
Theater of Marcellus, 270
Trevi Fountain, 269
Vatican, 262, 271
Vatican Museum, 271

Sicily, 183
Turin, 249, 279
Venice, 253–59
  Cathedral of San Marco, 255
  Palace of the Doges, 254
  Palazzo Reale, 258
  Piazza di San Marco, 254
  Santa Maria dei Frari, 256
  Santa Maria dei Gesuiti, 256
  Santa Maria del Carmine, 256
  Vesuvius, 275
Itō Hirobumi, 202, 208, 232
Iwakura Mission, xlvi, 151, 191, 193, 198, 199, 200, 201, 202, 203, 204, 208, 209, 211, 216, 217, 219, 220, 227, 234, 237, 280, 288, 294, 296
Iwakura Tomomi, 193, 198, 200, 208, 219, 231, 233, 234, 236, 292
Iwasaki Mineko, xxiv
Iwashita Chōjūrō, 227, 239
Izawa Heikyū, xxvii
jigoku, 39, 140

Joan of Arc, 286
kabuki, 58, 89, 97, 98, 100, 101
kagema, 5
Kagetsu shinshi, ix, xliv, xlv, lii, 76, 141, 142, 311, 336
Kamei Hideo, xxxvi
Kamizawaya, 244
Kanbe Yoshikata, 281, 297
kanbun, xi, xxxi, xxxii, xxxi–xli, xlii, l, lii, lv, lviii
kanbun fūzokushi, xxxii, xxxvi, xl, xli
kanbun gesaku, xxxv, 11, 340
Kanda River, xv
Kanematsu Naoshige, 215, 283
Kansei reforms, xii
kanshi, x, xi, xxviii, xlvi, l, li, lii
kanshibun, xi–xii, xii, l, lii
karyūkai, xvi, xxxiii, 57, 65, 67, 115, 140
Katsuragawa Hoshū, xli, 40, 72, 130, 149
kawabiraki, 53, 68, 340
Kawada Ōkō, 141
Kawaji Kandō, 199, 201
Kawaji Toshiyoshi, 150, 151, 206, 239, 287

Kawamura Sumiyoshi, 295, 299
Kawarazaki Gonjūrō. *See* Ichikawa Danjūrō IX
Kawazu Sukeyuki, 191, 198, 219, 230, 231, 243
ken, 37, 340
kenban, 46, 341
Kido Takayoshi, 198, 202, 210, 219, 227, 233
Kikuchi Dairoku, 149, 289, 293, 296, 302
Kikuchi Sankei, 76
Kinokuniya Bunzaemon, 112, 114
Kishira Kaneyasu, 150
Kiyomoto, 33, 341
kojitsuke, 51, 96
Komaki Masanari, 157
Komatsu Seiji, 201, 202, 204, 215, 223
Komeda Keiji, 208, 209, 211, 214, 215
Komuro Shinobu, 206, 210, 296
Kōno Togama, 150, 206
kōshaku, 15, 341
Koyama, Noboru, 329

Kumagai Naotaka, 198
Kume Kunitake, xlvi, 199, 202, 317
kundoku, xi, lii, lv
Kunii Tadao, 234
Kurimoto Joun, xli, 189, 198, 201, 236
Kurimoto Teijirō, 189, 192, 195, 197, 201, 202, 208, 210, 215, 222, 223, 226
kusazōshi, 49, 58, 341
Kusuyama Kōichirō, 234
Kusuyama Takasaburō, 335
Kuwabara Kaihei, 157
kyōka, 19
Legge, James, 158
Li Bo, 96, 190, 261, 278, 322, 324
Li Qian, 142
Li Shiniang, 58, 66, 130
Liu Yiqing, 126
Liu Yuxi, 337
Liu Zongyuan, 135
Longfellow, Charles A., xx, xxiii, 58
Louis XIV, 196, 246, 286
Louis XV, 196

Louis XVI, 196, 219, 246
Lu You, 123
Lü Zhu, 65
machi-geisha, xviii, 343
Mac-Mahon, Marshal, 246
Maeda Ai, xxx, xlv, 312
Malacca, 164, 167
Mao Xixi, 65
Marie Antoinette, 196
Markus, Andrew, lix
Masuda Katsunori, 150, 151, 201, 289, 291, 295, 299
Masuda Sayo, xxv
Masuno Sukezō, 300
Matsuchi, 3
Matsuda Masahisa, 151, 198, 246
Matsudaira Norikata, 77
Matsuki Kōan. *See* Terashima Munenori
Matsumoto Hakka, xlii, 148, 149, 152, 160, 179, 181, 184, 192, 193, 195, 202, 210, 222, 244, 245, 255, 257, 282, 284, 287, 320
Matsumoto Judayū, 200
Matsumoto Tamenosuke, 200

Matsumura Toshisaburō, 242, 243
Mediterranean Sea, 179, 181, 182
Mei Kong, 150, 159, 332
Meiji Restoration, 80, 139
Meirokusha, 149, 286
Mencius, 24
mitate, 90
Mitsui-gumi, 242, 244, 292
Mitsukuri Genpo, 199
Mitsukuri Gyokkai, 104
Mitsukuri Shūhei, 149, 188, 210, 289, 302
Miwa Hoichi, 258
Miyoshi, Masao, 317
Mizuno Jun, 157
Mizuno Tadakuni, xxxii
Mori Arinori, 226, 286, 302
Mori Kinnojō. *See* Mori Arinori
Mōri Motoisa, 191
Mori Ōgai, 148
Mori Shōgo, 234
Mori Shuntō, 313, 316
Mukōyama Kōson, 157
Murata Fumio, 180
Nagai Hōzan, 125

Nagai Kafū, xiv, xxviii, xxix, 312
Nagano Keijirō. *See* Komeda Keiji
Nagaoka Seisuke, 191
Nagaoka Yoshiyuki. *See* Nagaoka Seisuke
Nagasawa Korekazu, 297
nagauta, 33, 84, 342
najimi, 94, 342
Nakae Chōmin, 194
Nakagawa Otsuyū, 27
Nakai Hiroshi, 157, 283
Nakajima Saikichi, 241, 242
Nakajima Suidō, 4
Nakamura Nakazō III, 100
Nakayama Jōji, 254, 258
Nakayama Umonta. *See* Nakayama Jōji
Nakazō. *See* Nakamura Nakazō III
Namura Taizō, 150, 151, 186, 192, 193, 227, 238, 241, 246, 281, 282, 287
Napoleon I, 184, 185, 196, 211, 251, 255, 266, 283, 289, 294, 296, 303
Napoleon III, 196, 200, 212, 213, 219, 222, 224, 296
Narushima Kenkichi, 189, 234, 258, 280, 281, 282, 283, 284, 286, 287
Narushima Nobu, 312
Narushima Ryūhoku
  canonicity, x–xi
  diary, 26–27
  Diary of a Journey to the West, xiv, xli–lvii
  publication, 311–13
  Keibyō ippan, 3, 123
  New Chronicles of Yanagibashi, xii–xiv, xv–xli
  pirate editions, xxix, 80
  publication, xxviii–xxix
  Ryūhoku shishō, 313
  service to shogunate, 77–78
  sobriquets, 3, 148
Narushima Toshirō, 312
Nelson, Horatio, 289
Nero, 263, 264, 268
newspapers, 133, 140, 252, 334–36
Nishi Amane, 151
nishikie, 252

Nishimura Katsurō, 211, 223
Nishimura Katsuzō, 211
Nishimura Uhei, 149
Nishioka Yumei, 296
Nishiyama Atsuhisa. *See* Tomita Atsuhisa
nitari, 14, 342
Nitta Shizumaru, 151, 190, 208
Nitta Tadazumi, 151
Noguchi Tomizō, 211
Noh, 19, 31, 89, 246, 343
Numa Morikazu, 150, 151, 166, 186, 198
obelisks, 262, 263, 268
Okada Yoshiki, 288
Okiku, 58–61
Okkotsu Kenzō, 293, 299, 300, 301
Okkotsu Taiken, 294
Okkotsu Wataru, 294
Ōkōchi Teruna, 136
Ōkubo Toshimichi, 198, 219, 280
okujusha, ix, 77, 340
Ōkura Kihachirō, 223, 226, 227, 230, 285, 286, 288, 290, 291
Ōno Mitsutsugi, 312

Ōno Naosuke, 191
Ono Tomogorō, 200
Ono Yaichi, 191, 216, 222, 226, 227, 229, 230, 231, 234, 236, 237, 238, 239, 242, 244, 245, 247, 250, 272, 273, 280, 282, 283, 287, 303
Ono Yaiichi, 191
Ono Zenjirō, 223, 245, 302
Ono Zensuke, 244, 302
Ono-gumi, 223, 242, 244, 302
opera, 245, 270
Osada Keitarō, 189, 195, 201, 204, 208, 215, 216, 217, 223, 227, 231, 232, 233, 234, 236, 239, 246, 280, 281, 282, 283, 285, 286, 287
Osada Tōichi, 296
oshaku, 32
Ōshima Ryūichi, 312
Ōshima Shin, 78
Ōtani Kōei. *See* Gennyo
Ōtomo. *See* Ōya Tomoemon V
Ōtomo Hirotsugi. *See* Ōya Tomoemon V
Ōtori Keisuke, 290, 298
Ōtsuki Bankei, 104, 184

Ouyang Xiu, 135
Ōya Tomoemon V, 98
Pacific Mail Steamship Company, 320, 328
Paris Commune, 196, 219, 246
Perim Island, 178
physicians, 35, 37
prisons, 220, 221, 222, 255, 262, 298, 300
prostitution, xv, xvii, xx, 5, 10, 26, 41, 56, 110, 140, 170, 194, 195, 207, 240, 244, 247, 250, 273, 276, 277, 279, 340
Qu Yuan, 81
Rai San'yō, 152, 184
railroad, 108–9
rakugo, 15
Red Sea, 176, 177
rickshaw, 107–8
Roches, Léon, 189
Rosny, Léon de, lx, 210, 222, 235, 236, 244, 284, 302, 318
Ryōgoku, 82, 88, 118, 127, 128, 129, 130
Ryōgoku Bridge, 3, 8, 9, 53, 68, 70, 109, 122
Saitō Chikudō, 184

Saitō Gesshin, 217
Sakata Kan'ichirō, 193, 194, 217, 230, 232, 236
Sakura Tsuneshichi, 243
Sameshima Naonobu, 189, 191, 226, 286, 287
San'yūtei Enchō, 106
Sangaku, 246
Sanskrit, 158, 216, 236, 244, 334
Sarugaku, 343
Sasaki Takayuki, 216
Satō Shizuo, 191, 195
Satow, Ernest, 211
Savatier, Paul Ludovic, 156
Sawamura Tanosuke III, 98, 106
Sawamura Tosshō II, 98, 100
Scott, Winfield, 323
Seisen Hakuseki Sanjin In, 136
Seki Sekkō, xxvii, 76
Seki Shinzō, xlii, 148, 149, 152, 163, 166, 210, 222, 289, 297, 298, 302, 303
Senju, 66
senryū, 28

Shibusawa Eiichi, 178, 241, 245
Shibusawa Kisaku, 211, 241, 242, 245
Shibusawa Sōgorō, 245
Shimabara, 140
Shimada-gumi, 242, 244
Shimaji Mokurai, 193, 194, 198, 202, 207, 208, 210, 216, 230, 231, 232, 234, 235, 237, 241, 242, 245, 290, 317
Shimizu Kihei, 242, 243
Shimooka Renjō, 330
Shinagawa, 5, 10
Shinbashi, xxi, 127
Shinchi, 5
Shinmei, 5
Shioda Saburō, 201, 223, 227, 231, 242
Shionoya Tōin, 157
shirabyōshi, 66
shirukoboshi, 13, 343
Shizuza, 66
shogakai, 20, 124
shubi no matsu, 69
shunga, 100, 271, 274, 277, 344
Sima Qian, 135
Singapore, 164–67, 167, 169

Société d'ethnographie, 235, 244, 284
Sonzogno, Edoardo, 251, 252
Sri Lanka, 168, 169–72, 172, 178
   Bōgahā Temple, 170, 171
   Point de Galle, 169
Su Dongpo, 130, 135, 147, 175
Su Xiaoxiao, 65, 86, 143
Suez Canal, 179–82
Sugi Magoshichirō, 188
Sugimoto Kōseki, xxvii
Sugiura Yuzuru, 178
Sugiyama Shūtarō, 204, 206
Sumatra, 164, 168
Sumida River, xv, xvi, xx, xxvii, 3, 67, 70, 88, 99, 128
Summers, James, 294, 318
sumo, 98
Sun Bin, 135
Suzuki Kan'ichi, 296
Tachibanaya Isobē, 149
taikomochi. See *hōkan*
Taiwan, 153, 157
Takabatake Bizan, 281, 282, 283, 284, 287, 299, 300, 302
Takabatake Gorō. *See*

389

Takabatake Bizan
Takahashi Shin'ichi, 157
Takahashi Shinkichi, 157
Takamiyama. *See* Takasago Uragorō
Takao, 89
Takasago Uragorō, 98
Takasaki Masakaze, 211, 217, 243, 286, 287
Takeda Masatsugu, 288, 289, 291, 293, 294, 295, 297, 298, 299, 300, 302
Takeuchi Gendō, 128
Takeuchi Zaijirō, 234
Takizawa Bakin, 20
Tamura Sōtatsu, xxvii
Tanabata, 69, 109
Tanabe Taichi, 78, 200, 202, 203, 208, 215, 223, 233
Tanaka Kenzaburō, 254
Tanaka Yoshio, 192
Tao Yuanming, 154
Tateishi Onojirō. *See* Komeda Keiji
Tateishi Tokujūrō, 209
Tejima Eijirō, 288, 289, 290, 297, 302

Tejima Seiichi, 288
Tenpō Reforms, xxxii, 5, 41, 85
Terajima Munenori, 302
Terakado Seiken, 4, 6
    Edo hanjōki, xxx, xxxii, lix, 4, 100, 133
Terashima Munenori, 202
Thiers, Louis Adolphe, 196, 296
Tokiwazu, 33, 344
Tokugawa Akitake, 155, 192
Tokugawa Iemochi, xxvi, 76
Tokugawa Iesada, xxvi
Tōkyō chinbun, 335
Tomimoto, 33, 344
Tomita Atsuhisa, 295
Tomita Tōzan, 199, 204
Tomoe, 19
Tosshō. *See* Sawamura Tosshō II
Tsubouchi Shōyō, xxxiii
Tsuburi no Hikaru, 19
Tsukioka Yoshitoshi, xxii
Tsuruta Akira, 150, 151, 186, 206, 227, 241, 246, 282, 287
Turkey, 183, 236, 237
Ueda Bin, 294

Ueda, Atsuko, xxxiii
Umegami Kōen, 193, 194, 208, 230, 231, 232, 234, 290
United States, 87, 104
   Elkhorn River, 323
   Great Salt Lake, 326–27
   Green River, 326
   New York City, 307
      Central Park, 320–21
   Rocky Mountains, 325–26, 326
   Sacramento, 328
   San Francisco, 320, 328
   Sierra Nevada, 327
Utsunomiya Saburō, 199, 201, 216, 222, 227, 243
Vietnam, 161–64
   Saigon, 165
Vittorio Emanuele II, 259, 266, 272, 296
wakaimono, 21
Wang Han, 190
Watanabe Yoshinori, 284
Wellington, Duke of, 290, 292, 297, 303
White Star Corporation, 298, 299, 301

Xie Anshi, 64
Xixi Shanren
   Wumen huafanglu, 75
Xue Tao, 32, 66, 86, 143
yakata, 13, 68, 343, 344
Yamada Akiyoshi, 191, 198
Yamaguchi Naoyoshi, 208
Yamauchi Yōdō, 87
Yamazaki Ransai, xxx
Yanagawa Shunsan, 72, 106, 130
Yanagibashi, xiii, xv–xxii, xxviii, 7, 9, 58, 61, 69, 75
   bathing, 22
   restaurants, 19–23, 80–83
yanebune, xxi, 8, 13, 345
Yang Guifei, 125
yashiki, 13, 345
Yasukawa Shigenari, 296, 298
Yoda Gakkai, 142
Yokohama, 108, 113, 320, 328, 334
Yokoyama Magoichirō, 223, 285, 302, 303
yose, 240, 345
Yoshichō, 5
Yoshida Jirō, 291, 303

Yoshida Kiyonari, 290
Yoshiwara, xvi–xviii, xxii, 5, 8, 10, 16, 46, 47, 51, 54, 55, 85
yotsude, 14, 107, 345
Yu Huai, 61, 75
  Banqiao zaji, xxx, 43, 53, 58, 66, 70, 75, 130
Yuan Mei, 114
Yūmeirō, 58
Zhang Chao, 141
Zhu Xi, 143

www.ingramcontent.com/pod-product-compliance
Lightning Source LLC
Chambersburg PA
CBHW052041220426
43663CB00012B/2399